AFRICAN RE-GENESIS

AFRICAN RE-GENESIS

CONFRONTING SOCIAL ISSUES IN THE DIASPORA

Edited by

Jay B. Haviser

and

Kevin C. MacDonald

LONDON AND NEW YORK

First published by UCL Press in 2006 under ISBNs 978-1-84472-138-2 and 978-1-84472-39-9.

First published 2006 by Left Coast Press, Inc.

Published 2016 by Routledge
2 Park Square, Milton Park, Abingdon, Oxon OX14 4RN
711 Third Avenue, New York, NY 10017, USA

Routledge is an imprint of the Taylor & Francis Group, an informa business

Library of Congress Cataloging-in-Publication Data is available

Hardback (978-1-59874-217-6)
Paperback (978-1-59874-283-1)

Contents

Part III Archaeology and living communities

Part IV   Slavery in Africa: Other Diasporas

List of figures and tables

Figures

Tables

Notes on contributors

E. Kofi Agorsah is Professor of Black Studies and International studies at Portland State University, Portland, Oregon. Formerly Keeper of the Ghana Museum and Monuments Board, he served as Lecturer/Senior Lecturer in Archaeology at the University of Ghana (1983–87) and at the University of the West Indies, Jamaica (1987–92). Prof. Agorsah is a leading authority on the archaeology of Maroon Heritage.

Rose Mary Allen studied anthropology at the University of Nijmegen, the Netherlands, subsequently working for 20 years as researcher and policy-maker at the Institute of Archaeology and Anthropology of the Netherlands Antilles. Currently she is a lecturer at several institutes of higher learning on Curaçao. Her research focuses on the complexity of Afro-Curaçaoan social life in post emancipation Curaçaoan society.

Douglas Armstrong is a professor of Anthropology at Syracuse University and has been named Merideth Professor of Teaching Excellence and Maxwell Professor of Excellence. Professor Armstrong has been engaged in Caribbean archaeology for over 30 years, and has produced many publications on his fieldwork. His research published in this volume was funded by the Wenner-Green Foundation.

Allison Blakely is Professor of European and Comparative History and the George and Joyce Wein Professor of African American Studies at Boston University. His publications include *Blacks in the Dutch World: The Evolution of Racial Imagery in a Modern Society* (1994, Bloomington: Indiana University Press) and numerous articles on European dimensions of the Black Diaspora.

Steven A. Brandt is an associate professor at the University of Florida's Department of Anthropology. His interests include ethnoarchaeology, African food security, the archaeology of the Horn of Africa, and cultural heritage management in the developing world.

Caleb Adebayo Folorunso is a Reader in the Department of Archaeology and Anthropology, University of Ibadan, Nigeria. His publications include studies on comparative archaeology and on cultural resource management. His recent works include "The archaeology and ethnoarchaeology of soap and die making at Ijaye,

Yorubaland" and "Views of ancient Egypt from a West African perspective." He gained his PhD from the University of Paris—Sorbonne, France.

P. P. A. Funari is Professor of Archaeology at State University of Campinas, Brazil and Research Associate at Illinois State University and Barcelona University. He was co-editor of *Global Archaeological Theory* (2005, New York: Kluwer).

Dr R. Grant Gilmore III is currently Director of the St Eustatius Center for Archaeological Research (www.secar.org). He has a BA and MA from the College of William and Mary and a PhD from the Institute of Archaeology, University College London. His current research interests include Afro-Caribbean architecture, illicit trade, military sites, plantations and religious sites.

Fiona J. L. Handley completed her PhD, *Legacies of slavery: presenting the history of American slavery in the plantations and historic home of the Southern United States*, in 2004 at the Institute of Archaeology, University College London. She is currently an AHRC Research Fellow at the Winchester School of Art, University of Southampton.

Mark W. Hauser is a specialist in the technical study of low fired earthenwares associated with the African Diaspora. He is currently a visiting member of the faculty at De Paul University and a research associate at the Field Museum in Chicago.

Jay B. Haviser has been the Archaeologist for the Netherlands Antilles Government since 1982. He received his Doctorate in Archaeology from Leiden University, the Netherlands, in 1987, and his publications include *African Sites Archaeology in the Caribbean*. Dr Haviser is the President of the International Association for Caribbean Archaeology; Senior Regional Representative for the Caribbean and Central America of the World Archaeological Congress; and past President of the Museums Association of the Caribbean.

Aondofe Joseph-Ernest Iyo holds a PhD in African History from the University of Calabar, Nigeria. He is a senior lecturer and is Director of the Multicultural Studies Center, University of Belize (Belmopan). Dr Iyo has authored seven books: four on African History and three on Belizean History, as well as a number of contributions to edited books and scholarly journals.

Kenneth G. Kelly, Associate Professor at the Department of Anthropology, University of South Carolina, teaches both historical and African archaeology. His research has developed a Trans-Atlantic perspective on the archaeology of the African Diaspora, and its impacts in West Africa and the Caribbean through field projects in Jamaica, Guadeloupe, Martinique, Bénin and Guinea.

Paul E. Lovejoy, Distinguished Research Professor, Department of History, York University and holder of the Canada Research Chair in African Diaspora History, is Director of the Harriet Tubman Resource Centre on the African Diaspora (www.yorku.ca/nhp). He has published more than 20 books and 80 articles and papers, including (with DV Trotman) *Trans-Atlantic Dimensions of Ethnicity in the African Diaspora* (2004); (with R Law) *Biography of Mahommah Gardo Baquaqua: His Passage from Slavery to Freedom in Africa and America* (2001) and (with T Falola) *Pawnship, Slavery and Colonialism in Africa* (2001).

Kevin C. MacDonald is Senior Lecturer in African Archaeology at the Institute of Archaeology, University College London. He received his Doctorate in

Archaeology from Cambridge University in 1994. A veteran West African field researcher in both prehistoric and historic Archaeology, his publications include *The Origins and Development of African Livestock: archaeology, genetics, linguistics and ethnography* (with Roger Blench). His research interests include the archaeology and history of African states and pastoralists, as well as the African Diaspora in French Colonial North America.

Gertrude Marie "Trudi" Martinus-Guda was born in Paramaribo, Suriname, and has a Masters in Cultural Anthropology , Utrecht, The Netherlands (1968). Her publications are primarily concerned with the oral traditions of Suriname.

John P. McCarthy was the editor of the *African American Archaeology Newsletter* between 1996 and 2000. He has worked for a number of cultural resource management firms in the northern United States, with a research specialism in the archaeology of the African Diaspora in America.

Philip D. Morgan is Sidney and Ruth Lapidus Professor in the American revolutionary era at Princeton University. He is the author of *Slave Counterpoint: Black Culture in the Eighteenth-Century Chesapeake and Low Country* (1998, Chapel Hill: University of North Carolina Press).

David W. Morgan currently is the Chief of Archaeology and Collections with the National Park Service's National Center for Preservation Technology and Training, and he also holds an affiliated faculty position at Northwestern State University of Louisiana. He received his master's from the University of Alabama and his doctorate from Tulane University and has conducted both historic and prehistoric archaeological research in the southeastern United States.

Neil Norman is a doctoral candidate at the Department of Anthropology, University of Virginia. He has conducted archaeological research in the southeastern United states, Tanzania, and the Republic of Benin. His research interests include ethnoarchaeology, urban modeling, and issues of historic memory and landscape as they relate to the trans-Atlantic Diaspora.

Brempong Osei Tutu has a masters in African Archaeology from the University of Ghana (Legon), and is currently working towards a PhD at the Department of Anthropology, University of Syracuse. His areas of interest are material culture studies and public policy in archaeology, in particular the relationship between tourism, development and the management of the past as a resource in conflict.

Armin Schwegler is Professor of Spanish Linguistics at the University of California, Irvine. Raised in Switzerland, he has researched Afro-Hispanic languages and culture for the past 20 years. His latest book, *Lengua y ritos del Palo Monte Mayombe: dioses cubanos y sus Fuentes africanas* (2005), studies the Afro-Cuban ritual language of Palo Monte.

Jonathan R. Walz is a doctoral candidate in the Department of Anthropology at the University of Florida, USA. His dissertation concerns historical representations and the later archaeology of the Pangani Basin, northeast Tanzania. Other intellectual pursuits include Indian Ocean histories and heritages as well as diasporas linked to Africa.

Preface and acknowledgments

The impetus for this present volume came from the World Archaeological Congress (WAC) Intercongress on the African Diaspora held at Curaçao, Netherlands Antilles, in the spring of 2001. Therefore our appreciation is extended to the Jacob Gelt Dekker Institute for hosting that event. However, this work is not a conference proceedings. New papers have been added, and original papers have been substantially revised. This volume showcases how archaeology and allied disciplines are working not only for a better understanding of the Diaspora's past, but also to interpret and make these findings relevant to living communities.

We wish to express our heartfelt appreciation to the WAC Executive Council, in particular Professor Peter Stone of the International Centre for Cultural and Heritage Studies, University of Newcastle and Professor Peter J. Ucko of the Institute of Archaeology, University College London, for their commitment to the completion of this volume. We hope that the fruits of this labor will promote a more profound appreciation of the Diaspora's enduring African Heritage and its contribution to humanity.

1   Introduction

An African re-genesis

JAY B. HAVISER AND KEVIN C. MACDONALD

Four times Wagadu stood there in all her splendour. Four times Wagadu disappeared and was lost to human sight: once through vanity, once through falsehood, once through greed and once through dissension … Four times she turned her face. Once to the north, once to the west, once to the east and once to the south … Those are the directions whence the strength of Wagadu comes, the strength in which she endures no matter whether she be built of stone, wood, earth or lives but as a shadow in the mind and longing of her children …
Wagadu is the strength that lives in the hearts of men …

("Gassire's Lute," *African Genesis: Folk Tales and Myths of Africa,*
Frobenius and Fox 1937: 97)

African re-genesis

Whereas the above quotation from *African Genesis* forms part of the oral historiography of West Africa's Sudanic empires, it is equally apt for considering the phoenix-like nature of African Diaspora communities. Ripped from motherland and family, ethnically mixed to quell the potential of uprisings, and brutalized by regimes of hard labor, the heart—the spirit—of Africa did not stop beating in the New World. Rather, it survived and has reemerged, changed by contacts with new cultures and environments we would argue, but still part of the continuum of African tradition: an African re-genesis.

Since the seminal work of Herskovits (1958), historians, anthropologists, and archaeologists have all struggled with questions of African cultural survival and metamorphosis in the New World. As Mintz and Price (1976: 52) put it:

If African-American cultures do in fact share such an integral dynamism, and if, as we shall argue, their social systems have been highly responsive to changing social conditions, one must maintain a sceptical attitude toward claims that many contemporary social forms represent direct continuities from the African homelands.

Over the past half century, quests for unmodified *retentions* of African culture in the New World have given way to attempts at understanding creolized or culturally mixed *syncretisms* of diverse African, European, and Native American populations (though not all agree with this trend, see Iyo Chapter 5, in this volume). Archaeologists have only belatedly begun to question naïve notions of cultural equivalency between New World archaeological manifestations and discrete, or indeed *generalized*, African cultures (e.g. the [in]famous case of the 'Bakongo Cosmogram': DeCorse 1999; Ferguson 1999; see also Morgan, Chapter 6, in this volume). Rather, it is at last becoming evident that the temporal and geographic comparative reach of archaeology may allow it to form unique perspectives on broader trends in the transformation and (re-)emergence of African Diaspora cultures. Archaeology is an important witness, and in some cases the solitary witness, to the inevitable and inexorable transformations that confronted culturally diverse Africans and their descendents. We must go beyond asking "where is Africa in these archaeological remains?" to considering all material culture as representative of cultural negotiations between small groups of peoples (Europeans, Africans, and Native Americans) under regionally and temporally unique circumstances. Ethnic and linguistic diversity in enslaved communities, interactions with Europeans and Native Americans, and increasing generational removal from the homeland gradually made the *un-modified* retention of African culture in the New World increasingly unlikely.

For example, from an Africanist perspective, the almost entirely undecorated nature of "Afro-colonowares" is unexpected. Where are the richly and diversely decorated wares of the mother continent? Where are the cord roulettes, the stamps, the paints? It is only when one looks broadly that an interesting pattern becomes apparent. Such motifs are documented in small numbers of sherds from seventeenth-century Jamaica (Meyers 1999; Mark Hauser personal communication—but see DeCorse and Hauser 2003). Afterwards any such direct parallels rapidly vanish. Likewise, in southeastern USA, undecorated pottery that may be termed "colonoware"—whether of African or Native American manufacture—appears to diminish gradually with time, virtually disappearing in the nineteenth century (Singleton 1988).

Why aspects of African culture *did* survive is almost as important as the fact that they did. Are more abundant retentions/syncretisms of African cultures indices of "less-disrupted" societies or gestures of resistance and assertions of group identity in difficult circumstances? The contextualization of changing trends in material remains within broader socioeconomic circumstances can be very informative. A good example of this is the reemergence of African cultural characteristics in the late Antebellum cemeteries of Philadelphia—at a time of increasing racial tension and economic competition in free African communities (see McCarthy, Chapter 15, in this volume).

In some places and times links to Africa may only be visible at a social, organizational, or perhaps cognitive level (see Haviser, Chapter 4, in this volume). Elsewhere, such as in the Columbian Palenque, more marked linguistic and mortuary continuities may exist to the present day (see Schwegler, Chapter 18, in this volume). An implication of all of this is that Diaspora Archaeology must continue to expand not only geographically and temporally, but also conceptually, to sense trends in the variation and transformation of African New World culture. Indeed, a longstanding emphasis on the archaeology of eastern North America—potentially one of the most acculturated zones of the Diaspora—has led to a certain skewing of expectations and theoretical perceptions. More globally, scholars have often neglected the archaeological potential for tracing subsistence changes wrought by Africans in the New World. The inception of African agricultural and culinary innovations would seem to be particularly amenable to consideration via the archaeological record. Overall, we need comparative data from elsewhere in the American South, as well as from the relatively neglected, though demographically paramount, Central and South American Diaspora communities. It is hoped that this volume will begin to redress this balance with field research contributions from Brazil (Funari), Suriname (Agorsah), Columbia (Schwegler), and Louisiana (MacDonald et al.).

To better appreciate the coping strategies of Africans in the New World, we need to understand both the local (plantation community level) mix of African ethnicities and the nature of the exterior communities with which they were (or were not) able to interact. To this end, we should be able to comparatively evaluate the potential impacts of local legal codes governing the lives of slaves, as well as local geographical circumstances and systems of provisioning and other trade. Gilmore, Armstrong, and Hauser (Chapters 8, 13, and 14, respectively, in this volume) all provide us with insights into the socioeconomic, and potentially cultural, impact of trade and maritime interactions of communities on the Caribbean islands. Gilmore in particular deals with changes in local law and regulation, which had telling effects on the mobility and social lives of the enslaved on St Eustatius.

Thus, our research questions should take into consideration factors such as the ethnic mix of the enslaved at a particular plantation or regional group of plantations, their generational removal from Africa, their gender balance, contacts with aboriginal groups, and restrictions placed upon them by their regime of enslavement. These elements are the constants without which we cannot comparatively measure archaeological responses. Without them we lack sufficient "control" to make sense of subtle dynamics within relatively small and isolated slave communities in the archaeological time frame.

Problems of presentation, questions of relevance

Regardless of discipline, all Diaspora research requires a relevance to modern communities and sensitivity to interplay with contemporary cultural identities. Matters concerning race and cultural diversity, though ostensibly defused by the vocabulary of political correctness, remain contentious. Indeed, the topic of racial relations has become to the twenty-first century what sex was to the nineteenth—something best not discussed in public, and better talked around than confronted directly. The presentation of historic sites involving slavery is imperative in an ongoing healing process, but to whom and how such sites are 'pitched' is an explosive question (Chappell 1999; Eichstedt and Small 2002; Haviser 2002).

Osei-Tutu and Handley (Chapters 2 and 3, respectively, in this volume) both deal with how a burgeoning African-American tourist trade in coastal West Africa is confronting (and being confronted by) continental African attitudes and heritage priorities. Issues of mass human deportation and attempted cultural genocide are not easy to deal with in a package tour or in a single cathartic confrontation with a "slave fort." There is undoubted difficulty for returning African-Americans to embrace as long lost family potential descendents of the same hierarchies who were culpable of their ancestors' initial enslavement. Or, for that matter, how does one explain the pain of slavery to mixed groups of African-Americans and Euro-Americans (whether the descendents of slave-owners or not) and avoid inciting even more racial tension? Can a specialized form of "slavery cultural tourism"—whether in Africa or the Americas—be formulated without descending into either platitudes of deflection and denial or rising to shrill cries of invective? The chapters of this book demonstrate that there are many gray areas and complexities regarding slavery and African-American culture not easily reduced to sound-bites or paragraphs on explanatory panels. For this reason priority needs to be put on teaching a more detailed and nuanced account of slavery at precollegiate levels, particularly concerning changes in the interactions of Africans, Europeans, and Native Americans over time.

Few aspects of American archaeological research are as fraught with controversy as the excavation of human remains. The past 20 years have witnessed an increase in public involvement in the determination of scientific access to ancestral burials (Layton 1989; Fforde and Hubert 2004). The case of the New York African Burial Ground is the first prominent case wherein African-American community groups asserted their rights in determining both who could study their historic dead and how they were ultimately re-interred (Blakely, Chapter 7, in this volume). What is perhaps most interesting about this now famous episode from the 1990s is that it demonstrated the strength of "public will" regarding archaeological research on the African Diaspora. Indeed, the public interface of many current Diaspora archaeological projects speaks to the broader relevance of what we archaeologists can elucidate about the undocumented pasts of the African New World.

We have very few written accounts of slavery from the perspective of the enslaved (for an analysis of a remarkable exception, see Lovejoy, Chapter 9, in this volume). In the USA, African-American oral histories were not collected systematically until between 1936 and 1938 when they were recorded by the Works Progress Administration (WPA). Some 2,194 interviews were conducted of survivors of slavery (Blassingame 1977). This extremely useful resource, though skewed by interviewers and their techniques, might be considered to have been too little, too late. However, in many parts of the Diaspora, particularly in South America and the Caribbean, a great deal of active research desperately needs doing on living traditions and historic events within living memory. Both Martinas-Guda and Allen (Chapters 10 and 11, respectively, in this volume), demonstrate the utility of working to document memories and tradition of Diaspora experience, with their consequent illumination of processes of ongoing cultural change. Yet, such work also has strong benefits at the level of community involvement for a variety of projects and could usefully be incorporated in most research schemes. Dialogue with groups that have too long been disenfranchised by academia, can start simply by listening to what they have to say.

Africa and the Diaspora

Finally, we should consider the rather neglected relevance of research in Africa itself for our understanding of the broader Diaspora. Not only is the study of the cultural diversity of the continent essential for understanding the African New World, Africa also holds within it many internal Diasporas brought about by the endemic practice of slavery and slave raiding extending back into the first millennium AD (Lovejoy 2000). What began in parts of the continent as systems of "rights in persons" based on age, gender, and indebtedness intensified in some areas to become mainstays of political organization—with slave armies and enslaved agricultural work forces (Miers and Kopytoff 1977; Meillassoux 1991). Yet, it is becoming increasingly evident that the Trans-Atlantic slave trade diversified and deepened these internal slave labour systems and, particularly along the West African coast, had profound repercussions for sociopolitical organization and economy (Thornton 1998; Lovejoy 2000). An archaeology of these historic processes has only just begun (cf. DeCorse 2001; Kelly 2004). One such new archaeological study, included in this volume, deals with settlement changes in the interior of West Africa during the era of the Atlantic Slave Trade (cf. Folorunso, Chapter 20). The growth of African Historical Archaeologies should be of particular importance to practitioners of Diaspora Archaeology.

One of the weaknesses of analogies routinely made between the Diaspora and the continent is the poverty of our knowledge of historic African material cultures. Most archaeological research heretofore has concentrated on subjects of entirely different timescales: the origins of modern humans, the advent of food production, and the first sub-Saharan states. We therefore know a good deal about what African ceramics and metalwork looked like around ca. AD 1000, but we know comparatively little of what it was like ca. AD 1700. Increased research should begin to close the gap that exists between contemporary ethnoarchaeological studies and archaeologies of early African states, and may prove eyeopening for understanding African cultural elements in the New World.

The ethnoarchaeological and historical archaeological work of Kelly and Norman (Chapter 19, in this volume) provides an admirable example of how well-informed research on contemporary and historic material culture can have double relevance to Africanists and "Diasporists." Their research seeks to understand the people behind the pots—particularly ritual pottery—and its (spatial) contexts. It makes a good model for similar studies, which are urgently needed on the continent, especially in that it treats a continental subject without forgetting potential extra-continental ramifications.

To complete this volume we solicited a major new contribution regarding slavery in East Africa and the virtually unknown, but substantial, Indian Ocean Diaspora (Walz and Brandt, Chapter 21). Lovejoy (2000: Table 3.1) estimates that ca. 1,000,000 Africans forcibly left the continent via the Red Sea and the Indian Ocean between 1500 and 1800, moving into the Arab world and beyond. The pathbreaking research of Walz and Brandt gives perspective to the truly global scale of the dispersion of Africans and elements of African cultures during the second millennium AD. The remembrance of this forgotten Diaspora makes it clear that the slave trade was neither exclusively Trans-Atlantic nor West African.

In closing, we would like to express our hope that the spirit of inter-disciplinary and inter-regional collaboration that enriched the creation of this volume (and the WAC Intercongress which inspired it) will continue to grow. The multifaceted and, indeed, global nature of past, present, and future African cultures demands it.

References

Blassingame, John W. (ed.) (1977) *Slave Testimony: Two Centuries of Letters, Speeches, Interviews, and Autobiographies*, Baton Rouge, LA: Louisiana State University Press.

Chappell, Edward A. (1999) "Museums and American slavery," in T.A. Singleton (ed.) *"I Too Am America": Archaeological Studies of African-American Life*, 240–258, Charlottesville, VA: University of Virginia Press.

DeCorse, Christopher R. (1999) "Oceans apart: Africanist perspectives on Diaspora Archaeology," in T. A. Singleton (ed.) *"I Too Am America": Archaeological Studies of African-American Life*, 132–155, Charlottesville, VA: University of Virginia Press.

DeCorse, Christopher R. (ed.) (2001) *West Africa during the Atlantic Slave Trade: Archaeological Perspectives*, London: Leicester University Press.

DeCorse, Christopher R., and Hauser, Mark W. (2003) "Low-fired earthenwares in the African Diaspora: problems and prospects," *International Journal of Historical Archaeology*, 7: 67–98.

Eichstedt, Jenifer L., and Small, Stephen (2002) *Representations of Slavery: Race and Ideology in Southern Plantation Museum*, Washington, DC: Smithsonian, Institution Press.

Ferguson, Leeland (1999) " 'The Cross is a Magic Sign': Marks on Eighteenth Century Bowls from South Carolina," in T. A. Singleton (ed.), *"I Too Am America": Archaeological Studies of African-American Life*, 116–131, Charlottesville, VA: University of Virginia Press.

Fforde, Cressida, and Hubert, Jane (eds) (2004) *The Dead and their Possessions: Repatriation in Principle, Policy and Practice*, London: Routledge.

Frobenius, Leo, and Fox, Douglas C. (1937) *African Genesis: Folk Tales and Myths of Africa*, New York: Stackpole and Sons.

Haviser, Jay B. (2002) "Welcome to Slaveryland: a call for ethical standards in the long-term partnership of African Diaspora heritage and the tourism industry," paper presented at the African Diaspora Heritage Trail Conference, Bermuda, and published in *Kristof*, 12,1: 17–36.

Herskovits, M. J. (1958) *The Myth of the Negro Past*, Boston, MA: Beacon Press.

Kelly, Kenneth (2004) "The African Diaspora Starts Here: Historical Archaeology of Coastal West Africa," in Andrew M. Reid and Paul J. Lane (eds) *African Historical Archaeologies*, 219–241, New York: Kluwer Academic/Plenum Publishers.

Layton, R. (ed.) (1989) *Conflict in the Archaeology of Living Tradition*, London: Unwin Hyman.

Lovejoy, Paul E. (2000) *Transformations in Slavery: A History of Slavery in Africa*, 2nd edn, Cambridge: Cambridge University Press.

Meillassoux, Claude (1991) *The Anthropology of Slavery. The Womb of Iron and Gold*, Chicago, IL: Chicago University Press.

Meyers, A. D. (1999) "West African Tradition in the Decoration of Colonial Jamaican Folk Pottery," *International Journal of Historical Archaeology*, 3: 201–223.

Miers, Suzanne, and Kopytoff, Igor (eds) (1977) *Slavery in Africa: Historical and Anthropological Perspectives*, Madison, WI: University of Wisconsin Press.

Mintz, S. W., and Price, R. (1976) *The Birth of African-American Culture: An Anthropological Perspective*, Boston, MA: Beacon Press.

Singleton, T. A. (1988) "An Archaeological Framework for Slavery and Emancipation," in M. P. Leone and P. B. Potter, Jr (eds) *The Recovery of Meaning: Historical Archaeology in the Eastern United States*, 345–370, Washington, DC: Smithsonian Institution Press.

Thornton, John (1998) *Africa and Africans in the Making of the Atlantic World*, 1400–1800, Cambridge: Cambridge University Press.

Part I Heritage and contemporary identities

2   Contested monuments

African-Americans and the commoditization of Ghana's slave castles

BREMPONG OSEI-TUTU

Introduction

Ghanaian authorities restored two of Ghana's "slave fortresses," specifically Cape Coast and Elmina Castles (Figures 2.1–2.4), as memorials to the tragedy of the slave trade in order to draw African-Americans to the country. In the process, state officials collaborated with international development agencies and implemented changes that sharply contrasted with the desires of many African-Americans. The project has exposed many complex issues and has led to unintended consequences. In particular, concerned African-Americans have expressed outrage over their marginalization from, and the subsequent handling of, a project that impacts their lives emotionally. They have objected to several aspects of the restoration project, which include:

1   The painting of the monuments and the provision of much brighter lights and modern visitor facilities such as restaurants and gift shops for tourists' convenience. They consider these changes as "Disneyfication" and desecration of shrines as well as acts of falsification and "white washing" designed to mask the evils of slavery (Deku 1993; Robinson 1994: 4; Tyehimba 1998: 28).

2   The designation of the monuments as "castles" despite the fact that they did not house any nobility.

3   The payment of fees for admission to experience the monuments, arguing that fees compromise the solemnity of the buildings.

4   An under-representation of the horrors of slavery in the castles.

For a growing number of African-Americans who make their painful pilgrimages to the castles for self-realization and spiritual purification the journey takes on a sacred quality (see Angelou 1986; *US News and World Report,* September 18, 1995: 33; Bruner 1996: 290–293; the *Washington Post,* July 26, 2000: A16–A17).[1] These constituents desire to experience the monuments in their "original" context to enable them to reconnect with their ancestry as well as to ensure a more intimate and meaningful experience (Robinson 1994: 4; Bruner 1996: 293).

The paradox created by the project is intriguing. On the one hand, the emphasis on African-Americans is a positive development in a tourism industry that rarely caters to

Figure 2.1 The canon-lined ramparts of Cape Coast Castle (photo: Osei-Tutu).

Figure 2.2 Elmina Castle and town from a nearby shoreline (photo: Osei-Tutu).

Figure 2.3   Elmina Castle, entrance (photo: Osei-Tutu).

Figure 2.4   Elmina Castle, interior courtyard (photo: Osei-Tutu).

black Diaspora travel needs (see Stewart 1994: 71; Housee 1999: 137). On the other hand, some African-Americans have accused the Ghanaian authorities of exploiting the tragedy of slavery for financial gains (see the *Washington Post*, April 17, 1995: A10 and October 9, 2000: A22; Hyatt 1997: 27; Phillips 2000: 153). How do the Ghanaian authorities ensure that African-American concerns are addressed without sacrificing the multifunctional history of the castles? My chapter examines these particular realms of tension over the restoration of the two monuments. The issues I discuss also relate to other Diaspora Africans, but I focus on African-Americans because they have specifically been targeted by Ghanaian authorities for heritage tourism.

Theory

This chapter explores cultural commoditization. Scholars who have examined this topic have highlighted the conflicts provoked by the commoditization of culture. They have also largely presented the tensions as those between middle-class Western tourists and local rural people, mostly from non-Western settings (e.g. Greenwood 1977; Kincaid 1988; Pattullo 1996; Hodder 1998; Lindknud 1998). Raminder Kaur and John Hutnyk (1999) have addressed the previously unexplored complex travel experiences of Diaspora peoples who travel to their "ancestral" homelands as tourists. Edward Bruner (1996) has specifically investigated the experiences of African-Americans in Ghana. My research builds and expands on Bruner's (1996) work by exploring how African-Americans contest the attempts by the Ghanaian authorities to restore Cape Coast and Elmina Castles in order to give recognition to their agency in the enterprise.

I take my theoretical inspiration, in part, from Davydd Greenwood's (1977) analysis of cultural commoditization. In particular, I highlight his emphasis on the dilemmas that result from the process of unpacking the tensions provoked by the restoration of Ghana's slave castles. But while Greenwood emphasized local people's protestations of the commoditization of their cultural landscape, I highlight also African-Americans' contestation of the restoration of Ghana's slave castles.[2] In doing so, I do not in anyway attempt to homogenize African-Americans. Rather I see them as a heterogeneous group with complex identities on a transnational landscape.

I also draw on transnationalism, specifically Diaspora theory, to delve into the spiritual, emotional, and psychological aspects of African-Americans who travel to Ghana to experience the slave castles. I bridge these two paradigms (i.e. cultural commoditization and Diaspora theory) to address the complexities of African-Americans' opposition to the restoration of and their subsequent passion for these monuments, and, to dissect competing interests and tensions provoked by this international project. In doing this, I strive to add to the scholarship on the African Diaspora and its relationship with Africa and African development (Zack-Williams 1995: 349) and help bridge the existing gap between Africa and the African Diaspora. I also contribute to the theorization of cultural commoditization, an area that has largely been conceptualized as an encounter between middle-class European-Americans and non-Western peoples.

Context

The Central Region Development Commission (CEDECOM, a regional development agency of one of the administrative regions of Ghana) initiated the restoration (and commoditization) of the two monuments. This happened soon after the United Nations Educational, Scientific and Cultural Organization (UNESCO) declared the monuments as World Heritage sites in 1990 (*New York Times*, November 25, 1990: 14; Hyatt 1997: 5). The project subsequently became an international collaborative effort involving the Ghanaian authorities, the United Nations Development Program (UNDP), and the United States Agency for International Development (USAID). The key Ghanaian agencies were CEDECOM, the Ghana Museums and Monuments Board (GMMB), and Ghana Heritage Conservation Trust (GHCT), a non-governmental organization (NGO). A number of US NGOs were also involved in the project.[3]

This collaborative effort aimed at restoring and preserving monuments that were in disrepair because of funding shortfall for their maintenance. The project involved stabilizing and repairing the fabric of the buildings to make them watertight. It also sought to refurbish rooms, install modern facilities, find uses for them, and present them more effectively to visitors (Hyatt 1997: 6).

As previously indicated, many African-Americans have opposed these changes. Their opposition has taken several forms including passionate newspaper comments. For example, in a letter published in *New African*, Imahkus Nzingah Okofu (formerly Imahkus Vienna Robinson), an expatriate African-American in Ghana, characterized the restoration as "renovation and destruction of an important monument of the African Holocaust" (1994: 4). Afrikadzata Deku (1993), an African-American scholar, described the project as a "teleguided falsification" in the name of preservation for the promotion of tourism. The protests culminated in a formal petition with 3,025 signatures of Diaspora Africans from around the world being presented to the Ghanaian government by a delegation of African-Americans in April of 1998. African-Americans were (and are) worried that changes in the monuments deprive them of the direct intimate experience of being able to see, smell, and feel the presence of their ancestors for spiritual reconnection and personal purification (Robinson 1994: 4).

Indeed the restoration of Ghana's slave monuments has a fascinating historical precedent that complicates the current controversies. In the 1970s, the African Descendants Association Foundation (ADAF, comprising African-American membership) of Ghana mobilized funds to restore Fort Amsterdam, also in the Central Region of Ghana, as a historical shrine for Africans in the Diaspora (*Ebony*, January 1972: 88–91). This fort, built by the British in 1631, was in disrepair at the time. Its restoration provoked controversies as well, but at that time it was white and local people who put African-Americans on the defensive. The project was perceived in some white circles as a foundation of a black power movement for anti-white propaganda (*Ebony*, January 1972: 89). On their part, the local residents protested that changes that would result from the project might anger the spirits that protected them (*Ebony*, January 1972: 91).

Discussion

Despite the concerns of those worrying about the consequences of current modifications to these buildings, there are those who would argue that these changes are merely a part of an ongoing process. Richard Handler and Eric Gable (1997) have argued that there really are no original monuments since buildings are always being restored for various reasons. They have discounted the existence of any original buildings at Colonial Williamsburg since the monuments have undergone continual restoration to ensure their preservation (Handler and Gable 1997: 222–224). Similarly, Cape Coast and Elmina Castles have a long history of modifications, having been rebuilt and expanded by the different European powers, which controlled them over the centuries (see Lawrence 1963: 18, 25; Anquandah 1982: 133; Schildkrout 1996: 36). Postcolonial governmental agencies have also utilized spaces in these monuments. In addition, the GMMB, the designated national institution responsible for these monuments, has been undertaking preservation work on them since Ghana's independence (see Kankpeyeng 1996: 3, 12–13). The recent involvement of international development agencies in the restoration project merely brought in much needed capital and expertise to reinforce previous efforts. As Vera Hyatt (1997: 6) notes, before the restoration project started, the two monuments were "dilapidated and in urgent need of repair."

Handler and Gable (1997: 222–224) have further argued that there is no necessary correlation between buildings *per se* and the experience of historical reality. What they consider more significant is the contextualization of buildings and the narratives that surround and make use of them. Indeed, according to Afrikadzata Deku (1993), "the importance of slave dungeons in Ghana/Africa is not the buildings but the collective knowledge, memory and external remembrance of the hell we suffered there as Africans."

John Tunbridge and John Ashworth (1996), as well as Nick Merriman (1996: 381) have noted how the commoditization of monuments can provoke conflicts. Merriman (1996: 391) attributes these tensions to the notion of monuments' empirical and transcendental significance. According to Merriman (1996: 382), monuments exist in physical forms as buildings as well as in peoples' minds in the form of collective memories, attitudes, and imaginations. Together these qualities endow the monuments with a meaning. The situation from Ghana's landscape suggests that physical experience of the castles makes a great deal of difference to African-Americans. Some of them claim that they can still hear the endless cry of pain of their ancestors whose presence they desire to experience when they visit the monuments (see Deku 1993; Robinson 1994: 4). African-American groups see Ghana's slave castles as shrines symbolizing the agonies and sufferings from the Atlantic slave trade.

I agree with James Young (1983) that issues involving slavery or the Holocaust can be extremely sensitive and controversial. African-Americans' prior involvement in the restoration of Fort Amsterdam requires a consideration of the issue of who has power to represent these monuments. Controversies over the exhibition *Harlem on My Mind* (Dubin 1999), the discovery of the African Burial Ground in New York

City (Harrington 1996; *Washington Post*, August 19, 1993: J01), and the planned excavation of the Foster property in Charlottesville in Virginia (*Washington Post*, October 10, 1993: F01) stemmed from what African-Americans perceived to be their lack of control over the fate of their heritage. The *Harlem on My Mind* exhibition was designed by mostly white curators to draw public attention to life in Harlem, particularly racism, between 1900 and 1968. Black Americans who critiqued the exhibition "frequently raised the issues of paternalism, self-determination, and the symbolic ownership of a group's history and identity" (Dubin 1999: 38). The African Burial Ground was stumbled upon in September 1991 when a site was being cleared for a federal office building in lower Manhattan in New York City. Black American scholars lobbied for transfer of control from white scholars to black investigators (Pearson 1999: 179). Michael Blakey, an African-American Professor of Anthropology at Howard University at the time, perceived this shift not only as a symbol of empowerment but also as insurance against the exploitation and disrespect of African-American history (*Washington Post*, August 19, 1993: J01; see also Blakely, Chapter 7, in this volume). The Foster property, which belonged to a free black family, was unearthed in 1993 when the University of Virginia was preparing a parking lot (*Washington Post*, October 10, 1993: F01). The University entrusted one of its white anthropology professors Drake Pattern (who specializes in African-American history) to investigate this site. The decision did not please some black Americans who agitated for a qualified black anthropologist to lead the investigation. The reason, according to Barbara Walker, President of the Afro-American Historical and Genealogical Association in Washington was that only black people have the requisite insight and spiritual sensitivities to investigate black history (*Washington Post*, January 18, 1994: D04). The black American photographer Roy DeCarava expressed these sentiments more succinctly in his reaction to the *Harlem on My Mind* exhibition when he said: "The fundamental thing is that blacks want to say their own things about themselves. White people, no matter how sympathetic, can't do it" (Dubin 1999: 38). Referring specifically to the restoration of Cape Coast and Elmina Castles, Imahkus Robinson (1994: 4) wonders why African-American history is being "white washed" by the very European-Americans who created and operated the Trans-Atlantic slave trade. Similarly, as the discussion thus far has shown, African-Americans also do not feel that Ghanaians have the requisite experience and sensitivity to represent the monuments.

It is significant to note that African-Americans have perceived the castles solely in terms of the Atlantic slave trade, which represents just a fraction of the complex history of the monuments. Dr. Francis Duah, the former Museum Director of these castles, has been critical of this bias (see *US News and World Report*, September 18, 1995: 33). Martha Norkunas (1993: 6) has argued that monuments tend to represent complex historical events. Cape Coast and Elmina Castles have served different functions and this means different utilization of space over time. They have been used as trading posts, slave dungeons, military fortifications, colonial administrative centers, prisons, schools, offices, and are now presented as tourist attractions. In terms of space utilization, the slave dungeons had previously served as storage rooms for nonhuman cargo while the slave auction hall used to be a Portuguese Roman Catholic church (cf. the *New York Times*, November 25, 1990: 14; Bruner 1996: 293; Schildkrout

1996: 36; Hyatt 1997: 29). Ghanaian museum officials insist that their efforts seek to project the multifunctional histories of these monuments.

Scholars such as Kwame Appiah (1992: 6–7), Kwame Arhin (as cited in the *Washington Post*, April 17, 1995: A10), and Edward Bruner (1996: 293) locate the complexity of these tensions within the different historical experiences of Ghanaians and African-Americans. They emphasize that even under colonization Africans lived in a society with an overwhelming black majority where black people were largely in charge of their own social and cultural institutions. Arhin argues that most Ghanaians did not even see the British colonial masters and have not endured centuries of slavery and legal segregation (*Washington Post*, April 17, 1995: A10). As such, for them racial problems were less salient. For African-Americans, on the other hand, daily life was and has been a painful struggle by a minority group against racism and economic marginalization within a dominant white society. Further, racism was the driving force behind the slave trade and colonialism and was also responsible for the deep-rooted racial stereotyping of peoples of Africa and of African descent (Dei 1998: 144; Ackah 1999: 12; Minter 2000: 200–210).

Conclusion

The case of Cape Coast and Elmina Castles reinforce the complexity of the use of culture as a commodity. The strong emotions the treatment of these sites has provoked among African-Americans show how controversial representations of slavery can be. The controversies over ownership, control, and authority demonstrate the web of complexity surrounding restoration projects and the way that power is transmitted through the process. It is odd that African-Americans were not consulted during the initial stages of the project given the sensitive issues surrounding it and the fact that the restoration project was particularly aimed at them. The omission may partly reflect the different sensibilities that Ghanaian officials and African-Americans bring to the enterprise. While the issues engendered sparked off heated discussions, they also made it possible for dialogues and compromises. For example, the Ghanaian authorities closed down the restaurant-bar in Cape Coast Castle out of respect for African-American concerns. In addition, new signs erected in front of both Cape Coast and Elmina Castles refer to these monuments as both castles and dungeons. This action is in recognition of African-American sentiments that the monuments were not just castles but also dungeons. But while African-Americans have the political clout to influence changes, the ultimate decisions and their implementation rest with Ghanaian officials. It is hoped that Ghanaian representations of the monuments, with more reverential attention to the slavery heritage aspect, will ultimately be acceptable to African-Americans.

Notes

1 1993 statistics show that 67 percent of the 17,091 visitors to Elmina Castle were Ghanaians, 12.5 percent were Europeans, and 12.3 percent were North Americans, including a substantial number of African-Americans (Bruner 1996: 290).

2 Anthropologists have often highlighted the complexity of heritage tourism. The landscape is bound to become even more complex when Diaspora populations are involved in the analysis since the return of any Diaspora group to its "ancestral" homeland is, in itself, always problematic (see Angelou 1986; Naipaul 1987; Safran 1991: 83–84; Kasinitz 1992; Harris 1993: 6; Shepperson 1993: 44; Skinner 1993: 11; Clifford 1994: 311; Bruner 1996; Gershoni 1997; Brown 1998; Kaur and Hutnyk 1999; Vickerman 1999: 137–163; Akyeampong 2000: 185–186). Also, as Bruner (1996) shows for African-Americans who return to Ghana, the terrain becomes even more controversial when the Diaspora group is confronted with the unexpected representations of slavery that await them.

3 Conservation International (CI), the International Council on Monuments and Sites (US/ICOMOS), the Debt for Development Foundation, and the Smithsonian Institution under the leadership of the Midwest Universities Consortium for International Activities, including the University of Minnesota Tourism Center for Tourism Development.

References

Ackah, William B. (1999) *Pan-Africanism: Exploring the Contradictions. Politics, Identity and Development in Africa and the African Diaspora*, Aldershot: Ashgate.

Akyeampong, Emmanuel (2000) "Africans in the Diaspora: the Diaspora and Africa," *African Affairs*, 99: 183–215.

Angelou, Maya (1986) *All God's Children Need Traveling Shoes*, New York: Vintage Books.

Anquandah, James (1982) *Rediscovering Ghana's Past*, Harlow and Accra: Longman and Sedco.

Appiah, Kwame A. (1992) *In My Father's House: Africa in the Philosophy of Culture*, Oxford: Oxford University Press.

Brown, Jacqueline N. (1998) "Black Liverpool, Black America, and the gendering of diasporic space," *Cultural Anthropology*, 13, 3: 291–325.

Bruner, Edward M. (1996) "Tourism in Ghana: the representation of slavery and the return of the Black Diaspora," *American Anthropologist*, 98, 2: 290–304.

Clifford, James (1994) "Diasporas," *Cultural Anthropology*, 9: 302–338.

Dei, George J. S. (1998) "Interrogating 'African development' and the Diasporan reality," *Journal of Black Studies*, 29, 2: 141–153.

Deku, Afrikadzata (1993) "The Truth about Castles in Ghana and Africa," *Ghanaian Weekly Spectator*, May 8: 5, May 15: 14.

Dubin, Stephen C. (1999) *Displays of Power: Memory and Amnesia in the American Museum*, New York: New York University Press.

Ebony, January 1972, "A shrine to slaves: Black Americans restore Ghana's old fort," 88–91.

Gershoni, Yekutiel (1997) *Africans on African-Americans: The Creation and Uses of an African-American Myth*, New York: New York University Press.

Greenwood, Davydd J. (1977) "Culture by the Pound. An Anthropological Perspective on Tourism as Cultural Commoditization," in Valene L. Smith (ed.) *Hosts and Guests: The Anthropology of Tourism*, 129–138, Philadelphia, PA: University of Pennsylvania Press.

Handler, Richard and Gable, Eric (1997) *The New History in an Old Museum: Creating the Past at Colonial Williamsburg*, Durham, NC: Duke University Press.

Harrington, Spencer (1996) "An African Cemetery in Manhattan," in Brian Fagan (ed.) *Eyewitness to Discovery: First Person Accounts of More than Fifty of the World's Greatest Archaeological Discoveries*, 324–333, Oxford: Oxford University Press.

Harris, Joseph E. (1993) *Global Dimensions of the African Diaspora*. 2nd edn, Washington, DC: Howard University Press.

Hodder, Ian (1998) "The Past as Passion and Play: Çatalhoyuk as a Site of Conflict in the Construction of Multiple Pasts," In Lynn Meskell (ed.) *Archaeology Under Fire: Nationalism, Politics, and Heritage in the Eastern Mediterranean and Middle East*, 124–139, London: Routledge.

Housee, Shirin (1999) "Journey Through Life: The Self in Travel," in Raminder Kaur and John
    Hutnyk (eds) *Travel Worlds: Journeys in Contemporary Cultural Politics*, 137–154, London:
    Zed Books.
Hyatt, Vera (1997) *Ghana: The Chronicle of a Museum Development Project in the Central Region*,
    Washington, DC: The Smithsonian Institution.
Kankpeyeng, Benjamin (1996) *Archaeological Resources Management in Ghana*, unpublished
    Master's thesis, Department of Anthropology, Syracuse University, Syracuse.
Kasinitz, Philip (1992) *Caribbean New York: Black Immigrants and the Politics of Race*, Ithaca, NY:
    Cornell University Press.
Kaur, Raminder and Hutnyk, John (1999) "Introduction," in Raminder Kaur and John Hutnyk
    (eds) *Travel Worlds: Journeys in Contemporary Cultural Politics*, 1–13, London: Zed Books.
Kincaid, Jamaica (1988) *A Small Place*, Toronto: Collins Publishers.
Lawrence, Arnold Walter (1963) *Trade Castles and Forts of West Africa*, London: Jonathan Cape.
Lindknud, Christian (1998) "When Opposite Worldviews Attract: A Case of Tourism and
    Local Development in Southern France," in Simone Abram and Jacqueline Waldren (eds)
    Anthropological Perspectives on Local Development: Knowledge and Sentiments in Conflict,
    141–159, London: Routledge.
Merriman, Nick (1996) "Understanding heritage," *Journal of Material Culture*, 1, 3: 377–386.
Minter, William (2000) "America and Africa: beyond the double standard," *Current History* 99,
    637: 200–210.
Naipaul, Vidiadhar S. (1987) *The Enigma of Arrival: A Novel*, New York: Knopf.
New York Times, November 25, 1990: 14 "The slave fortresses of Ghana: monuments to a tragic
    past."
Norkunas, Martha K. (1993) *The Politics of Public Memory: Tourism, History, and Ethnicity in
    Monterey, California*, Albany, NY: SUNY Press.
Pattullo, Polly (1996) *Last Resorts: The Cost of Tourism in the Caribbean*, Kingston, Jamaica: Ian
    Randle Publishers.
Pearson, Mike (1999) *The Archaeology of Death and Burial*, College Station, TX: Texas A&M
    University Press.
Phillips, Caryl (2000) *The Atlantic Sound*, New York: Knopf.
Robinson, Imahkus (Imahkus Nzingah Okofu) (1994) "Ghana—don't white wash the slave
    trade," *New African*, 324, 1994: 4.
Safran, William (1991) "Diasporas in modern societies: myths of homeland and return,"
    Diaspora, 1,1: 83–99.
Schildkrout, Enid (1996) "Kingdom of Gold," *Natural History*, 105, 2: 36–47.
Shepperson, George (1993) "African Diaspora: Concept and Context," in Joseph E. Harris (ed.)
    Global Dimensions of the African Diaspora, 2nd edn, 41–49, Washington, DC: Howard
    University Press.
Skinner, Elliott P. (1993) "The Dialectic between Diasporas and Homelands," in Joseph E.
    Harris (ed.) *Global Dimensions of the African Diaspora*, 2nd edn, 11–40, Washington, DC:
    Howard University Press.
Stewart, Rowena (1994) "The Empowerment of African-American Museums," in Jane R.
    Glaser and Artemis A. Zenetou (eds) *Gender Perspectives. Essays on Women in Museums*,
    71–76, Washington, DC: The Smithsonian Institution Press.
Tunbridge, John E. and Ashworth, Gregory John (1996) *Dissonant Heritage: The Management of
    the Past as a Resource in Conflict*, New York: Wiley.
Tyehimba, Cheo (1998) "Scarred walls of stone," *American Legacy*, 4, 2: 22–30.
US News and World Report, September 18, 1995: 33.
Vickerman, Milton (1999) *Crosscurrents: West Indian Immigrants and Race*, New York: Oxford
    University Press.
Washington Post, August 19, 1993: J01, "Voices from the Grave: Howard to study bones of
    Colonial African Americans."
Washington Post, October 10, 1993: F01, "Catherine's Ghost: while bulldozing a parking lot, the
    University of Virginia ran into a problem. It was as old as slavery and racism."

Washington Post, January 18, 1994: D04, "Blacks Protest Excavation Team."

Washington Post, April 17, 1995: A10, "U.S., African Blacks differ on turning slave dungeons into tourist attractions."

Washington Post, July 26, 2000: A16-17, "Back to Land of No Return"

Washington Post, October 9, 2000: A22, "Modern Slave States."

Young, James E. (1983) *The Texture of Memory: Holocaust Memorials and Meaning*, New Haven, CT: Yale University Press.

Zack-Williams, Alfred (1995) "Development and diaspora: separate concerns?," *Review of African Political Economy*, 65: 349–358.

3 Back to Africa
Issues of hosting "Roots" tourism in West Africa

FIONA J. L. HANDLEY

Introduction

Tourism is a phenomenon that has come under increasing scrutiny in the contemporary world. It crosses multiple disciplinary boundaries from economics, tourism, and leisure studies to anthropology. Because it involves the movement of people and ideas around the world it is frequently analyzed in the light of globalization and thus has been subject to what could be described as postmodern critiques (MacCannell 1992; Robertson *et al.* 1994; Urry 1995; Rojek and Urry 1997). At one level this chapter makes a contribution to this goal, since the tourism of immigrants and exiles back to their country of origin has recently been recognized in this discourse. However, this chapter will examine one group of returnees who are usually unable to narrow their genealogical heritage beyond the broad area of West Africa. Whereas it may seem obvious why recent immigrants want to return to see family, friends, and places that they, their parents, or their grandparents remember, the phenomena of African-Americans returning to Africa is less straightforward. With the exception of some illegally smuggled slaves, there is a temporal gap of nearly 200 years between the present and the direct slave trade between the USA and Africa. One way to begin to comprehend this phenomenon is through a consideration of the long lasting links between Africa and its Diaspora in the Americas.

The West's understanding of Africa has been constructed over many decades through ethnography and physical anthropology (see Mudimbe 1988, 1994; Coombes 1994), and compromised by colonial research envisaged to allow the colonizer to control the colonized (e.g. Said 1978). "Colonized" Africa played a significant role in the creation and construction of modern African-American identity. Over the past two centuries there have been several Back-to-Africa movements and many instances of small groups organizing their own return to the continent. All were linked to socioeconomic conditions in the USA, with interest in migration reflecting both the debased status of black people of the time (Redkey 1969: 22) and how Africa itself was perceived. As has been hinted at earlier, the African-American community followed other Americans by holding a vision of Africa clouded by stereotypes and sentimentalism (Okoye 1971). Africa was seen as a heterogeneous, peaceful place where people lived simple, un-Christian lives in rural harmony. The stereotype of

Africa as an uncivilized place did not encourage migration, although it did inspire a missionary urge in some. Pride in fighting inequality and a hope of sharing the riches of the land they had helped create had to be weighed up against freedom from persecution, fear of the unknown, and leaving family and friends. While there was no clear-cut African-American stance on the matter, for a variety of reasons people did hunger for return.

The American Colonization Society, founded in 1816, was the first organization to attempt to systematically return African-Americans to Africa. The society, which was a curious and unholy mixture of prominent white men such as Thomas Madison, Abolitionists, and racist segregationists, raised enough money to send its first ship to West Africa, to what became Liberia, in 1820. These early trips were fairly disastrous, but over time Liberia was "settled" and became more stable, and in the following decade over 2,000 settlers arrived. Colonization continued through the mid-nineteenth century, then saw a sharp rise after the deterioration of race relations in the South at the end of Reconstruction in 1877 (Redkey 1969: 21). By the end of the nineteenth and the beginning of the twentieth centuries national debates about the future of African-Americans were being held by high profile blacks, with fierce pro-colonization stances taken by Bishop Henry Turner and Edward W. Blyden. Their mantle was taken up by Marcus Garvey, who, in 1919, founded the Black Star Line, a shipping company whose purpose was to return blacks to Africa. All of these schemes had small successes but quickly ran into problems, eventually culminating in the current problems of Liberia—a country torn by generations of immigrant exploitation of indigenous communities.

As the twentieth century progressed, these developments moved in a new direction, with an increasing concern for uniting black Africans and African-Americans in their nationalist struggles against white oppression. This movement, termed Pan-Africanism, was epitomized by concerns for artistic and cultural authenticity (*négritude*) and a growing body of scholarship by Africans about Africa that questioned traditional Western attitudes toward the continent and its history (see Howe 1998; Ackah 1999). By the 1960s, Pan-Africanism was bearing fruit, with the Civil Rights Movement in the USA starting to gain equal rights for African-Americans and the rapid expulsion of European colonial powers from Africa. Many of the new African leaders developed a close relationship with African-American Civil Rights leaders in a mutually supportive relationship and the vision of a land governed by blacks again led some black Americans to return to Africa, most notably Stokely Carmichael, later known as Kwame Ture, a prominent member of the Black Panthers, who emigrated to Guinea in 1969.

"Roots"

The new African awareness that the Civil Rights Movement engendered in the USA resulted in a new pride in Africa, demonstrated through, for example, the use of Kente cloth and cowrie shells in clothing and jewelry. Some visible, if superficial, cultural connections were being made, although the historical connections between Africa and African-Americans were still difficult to deal with. But one book and its accompanying television series changed this situation. In 1976, Alex Haley published *Roots: The Saga of an American Family.* The book is a narrative based on Haley's own family history and the stories said to have been passed down by them through the generations. While it reads as fiction, it becomes clear at the end of the book that it is a true story. Haley himself appears as a kind of historical detective, tracing his family's history through the clues passed down to him about his African ancestor Kunte Kinte. He heads off to Gambia, hoping that the Kamby Bolongo River, held within his family's traditions, is the River Gambia:

> Then we went on, and upon arriving at a little village called Alvreda, we put ashore, our destination now on foot the yet smaller village of Juffure, where the men had been told that this griot lived. There is an expression called "the peak experience"—that which emotionally, nothing in your life ever transcends. I've had mine, that first day in the back country of black West Africa ... "About the time the King's soldiers came"— another of the griot's time-fixing references—"the eldest of these four sons, Kunta, went away from his village to chop wood ... and he was never seen again ..." And the griot went on with his narrative. I sat as if I were carved of stone. My blood seemed to have congealed. This man whose lifetime had been in this back-country African village had no way in the world to know that he had just echoed what I had heard all through my boyhood years on my grandma's front porch in Henning, Tennessee ... of an African who always had insisted that his name was "Kin-tay," who had called a guitar a "ko," and a river within the state of Virginia, "Kamby Bolongo"; and who had been kidnapped into slavery while not far from his village, chopping wood, to make himself a drum ... I don't remember hearing anyone giving an order, I only recall becoming aware that those seventy-odd people had formed a wide human ring around me, moving counterclockwise, chanting softly, loudly, softly; their bodies close together, they were lifting their knees high, stamping up reddish puffs of the dust.
>
> (Haley 1977: 628–631)

Haley's emotional recounting of this experience in the book and subsequent TV series made *Roots* a phenomenal success. Haley had co-authored the *Autobiography of Malcolm X*, but little prepared him for the success of this book. The publisher's initial print run in 1976 of 200,000 copies—a figure unprecedented for a book by a black author—was quickly sold out, and within the first year of publication more than a million hardcover copies had been sold. By 2000 it had sold 8.5 million copies in 26 languages (Bundles 2001). Contributing to this success was the TV mini-series *Roots*, which was screened in late January 1977 on ABC. Of the eight episodes screened on consecutive nights, 85 percent of American households tuned into some or all of the scheduling:

> On each successive night, as restaurants lost business and bar owners switched their overhead television sets from basketball to *Roots*, the audience mushroomed until the Sunday night finale reached 100 million viewers. By the week's end, in a deliciously ironic triumph, *Roots* had

toppled *Gone with the Wind*—which had made its television debut just a year earlier—from its perch at the top of the nation's ten most watched programs.

(Bundles 2001: 13)

As one author later wrote: "it was all my friends and co-workers could talk about. They watched it at night and talked about it in the morning—about Africa, about slavery, about finding their ancestors" (Redford and D'Orso 2000: 2). Not surprisingly, *Roots* attracted proportionally more black than white viewers but apparently reached a large white audience and created more white interest in, knowledge about, and tolerance for, the black experience (Merelman 1995: 263). *Roots* weeks were organized in 30 cities, and the National Archives, which houses census manuscripts for genealogical research, reported that the number of letters they received had tripled, and applications to use the archive had risen by 40 percent (Rushdy 2001: 15). The book continues to be cited as a key text in understanding the African-American experience (Ruffins 1992: 569; Curtis 1996: vii; Redford and D'Orso 2000; Durant 2002: 79) because, as Dee Parmer Woodtor states:

> African Americans do not have one epic story to explain their capture from Africa, their enslavement and subsequent freedom in the Americas. Nor do many of us have family stories that tell of our ancestors in epic form. What we have are bits and pieces of stories or maybe individual stories based on individual achievements. *Roots* came closest to telling this story in epic form, for *Roots* was the story of nearly every African American family. Kunta Kinte was a symbol of the first African and his exploits, trials, tribulations, and victories in the United States. In a major way, *Roots* is our epic story.
>
> (Woodtor 1999: 11)

Roots launched a generation of African-American family historians and turned many heads towards Africa:

> By all means, if you are an African-American, try to trace your roots back to Africa. You may be one of the lucky ones who get the thrill of a lifetime finding evidence of their own past among one of Africa's indigenous cultures. Certainly, go to Africa if you ever get the chance, whether or not you intend to do some serious genealogical research. After all, if you are an African American, then Africa is the first home of your ancestors. You are connected to that land by blood.
>
> (Johnson and Cooper 1996: 8)

Roots, through demonstrating how genealogy could be used, created a direct link between African-Americans and Africa. It substantiated a connection that had always been felt in the African-American community and demonstrated the possibilities of a visit to the continent for those African-Americans with disposable income. How then did African countries respond to this interest?

Africa and "Roots" tourism

While African countries shared a common political bond with American blacks through the 1960s, initial enthusiasm for Pan-Africanism was put aside as the new nations dealt with the more prosaic problems of running countries divided not between white and black but along "tribal" or ethnic lines. One of the major problems faced by West African nations has been finding economic stability, and many countries turned toward the world's fastest growing industry—tourism. Africa has huge potential as an international tourist destination, but is underdeveloped in terms of infrastructure and the creation of destinations (Travel and Tourism Analyst 1996). Tourism has played an important role in the economies of countries such as Kenya and the Gambia since the 1960s, and more recently tourism has been repositioned as a central developmental strategy in many sub-Saharan African nations, including the Gambia, Ghana, Mali, and Senegal.

The Gambia Incorporated is the Gambian Government's economic vision of Gambia in the twenty-first century, and it focuses strongly on tourism. Tourism is the fastest-growing segment in the Gambian economy, contributing to 12 percent of the GDP, and indirectly employing 10,000 Gambians. Tourist arrivals are close to 100,000 per year (Gambia 1996). While the Gambia has a long history as a winter sun destination attracting Northern Europeans to the beaches around Banjul, the potential benefits have been limited by both the seasonal and geographical concentration of the market. Attempts to distribute the market more evenly have resulted in a focus on the country's heritage, especially St James Fort, a slave fort situated on an island in the river Gambia. The Gambia also has a singular tourist attraction in the village of Juffure, which was where Alex Haley heard the local *griot* recount the village's history and mention the disappearance of Haley's ancestor Kunta Kinte. The immense interest in this story led to a Gambian tourist office being set up in New York as long ago as the 1970s (Gamble 1989: 50). While this initial attempt did not result in the office becoming permanent, this theme has been further developed through the creation of a *Roots Homecoming Festival*, which began in 1996. The festival, 'now known as the *International Roots Festival,*' is celebrated in the low tourist season in the early summer and consists of seminars on Gambian history, music evenings, as well as a day trip called "Kunta Kinteh's Trail of No Return" to the St James Fort and the village of Juffure. There is also a trip to Kanilai for a "Jola initiation/rites of passage ceremony" (Roots Festival 2002). The 8th *International Roots Festival* is planned to take place in 2006.

Ghana has a shorter history of involvement with tourism, but tourist arrivals in the country leapt from 85,000 in 1985 to 325,438 in 1997, and by 2010 tourism is expected to be Ghana's number one foreign exchange earner. There is now a 15-year Integrated National Tourism Development Program in place that identifies historic monuments relating to slavery as a potential market. The development of the slave forts including Cape Coast Castle and Elmina and the building of a museum and a museum shop along the stretch of coast between Accra to Half Assini were part of a cultural and ecological conservation project funded by the United States Agency for International Development (USAID), which began in 1997. Visits to these sites rose from 20,000 in 1992 to 40,000 in 1997 (Africa Online 1998). Ghana remains an expensive place to get to: there are no charter flights into Accra from Europe though there are now twice-weekly flights from the USA. Although the Ghanaian tourism office went on a US promotion campaign in 1995, at present the American market is not specifically targeted. Despite this, Ghana still attracts "Roots" tourists by being the most accessible country along this stretch of coast and by being the West African country most Americans are familiar with from the 1960s emigrations of prominent African-Americans such as Maya Angelou. Since 1998 Ghana has hosted an annual Emancipation Day celebration on August 1st, involving memorial ceremonies and trips to "slave castles." By 2002 this had expanded to include trips to slave markets in the interior, wreath-laying ceremonies at prominent locations in Accra, and a Vigil/Reverential Night at Cape Coast Castle (Ghana Ministry of Tourism 2002a). There is also a visit to the tombs of Crystal and Carson, two skeletons of slaves brought from Jamaica and the USA, who were re-interred in 1998. August 1 refers to the emancipation of slaves in the British Empire and is thus usually celebrated in the Caribbean; however, the festival attracted 200 African-Americans to Ghana in 2002 (Ghana Ministry of Tourism 2002b). As well as the government-organized events, there are ceremonies and trips run by local businesses (Bruner 1996).

Several countries in the region, together with Ghana and the Gambia, have sites associated with slavery, which are being incorporated into the tourist infrastructure. Benin is making tentative attempts to develop international tourism at the town of Ouidah and has a slave route from the museum down to the beach where the boats landed to trade their wares and purchase slaves who were then taken out to the slave ships in the deeper water. There is a memorial in the form of an arch that can be walked through, known as "The Point of No Return."

Senegal is home to probably the best-known slavery site in West Africa, the Maison des Esclaves at Gorée Island. Gorée, a World Heritage Site, was where US President Bill Clinton finished his 1998 African tour, and where his successor, George W. Bush, gave a speech on America's role in the slave trade at the beginning of his trip in 2003. The view from the hatch—another Point of No Return—is an emblematic image. Some tours operate out of the USA to come here, but it seems that there is no specific Government program to encourage this kind of tourism.

Like other West African countries, local sensitivity toward this history of slavery is difficult to gauge. Pamela Thomas was told while at Gorée that "probably 80–90% of the people in Senegal have no idea that you were taken from Africa because of the slave trade" (Thomas 1998: 18) and the following quote from the Ghanaian Minister of Tourism, Hon. Kwamena Bartels to the Ghanaian media is suggestive:

> I hope you will ensure that information on the Emancipation Day Celebrations will be effectively and widely disseminated so that the average Ghanaian will know when and where to join the celebration. This is also very important because much as we welcome external visitors to the country, there is the need to encourage our local citizens to take part in the celebrations in order to give the event a national character.
>
> (Ghana Ministry of Tourism 2002a)

That West Africans don't celebrate the end of slavery in the New World is perhaps obvious, although it is interesting that the Minister is trying to involve them in the festival to encourage feelings of "African Unity" (Ghana Ministry of Tourism 2002b). What is certain is that if it were not for the pressure or attention brought to the subject of slavery by the Diaspora, these programs would not exist. Indeed, from one perspective it is strange that African Unity can traverse not just the divide of time or distance but also that the ancestors of the West Africans welcoming African-Americans back were the original captors and enslavers. As Henry Louis Gates Jr states: "we feel at home here because we are surrounded by black people, that's why we come. But the memory of slavery and what our ancestors must have gone through is always lurking, even a pretty little harbor town like Elmina is dominated by its slave castle. And for us a slave castle is like Auschwitz" (Gates 1999).

The African-American experience in Africa

As the foregoing suggests, Diaspora tourism in Africa is not a straightforward experience. The meeting between the tourist and the local community at the tourist destination is central to definition of the experience. The anthropology of tourism has focused on authenticity, in particular how traditional cultures have to be "commodified" for the tourist (Cohen 1988). To varying degrees this relationship has also been characterized as damaging to indigenous cultures, exploitative, even as a kind of neocolonialism. What runs through these definitions is the concept of tourism as the West's search for contact with the authentic premodern "other" (MacCannell 1992), but the meeting of African-Americans and Africans in a tourist space questions this definition. Certainly there are some elements of local culture that are merely commodified for tourists, but some of the tourist practices are entirely new (expressly invented) activities. Part of what takes place is appropriate local behavior for a celebration or memorial, but the places visited and things talked about have no local cultural currency, and events such as the vigils in slave castles are entirely new.

For that matter, the relationship between Africa and African-Americans is not the one traditionally understood in the anthropology of tourism. Both have been "othered" in Western discourse through the use of stereotypes that are rooted in notions of Africans as primal and uncivilized. Both have been oppressed by people of white European descent, both are now liberated. And as explained earlier, there is a deep bond running between the communities. Evidently then, black visiting black in a black-run country is very different from traditional tourist scenarios, and at the most minimal level would create a different set of expectations and preconceptions. Most profoundly, the return to Africa is deeply symbolic for African-Americans, a sensation that can only find possible parallels in the tourism of the devotee to religious sites. Precisely because most African-Americans cannot point to one place on a map as their point of origin, their whole experience of meeting Africans and seeing Africa can be read through the subtext of "*this could have been me … they could be my distant relations.*" Gwendolyn Hackley Austin went to the Gambia and describes her feeling of immediacy with her enslaved African ancestor "I left the village of Gandiaye with mixed emotions. Although I never knew the African lady, I felt a closeness to her while in the village. I do not know for certain that she ever lived there ..." (Austin 1987: 69). Renée Kemp went to Ghana and states: "there is something else about the atmosphere here—an eerie feeling that causes me to turn and look for someone standing beside me even when I know I am alone" (Kemp 2000: 17). Both Austin and Kemp were on organized tourist packages, the kind of tourism that has been dismissed so widely in most anthropological literature (e.g. Ritzer and Liska 1997). But as one commentator, Tim Edensor, has pointed out "certain sites are so 'full' of meaning that they cannot be rendered superficial through their commodification" (Edensor 1998: 6).

The package may be inauthentic, but it is the route to profound feelings. All of the tours cover sites that are especially symbolic, and all of these generally have an area within them that is singled out for the encountering of particularly deep emotions. These are frequently views across the sea, such as the hatch at Gorée, at Cape Coast Castle, and the constructed view through the arch at Ouidah. These are presented in terms of being "The Point of No Return," and symbolize the crossing of a threshold, off the land of Africa into a new life. At Cape Coast Castle Renée Kemp states: "it is at the 'Door of No Return' that I understand with a rush of sadness exactly how I have come to be an African in America. Through this door, hundreds of years ago, a brown-skinned girl who looked just like me was marched from the dungeon and onto a waiting ship, bound for the Americas" (Kemp 2000: 23).

The intense feelings experienced by African-Americans upon reaching Africa suggest that this might be a very fruitful cultural meeting ground. This potential, unsurprisingly, is compromised through several factors. Many African-Americans' image of Africa is informed by the "Imaginary Africa" (Okoye 1971) created, it is fair to say, through their experience in the Diaspora rather than from information about Africa itself. The reality of arriving in a poor, developing country is shocking, and what is immediately striking are the differences rather than the similarities. Many are confused that Africans respond to them primarily as Americans, rather than as fellow blacks. Edward Bruner explains that in Ghana, African-Americans are referred to as *obruni*, meaning whiteman, a word that describes Europeans, Americans, and Asians regardless of skin color, but also means foreigner. The exceptions are black Africans of other continental African nations, who are referred to by a different name for stranger (Bruner 1996). The unbreakable association not with Africa, but rather with America is ironic considering the motivations of many African-Americans longing to slip into the crowd and feel at home. Cultural differences are also displayed through tourist interactions of taking photos, buying souvenirs, and spending money, which draw attention to the extreme differences in lifestyles and aspirations of host and guest. Pamela Thomas recounts her uncomfortable experience on arriving in Senegal, when a young Senegalese man asks her if it is her first time in Senegal. " 'Yes', I replied, breathlessly. 'My first time'. 'Welcome to Senegal', he replied. 'Welcome to the Motherland'. And as I turned to him with tears in my eyes, he said, 'Give me a dollar' " (Thomas 1998: 17). Most problematic of all, while African-Americans seek fulfillment in Africa, they may be confronted by Africans who dream of the USA.

More importantly for the host–guest relationship, the act of return recalls the departure. Presentations at the historical sites make it clear that it was Africans who sold their fellow Africans into slavery, facts which trouble the bond of common experience and instead raise questions of culpability. In a TV series on the history of West Africa, African-American academic Henry Louis Gates Jr interviews a tourist after their tour of Elmina where these facts were presented. She says: "I think I was surprised and hurt and angry and everything because these were people that I sort of had a fantasy about, as our ancestors, and your ancestors don't sell you. So that fantasy was sort of blown away" (Gates 1999). Visitors expecting to be reassured through mutual recognition of a common enemy are confronted not with a salve to trauma, but the potential opening of new, unexpected wounds. Old ones too can be reopened, as the horrors of both the conditions at the forts and the Middle Passage are re-enacted and imagined. Bruner reports that this has led to attacks on white tourists by African-American tourists at Elmina (Bruner 1996: 296).

The *relative* importance of slavery to both communities is also emphasized. To West Africans, the enslavement and disappearance of Africans was but one important event in a long, dynamic history. To the Diaspora, enslavement is the defining moment of their common identity and the reason for their return to Africa. This division is just a starting point for the contentious decisions about which history to present and how to present it. The deep emotion that many "Roots" tourists feel is difficult to translate into traditional presentations and may suggest that these places are best left almost uninterpreted, because words can never do them justice. Yet their immense educational value implies that they should be accessible and understandable to as many people as possible, a scenario that does not fit well with minimal interpretation for the purposes of quiet reflection. But too great a focus on the horrors of slavery may dissuade visitors, and the "middle ground" of a general historical presentation focusing on slavery could easily become non-challenging and insensitive. For example, the slave holding areas in the Cape Coast Castle in Ghana are notorious for their horrible smell many years after their last captives left. The question of whether this very vivid sign of the centuries of abuse that went on within their walls should be cleaned up is one that continues to be debated (Osei-Tutu 2003).

"Roots" tourism also questions another tenant of tourism as traditionally understood. Going on holiday—"going away"—is understood as an event involving leaving home. But this kind of tourism suggests that "going away" is in fact returning home. Urry (1995: 32, my italics) cites departure from home and the everyday as central to defining the tourist gaze: "the journey (is) to … sites which are outside the normal places of residence and work. Periods of residence elsewhere are of a short term and temporary nature. *There is a clear intention to return 'home' within a relatively short period of time.*" Yet this contradicts the definition of diasporic identity which is molded around a mythic homeland, a "home" which is not where the diasporic subject dwells (Clifford 1997: 247). "Roots" tourism consciously disturbs the polarities of "home" and "away" and "here" and "there," and highlights the multiplicity of diasporic identity recently identified in much postcolonial literature (Gilroy 1993; Hall 2000). But, if diasporas are defined by a geographic displacement, then surely traveling will at least help develop some answers, even if the "origins" in Africa being sought can never truly be found.

Conclusion

Generations have passed since the last enslaved Africans left their homeland to go to the Americas, but the African-American community is still very aware of its ties to this continent. During this period, individuals have taken it upon themselves to become closer to their homeland, through using Africa as a cultural referent, by engaging with common political goals and through physically returning. The growing awareness in the 1970s of the history of slavery and the possibilities of genealogical research led to a renewed interest in Africa, and the advent of affordable international tourism made holidays to Africa a possibility for some African-Americans.

"Roots" tourism subverts traditional definitions of tourism. Pan-Africanism may create a bond demonstrated through the direct marketing of destinations to African-Americans, but it does not seem to operate at the face-to-face level within the tourist space. The high expectations of tourists who want to disappear into the crowd or to feel as if they have returned home are continually compromised by the tourist structure. But while they do not have the experience they were expecting, they do have a tangibly different one to other groups of visitors because their expectations are so very different and because of the visit's central importance to their individual and community identity. "Roots" tourism may take place within the structures of contemporary global tourism, but, while the tourist product is still commodified in West Africa, the experience of tourists there cannot be described as inauthentic because whatever the outcome, whether it is upsetting, shocking, or rewarding, the encounter is always both deeply personal, transformative, and communally symbolic.

Acknowledgments

I would like to thank the Royal Historical Society, the Institute of Archaeology (University College London), and the Arts and Humanities Research Board for funding my attendance at the conference for which this chapter was initially prepared.

References

Ackah, W. B. (1999) *Pan-Africanism: Exploring the Contradictions*, Aldershot: Ashgate.
Africa Online (1998) "USAID's briefing to the President–overview," *African Online*, available at http://www.africaonline.com.gh/Usaid/ghana.html (accessed February 5, 2001).
Austin, G. H. (1987) "The African lady," *Journal of Afro-American Historical and Genealogical Society*, 8: 61–69.
Bruner, E. M. (1996) "Tourism in Ghana: the representation of slavery and the return of the Black Diaspora," *American Anthropologist*, 98, 2: 290–304.
Bundles, A. L. (2001) "Looking back at the *Roots* phenomenon," *Black Issues*, 3, 4: 12–15.
Clifford, J. (1997) *Routes: Travel and Translation in the Late Twentieth Century*, London: Harvard University Press.
Cohen, E. (1988) "Authenticity and Commodification in Tourism," *Annals of Tourism Research*, 15: 1–386.

Coombes, A. E. (1994) *Reinventing Africa: Museums, Material Culture and Popular Imagination*, London: Yale University Press.

Curtis, N. C. (1996) *Black Heritage Sites: The South*, New York: The New Press.

Durant, T. J. (2002) *Our Roots Run Deep: A History of the River Road African American Museum*, Virginia Beach, VA: The Donning Company Publishers.

Edensor, T. (1998) *Tourists at the Taj: Performance and Meaning at a Symbolic Site*, London: Routledge.

Gambia, Republic of the (1996) *The Gambia Incorporated: Vision 2020*, Banjul: The Gambian Government.

Gamble, W. P. (1989) *Tourism and Development in Africa*, London: John Murray.

Gates, H. L. Jr (1999) "Slave kingdoms. One episode of the TV series," *Wonders of the African World with Henry Lewis Gates Jr*, Wall to Wall Television (first aired in the USA October 1999).

Ghana Ministry of Tourism (2002a) "Speech delivered by the AG. Minister of Tourism, Hon. Kwamena Bartels on the Occasion of the Media Launch of Emancipation Day 2002 on Thursday 13th June 2002," *Ghana Ministry of Tourism*, available at http://www.ghanatourism.gov.gh/special/minister_speech.asp (accessed June 22, 2003).

Ghana Ministry of Tourism (2002b) "Emancipation: our heritage, our strength," *Ghana Ministry of Tourism*, available at http://www.ghanatourism.gov.gh/special/minister_speech.asp (accessed June 22, 2003).

Gilroy, P. (1993) *The Black Atlantic: Modernity and Double Consciousness*, London: Verso.

Haley, A. (1976) *Roots: The Saga of an American Family*, New York: Doubleday and Company.

Hall, S. (2000) "Cultural Identity and Diaspora," in N. Mirzoeff (ed.) *Diaspora and Visual Culture: Representing Africans and Jews*, 21–33, London: Routledge.

Howe, S. (1998) *Afrocentrism: Mythical Pasts and Imagined Homes*, London: Verso.

Johnson, A. E., and Cooper, A. M. (1996) *A Student's Guide to African American Genealogy*, Phoenix, AZ: Oryx Press.

Kemp, R. (2000) "Appointment in Ghana: an African-American woman unravels the mystery of her ancestorsv" *Modern Maturity*, July–August,: 17–23.

MacCannell, D. (1992) *Empty Meeting Grounds: The Tourist Papers*, London: Routledge.

Merelman, R. M. (1995) *Representing Black Culture: Racial Conflict and Cultural Politics in the USA*, London: Routledge.

Mudimbe, V. Y. (1988) *The Invention of Africa: Gnosis, Philosophy, and the Order of Knowledge*, Indianapolis, IN: Indiana University Press.

Mudimbe, V. Y. (1994) *Idea of Africa*, London: James Currey.

Okoye, F. N. (1971) *The American Image of Africa: Myth and Reality*, Buffalo, NY: Black Academic Press.

Osei-Tutu, B. (2003) "Monuments and the experience of historical reality. African Americans and Ghana's slave castles on a transnational landscape," paper presented at the 5th World Archaeological Congress, Washington, DC, June 21–26.

Redford, D. S., and D'Orso, M. (2000) *Somerset Homecoming: Recovering a Lost Heritage*, Chapel Hill, NC: University of North Carolina Press.

Redkey, E. K. (1969) *Black Exodus*, London: Yale University Press.

Ritzer, G., and Liska, A. (1997) " 'McDisneyization' and 'Post-Tourism': complementary perspectives on contemporary tourism," in C. Rojek, and J. Urry (eds) *Touring Cultures: Transformations of Travel and Theory*, 96–109, London: Routledge.

Robertson, G., Mash, M., Tickner, L., Bird, J., Curtis, B., and T. Putnam (eds) (1994) *Travellers' Tales: Narratives of Home and Displacement*, London: Routledge.

Rojek, C., and Urry, J. (eds) (1997) *Touring Cultures: Transformations of Travel and Theory*, London: Routledge.

Roots Festival (2002) *Roots Festival Official 2002 Program*, The Department of State for Tourism and Culture of the Government of the Gambia, available at http://www.rootsfestival.gm/Announcements/announcements.html (accessed July 18, 2003).

Ruffins, F. D. (1992) "Mythos, memory, and history: African American preservation efforts, 1820–1990," in I. Karp, C. M. Kreamer, and S. D. Lavine (eds) *Museums and Communities: The Politics of Public Culture*, 506–611, Washington, DC: Smithsonian Institution Press.

Rushdy, A. H. A. (2001) *Remembering Generations: Race and Family in Contemporary African American Fiction*, Chapel Hill, NC: University of North Carolina Press.

Said, E. W. (1978) *Orientalism: Western Concepts of the Orient*, London: Penguin.

Thomas, P. J. (1998) "Postcards from home—Senegal: six African Americans search for a connection in West Africa," *Pathfinders Travel*, Fall/Winter: 16–20.

Travel and Tourism Analyst (1996) "Market segments: Europe to sub-Saharan Africa," *Travel and Tourism Analyst*, 5: 46–64.

Urry, J. (1995) *Consuming Places*, London: Routledge.

Woodtor, D. P. (1999) *Finding a Place Called Home: A Guide to African-American Genealogy and Historical Identity*, New York: Random House.

4 Cognitive issues related to interpreting the African Caribbean

JAY B. HAVISER

Introduction

With this chapter I would like to re-evaluate not only how we interpret African-American identity, but more precisely I would like to challenge the very structure of those interpretations. I will do this by identifying specific cognitive processes that define the African-descendant societies of the Caribbean. One of the fundamental principles for this presentation is the recent sociopsychological research of Nesbitt *et al.* (2001), which contrasts Western thought and Eastern thought and questions whether cognitive processes are actually universal for all cultural groups, as has been assumed in the history of psychological research. They suggest that social organization affects cognitive processes in two basic ways: indirectly by focusing attention on different parts of the environment, and directly by making some kinds of social communication patterns more acceptable than others (Nesbitt *et al.* 2001). The basic premise of their study showed that Eastern thought is more holistic, attending to the entire environment and assigning causality to it, making relatively little use of categories and logic, and relying on "dialectical" or "experiential" reasoning. On the other hand, Westerners are more analytic, paying attention primarily to the object and the categories to which it belongs, and using rules, including formal logic, to understand behavior. For this chapter, I am suggesting that the same contrasts of cognitive perception are applicable between the Europeans and Africans in the colonization of the Americas, and these have carried over into the present, with recognition of a distinctive hybridization. Although hybridization is a crucial factor in sociocultural developments in the African Caribbean, it still remains that the basic dichotomy between cognitive perceptions was, and continues to be, significantly imbalanced. This is of course recognizing that there exist ethno-specific and temporally variable expressions of these deep cognitive perceptions manifested in Africa, Europe, and the Americas. Throughout history, most of the interpretations about African aesthetic and cultural expressions in the Caribbean have been from a primarily Western European or American perspective. Scientists and professionals have spent years and volumes of publications explaining African-Caribbean peoples to the world but few have asked the African-Caribbean peoples themselves how they perceive their own societies.

This chapter also follows closely a lecture given by Simon Ottenberg at the University of Legon (Ghana) in 1971, which supports the African parallel to the Asian example noted by Nesbitt *et al.* (2001). By using Ottenberg's (1971) lecture outlining African aesthetic expressions for West Africa and supplementing that with the cognitive process contrasts noted by Nesbitt *et al.*, I am supporting an interpretation of the "Revisionist Approach" to African Diaspora studies as suggested by Paul Lovejoy (1997). The Revisionist Approach seeks to emphasize the reformation of a new culture and society in the Americas with the maintenance of ties and associations with the African homeland. I would carry that further to the need for a redefinition of African cognitive-based evaluations when trying to identify African elements in the societies of the Americas.

One stimulus for this discussion was raised by the documentation of "Places of Memory for African Heritage" in the Caribbean. This is a current UNESCO-African Slave Route–Museums Association of the Caribbean (MAC) program that has generated many questions about the interpretation of African aesthetics for the region. The UNESCO–MAC survey results stem from 23 island nations in the region and have identified 319 African Heritage sites in the Caribbean for listing as significant places of memory and potential tourist destinations relating to the "African Slave Route," which is the goal of this project.

From conducting this survey, it has become ironically obvious that of the hundreds of books published on African-Caribbean aesthetics most are collections of photographs with little detailed textual background of the peoples. Indeed, often the same photographs appear in book after book. Thousands of African-Caribbean folktales have been published but few with interpretation and explanation of what is actually interesting, pleasing, or repelling to the African-Caribbean listener or speaker. The collecting of these sorts of superficial images leads to little aesthetic understanding of the peoples themselves and simply reinforces a European orientation. One aspect of resistance to change in these interpretations has been a Western emphasis on being "politically correct," which avoids discussion of some topics or aspects of culture and also sometimes intentionally redefines expressions. An example being the modern Bush Negroes of Suriname, who themselves reject the name "Maroons" given to them by contemporary Western anthropologists as being applicable to their ancestors but not themselves.

African causal phenomena behind historical events in the Caribbean (such as slave resistance) are often overlooked, in deference to European explanations. One example of this is the great emphasis placed on the importance of the French Revolution for the Haitian liberation by Africans, yet the neglect of the militaristic precedent of various Sahelian conflicts and the Kongo civil wars, which provided warriors for the incoming slave populations of the Americas (Thornton 1993, 1998). The key oversight here is the imbalance of interpretation toward a Eurocentric orientation, ignoring the continued information exchange being transmitted by successive waves of new Africans arriving from Africa, informing the resident Africans in the Americas of events in the homeland (Lovejoy 1997).

A New Paradigm

Thus, Euro-Americans have evolved a traditional tourist packaging of African-Caribbean culture, as isolated images of life and art, with minimal appreciation for the complexity of interrelated factors that comprise the basis for those images. In the past, most African Heritage site recording has been an example of this Eurocentric misrepresentation that has existed for so long. Therefore, following the suggestion of Doudou Diene, former director of the UNESCO Slave Route Project, it was proposed that we must create a *New Paradigm* for understanding Places of Memory in the Caribbean in such a way that the African, and other non-Western, contributions are given the proportional recognition that they deserve, and that they are presented in a form that is compatible to the African aesthetic and cognitive perspective.

Clearly, one important step in this direction is to break away from Euro-American systems of categorical analysis when trying to interpret African contributions in the Caribbean. The Euro-American analytic approach segregates aesthetic expressions into neat, isolated categories for study and identification (i.e. there are separate categories for masks and dances). However, the African aesthetic and cognitive appreciation of expressions are far more interrelated and holistic—a mask is part of a costume, a costume is part of a dance, a dance is part of a community expression. This understanding allows a blending of all the contributions into a more proper African-oriented perspective. The African focuses on the relationships among objects and events in the broader environment, while the Euro-American approach focuses on categories and rules which help them understand and explain objects independent of their contexts. A further example of this is with the contrasting views of medicine: the African uses a holistic approach for the cure of the entire body/spirit of specific ailments, whereas the Westerner analytically segregates the physical mechanism into specific identifiable problems that can be surgically removed or treated apart.

What is required now is to both re-evaluate how we should interpret African contributions to descendant cultures of the Americas and to restructure how those cultures are presented to the outside world. What were once called British, Spanish, Dutch, and French forts, within the New Paradigm, must now be presented as forts built primarily by Africans with extensive contributions of African craftsmen, funded and designed by the Europeans. What for many may seem to be an open patch of land on a hillside, from a holistic African-Caribbean perspective, could be a sacred gathering place for the reconfirmation of African identity. A plantation setting or mining operation is a place where Africans were the largest population, where Africans produced the goods and means of survival, and where Africans were able to reformulate their heterogeneous backgrounds into a newly formulated identity.

It is interesting to note Karen Fog Olwig's observations that many African-Caribbean populations who evolved out of colonial systems do not perceive themselves as autonomous entities bound to the soil of their ancestors, but rather as semi-autonomous marginalized societies, physically and socially scattered in niches of the (old) colonial infrastructure (Fog Olwig 1993:362). She further notes that these cultural systems, which emerged at the margins of the colonial infrastructure, are not so easily called upon to support national institutions, which are the expressions of the former colonial order. She suggests that the problems for creating National cultures in newly independent nation-states in the region is due less to a lack of common pasts and lifeways than to the difficulty of presenting and interpreting the shared pasts in National project concepts (Fog Olwig 1993: 362). This situation has been further complicated by an increase in unethical commercial exploitation of African Heritage for economic profit at private museums and projects in the Caribbean, owned by Europeans and Americans (Haviser 2002). The UNESCO–MAC Places of Memory survey has tried to bridge this deficiency by allowing African-Caribbean peoples to identify their own past. When geographical and social spaces are identified as important places of memory, it is often found that they are scattered to retreats incapable of exploitation and thus outside the European control. It should be remembered that the illusion of control is a vital aspect of Western philosophy, such that their view of the control of objects in the environment gives them a sense of confidence, whereas the Asian (and I propose in many cases African) view, is the opposite: it is difficult to separate objects in the environment from the environment itself. In those niches created by the enslaved Africans were spawned semi-autonomous spheres of life with parallel adaptive strategies, which formed the basis of African-Caribbean communities (Haviser 1999). An example of this would be the Jamaican Maroons who experienced a reinforcement of social cohesion during the conflicts and isolation of the slavery period.

Another aspect of the shared past is that enslaved Africans were also able to gain a place of recognition for their unique culture expressions within the colonial society, by publicly interpreting them through European-derived social functions, like activities on the Sabbath (Fog Olwig 1993: 364). Slaves exploited the local markets, initially established for white traders, so extensively that they eventually became known as "slave's markets." These too are important places of memory. From the holistic view we must recognize that these markets were far more than places of trade; they were gathering places for information exchange and social relations, inter-relating people from various marginalized niches.

After emancipation, there was a dramatic increase in the social marginality for African-Caribbean peoples, as they were forcibly introduced to European middle-class norms of respectability, which had been vague or non-existent within the earlier African-Caribbean identity formation (Fog Olwig 1993). The social complexity of these forced adaptations to the newly confronted social norms and European notions of what constitutes "freedom," are manifested in many of the current expressions of "African Heritage Sites" as being associated with great houses and forts, rather than folk houses and fields. This results in part from the previously stated dichotomy of African perception as more collectivist and oriented towards the group or "situation-centered," with a Western view being more "individual-oriented" with a conquering attitude toward their environment (Nesbitt et al. 2001).

When trying to reconstruct the paradigm of image for the Caribbean, we can use the metaphor that Western aesthetic expressions are primarily "enclosed" spatially. They either take place in the frame of a square or cube: the box stage of the theatre, the frame of a picture, the room of a museum, or the cinema screen (Ottenberg 1971:8). African aesthetics take place within more fluid borders in which the boundary of action may change, as in the procession of a dance in an open plaza, and it is often curved or elongated, with some mixing of the viewer and participant roles. The subtlety of this fluid perspective applies to the social as well as physical expressions in the Caribbean and accentuates the logical versus experiential knowledge understandings of these two groups. Where Africans are more heavily influenced by prior beliefs and experiences for judging the soundness of formal arguments, the Westerners are more capable of ignoring previous beliefs, setting aside experience, for reasoning based on logical rules (Nesbitt *et al.* 2001). The Africans tend to group objects and events on the basis of functional relationships and as "part-whole" relationships (A is part of B). While the Europeans tend to group objects on the basis of category membership (A and B are both X's), objects are seen as having individual properties that are themselves then considered universal (such as whiteness, hardness). The gist of this presentation is that the African perception is one of striving for stability in social relations, with social needs influencing intellectual stances, thus seeking compromises to solve problems and to reconcile seeming contradictions in the world. On the other hand, the European perception is more inclined to reject one, or both, of two propositions construed as contradicting one another (Nesbitt *et al.* 2001). Such contradictions in logical versus experiential knowledge are at the heart of complexities in discussing and interpreting African Heritage in the Americas.

Closing comments

The concept of *Ambiguity* has been the greatest concern for outside observers of the UNESCO–MAC Places of Memory inventory project. However, I would argue that an appreciation for an ambiguous interpretation is, in fact, at the heart of the New Paradigm for an African-Caribbean view of aesthetic expression. The very definition of ambiguous is to "have several possible meanings or interpretations." It is the Western approach to attempt a systematic analysis in the desire for a precise empirical understanding of concepts and expressions. Yet from the African approach the ability to make an understandable ambiguous statement is stimulated and cultivated. Masks are deliberately made with expressionless faces, so that they may be used in a variety of contexts. For the African aesthetic an expression should be at a point somewhat between absolute abstraction and absolute likeness, for which the Yoruba have the term *Jijora*. If an expression, such as a mask, is too specific to an individual person, it is not appreciated; neither can it be seen as a human or chief if it is too abstract. Clearly, there is a dynamic to the range of these aesthetic evaluations, not only among the artists, but also for the appreciation of society in general, and this is vital to an understanding of African aesthetics in the Caribbean. Indeed, the subtle ambiguities of each island in formulating their own representations of self-prescribed African Heritage places of memory is one of the very essences of the richness of our African-Caribbean culture to be presented to the outside world.

There is clearly a need for more direct African historical inclusion in the reconstruction of Caribbean cultures, to correct the bias of exaggerated emphasis on gravitation toward Europe and the Americas, which distort interpretations of creolization processes in the Americas. The Revisionist Approach, being supported here, directly challenges the marginality of African history and internal New World African social dynamics to developments in the Diaspora. The sociopsychological insights presented here further compliments that with a renewed appreciation of the very process of analytic research of Africans and African descendants, thereby hopefully opening a more holistic understanding of the African Diaspora itself, and more correct presentation of the African contribution to the cultures of the Americas.

References

Fog Olwig, Karen (1993) "Defining the National in the transnational: cultural identity in the Afro-Caribbean Diaspora," *Ethnos*, 58, 3–4: 361–376.

Haviser, Jay B. (1999) *African Sites Archaeology in the Caribbean*, Princeton, NJ: Markus Wiener Publishers.

Haviser, Jay B.(2002) "Welcome to Slaveryland: A call for ethical standards in the long-term partnership of African Diaspora heritage and the tourism industry," *Kristof*, 12, 1: 17–36.

Lovejoy, Paul (1997) "The African Diaspora: Revisionist interpretations of ethnicity, culture and religion under slavery," *Studies in the World History of Slavery, Abolition and Emancipation*, 2, 1, available at, http://www.hnet.msu.edu/~slavery/essays/esy9701love.html (accessed August 18, 1998).

Nesbitt, R., Peng, K., Choi, I., and Norenzayan, A. (2001) "Culture and systems of thought: holistic versus analytic cognition," *Psychological Review*, 108, 2: 291–310.

Ottenberg, Simon (1971) "Anthropology and African Aesthetics," paper presented at the University of Legon, Ghana, January 28, 1971 (copy on file with J. Haviser).

Thornton, John (1993) "I am the subject of the King of Kongo," *Journal of World History*, 4: 2: 181–214.

Thornton, John (1998) *Africa and Africans in the Making of the Atlantic World, 1400–1800*, Cambridge: Cambridge University Press.

5 Historiographical issues in the African Diaspora experience in the New World

Re-examining the "Slave Culture" and "Creole Culture" theses

JOSEPH-ERNEST AONDOFE IYO

Introduction

In this chapter I explore how the Middle Passage and the experience of slavery were capable of eroding African customs, traditions, and cultures, or the memories of their customs, traditions, and cultures in a new environment. I question the theory of racial, ethnic, and cultural transformation—the so-called Creolization theory, which seeks to emphasize assimilation, both cultural and biological. Finally, I question why it seems that only Africans are portrayed as having undergone such a transformation in the New World.

To answer the above questions, I have attempted to reconstruct a chronological sequence of events, which culminates in the so-called transformation of Africans in the New World. Africans were subdivided into innumerable categories at the whims and caprices of the conqueror and slave master, with this process following a number of stages:

1 First, the so-called transformation began as a racist doctrine to justify slavery.

2 Second, from a racist doctrine arose an ideological necessity to explain the phenomenon of cultural and social devaluation of everything African.

3 Third, from an ideological standpoint arose the need for a methodology to divide and control African-born vis-à-vis New World-born Africans.

4 Fourth, from a methodological device arose the need for a new historiography to explain the phenomenon of cultural and biological hybridization ("Creolization"). As the numbers of the Mulatto population continued to grow in the plantations of the Americas, and as racism became a way of life, the theory of the transformation of the "Creolized" segment became necessary to justify their occasionally elevated status as "Head Nigger in Charge" (HNIC) in the plantation society.

5 Fifth, after slavery, a new historiography successfully transformed the minds of the descendants of enslaved Africans to a point whereby it became fashionable

to deny any connection to an "uncivilized" and "barbaric" race in a continent described by many as "Dark and without history" (cf. Erim and Uya 1948).

6 Sixth, the further deterioration of the image of Africa and Africans on CNN and allied media in the postmodernist period has made it even more fashionable for descendants of enslaved Africans to be anything except African.

Suffice it to say that "Creole" as contested ethnic category in the Caribbean has created a "sharing of two worlds": one European (as evident in how some Creole insist on being classified as either Euro-Creole or Afro-Saxons)[1] and the other African (with this group in recent years coming to prefer the term "Black" over African). And yet, on another level, there was and still is a group that can be truly classified as "marginalized" Africans, unwilling to break with the familiar past, the known, the familiar African world rich in traditions, religion, music, dances, and culture. Such a love of African heritage has been transferred generationally from African mothers and fathers on down to the present generation. These traditions and cultures, as rightly observed by Stuckey (1987: 23–24), were important features of the African cultural heritage in the Americas, which provided a means by which the new reality of slavery in the Americas was interpreted and their spiritual needs at least partially met. Jama Adams (1999: 3) tends to support the view that, "Existing within this space (a psychological space in which a people can reflect not only on their experience but can also practice life of the mind) are elements of tradition and technical skills that keep the impulse of the lost endemic homelands alive. It is these elements that give grounding to an Afro-Caribbean or an Indo-Caribbean identity." Harold Courlander (1996: 2) sums up this view when he states that even though

> it is abundantly evident that many tangible elements of African ways, customs, attitudes, values and views of life survived the Atlantic crossing, ... This does not mean that Haitians, black Cubans or black North Americans are Africans, for they are products not only of their African past but of the European cultures on which they have so heavily drawn and, most important of all, of their unique collective experience in the New World.

Courlander (1996: 2) concludes, "In speaking broadly and familiarly of Afro-America, therefore, we are not referring to a common genetic inheritance but to cultural inheritance, which is to say an inheritance of experience." According to this view, there is no one self but instead a multiplicity of selves that reflects the subjects's multiple involvements and affiliations. This is a poor attempt to refute essentialist arguments of identity: the irreducible ethnic essences that define given peoples such as Native Americans and Jews worldwide (cf. Gilroy 1993).

Ashamed of their African ancestry, African-Americans both in the Caribbean and North America have written prodigiously to justify why and how their ancestors de-Africanized and became Creolized in the New World. By subscribing to Creole and "Black" identity (culture and biology), many Africans in the New World have sought to smooth the "primitive" edges off their "Africanness" in the Western Hemisphere. This is perhaps what Courlander (1996: 6) means when he stresses that, "It is of course true that having a dark skin and other distinguishing racial attributes was a particular disability to slaves and their descendants in the Western Hemisphere. The fact of their being black had a direct bearing on their experience, which, in turn, left a mark on their lives and their literature"—including their present denial of being African.

It is therefore my contention that the "Creole Culture" theory is merely a minor shift from previous colonial discourse, which sought to deny Africans (and Africanisms) a social space in the New World. "Creole Culture" reifies a view of Africans' capacity to mindlessly assimilate "superior" white cultures. This is a view that many Africans in the Diaspora (writers, in particular) have come to accept a priori. That many of them have made a good living in academia as a consequence is hardly surprising. More importantly, few Africans in the New World have forgiven Africans in the Continent for their "complicity" in the Slave Trade.

Despite attempts by the integrationists and the "Talented Tenth" to perpetuate the theory of de-Africanization of Africans in the Americas, there have been others who have stressed a willingness to be "Negro with every drop of blood and every stir of soul" (Robeson 1934).

Even though Brathwaite (1978: 45) has articulated the view that, "There can be little argument anymore about African Survivals in the Caribbean/New World," it is doubtful whether his conclusion is universally true. According to him, "the scholarship and literature of African survival in the Caribbean and the New World has grown and gained a new resonance of confidence" (Brathwaite 1978: 45) While it may be true that the scholarship and literature of African survival has grown, there is little attempt to filter these for the ordinary people who were brought up in a tradition of self-denial. This is the group that is becoming more and more confused and ignorant about its ethnicity and heritage.

To use biology as an ethnic marker or even a racial marker, as many writers on the African Diaspora have done, is ahistorical and hypocritical. Biologically and historically, there is nothing like a "pure race" or a "pure tribe." Even culturally, no group today can regard itself as culturally pure. What many scholars have described and characterized as "Slave Culture" and "Creole Culture" in the New World can therefore best be described as Pan-African culture (Stuckey 1987) dosed with white Anglo-Saxon and Latin,[2] and indigenous cultures in some cases.[3]

African continuity versus discontinuity

The major thrust of this chapter is to contest the view that the cultures that emerged in the plantations of the New World in general, and Belize in particular, were not a real continuation of African life (as suggested by Courlander 1996, among many others). The "Slave Culture" thesis evolved out of the pseudo-scientific racism of the nineteenth and twentieth centuries.[4] I have also argued elsewhere that the "Creole Culture" is essentially a post-structuralist and postmodernist view of this old African continuity problematic (Iyo 2000). Indeed, what the Creole theoreticians are describing and characterizing as "Creole Culture" is a negation of Hertskovitsian structuralism, which admittedly still has many followers. We are not denying that the

"Negroes in the New World are the inheritors of Spanish, Portuguese, French, Dutch, English and other traditions as well" (Courlander 1996: 5). We are contesting the view that "it is a body of Africanisms, not Africans, that has survived in the New World." (Courlander 1996: 2).

Historically, race and ethnicity have always been defined by the hegemonic powers, albeit arbitrarily. Race and ethnicity are today defined as biological constructs (ahistorical) or social constructs (elusive, dynamic, and multilayered), as opposed to the still extant essentialist view (which has been used to define "Jews" and "Arabs," for example). Sterling Stuckey's (1987) structuralist analysis and interpretation of African cultural continuity in the USA, though weak in some cases is, nevertheless, important for my analysis of the Belize case study (Iyo 2000). His interpretation of the parades of governors in New England, and John Kunering in North Carolina, is similar to what obtained in early-nineteenth-century Belize (Iyo 2000).

It is, therefore, instructive to stress that while the above traditions professing "identity" were important in Belize among enslaved Africans, other African cultural practices such as *obeah* (African traditional religion misinterpreted as witchcraft, widely practised during and immediately after slavery, but now carried on behind closed doors), the wakes (an important African mourning and funeral rite), *Sambai* music and dance (which started as fertility cult but has been transformed into a form of entertainment in Gales Point village of Belize), and the different versions of *Ananse* folktales, together with several African derived cuisines were, and still are, important features of direct African cultural continuity. These are the same features that Creole theoreticians have swept under the rubrics of Creolization (Iyo 2000).

Creolization theory is simply an attempt to de-Africanize: an attempt that started immediately after emancipation (Shoman 1995). Indeed, after emancipation, many ex-slaves in Belize, for example, with no obvious European ancestry, began to invent white (Scottish) paternal ancestry[5] in order to gain acceptance and also to participate in the "colonial experiment," which started in 1862. Evidence suggests that, even those whose white ancestry was not in doubt, still faced—with varying degrees—discrimination from the new white settlers (referred to as *Baymen*). Indeed, Shoman (1995: 60) tells us that: "The Free Coloured in Belize had been petitioning the King for equal status with Whites as were their counterparts in other West Indian Colonies." Extant records demonstrate how George Hyde (the son of an eminent old white settler, James Hyde) was discriminated against "on the sole ground of his mother being a woman of colour." (Shoman 1995: 61).

Deconstructing African slavery in the New World

We cannot treat African slavery without an understanding of the environment in which slaves were nurtured before transportation to the Americas. Certainly, several factors influenced African slaves in their new abode:

1 The strong sense of family and community life in Africa before transportation to the Americas can no longer be ignored.

2 The momentary disconnection of that sense of family and community at the initial stage upon disembarking the ships in the Americas must have had a devastating impact on their psychological and sociological make up.

3 After the initial shock, some cultural means were found to survive the concentration camp-like plantations (see Lewis 1971).

The West and Central Africans who were enslaved and sent to the New World had a long tradition of extended family support networks, an ancient tradition of political complexity, diverse agricultural systems, long distance external trading networks, metal working dating back to the first millennium BC, and ancient traditions of ceramic-making, weaving, and so on (Connah 2001). Their "employment" or deployment in some of these trades and professions only helped to reinforce/improve such technologies in the New World (Herskovits 1941; Bastide 1971; Goucher 1993). Additionally, there is evidence of slaves maintaining varying degrees of matrimony (in some occasions, what many Africans considered as polygamy was inadvertently encouraged by the slave masters for reproductive, and hence, economic reasons). Indeed, there is also evidence of the reconstitution of family structures on the plantations and maintenance of African traditions by the use of coded language under the cover of night, or, in some remote corner of the plantation. Many of these cultural "innovations"—innovations that have roots in the African psyche—have apparently escaped many Creole theoreticians. Some scholars schooled in the Eurocentric tradition, saw, or still see slaves as mere property (compare the approaches of Herskovits 1941; Patterson 1967; Wilentz 1992). Indeed, Africans, as far as some scholars are concerned, were and are still incapable of generational continuity or cultural retention/continuity.

The co-modification of Africans has become so pervasive that even an Afrocentric scholar like Gay Wilentz argues both for and against African continuity in the Diaspora. Perhaps the following quotations will help illustrate this problematic. Wilentz (1992: xi–xii) writes on the one hand that: "the passing on of cultural values and personal history [is] traditionally a woman's domain." Yet, she opines on the other hand that "when Black women began to write creative works they looked back to their foremothers to recreate these stories ... but since *the line had been broken by their dispersion* [emphasis added] into the Americas, they have had to make a *larger imaginative leap* [emphasis supplied] than their African sisters." However, I would contend that African women performed these cultural roles admirably, and without interruption, throughout slavery and even after slavery.

The argument therefore, that, generational transfer was impossible simply because of the tender age of the majority of Africans transported to be enslaved in the Americas is clearly based on a lack of understanding of African cultural traditions and a deliberate attempt to deny Africans tenacity and creativity. It needs stressing too that, in precolonial, colonial, and postcolonial Africa, elders have always passed on their knowledge to the incoming generation through the apprenticeship system—a system that was abused after emancipation in the New World.[6] Indeed, in Africa then, and even now, any child of 7 years of age was and is already on their way to being well versed in the chosen field of apprenticeship be it blacksmithing, carving, or pottery.

Also, to directly compare the artifacts and other works created by Africans during and after slavery with contemporary pieces in present-day Africa, as some archaeologists and anthropologists are now attempting to do, seems rather ahistorical! However, this is not always the case. It has been argued that, "Many archaeologists, if they make any direct comparisons, do so mainly with historical African assemblages dating to the time of slavery, rather than contemporary assemblages. One could also argue that not to make such comparisons with Africa would support a theory of non-continuity" (K. C. MacDonald personal communication).

It is my contention that neither Africans in the continent nor those transported to the Americas were static in their thinking and creativity. Indeed, the transmigration and transformation of *Ananse* (the Akan spider trickster story) and the Bantu *Brer* Rabbit and *Brer* Tiger in the New World can only be understood as products of generational continuity modified to suit the new environment and the new sociological setting. It is therefore important to stress that, even in Africa, these folktales have transformed dramatically to accommodate the changes in the society.

Toward a less ethnocentric approach

The subject of African culture in the New World has received a disproportionate space in books and scholarly journals. By the tone of the debate, it appears that the subject is far from being put to rest.[7] The debate between those who insist that the Middle Passage and the experience of slavery were so momentous that Africans metamorphosed into something else ("Creolized") and those who hold the view that African continuity in the New World was possible continues with variation to the present day. Clearly methodology is at the heart of this problematic. Certainly, there were instances of old African traditions becoming modified due to the intense pressure from the white slave-owning class. Pressures from new environments also acted as catalysts for adjustments to African traditions and customs. There were also instances when these pressures proved too strong for wholesale preservation of the African traditions and customs. This was particularly true of the period immediately after the Haitian Revolution. But one should not proceed too far down this road.

Arnold Toynbee, who is characterized by Forsythe (1975: 13–14) as one of the most racist historians of his day, wrote that:

> The ... impact of the Western Civilization upon the other living societies ... was so powerful and so pervasive that it turned the lives of all its victims upside down and inside out—affecting the behavior, outlook, feelings, and beliefs of individual men, women and children in an intimate way, touching chords in human souls that are not touched by mere external material forces—however ponderous and terrifying.
>
> (Toynbee 1948: 214)

Evaluations, such as Toynbee's, regarding the consequences of slavery and colonialism for the devaluation of the African have worked to weaken arguments for cultural retention or continuity in the New World. According to this view, the impact of slavery was so pervasive that it utterly destroyed African customs, cultures, and traditions and left a gaping void only to be filled by European culture. Mintz and Price (1981: 1), in apparent support of this Eurocentric view, have argued that,

> No group, no matter how well equipped or how free to chose, can transfer its way of life and the accompanying beliefs and values intact, from one locale to another. We assert further that the conditions of transfer, as well as the characteristics of the host setting, both human and material, will set some limits on the variety and strength of effective transfers. It goes almost without saying that Europeans and Africans participated in highly differentiated ways in the process of New World settlement. Though it may appear at the outset that the continuity and the strength of transferred cultural materials weighted much more heavily in favor of the Europeans than of the Africans, we would contend that a more sophisticated treatment of the content of transferred materials would fail to support so simplistic a conclusion. In fact, the character of transfers and their subsequent transformations may argue at times for greater continuity in the case of Afro-America than in that of Euro-America, considering the circumstances under which the transfers occurred, and the settings within which they took roots.

Mintz and Price's insistence that Africans transported to the New World cannot be said to have *shared a culture* (emphasis in the original) in the sense that European colonists in a particular area can be said to have done so is deeply flawed. It is hypocritical for Mintz and Price to identify compatibility in culture in (multi-ethnic) Europeans but fail to identify such compatibility with respect to Africans. It is true that "Africans were drawn from different parts of the African continent, from numerous tribal [sic] and linguistic groups, and from different societies," but it is also true that, "The cultures and histories of [African] nations are similar in many respects—indeed, despite the differences—most people would agree that there is something called African culture" (Iyo 2000: 20). As Stuckey (1987: 3) states:

> The final gift of African "tribalism" [sic] in the nineteenth century was its life as a lingering memory in the minds of ... slaves. That memory enabled them to go back to the sense of community in the traditional African setting and to include all Africans in their common experience of oppression in North America. It is greatly ironic, therefore, that African ethnicity, an obstacle to African nationalism in the twentieth century, was in this way the principal avenue to black unity in antebellum America ... During the process of their becoming a single people, Yoruba, Akan, Igbo, Angola, and others were present on slave ships to America and experienced a common horror ... As such, slave ships were the first real incubators of slave unity across cultural lines, cruelly revealing irreducible links from one ethnic group to the other, fostering resistance thousands of miles before the shores of the new land appeared on the horizon.

From what has been said so far, it is evident that some of the approaches which have sought to examine African cultures and traditions in the New World have been ill-constructed. We can no longer deny that some of the earlier works of scholars in the field of the African Diaspora cannot stand rigorous scrutiny today. Intellectual obscurantism, vulgar theorizing, and ethnocentric sentiments have been the hallmarks of Eurocentric interpretation of Africa and its people wherever they are found. For example, some scholars[8] still argue against the sociocultural consciousness of African slaves. Many early writers argued against generational continuity and hence the impossibility of slaves to give their children African names according to the ethnic group they came from or the day the child was born—arguments we now know to be false.[9] Not many scholars, have, for example, explained why New World rivers, creeks, lagoons, and, in some cases, villages have African names.[10] Why, one may ask, have scholars not been able to interpret these phenomena as symptomatic of continuity in African cultural expressions?

The answer is as follows: the task of exploring works of cultures suppressed by a "dominant culture" not only requires interdisciplinary methodology, but more importantly, a more objective search for the elusive truth. Gender also plays a role. It is a truism that not many Euro-American scholars have tried to investigate how African cultural traditions were passed down from the African mother to the African slave mother on to present generations. Gay Wilentz (1992; xiv) underscores this point when she stresses that, "to look back through our mothers is seen as a woman's domain. Orature and consequently, literature are part of a woman's daily struggle to communicate, converse, and pass on values to their own and other children, and one another." Indeed, in both Africa and in the New World, women were, and still are, major transmitters of customs and values—(such is certainly the case amongst the Garafuna of Belize). They were, and still are, the primary and constant agents of child socialization. Women also fulfil central roles as *griots*, craftspeople, herbalists, and instructors on African spirituality. However, the case of the Mande peoples (of Mali, Guinea, etc.) where both men and women share these roles is also instructive (Frank 1998).

It is also important to stress that, in the examination of the survival of African spirituality in the New World, one need to be cautious about the division between the secular and the sacred. Whereas this division is prominent in Western culture and philosophy, it is nonexistent in African thought and philosophy (Wiredu 1980; Andah 1988). Indeed, much of the numerous slave resistances in the New World were often motivated by a strong sense of religiosity. It was indeed the realization of the importance of African religion on the part of the white slave masters in Belize that occasioned the ban of *gumbay* drumming and *Obeah* (African traditional religion misinterpreted as witchcraft in many books). Suffice it to stress that African religiosity is still evident in the *Dugu* and other ceremonies practised by the Garinagu of Belize.[11]

Conclusions

The fundamental question raised in this chapter is why only the descendants of enslaved Africans are said to have undergone a metamorphosis, or "creolization" in the

New World. I have noted that there is no denying the fact that the processes of miscegenation, acculturation, hybridism, and assimilation have occurred everywhere in history. I have also stressed the bankruptcy of "Pure Tribe" and "Pure Race" theories. Yet, I have also argued that it is unfounded to say that Africans in the Diaspora are no longer Africans but a new people "native to the Caribbean" (Smith 1965: 5–6) because of miscegenation, acculturation, and assimilation.

The attempt here is to stimulate rethinking within the post-structuralist and postmodernist schools of thought, whose view of race and ethnic identity is a negation of the essentialist view. My work is by and large an implicit rebuttal of Paul Gilroy's (2004) rejection of any notion of ethnic solidarity, or any essential identity around blackness, speaking instead of a multiplicity of ways of being black, some in open contradiction to others. I also reject Balibar's insistence that we live in a world of multiple belongings, with intense competition for commitment to identity (see Balibar and Wallerstein 1991). Whereas it may be true that many black intellectuals have written powerfully about hybridism and transgression in African-American culture, the call for a postmodern identity is tantamount to surrendering to the "one-drop rule." If the "one-drop rule" were to be applied to all continental African ethnic groups, none of the culture groups in Africa today would be considered monolithically and homogeneously Igbo, Hausa, Tiv, and Yoruba. This is because inter-ethnic marriages and inter-ethnic cultural sharing among African groups have been going on for centuries.

Thus, as Michael Dyson (2003: 71–72) rightly observes,

> Jorge's belief that, by considering themselves black, African Americans are surrendering to the "one-drop rule" misses the point of history and the context of culture. History suggests that there are criteria that are objective—if by objective we mean actually existing material, cultural and political forces independent of the subjective perceptions, wishes, or views of individuals or groups—that shape the lives and destinies of black life. There are socially constructed norms—which, contrary to popular misconception, make them no less concrete or influential in their impact than if they are conceived to be permanent, necessary features of the social landscape—that mediate the relations of race, norms that help determine how black people are seen and judged. So even if black identity is up for grabs—a statement with which I largely agree, although with decidedly different political resonance, since I've argued in my book about the fluidity of the boundaries of black identity—it has real historical and cultural limitations.

If the impact of Western culture through the agents of slavery and colonialism packaged as a "civilizing mission" and the "white man's burden" has created so-called multiple-selves (apologies to McBobbie 1999) or multilayered ethnic constructs, can this not be said equally of Africa and the New World? Are we not all products of "multilayered ethnic constructs" in the New World? It is, in deed, both hypocritical and contradictory to consider Asian Indians as distinctly East Indians despite their long sojourn in the Americas and then refer to the descendants of enslaved Africans as everything except African. Both groups have undergone miscegenation and assimilation in the Americas. If the Asian Indians are a product of M. G. Smith's (1965) classic plural model in the Caribbean, why can't the same be applied to the descendants of enslaved Africans?

M. G. Smith (1965: 112) noted that plural societies in the British West Indies in the 1820s

> Were differentiated culturally—that is, by there adherence to different institutions ... In effect the population of a British West Indian colony at this period was culturally pluralistic—that is to say, it contained sections which practiced different forms of the same institutions. Thus the population constituted a plural society, that is, a society divided into sections, each of which practiced different cultures.

M. G. Smith's eloquent testimony of how the Caribbean society was historically and culturally constructed with no single organizing principle than that of power, political domination, and unequal incorporation has generated a healthy debate between the integrationists and the pluralists, between the consensus theorists and conflict theorists. It stands that there was never a consensus between the dominant and the dominated classes, the white master and the African slave. It would thus be presumptuous for us to assume that post-structuralism and postmodernism will bridge the historiographical problematic of African Diaspora experience. This is because the debate is still one of power versus powerlessness, white dominant power versus African powerlessness. The Creole ethnic and cultural construct is therefore an escapist theoretical abstraction: a racialist reaction to racism.

Notes

1 Whereas Central Statistical Office has standardized ethnic and racial categories, many young Belizeans (age 12–17) currently cannot classify themselves by any of the existing ethnic categories. This is based on a survey of high school students in Southside Belize City, January 2003. Post-structuralism and postmodernism seek to explain the phenomenon of racial and ethnic identity as a process that does not really result in a final product but rather that individuals are constantly reinventing and reconfirming old and new aspects of multiple selves. Refer to Dyson (2003). Reflecting on this phenomenon in a paper titled, "The construction of identities among Caribbean-Americans" Jama Adams (1999: 3) notes,

> While these elements (African and Indian) exist as a powerful substrate, informing the outlook and actions, they often lack fertile institutional space in which to fully develop. Alongside these life-maintaining elements exists some of the internalized aspects of the Euro-American worldview that forces all Caribbean peoples to question the relevance and efficacy of these immortal but elusive aspects of the collective psyche.

2 The disappearance of African as a racial or ethnic group in much of Latin America is due to a form of ethnic cleansing. cf. Purcell, 1987.
3 The Garifuna (formerly known as the black Caribs) of Central America and the Black Indians of North America are cases in point here. Even though biologically their mixture with the indigenous peoples has been determined to be minimal, their interpretation and contestation

of who they are has left no one in doubt that they like their Creole cousins are ashamed to be ascribed as Africans. The Garifuna culture is still predominantly African at this time of writing. For a detailed critique on these aspects refer to Iyo (2000).

4 I am indeed indebted to Philip Curtin's (1960) article, " 'Scientific' racism and the theory of empire," in the *Journal of the Historical Society of Nigeria*, 2, 1: 40–51. The paper, in more ways than one, inspired me to begin to question the Eurocentric historical scholarship, which pervaded as historical "truth" in the academia.

5 Practically every black family that I have interviewed in Belize has claimed Scottish paternal ancestry. I have argued elsewhere that the numbers do not add up. In much of the slavery period, whites always numbered approximately between 250 and 300 (and how many of these Scottish?) compared to blacks that always numbered approximately between 2000 and 3000.

6 The majority of ex-enslaved Africans in Belize, for example, had worked all their lives in given trades only to be compelled to serve as apprentices in the same trades with the same masters after Emancipation in 1839.

7 See for example the issue of *Caribbean Quarterly*, 44, 1 and 2 (1998).

8 Bastide (1971), for example, argued persuasively that although the evidence for ethnic origins may be of great interest historically speaking, it offers little value to the ethnology. Refer to a critique of this view in Iyo (2000: 28).

9 The Belize Case Study (Iyo 2000) has demonstrated that contrary to popular belief that all enslaved Africans lost their African names on the other side of the Atlantic, those in Belize not only retained, but were also in a position to give their children African names denoting days of their birth. A perusal of Slave Census Registers from 1791 to 1832 clearly demonstrates how enslaved Akan were able to continue to name their children according to gender and days of the week. Other groups, including those of Igbo (called Eboes in Belize and spelt as such in the Slave Registers) origin, of Angolan (called Mungolas and spelt as such in the Slave Registers) origin, of Yoruba (called Nangoes and spelt as such in the Slave Register) and those of Congo (called Congoes and spelt as such), etc. continued with the practice of naming their children after the name of their ethnic groups.

10 Refer to my interpretation of these phenomena including the African derivation of the name Belize, which independent Belize now answers to, in Iyo (2000: chapter 1). Other place names include the former Eboe Town—after Igbo—in the heart of Belize Town, Nago Bank, Yoruba in origin, Quamina Creek and Quashie Creek, Akan, etc.

11 The debate on whether the Garifuna are indigenous to America or African is outside the scope of this chapter. Suffice to stress that the debate remains one created and sustained by Eurocentric anthropologists in their attempt to create divisions between the different shades of African descended peoples of the Americas.

References

Adams, Jama (1999) "The construction of identities among Caribbean-Americans," *Caribbean Quarterly*, 45, 4: 1–11.

Andah, Bassey (1988) *African Anthropology*, Ibadan: Shaneson C. I. Limited.

Balibar, Etienne and Wallerstein, Immanuel (1991) *Race, Nation, Class: ambiguous identities*, Chris Turner translator, London: Verso.

Bastide, Roger (1971) *African Civilizations in the New World*, London: C. Hurst & Company.

Brathwaite, Edward Kamau (1978) "The spirit of African survival in Jamaica," *Jamaica Journal*. 42: 45–63.

Connah, Graham (2001) *African Civilizations: An Archaeological Perspective*, 2nd edn, Cambridge: Cambridge University Press.

Courlander, Harold (1996) *A Treasury of Afro-American Folklore. The Oral Literature, Traditions, Recollections, Legends, Tales, Songs, Religious Beliefs, Customs, Sayings, and Humor of Peoples of African Descent in the Americas*, New York: Marlowe & Company.

Curtin, Philip (1960) "Scientific racism and the theory of empire," *Journal of the Historical Society of Nigeria*, 2, 1: 40–51.

Dyson, Michael (2003) *Reflections on Philosophy, Race, Sex, Culture and Religion: Open Mike*, New York: Basic *Civitas* Books.

Erim, Erim O. and Uya, Okon (eds) (1948) *Perspectives and Methods of Studying African History*, Nigeria: Fourth Dimension Publishers.

Forsythe, Dennis (ed.) (1975) *Black Alienation Black Rebellion*, Washington, DC: College and University Press.

Frank, Barbara (1998) *Mande Potters & Leatherworkers: Art and Heritage in West Africa*, Washington, DC: Smithsonian.

Gilroy, Paul [1993] (2004) *The Black Atlantic Modernity and Double Consciousness*, Cambridge, MA: Harvard University Press.

Goucher, Candice L. (1993) "African metallurgy in the Atlantic world," *African Archaeological Review*, 11: 197–215.

Herskovits, Melville (1941) *The Myth of the Negro Past*, Boston, MA: Beacon Press.

Iyo, Joseph (2000) *Towards Understanding Belize's Multicultural History and Identity*, Belize: University of Belize Press.

Lewis, Mary A. (1971) "Slavery and Personality," in Anne J. Lane (ed.) *The Debate Over Slavery. Stanley Elkins and His Critics*, 75–86, Urbana, IL: University of Illinois Press.

McBobbie, Angella (1999) "Different, youthful, subjectivities," *Caribbean Quarterly*, 45, 4: 1–12.

Mintz, Sidney W., and Price, Richard (1981) *An Anthropological Approach to the Afro American Past: A Caribbean Perspective*, Philadelphia, PA: Institute for the Human Issues.

Patterson, Orlando (1967) *The Sociology of Slavery: An Analysis of the Origins, Development and Structure of Negro Slave Society in Jamaica*, London: MacGibbon and Key.

Purcell, Trevor (1987) "Structural transformation and social inequality in a plural society: the case of Lima, Costa Rica, where Jamaican immigrants are deliberately assimilating into the Hispanic group," *Caribbean Quarterly*, 33, 1 and 2: 20–43.

Robeson, Paul (1934) "I Want to Be African," in E. G. Cousins (ed.) *What I Want from Life*, 71–77, London: George Allen & Unwin.

Shoman, Assad (1995) *Thirteen Chapters of a History of Belize*, Belize: The Angelus Press Limited.

Smith, M. G. (1965) *The Plural Society in the British West Indies*, Berkeley, CA: University of California Press.

Stuckey, Sterling (1987) *Slave Culture Nationalist Theory and the Foundations of Black America*, New York: Oxford University Press.

Toynbee, Arnold (1948) *Civilization on Trial*, New York: Oxford University Press.

Wilentz, Gay (1992) *Black Women Writers in Africa and the Diaspora*, Indianapolis, IN: Indiana University Press.

Wiredu, Kwesi (1980) *Philosophy and an African Culture*, Cambridge: Cambridge University Press.

Part II   Historical and anthropological perspectives

6 Archaeology and history in the study of African-Americans

Philip D. Morgan

Introduction

An active debate, very much alive today, concerns how much African heritage African-Americans have maintained. A polarizing tendency is often evident. Some scholars have been dubbed "creation theorists" for allegedly paying too much attention to the cultural creativity of enslaved Africans in the New World at the expense of what Africans brought with them. On the other side are the so-called continuity theorists, some of whom take a militantly Africa-centric position, stressing the continuing role of African ethnicities in the Americas. A middle ground surely exists, but a real and sometimes rancorous argument is afoot, revolving about the staying power of African ethnicities versus the innovative processes of creolization in the New World (Price 2001; Chambers 2002; Lohse 2002; Hall, 2005).

Without doubt, one of the most exciting developments in African-American history is the attempt to trace connections between specific homelands in the Old World and specific destinations in the New. Linking particular locales in Africa with particular sites in the Americas is very much on the agenda for many scholars. One of the engines driving this development is new information on the precise workings of the Trans-Atlantic slave trade.

History of the Trans-Atlantic slave trade

Historians of the Trans-Atlantic slave trade have emphasized its specialized, patterned character. It was no random, unsystematic business. In general, the slave trade of any African region was heavily centered at one or two places. About 80 percent of all slaves from the Bight of Biafra left from just two outlets, Bonny and Calabar. Ships leaving on a slave voyage would normally trade in only one African region, though occasionally at several locations in that region. Only about one in 10 slave vessels traded at two or more ports, and only one in 20 traded across regional boundaries. One reason that most slavers headed for specified destinations is that Africans in different coastal regions had distinct preferences for merchandise. Similarly, most Trans-Atlantic ships disembarked their migrants at a single port in the Americas. Over 95 percent of slave ships landed all their slaves at one place. And usually one or perhaps two ports in an American territory garnered most arrivals. Almost nine out of 10 Africans entered Jamaica through Kingston (Eltis and Morgan 2001).

As historians explore precisely where Africans came from, with precise regional and port information, wherever possible—and it often is possible—and pay particular attention to timing, the most discrete periods they can manage, so the chances of exploring regionally specific African cultural traits in particular places in the Americas are enhanced.

Many Africans arrived in a particular New World setting alongside Africans from the same coastal region. Particularly early in the history of many slave societies, one or two African regions supplied most slaves. Thus, in the third quarter of the seventeenth century, for example, three-quarters of the Africans landing in Barbados came from just two regions: the Bight of Biafra (supplying 48 percent) and the Bight of Benin (28 percent). In the first quarter of the eighteenth century, four-fifths of Jamaica's Africans came from just two regions: the Gold Coast (46 percent) and the Bight of Benin (34 percent). In the first quarter of the eighteenth century, just one region, the Bight of Biafra, supplied about 60 percent of Africans to the York Naval District in Virginia, which received more of the colony's Africans than the colony's other four naval districts combined. Africans from the same coastal region, then, often predominated in specific American locales, particularly early in time (Eltis *et al.* 1999; Eltis 2001; Walsh 2001). A basis for shared communication thus existed.

The proportions of men and women, adults and children varied markedly in shipments from different regions of the African coast. The proportion of males sailing from Upper Guinea (Senegambia to the Windward Coast) was larger (almost 75 percent) than elsewhere and the proportion of children smaller (just 6 percent). West-Central Africa, Angola, Kongo, by contrast had more children (over 20 percent) among the slaves leaving its shores than other African coastal regions. In the Bight of Biafra women were almost as numerous as men among slaves carried to the Americas. Ratios did change over time but if we can plot when people were coming from particular regions of the African coast we will have a reasonable proxy of at least some of the building blocks for family formation and demographic growth (Eltis 2001; Nwokeji 2001).

Connecting particular African and American locales is therefore a valuable and potentially fruitful exercise. It means of course that we all need to become expert as much as possible in the relevant regional cultures that fed into any particular American slave society. It will also be necessary to draw on archaeological work on both sides of the Atlantic with as much regional specificity as possible. Good examples of such studies, only just beginning to appear, include those by Kelly (1997a, b) and DeCorse (2001).

Implications and cautions

It will be important too to be as regionally specific as possible on the American side of the Atlantic. We are learning not just about differences between colonies but also about more precise local differences—between established plantation areas and frontier zones, between tidewater and piedmont, between lowlands and highlands, between urban and rural, between small farm and large plantation. Nevertheless, I now want to offer a few caveats about what can be termed the rage for regionalism, this search for spatial specificity on both sides of the Atlantic.

First, although many Africans arriving in the Americas, like Europeans, shared a distinctive local, perhaps "ethnic" identity, the conception of homogeneous peoples being swept up on one side of the ocean and set down *en masse* on the other is problematic. Ethnic mixing and the reconstitution of identity started well before the coerced migrants ever set foot on a ship. Because many African slaves came in tortuous and convoluted ways from the interior to the coast, whatever ethnic identity they originally had was undoubtedly in flux. Identities were reshaped as slaves moved to the coast, a process often taking months, occasionally years—and as they awaited shipment in the barracoons and in the holds of ships as loading proceeded. Africans employed pidgin and even creole languages on the coast as they tried to communicate with one another. Many slaves became identified by their port of embarkation—Calabars, Cormantees, Pawpas or Popos, and so on—but such identifications masked diversity. Even when New World ethnonyms such as "Lucumi" and "Nago" (both used to describe people today termed "Yoruba") can be traced to particular African groups or places, they were not alternative names for the same people; Lucumi referred primarily to southern, and Nago to western, Yorubaland (Law 1997).

Second, the scale of linguistic and cultural diversity within particular African regions must also be taken into account. The Bight of Biafra region, for example, was home to at least four major languages—Yoruba, Igbo, Edo, and Ijo—and their respective dialects, together with many other minor languages including Efik, which were spoken by many who came to the New World as slaves. To point to the predominance of the Bight of Biafra as a region of origin for a particular New World locale's slave population is therefore not to say that slaves from that region shared much of a shared identity or a mutually intelligible language. The proportion of Igbo speakers among slaves entering the Chesapeake, for example, has been recently estimated at about a quarter (Northrup 2000). Some recent archaeological investigations suggesting that certain deposits seem similar to Ibo ancestor shrines, or that certain incised spoon handles are similar to the symbols used by Ibo diviners, or that so-called root cellars or subfloor pits can be traced to an Ibo practice of concealing valuables under floors, not in cellars or pits, seem to me to be stretching credibility (Samford 1996). Nor am I much persuaded by claims that a group of artifacts left in a corner of a building at a former slave quarter in Texas, dating to the 1850s at the earliest, including such objects as seashells, beads, doll parts, bird skulls, medicine bottles, and so on are "virtually identical to those used by modern-day Yoruba diviners for healing and other rituals" (Brown and Cooper 1990: 16–18).

Third, just as identities were in flux in Africa, inevitably they were extraordinarily fluid in the Americas. Ethnogenesis did occur but in extremely complicated ways. Thus, for example, many Africans from the Bight of Biafra who had never heard the name Igbo in their own lands and identified themselves instead by their villages or districts yet came to accept the term when forced abroad. They may even have incorporated people and cultural traits from places far remote from the Bight of Biafra. Perhaps the most famous Ibo of the eighteenth century, Olaudah Equiano, seems to have participated in the invention or reconstitution of his identity. Equiano may well have been a native of South Carolina rather than of the Bight of Biafra. That he chose to become an Ibo says much of the importance of that group in his life (Carretta 1999, 2005). Similarly, consciousness of Yoruba ethnicity first emerged among the Displaced African Diaspora, and the "Lucumi" of Cuba included some non-Yoruba groups. Ethnic identities in America were more wide-ranging and inclusive than they had been in Africa (Law 1997).

Fourth, one reason for this development was the continuing influx of peoples from ever more diverse places in Africa. Even if one or two African coastal regions often dominated the early history of a New World slave society, over time more mixing occurred. By the last quarter of the eighteenth century in Barbados, for example, the two leading African regions supplied only just over a half of the island's Africans, and the dominant supplier was now West-Central Africa (at 37 percent), a region that had provided no slaves to the island a century earlier. By the 1730s in York Naval District, Virginia, the Bight of Biafra, though still the primary supplier, was providing less than half of the incoming Africans; West-Central Africa, Senegambia, the Windward Coast, and Gold Coast provided the rest. Moreover, most other naval districts in Virginia received Africans from a much wider range of regions than did York. Increasing heterogeneity is the dominant feature of African migration into most North American and Caribbean regions (Eltis *et al.* 1999; Eltis 2001; Walsh 2001).

Finally, just as I would see ethnic identities as fluid and permeable, so I think social and cultural development for any group in North America and the Caribbean involved borrowing, adaptation, modification, and invention. Slaves were the most ruthless *bricoleurs*: picking and choosing from a variety of cultural strains, precisely because they came from such diverse origins, were thrown together in the New World, and were denied the resources to recreate institutions, languages, and family structures known in their homelands. Their plasticity was of an extreme kind, because they were subjected to an extreme horror. Developing significant creole populations within their midst entailed yet further transformations. The movement of slaves from region to region further enhanced the mix. The extent of cultural fusion, syncretism, and blendings in which all newcomers engaged is perhaps best summed up in the term creolization, and I believe it will still be the central New World story, even when we have depicted African and European peoples with all the ethnic and regional particularity we can muster.

Conclusions

Looking over recent archaeological research, I would emphasize four issues of context and comparison.

The first is the balance to be struck between ethnic or regional African traits and general West or West-Central African cultural principles. Consider one specific ethnic symbol that gets deployed, over-deployed I contend, in a number of archaeological contexts: the Bakongo cosmogram (see Ferguson 1992, 1999). One of the more plausible applications is Leland Ferguson's interpretation of the marks and scratches on just over 20 colonoware sherds in the South Carolina lowcountry: many of the incisions were made after firing, which seems to indicate owners' rather than makers' marks; their predominantly underwater provenience suggests ritual usage; they were made on bowls, not jars; and West-Central Africa was a major supplier of slaves to the region especially early in the eighteenth century. Nevertheless, as Ferguson admits, syncretism, the incorporation of Christian and Native American meanings, may be just as important as any attribution to the Bakongo. This syncretic argument assumes more force if Carl Steen (1999) is correct in suggesting that Indian women, who as late as 1730, comprised a significant minority of lowcountry slaves, contributed significantly to colonoware pottery production in the region. Furthermore, the ideas involved in Bakongo cosmology, the division between the living and the dead, were extremely complex, while the symbols were quite simple. Can one infer a cosmological system from a few scratches and incisions, particularly when similar marks have been found on ceramics in other cultural and historical settings?

In other cases than that posited by Ferguson, the "discovery" of the Bakongo cosmogram seems far-fetched. Here is my list of recent attributions based on the finding of a cross or x mark in archaeological assemblages: a single European-manufactured sherd in the Bahamas (Wilkie and Farnsworth 1999; Wilkie 2000); a small handmade skull figurine in Loudoun County, Virginia (Fennell 2000); the handle of a teaspoon, a clay marble, and a Chinese coin at Locust Grove, Kentucky (Young 1997); three limestone marbles at the Hermitage plantation near Tennessee (Russell 1997); a pocketknife handle from a slave quarter at Somerset Plantation in North Carolina (Samford 1996); pewter spoons at Kingsmill Plantation in Virginia and Garrison Plantation in Maryland (Klingelhofer 1987; Samford 1996); and another spoon found at the bottom of the East River in New York City (Wall 2000). The placement of putative spiritual objects in northeastern corners of rooms at slave-related sites in Virginia and Maryland are said to have been inspired by the northeastern quadrant of the Bakongo cosmogram, corresponding to birth and life (Leone and Fry 1999; Samford 1999). Of some objects—a bottle containing a button, several cloth, sugar, and tobacco bags holding plant material, and an iron knife—found in some interior and exterior walls of two quarters, one in North Carolina and the other Virginia, one historical archaeologist has claimed that they "are meaningless until related to cultural practices of the Bakongo" (Samford 1996: 107). All of these works derive their inspiration from Robert Farris Thompson (1983: 106–116). But, in some of these places (and times), it might be difficult to find even a few West-Central Africans or their descendants.

African archaeologists often criticize their Americanist colleagues for their tendency to generalize about African cultures, for failing to reflect the complexity and variety of Africa. At the same time, perhaps, they should be applauding American archaeologists for beginning to strive to uncover certain African deep-level principles and fundamental ways of thinking. Yet, it may be a fool's errand, to search for such a specific, such a precise ethnic trait, as the Bakongo cosmogram (see also Saraceni 1996; Wilkie 1997).

A second issue is the balance to be struck between African continuities and creolization. Arguably, the spotlight shone on the small minority of ceramics found at slave sites that might have been made by Africans and their descendants in the

Americas puts in the shadow the vast majority of ceramics that are of European manufacture. As Merrick Posnansky (1999) notes, no transfer of sophisticated African ceramic skills to the Americas seems to have occurred. Relatively few mature women with well-honed pottery skills made it to the New World. Colonoware was usually decoratively impoverished, and, in Matthew Hill's (1987) words, is remarkable not for being distinctively African but for being distinctively non-European (but, see Meyers 1999).

Once our gaze turns from the search for continuities to the actual makeup of most ceramic assemblages at slave sites, inventive interpretations stressing cultural creativity begin to surface. Wilkie and Farnsworth, for example, observe a predominance of polychrome decorated vessels and handpainted wares among the European-made ceramics preferred by Bahamian slaves (Wilkie and Farnsworth 1999; Wilkie 2000). Because of their own aesthetic principles, it is said that West Africans favored the chevrons, bands, and dots commonly found in annular/mocha wares produced by English potters. Higman (1998) finds that geometric design elements used on some of the European ceramics excavated at New Montpelier in Jamaica were mimetic analogs of West African patterns found in stamped adinkra cloth. It is instructive, however, that the Bahamian slaves studied by Wilkie and Farnsworth preferred browns and oranges rather than the blue-decorated wares common among their owners, whereas at Montpelier, studied by Higman, shades of blue dominated the pearlware and whiteware common there, and their slaves' taste is akin to that preferred by the British poor. Jean Howson (1995) has shown that slaves in Montserrat preferred transfer-printed plates favoring exotic scenes and transfer-printed bowls patterned with repetitive geometric motifs or bearing multicolored stripes characteristic of mocha and banded wares. The bowls in particular, she argues, reflected a West African aesthetic—favoring bold, repetitive, and stylized motifs.

A third issue is the need for more comparisons between African-Americans and that strata of white society closest in status to slaves. Only then will it be possible to determine what is distinctively African-American, as opposed to what is shared among poor folk. Comparisons to other groups—especially poor whites, overseers, tenants, artisans, small landowners—are essential. John Otto (1984) pioneered this kind of work, but I do not see all that many archaeologists following his lead. I like Barbara Heath's (1999a) close investigation of a white artisanal house at Monticello, showing that architecturally these whites had more floor space, greater privacy, and more comforts than the slaves, but seemingly their diet was worse than that of the enslaved. This last suggestion gains some support from height data. By the late eighteenth century, native-born North American slaves were almost the same height as whites, with the mean height of adult male slaves being about 67.2 in, making them taller than almost all Europeans (indeed only European aristocrats were as tall), taller than those slaves born in the Caribbean, and much taller than those born in Africa (Sokoloff and Villafor 1982). In the early nineteenth century, American-born slaves were, on average 1.6 in taller than even the Yoruba, the tallest ethnic group in Africa (Komlos 1994, 1995; Eltis 1982, 1990).

Lastly, broader comparisons in general are required. Archaeology is, by its very nature, site specific; its focus, like some historical work, is microcosmic. Inter-site comparisons on a regional basis are obviously in order. Thus, I believe projects such as the Digital Archaeological Archive of Chesapeake Slavery, presently being conducted at Monticello's Archaeology Department, which is standardizing all the artifacts generated at 20 sites in Virginia, is the way of the future (see www.daacs.org). I will confess to being frustrated when I read particular studies of colonoware, or whatever term one wants to use for the local ceramics often made by African-Americans whether in South Carolina, Barbados, Antigua, St Eustatius, Jamaica, or Dominica, because rarely does anyone try to compare these local ceramic traditions in a full comparative context. We know of some basic similarities: hand-modeling for the most part, firing without a kiln, and the non-application of glazes. We know that there are more diverse forms on St Eustatius and Jamaica than on the other islands (Heath 1988; Heath and Armstrong 1999; Heath 1999b; Hauser and DeCorse 2003; Hauser Chapter 14, in this volume). But surely somebody could now offer a general study, pointing out generic similarities and local variations. Morgan and MacDonald (2004) caution, however, that they "expect to see many different unique (micro-) regional stories, rather than a single generalized phenomenon."

At a time when slavery is increasingly viewed in an Atlantic, and often global, perspective, the greater the comparative focus the better. Scholars of African history such as John Thornton, Paul Lovejoy, Robin Law, and Ray Kea—just to mention a few—have recently been turning their sights toward the Diaspora, while historians of the Americas have gradually realized that they must understand Africa as much as Europe. Slavery has been studied comparatively more than any other Atlantic institution. It will be good to see historical archaeologists embrace these goals.

References

Brown, Kenneth L., and Cooper, Doreen C. (1990) "Structural continuity in an African-American slave and tenant community," *Historical Archaeology*, 24: 7–19.

Carretta, Vincent (1999) "Olaudah Equiano or Gustavus Vassa? New light on an eighteenth-century question of identity," *Slavery & Abolition*, 20, 3: 96–105.

Carretta, Vincent (2005) *Equiano the African: Biography of a Self-Made Man*, Athens: University of Georgia Press.

Chambers, Douglas B. (2002) "The significance of Igbo in the Bight of Biafra slave trade: a rejoinder to Northrup's 'Myth Igbo'," *Slavery & Abolition*, 23, 1: 101–120.

DeCorse, Christopher R. (2001) *An Archaeology of Elmina: Africans and Europeans on the Gold Coast, 1400–1900*, Washington, DC: Smithsonian.

Eltis, David (1982) "Nutritional standards in Africa and the Americas: heights of Africans, 1819–1839," *Journal of Interdisciplinary History*, 12: 453–475.

Eltis, David (1990) "Welfare trends among the Yoruba in the early nineteenth century: the anthropometric evidence," *Journal of Economic History*, 50: 521–540.

Eltis, David (2001) "The transatlantic slave trade: a new census," *William and Mary Quarterly*, 3rd series, 58: 17–46.

Eltis, David, and Morgan, Philip D. (ed.) (2001) "New Perspectives on the Transatlantic Slave Trade," *William and Mary Quarterly*, 3rd Series, 58: 3–251.

Eltis, David, Behrendt, Stephen D., Richardson, David, and Klein, Herbert S. (eds) (1999) *The Trans-Atlantic Slave Trade: A Database on CD-Rom*, Cambridge: Cambridge University Press.

Fennell, Christopher C. (2000) "Conjuring boundaries: inferring past identities from religious artifacts," *International Journal of Historical Archaeology*, 4, 4: 281–313.

Ferguson, Leland (1992) *Uncommon Ground: Archaeology and Early African America, 1650–1800*, Washington, DC: Smithsonian.

Ferguson, Leland (1999) " 'The Cross Is a Magic Sign': Marks on Eighteenth-Century Bowls from South Carolina," in Theresa A. Singleton (ed.) *"I, Too, Am America": Archaeological Studies of African-American Life*, 116–131, Charlottesville, VA: University of Virginia Press.

Hall, Gwendolyn Midlo (2005) *Slavery and African Ethnicities in the Americas: Restoring the Links*, Chapel Hill: University of North Carolina Press.

Hauser, Mark, and Armstrong, Douglas (1999) "Embedded Identities: Seeking Economic and Social Relations through Compositional Analysis of Low-Fired Earthenware," in Jay Haviser (ed.) *African Sites Archaeology in the Caribbean*, 65–93, Kingston: Ian Randle Publisher.

Hauser, Mark and DeCorse, Christopher R. (2003) "Low-Fired Earthenwares in the African Diaspora: Problems and Prospects," *International Journal of Historical Archaeology*, 7, 1: 67–98.

Heath, Barbara J. (1988) *Afro Caribbean Ware: A Study of Ethnicity on St. Eustatius*, unpublished PhD dissertation, University of Pennsylvania.

Heath, Barbara J. (1999a) " 'Your Humble Servant': Free Artisans in the Monticello Community," in Theresa A. Singleton (ed.) *"I, Too, Am America": Archaeological Studies of African-American Life*, 193–217, Charlottesville, VA: University of Virginia Press.

Heath, Barbara J. (1999b) "Yabbas, Monkeys, Jugs, and Jars: A Historical Context for African Caribbean Potterys on St Eustatius," in Jay Haviser (ed.) *African Sites Archaeology in the Caribbean*, 196–220, Kingston: Ian Randle Publisher.

Higman, B. W. (1998) *Montpelier Jamaica: A Plantation Community in Slavery and Freedom, 1739–1912*, Kingston: The Press University of the West Indies.

Hill, Matthew (1987) "Ethnicity lost? Ethnicity gained? Information functions of 'African ceramics,' " in R. Auger, M. F. Glass, S. MacEachern, and P. McCartney (eds) West Africa and North America, in *Ethnicity and Culture: Proceedings of the Eighteenth Annual Chacmool Conference*, 135–139, Calgary: Archaeological Association, University of Calgary.

Howson, Jean (1995) *Colonial Goods and the Plantation Village: Consumption and the Internal Economy in Montserrat from Slavery to Freedom*, unpublished PhD dissertation, Department of Anthropology, New York University.

Kelly, Kenneth G. (1997a) "The archaeology of African-European interaction: investigating the social roles of trade, traders, and the use of space in the seventeenth-and eighteenth-century Hueda Kingdom, Republic of Benin," *World Archaeology*, 28, 3: 351–369.

Kelly, Kenneth G. (1997b) "Using historically informed archaeology: seventeenth and eighteenth century Hueda/European interaction on the Coast of Benin," *Journal of Archaeological Method and Theory*, 4, 3–4: 353–366.

Klingelhofer, Eric (1987) "Aspects of early Afro-American material culture: artifacts from the slave quarters at Garrison Plantation, Maryland," *Historical Archaeology*, 21: 112–119.

Komlos, John (ed.) (1994) *Stature, Living Standards, and Economic Development: Essays in Anthropometric History*, Chicago, IL: University of Chicago Press.

Komlos, John (1995) *The Biological Standard of Living in Europe and America, 1700–1900*, Aldershot: Variorum.

Law, Robin (1997) "Ethnicity and the slave trade: 'Lucumi' and 'Nago' as ethnonyms in West Africa," *History in Africa*, 24: 205–219.

Leone, Mark P., and Fry, Gladys-Marie (1999) "Conjuring in the big house kitchen: an interpretation of African American belief systems based on the uses of archaeology and folklore sources," *Journal of American Folklore*, 112: 372–403.

Lohse, Russell (2002) "Slave trade nomenclature and African ethnicities in the Americas: evidence from early 18th century Costa Rica," *Slavery and Abolition*, 23, 3: 73–92.

Meyers, A. D. (1999) "West African tradition in the decoration of colonial Jamaican folk pottery," *International Journal of Historical Archaeology*, 3: 201–223.

Morgan, David W., and MacDonald, Kevin C. (2004) "Colonoware in Western Colonial Louisiana: makers and meaning," paper presented at the 37th Annual Conference on Historical and Underwater Archaeology, St Louis, Missouri.

Northrup, David (2000) "Igbo and myth Igbo: culture and ethnicity in the Atlantic world, 1600–1850," *Slavery & Abolition*, 21, 3: 1–20.

Nwokeji, G. Ugo (2001) "African Conceptions of Gender and the Slave Traffic," *William and Mary Quarterly* 3rd Series, 58: 47–68.

Otto, John S. (1984) *Cannon's Point Plantation, 1794–1860: Living Conditions and Status Patterns in the Old South*, Orlando, FL: Academic Press.

Posnansky, M. (1999) "West Africanist Reflections on African-American Archaeology," in T. A. Singleton (ed.) *"I Too Am America": Archaeological Studies of African-American Life*, 21–38, Charlottesville, VA: University of Virginia Press.

Price, Richard (2001) "The miracle of Creolization: a retrospective," *New West Indian Guide*, 75: 35–64.

Russell, Aaron E. (1997) "Material culture and African-American spirituality at the hermitage," *Historical Archaeology*, 31, 2: 63–80.

Samford, Patricia (1996) "The archaeology of African-American slavery," *William and Mary Quarterly*, 3rd Series, 53: 87–114.

Samford, Patricia (1999) " 'Strong is the Bond of Kinship': West-African-Style Ancestor Shrines and Subfloor Pits on African-American Quarters," in Maria Franklin and Garrett Fesler (eds) *Historical Archaeology, Identity Formation, and the Interpretation of Ethnicity*, 71–92, Williamsburg, VA: Colonial Williamsburg Research Publications.

Saraceni, J. E. (1996) "Secret religion of slaves," *Archaeology*, 49, 6: 21.

Sokoloff, Kenneth L. and Villaflor, Georgia C. (1982) "The early achievement of modern stature in America," *Social Science History*, 6: 453–481.

Steen, Carl (1999) "Stirring the ethnic stew in the South Carolina backcountry: John de la Howe and Lethe Farm," in Maria Franklin and Garrett Fesler (eds) *Historical Archaeology, Identity Formation, and the Interpretation of Ethnicity*, 93–120, Williamsburg, VA: Colonial Williamsburg Research Publications.

Thompson, Robert Farris (1983) *Flash of the Spirit: African and Afro-American Art and Philosophy*, New York: Random House.

Wall, Diana diZerega (2000) "Twenty years after: re-examining archaeological collections for evidence of New York City's colonial African past," *African-American Archaeology*, no. 28 (Spring): 2–6.

Walsh, Lorena S. (2001) "The Chesapeake slave trade: regional patterns, African origins, and some implications," *William and Mary Quarterly*, 3rd Series, 58: 139–170.

Wilkie, Laurie A. (1997) "Secret and sacred: contextualizing the artifacts of African-American magic and religion," *Historical Archaeology*, 31: 81–106.

Wilkie, Laurie A. (2000) "Culture bought: evidence of creolization in the consumer goods of an enslaved Bahamian family," *Historical Archaeology*, 34: 10–26.

Wilkie, Laurie A., and Farnsworth, Paul (1999) "Trade and the construction of Bahamian identity: a multiscalar Exploration," *International Journal of Historical Archaeolog*, 3, 4: 283–320.

Young, Amy L. (1997) "Risk management strategies among African-American slaves at Locust Grove Plantation," *International Journal of Historical Archaeology*, 1, 1: 5–37.

7   *Putting flesh on the bones*

*History–Anthropology collaboration on the
New York City African Burial Ground Project*

ALLISON BLAKELY

Parameters of the project

Since 1993 researchers in the fields of anthropology and history have been conducting research focusing on the remains of some 400 individuals and hundreds of various artifacts from a burial ground in lower Manhattan that dates from the early eighteenth century and was used almost exclusively for blacks. The African Burial Ground was unearthed by chance in 1991 and 1992 during preparation for construction of an office tower for the United States General Services Administration (GSA). Examination of skeletal remains from this site, coupled with archival research, revealed that these burials were of free and enslaved African people buried from early in the British colonial period until the closure of the cemetery in 1794. Until this recent discovery only a few scholars in the fields of colonial New York history and African American studies knew of this cemetery's existence. In response to protest from black community organizations, excavation was temporarily delayed to allow for careful removal and sampling of what is estimated to be a 5 ½-acre plot containing more than 10,000 burials. The remains will be eventually re-interred at the burial ground site in a space provided next to the completed office building. The site has been designated a city and national landmark with a federal steering committee appointed. Meanwhile, the 400 remains were transported to Howard University's W. Montague Cobb Biological Anthropology Laboratory for the research that is currently in progress, led by Anthropologist Dr Michael Blakey, and supported by a grant from the GSA. It is important to note that this final choice of research site came about only as a result of protest from African American community leaders such as the then New York Mayor David Dinkins, New York State Senator David Paterson, and Congressman Gus Savage of Illinois, after the GSA originally designated an all-white research team of anthropologists and archaeologists from Lehman College in New York (Scarupa 1995). Current research on this site features fascinating interplay between many academic disciplines, especially anthropology and history, and poses complex challenges of communication and interpretation for the scholars representing these two disciplines. The team of anthropologists led by Dr Blakey, a physical anthropologist, has from the outset included varied specialists in the investigation, including osteologists, dental radiologists, and chemists, molecular geneticists, archaeologists, botanists, African art historians, and historians.

This find offers the exciting possibility of gaining new information on African culture in colonial New York, including the specific African origins of the population. It should also provide means of assessing the degree of harshness of the enslaved's lives in America. Even before most of the research was begun, the dimensions of this find represented the most concrete evidence to date that Africans played a major role in the creation of this city from its beginnings and confirmed that slavery was far more common in this northern city than had earlier been thought. In the third year of the project's projected six years, a supplemental, smaller grant was awarded to Howard University's History Department so that it could help place the biological and anthropological findings into a historical context and provide documentary evidence that would explain the physical indications reflected in the skeletal and artifact analysis. The History Department's further objective is to provide a broader view of the lives of enslaved people in colonial New York. Toward that end, the research of the historians, led by Dr Edna Medford, has focused on the origins of New York's early African population through time: identifying political and social factors which determined acquisition of slaves; the social, cultural, and economic institutions the enslaved population had known in Africa; their living conditions and disease environments to which they had been exposed before their arrival in New York (including the Caribbean); and the nature of their response to a new and different socioeconomic, cultural, and legal reality in America. The historians participating have expertise on colonial America, Africa, the Caribbean, and the European slave trade. Also, during a visit to three West African countries in 1997, some of them established links with counterparts in several related disciplines at universities in Ghana, Cote d'Ivoire, and Senegal. This chapter is a brief summary of how anthropology and history have worked together in an effort to maximize the knowledge gained from this burial ground, and to highlight some of the methodological and practical questions raised by this collaboration.

Reconstructing the early history of Africans in New York

While the African Burial Ground appears to date from the late seventeenth century and beginning of the eighteenth century, it is instructive to also glance briefly at the Dutch period of New York's initial founding in the seventeenth century, because it was here that the basic patterns of life that continued into the eighteenth century became set. The Dutch colonies which emerged in West Africa and the Americas resulted from Dutch entry into the lucrative new trade in African slaves and New World sugar and tobacco. New Netherlands, the North American colony of the Dutch, actually predated the founding of the West India Company and only intermittently received its careful attention. Nevertheless', New Netherlands' half century of life was an interesting variation as a projection of Dutch society abroad. The site for this colony was originally discovered by the Englishman Henry Hudson in 1609, while he sought a new route to Asia for the Dutch East India Company. Although the area was called New Netherlands as early as 1614, the permanent European settlers were about 30 families of French-speaking Walloons who settled on

Manhattan Island in 1624, founding New Amsterdam. The West India Company purchased the island from the Indians in 1626 for 60 guilders and the Amsterdam Chamber of Commerce began to promote colonization around Fort Amsterdam in 1629. By 1630 there were about 300 Europeans there, still mostly Walloons.

As early as 1615 Amsterdam merchants founded a New Netherlands trading company. It experienced some success before the founding of a national trading company with its monopoly in 1621. The economy of New Netherlands was initially based on the fur trade with the Indians, becoming the best North American source of furs for the first half of the seventeenth century. In its final two decades under the Dutch the colony grew to around 9,000 people, was centered on an agricultural economy, and had increasingly more commercial ties with the Netherlands. Although the territory stretched for more than a 100 miles along the coast, the population was centered around just a few towns; the spaces between were still Indian country. New Amsterdam received a municipal charter and government in 1653, placing its burgomasters and other officials under the colony's director-general, who was appointed by the West India Company (New York Historical Society 1982; Rink 1986).

As much as half of the population of New Netherlands may have been non-Dutch: German, Norwegian, Swedish, Finnish, French, Danish, and British (Cohen 1981). Indeed, mid-seventeenth century maps of the region of North America show New France, New England, New Netherlands, New Belgium, and New Sweden as neighbors.[1] In the course of its existence the Dutch colony would be periodically at war with bordering New England and New Sweden, as well as local Indians, before finally falling to the English in 1664. Thus, this colony was awash in the swirl of international economic competition. Director-general Willem Kieft, who directed the colony from 1638 to 1647, counted 18 languages spoken there. By 1630, enslaved Africans were also brought to New Netherlands from the Caribbean, and some directly from Africa. Although there were slave markets in the region of New Amsterdam, most of these captives went to tobacco growers in the nearby southern colonies. This northern colony lacked the types of agriculture that welcomed slave labor. There are no firm estimates of the black population of New Netherlands, slave or free. Various estimates of the enslaved African population of New Netherlands range as high as 40 percent of the population of its main city, New Amsterdam.

Peter Stuyvesant, the director-general from 1647 to 1664, had 40 slaves in 1660, employed in farm labor and domestic work. He was probably the largest private owner. The West India Company was definitely the largest owner of slaves, just as it was of most other enterprises. Most of its slaves worked in all-male labor gangs, although there were also female slaves. Slaves carried out much of the construction in New Amsterdam: building forts and palisades, clearing land, burning lime, and farming the company plantation (New York Historical Society 1982: 20). In Fort Orange (present-day Albany, NY) the executioner was a black slave. It is generally agreed that slavery was somewhat milder in New Netherlands than in other European American colonies. The company developed a policy that allowed for limited manumission of its enslaved Africans. Some cases of intermarriage between blacks and whites were recorded. The Dutch Reformed Church allowed the children of some Christianized

Africans to be baptized. Sexual mixing outside marriage also occurred, as elsewhere. In all cases, however, the main consideration was the desire for order and efficiency, rather than humanitarian concerns (Goodfriend 1984).

After the bloodless British capture of New Netherlands in 1664, the English ruled New York until the end of the Revolutionary War in 1783. As was the case with the Dutch West India Company, a major commodity of the English Royal African Company was African captives. This transfer of power entailed no significant changes for the status of black slaves, and there is no historical evidence to indicate any major differences in the conditions of life for blacks in the colony during the eighteenth century. There is, however, considerable evidence that social tensions were mounting as slavery grew apace with the expanding colony. A slave uprising in 1712 left more than two dozen whites dead or wounded, and a trial in 1741 surrounding the alleged rebellion conspiracy saw more than 200 blacks arrested, 30 executed, and 71 shipped off (Davis 1984, 1985). Apart from such intriguing, indirect information, and the very fact of enslavement, there is little historical evidence on which to base a clearer picture of the conditions under which blacks lived in this era that would explain these outbursts of resistance. By mid-century there were probably around 100 free blacks on the island. The rest were enslaved, living in all sections of the lower end of the island, where the population in general was concentrated. In the final years of English rule there were over 3,000 blacks in New York City and nearly 4,000 in Albany County, as compared to 692 blacks in the city in 1703 (O'Callaghan 1849–1851). There was no slave quarter or black ghetto in the city before the American Revolution.

Initial results from the African Burial Ground

The silent messengers from the African Burial Ground now under scientific "interrogation" at Howard may provide helpful testimony toward a more detailed picture of what was happening in the lives of blacks in New York during these years. An example of how the disciplines of history and anthropology receive mutual benefit from collaboration may be seen in the ways that historical data can help overcome limitations in the anthropological analysis that result from a shortage of comparative skeletal databases on populations from Western and Central Africa. Most existing physical anthropological research has focused on East and South African populations and on hunter–gatherers who were peripheral to the Atlantic slave trade. This is the result both of research intensity (emphasis on questions regarding prehistoric human origins) and factors of preservation. Moreover, the traditional anthropological focus on race has led to lumping diverse groups into single categories for the generation of comparison indices. Historical information has alerted geneticists of the diversity of West and Central African populations brought as captives to the New World that need to be sampled for accurate assessments of cultural backgrounds. Of all the colonial cities on the British North American mainland in the eighteenth century, New York ranked second in the numbers of enslaved Africans who lived and labored there. Until the mid-eighteenth century most of those imported came from the West Indies; after that time, many arrived directly from the African continent, from a number of regions: the Guinea coast in West Africa, Congo and Angola in West-Central Africa, and even some from East Africa, including Madagascar. There has been little prior archaeological work on historic populations representing either Europeans or continental Africans that could allow comparison of the remains in question concerning relative living conditions. The samples that would provide the best comparison of relative health for the African population would of course come from European cemeteries in New York. These are precluded for obvious ethical and social reasons. Thus the investigators on the African Burial Ground remains must rely more on supplemental information from historical and other disciplines to formulate details about the origins and message of these remains.

An illustration of the type of information this sort of collaborative investigation can produce can be seen in the following excerpt from a report by Mark E. Mack and Michael Blakey:

> Burial 12 ... suffered from a number of dental pathologies. Many of her teeth were affected by severe caries. Periapical abscessing resulting in the spread of infection would have been likely, lowering her body's immunoresponse system to environmental insults. Reduced dietary intake due to masticatory pain would also contribute to disease risk ... Finally, her skeleton is riddled with sclerotic periostitis affecting her clavicles, humeri, ribs, vertebrae and innominates, indicative of a systemic infection. Her poor overall health should have negatively affected her child (Burial 14) both in utero and early life. Poor mineralization of the neonates's deciduous dentition and the simple, but sad fact that both the mother and newborn appear to have died shortly after childbirth is consistent with such effects. Our demographic studies show, moreover, that neonates and 30–35 year old females are in the highest risk categories for mortality for this population.[2]

This chilling analysis may prove quite instructive since half of the roughly 400 skeletons belonged to children under the age of 12, and nearly half of these were infants. Of the children who survived infancy, half show developmental defects in their dental enamel, resulting from prolonged or intermittent bouts of illness and malnutrition. A sampling of information from ongoing laboratory studies provide further illustrations of questions raised by the anthropologists for which historians may be able to suggest answers, or, conversely, which suggest answers for questions historians have about life at that time. Demographic data from the cemetery show that women who survived to 45 years of age had an increased chance of living into old age. The historical data says that Africans over 50 years of age were considered to be of little economic value and were often abandoned to the streets, but the condition of older women was somehow different from that of the men. Research aimed at assessing musculoskeletal indicators of work stress among the New York Africans suggests that men and women appear to have performed somewhat different tasks. For example, the cervical vertebrae of women are more likely to exhibit pathologies consistent with overloading of the neck while carrying items on the head.

Another ongoing study, seeking to weigh the impact of infectious disease, indicates that many individuals in the sample population were born in Africa or had spent a considerable period of time in the Caribbean. Syphilis is absent and yaws is relatively common. Historical documents often refer to yaws among African captives sent to New York, and rarely to syphilis.

The laboratory examination of the remains generally tends to affirm documentary evidence. Another skeletal analysis, treating the patterns of growth and development among subadults and adults, reveals significant differences between dental development rates (which is generally considered to be the most accurate indicator of subadult age) and rates of bone ossification, growth, and fusion. Infants and children in the sample frequently exhibit evidence of delayed growth and maturation. Historical evidence and skeletal analysis strongly suggest that observed inconsistencies between bone and dental ages among subadults are attributable to the severe stresses endured by these individuals. Premature mortality and infectious disease rate were high. About 80 percent of the children exhibit enamel defects resulting from the disease environment. Results of a separate study comparing dental evidence of health in putative African-born and American-born children suggest that adults exhibiting dental modifications indicative of African birth (e.g. tooth filing) were born and raised in a healthier environment than their notionally American-born counterparts.

One final example of how anthropological and historical data contribute to a fuller picture, a look at the fertility and population growth among the enslaved Africans, based on New York City municipal census data for the eighteenth century, reveals the virtual absence of natural increase in the city's African population prior to the American Revolution, as contrasted with Europeans, whose natural increase was slow but apparent. In the words of the combined team of anthropologists and historians:

> A host of stresses rooted in the political and economic circumstances of slavery in colonial New York appear to have placed strong limits on African fertility despite the large proportion of enslaved females brought to the colony. Mortality was clearly high for women of reproductive age, notably for adolescent girls and young women, and possibly for female children, thus eliminating much of the fecundity of the community. Skeletal evidence of arduous work and active and chronic infectious disease stresses in women of reproductive ages suggests further limits on the fecundity of surviving women. Infant mortality is approximately 18% of all mortality in the African Burial Ground population, most of which occurs during neonatal life, with an obvious negative impact on natural population increase. Historical chronicles also demonstrate that European enslavers in the more urbanized core of New York frowned upon childbearing among their enslaved women workers.[3]

Thus this collaboration between anthropology and history, in which historical evidence about fertility combines with skeletal studies, provides at least a basis for greater confidence concerning what has been suspected about the quality of life of the black population of New York during this distant age. Whereas the difficulty of obtaining comparative skeletal samples leaves unclear how this population's experience compared with that of the dominant group, it is known from historical data that the whites in New York's Trinity Churchyard had lived far longer than the Africans in the African Burial Ground. In any event, these findings remove any question that the black population was present and fully engaged in this important chapter of American history. Participation in the project itself has also taught valuable lessons to the historians and anthropologists. Perhaps the most important lesson is reinforcement of appreciation of the necessity of interdisciplinary studies for obtaining the most valuable results. Another is the opportunity it has provided for viewing a familiar topic from the perspective of a different discipline. For example, as a historian examining the minute details of the anthropological research, I found myself at times thinking that I had entered into a new perceptual dimension, one in which I was for the first time viewing history from the inside out, rather than visualizing along the surface. The seventeenth and eighteenth century Dutch notarial records with precise descriptions of cargoes of enslaved Africans I examined in archives in the Netherlands now came to life with new meaning. A major question this raises that I hope to pursue further is how can such collaboration between history and other disciplines become the norm rather than an exception? It should not be dependent on accidental discoveries of rare finds such as an African Burial Ground. Collaborative, interdisciplinary studies are more critically urgent for African Diaspora studies than for what might be termed "mainstream" history precisely because the aspects of history they seek to recapture have often been buried under other layers of history, and of historical amnesia, just as the African Burial Ground was buried in the earth under Manhattan.

Notes

1 For example a 1655 Jansz Visscher map is featured in the exhibit catalog of the exhibition *The Birth of New York: Nieuw Amsterdam 1624–1664*, which ran from October to December 1982 in New York, and February to March 1983 at the Amsterdams Historisch Museum.
2 Mark E. Mack and Michael L. Blakey, "The New York African Burial Ground Project: past biases, current dilemmas and future research opportunities," unpublished manuscript, 9–10.
3 Other evidence regarding the infant mortality suggests that the actual level is probably much higher than 18 percent. These data are from *AAPA Abstracts* of papers presented at the 2000 Annual Meeting of the American Association of Physical Anthropologists, and were published in supplement 30 to the *American Journal of Physical Anthropology* Annual meeting issue.

References

Cohen, David (1981) "How Dutch were the Dutch of New Netherland," *New York History*, 62: 51.
Davis, Thomas J. (1984) "These enemies of their own household," *The Journal of the Afro-American Historical and Genealogical Society*, 5, Fall/Winter: 133–147.
Davis, Thomas J. (1985) *Rumor of Revolt: The Great Negro Plot in Colonial New York*, New York: The Free Press.
Goodfriend, Joyce D. (1984) " 'Black families in New Netherland,' Proceedings of the sixth Annual Rensselaerswyck Seminar, 'Blacks in New Netherland and Colonial New York'," *Journal of the Afro-American Historical and Genealogical Society*, 5, Fall/Winter: 94–97.

New York Historical Society (ed.) (1982) *The Birth of New York: Nieuw Amsterdam 1624–1664*, Catalog for the Exhibition at the New York Historical Society, October–December New York: The Municipal Archives.

O'Callaghan, Edmund B. (ed.) (1849–1851) *Documentary History of the State of New York*, 5 Vols, Albany, NY: State of New York.

Rink, Oliver (1986) *Holland on the Hudson: An Economic and Social History of Dutch New York*, Ithaca, NY: Cornell University Press.

Scarupa, Harriet Jackson (1995) "Learning from ancestral bones: New York's exhumed African past," *American Visions*, February/March 18–21.

8   All the documents are destroyed!

Documenting slavery for St Eustatius, Netherlands Antilles

RICHARD GRANT GILMORE III

Introduction

St Eustatius, or *Statia* as it is known in the Antilles, has been studied by many historians as it was of primary importance in supplying war goods to the American rebels during their war for independence from Britain (Jameson 1903; Hartog 1976; Goslinga 1985; Tuchman 1988; Hurst 1996). The documents used by these historians were viewed with the goal of reconstructing trade routes and quantities and the military dimensions of life on the island. In contrast, archaeologists have not explored the wealth of documentary evidence available in the British Library, Clements Library at the University of Michigan, and especially the *Nationaal Archiefs* (Dutch National Archives) in The Hague, the Netherlands. Instead, they have presumed that the documents that would be helpful to their research on the island were destroyed due to hurricanes and neglect (cf. Hamelberg 1889; Bijlsma and Lee 1924; Meilink Roelofsz 1954–1955). However, as part of my doctoral research at University College London, I have examined documentary evidence in these libraries and have found much that is potentially helpful to archaeologists.

Historic documents are integral to historical archaeology. Yet, written records must be used carefully where slavery is concerned. They are typically written by the dominant class, which included slave owners (Singleton 1985, 1999). Thus, many accounts may project unduly positive or even idyllic images of what slave life was like. With this caveat in mind, societal information that can be gleaned from these records can stretch far beyond the typical demographic data examined by many historians. For example, how slaves were employed in the St Eustatius economy, to what extent they possessed freedom of movement, their responses to those in charge, and even how they entertained themselves are alluded to in these records. The material life of some slaves is also evident in the documentary record through descriptions of housing and the food they consumed. This information is found in primary sources such as wills, deeds, manumission papers, contracts, military records, laws and proclamations passed on the island, as well as travelogues written by visitors. In addition to these details regarding the social context of slavery on Statia, documentary sources also provide evidence regarding housing and food for slaves.

Document recording

Documents were recorded using both Microsoft Excel and Microsoft Word. Pertinent information about the contents of each document was recorded in Excel, including such things as property descriptions (e.g. size and location) and the owner's name and occupation. If the document was a deed or will and contained information regarding slaves, it was noted in the database and cross-referenced to a full transcription made in Word. In the Netherlands, documents were recorded in Dutch, French, and English—about half the documents being in Dutch. I have also translated elements of Schiltkamp's *West Indisch Plakaatboek* (West Indies Law book), which lists all of the laws and regulations passed by the various governments on St Eustatius between 1648 and 1816. Relevant maps and illustrations that I have found in libraries and archives have been digitally scanned.

Wills, inventories, and manumission papers from the Dutch National Archives

The Dutch National Archives contains extensive records from the time of both the Old West Indies Company (1636–1674) and the New West Indies Company (1674–1792). Additional documents held in the National Archives date to between 1792 and 1828 when St Eustatius came under the auspices of the Dutch Government. The majority are filed within the "Oud Archieven van St. Eustatius tot 1828" under the Toegangsnummer 1.05.13.01. Some documents are in French and English as a result of the island's occupation by these nations during the eighteenth century.

Wills, inventories, deeds, and manumission papers were issued to manage the conveyance of property. Property included both movable and immovable items, including chattels. Slaves were included in the latter category. Wills from St Eustatius are not much different than those written today. They consist of several parts that specify for whom the will is written, witnesses, and, most importantly, what property is to be conveyed. Inventories were taken before a property was sold by its owner, for tax purposes or upon the owner's death. The property lists contained in these inventories are quite helpful in reconstructing the numbers and purpose of plantation or urban buildings on a property as well as what they contained, and the numbers of livestock. Sometimes they also list the names, sex, age, and place of origin for slaves. For example, the slaves owned by Martin Dubrois Godet, Sr are enumerated in his will of January 21, 1782: "Gestorvene Slaaven & Slaavinnen: Gregory, Congo Trompe (from the Congo), Samde Kuyper (a cooper), Statius Mingo (from Statia), Jetta, Abigail, Maria St Johns (from St Johns in the Virgin Islands)" (Ouckama 1782b).

Occupations of slaves

In many cases, special skills or the occupations of the enslaved are also indicated. For example, in an inventory for December 28, 1792, 23 blacks and mulattos are listed who were employed in the Lower town as both ship workers and "canoe workers" (men who transported goods to and from ships in the anchorage) (Du Sart 1792b). Many slaves also worked as crewmen on ships. A 1782 ship's muster roll for the schooner "Adventure" lists six slaves as sailors out of a total crew of nine (Ouckama 1782d). The entire crew of the schooner "Catherine" with the exception of the captain consisted of slaves (Chabert and Ouckama 1782). This underscores the unusual relationship that many slaves may have had with the Statian merchants and seamen. Slaves working in commerce were permitted certain freedoms and monetary rewards in exchange for being entrusted with a merchant's goods. It was through this process that some slaves, including the famed Olaudah Equiano, were able to purchase their own freedom (Equiano 1999).

The "value" of various workers is noted in the inventories as well. The most valuable slave for William Moore was "Rush," a cooper. The next most valuable slave was "Francisco," who was a "sugar cooker." This position was generally the most specialized and valued position on West Indian sugar plantations as this profession was almost an art form (Craton and Walvin 1970: 106; Mintz 1985: 49). Next came Francois who was a "bomba," a position that I have not yet been able to find a translation for (although this may refer to his ethnic origins with the Bambara along the Niger River). Finally, among skilled slaves was Jack Barbados, a distiller. Presumably, Jack was from Barbados (Du Sart 1791b). Distilleries were particularly important on Statia's sugar plantations as they facilitated the transformation of sugar illegally exported from other colonies as a reexportable good in a duty-free colony.

In the 1791 will of Jacobus Seys, owner of "Peace and Rest" Plantation, a similar pattern emerges. Two of the most valuable slaves were Steven and Fortuyn, both of whom were "sugar cookers" (Du Sart 1791f). Interestingly, for a West Indian plantation, there was also a tailor named Manuel. He was valued at almost double the price of most other slaves (Du Sart 1791f). Not only would he be able to provide clothing for the slaves and the owner of the plantation, but also he could be a valuable moneymaking asset for his owner within the Statian economy. The inventory for Jan Swartz lists 11 slaves, one of whom was a barber (Du Sart 1790a). Barbers in the eighteenth century were not just hair cutters; they also offered many of the services now provided by surgeons and physicians. They were especially skilled at "bleeding." It may be that Swartz's barber provided additional income to his owner through his healing skills. The question remains whether these skills were European or African in origin.

Significantly, there is also evidence that slaves and freedmen participated in the mercantile trade on St Eustatius. A deposition, recorded for Benjamin Fox, indicates that he was a free Negro merchant living and working on St Eustatius (Du Sart 1791a). As noted above, many slaves worked in the warehouses along the shore, transporting goods to and from ships, and crewing ships plying the inter-island trade. This intimate contact with other tradesmen would have provided ample opportunity to become involved in profitable merchant activities.

The Slave's physical person

All aspects of a slave's physical person were possessed by slave owners including, to the belief of some owners, rights of sexual access. As a result, as in other colonies, there was a significant population of people of mixed race on Statia during the eighteenth and nineteenth centuries. These mixed race people were designated in inventories and in some cases the father can be inferred. Thomas Loe may very well have been the father of the "mulatto" Lucey who was listed in his January 1782 inventory and her mother may well have been Patience who was listed just above her in the inventory (Ouckama 1782a). He had died by March 1782, and all of the same slaves, including Lucey were listed in his wife's inventory (Ouckama 1782e).

Other inventories indicate that white residents freely cohabited with mulattos on St Eustatius. The merchant, Richard Owen, lived in town on Lot 31 with his free mulatto wife Johanna Maria Rigail and their four children Richard, Thomas, Edward, and Elisabeth (Du Sart 1791e). Interestingly, one of Johanna's free mulatto relatives, Franky Rigail, lived next door on Lot 30. As Johanna was able to sign the will as a witness, she was probably literate. The free mulatto Sarah Dixon and Mr Hendrick Schroder also lived together in Oranjestad on Lot 17 (Du Sart 1791d). In one "negro house" on their property, three adult female slaves and two of their children resided. In 1790, one of the most influential members of Statian society, Abraham Heyliger, left his house and its contents to two children of the mulatto woman Jane Aun "in consideration of services received of their mother" (Du Sart 1790b). The social implications of these activities are more akin to the conditions in French Louisiana or even Spanish colonies than those normally found in English colonial society. Free persons of mixed race on St Eustatius seem to have been able to enter the economic and social realms of the Statian elite with little social stigma.

Slave ownership

On Statia, wealthy individuals possessed large numbers of slaves. The former governor of the island, Abraham Heyliger, owned 151 "negroes, mulattos, and sambos" (Heyliger, Doncker, and Runnels 1786). When P. F. Martin drew his map in 1781, Heyliger owned 97 hectares or 5.1 percent of the island. According to his 1781 inventory, he owned seven houses in the Upper and Lower towns, in addition to six plots of land including "Golden Rock Plantation." By 1791, William Moore owned this plantation and had 56 slaves working on it (Du Sart 1791b). Thus, approximately 95 slaves belonging to Abraham Heyliger were distributed among his dozen urban residences or were employed in warehouses along the bay. It is probable that they were primarily leased to others to work in the warehouses.

Some poorer individuals owned only a portion of a slave. For example, Daniel Moniero was co-owner of a slave named Fortune with his brother Nobele who resided in Naples, Italy (Le Fer 1788). According to Moniero's 1788 inventory, Fortune and a young slave girl named Magdelene lived in a single residence at Mount Pleasants Plantation.

As in other colonies, some freed slaves owned slaves themselves. The free black Cloé, formerly the property of a "Mr. Rieboo," owned a slave called Marian (Ouckama 1782c). Her economic prowess is illustrated by the fact that she both purchased her own freedom and owned a number of houses that she rented to other free blacks on the island. Joseph How, another free black, owned four slaves (Ouckama 1784). The free person of color May Harvis, owned three slaves in her house in the New Town (*Nationaal Archiefs* 1797). The potential economic power of free Africans is illustrated by the purchase of Glassbottle Fort Plantation (including 14 slaves) by the free black woman, Frances Cuffey, for $3,000 in 1818 (Du Veer 1818). It is interesting to note that many of these free black slave owners were women. This also reflects the pattern observed in primary sources from the Dutch National Archives for property ownership on Statia in general—there were significant numbers of widows who owned substantial properties on the island during this time (Secretariële n.d.).

Slave dwellings
Wills and deeds also have the potential to indicate the quality of some slave dwellings. For example, in the inventory for Jacobus Seys, Sr there are "ten oak shingled negro houses" in which 42 slaves lived (Du Sart 1791c). A 1792 inventory for John Marlton also describes the building material for his slave houses (Du Sart 1792b). He owned 23 slaves who were housed in 10 separate dwellings, seven of which were made of wood. The entry for the other three does not specify the material that they were built from. John Bailen owned six slaves who were housed in two dwellings on his urban property in Oranjestad (Du Sart 1788).

Indentures
On St Eustatius, young free black boys were indentured (apprenticed) for a set period (5–7 years) in order to learn specialized skills such as carpentry, joinery, or blacksmithing. During this time they were expected to work for their teacher in any capacity that he asked in exchange for knowledge. At the end of the indenture the person was no longer bound to their teacher and could open up a business of their own or possibly join the same business where they were apprenticed. The 1792 indenture below is typical. A free Negro woman Fanny de Windt binds her son Adam for seven years to the free Negro Henry Basteann to learn the skills of a carpenter and joiner (Du Sart 1792a; note that I have retained the original grammar and spelling):

> On this day the eleventh of May in the year of our lord 1700 and Ninety two.

> Before Me Gerard du Sart, Second Secretary of this Island St. Eustatius, Notary Publick, and Sworn in interpreter of all Languages in Service of their High Mightynesses the States General of the United Netherlands, Residing and acting within the said island in presence of the undermentioned witnesses.

> Personally appeared Fanny de Windt, Also Cannegieter, free Negro Woman, Dwelling here on the one part and Henry Bastiaans, also Buntin, free Negro Man also dwelling here, on the other part;

> Signifying the appearers on both sides, their Intention to enter with one and other in the following contract of Engagement, and indenture of

apprentice ship, Respecting the first appeared her son, Named Adam, Also Bully, on the Terms hereafter mentioned to wit.

The appearer on the one part bindes her free Negro Son, Named Adam in the most solemn manner to serve the appearer on the other part the full and uninterrupted time and term of seven years beginning on this day the eleventh of May in the Year 1700 and ninety tow until the eleventh of May of the future year 1700 and ninety nine and such as apprentice to the Carpenter and joiners Busseness during which time the Said Adam also Bully is Engaged and bound to act, and to fulfil all the different departments of an apprentice, in the abovementioned business, with all the fidelity, punctuality, and obedience in his power as far as it shall be belonging to and may be required of him in that capacity on condition that the appearer on the other part, shall in the said term of seven years beginning and ending as before described, Instruct, teach and learn him, the said Adam also Bully the Intire Art and Histery of the Carpenter and Joiners business, and at same time during the prescribed term of seven years furnish him with good and sufficient meat, drink, washing, lodging, and cloathing such as is proper and elegible for him said Adam, also Bully as an apprentice to have and receive.

That on the other side the second appearer, Henry Basteann, also Buntin, by these presents engages himself to take as he actually takes here with, as apprentice, in his service, and carpenter and joiners Business the abovenamed free Negro Boy Adam, also Bully, for the term of seven years following having taken a beginning on this day the 11th of the month of May in the year 1700 and ninety tow and to Expere on the Eleventh of May in the year 1700 and ninety nine to come during wich time the appearer on the other part requires, demands and expects from the same free Negro Boy Adam also Bully an obedient deportment and faith full service and in which interval the appearer on the other part solemnly promises to Instruct the Same Adam also Bully in the art and learn and teach him the Histery of a Carpenter and Joiner and to Employ said Adam also Bully as is becoming an apprentice in said Business, and also during the aforestated term of seven years, to provide his thus indented apprentice with Good and sufficient meat, drink, washing, lodging and cloathing likewise is sucting and becoming an apprentice as aforesaid.

For the true and exact performance of the above Engagement and Indenture, the both parties bind their respective persons and all their possessions here or else where, according to Law.

Pass'd at St Eustatius aforesaid Date as above in presence of Lodewyk Aerton Dorner and Johannes Heyliger Lindesay Witnesses.

(Signed)

Lodewyk Aerton Dorner
Johannes Heyliger Lindesay

(x) This is the Mary of Fannay de Windt
Henry Bastian Bonton

Gerard du Sart
Secd Secretary

Adam de Windt became a carpenter's apprentice at the height of Statia's trading power
in the West Indies. The demand for his skills would have been very high during this
time, both among wealthy residents and on ships arriving in Oranje Bay in need of
repairs. His mother recognized that his increased earning potential would be a positive
asset to both his and her future. It is interesting to note that she took her son to be
apprenticed to a Free Negro carpenter and joiner as opposed to one of European
heritage. Also, it should be noted that it was no small economic risk for Henry Bastian
to enter into this contract with Fanny de Windt. He would be responsible for clothing
and feeding Adam for seven years! He must have been a reasonably successful skilled
workman to take on such a responsibility. It is evident then that people of African
heritage were able to not only obtain their freedom but also to establish successful
business ventures within the context of St Eustatius society. The next section provides
further evidence for the successes of people of color in this regard.

Government regulations

The most important source for government regulations and decrees on Statia is the
West Indisch Plakaatboek compiled by Jacob Schiltkamp and Jacobus Smidt (1973). The
authors have transcribed all of the laws passed by the governing council on the island
from 1648 to 1816. Laws passed between 1816 and 1844 are found in *Publicatien voor
het eiland St. Eustatius* (Departement van Kolonien 1857). As Statia changed hands
between the Dutch, English, and French many times during the seventeenth and early
nineteenth centuries, the laws are written in the language of the occupying nation at
the time the law was put into force. Many regulations in these volumes specifically
address issues relating to slavery. In referring to laws transcribed in Schiltkamp and
Smidt (1973) I use the number that they assigned to each particular regulation. For
example, "SE #34" refers to St Eustatius law number 34.

Laws governing slave commercial activities
It is evident from the regulations and acts passed on St Eustatius that slaves were ardent
participants in the vital commercial activities of the island. Slaves and free blacks sold
sugar in Statia's frequent auctions according to one decree passed under French rule in
1782 (Schiltkamp and Smidt 1973, SE #49). Unlike the Dutch, the French did not
permit a free trade in all commodities, especially sugar. The tenets of mercantilism
forbade this practice, and it was—for a time—prohibited on Statia.

The frenzied and unregulated trading atmosphere that existed on St Eustatius during
the 1785–1795 economic boom is reflected in several laws passed to limit this activity.
Apparently, anything not tied down was subject to sale by slaves, whites, and free
blacks alike. A regulation passed in 1790 (Schiltkamp and Smidt 1973, SE #78)

forbade the sale of "cattle and poultry" by slaves without written permission of the owner of the said items or of the slave's owner. Slaves also had to provide to their owners a list of the quantity and quality of goods that they wished to sell in town. A similar regulation was passed in 1811 (Schiltkamp and Smidt 1973, SE #187) with special reference to the sale of "small stock and poultry."

Some additional examples include a decree issued in 1769; slaves were required to carry a lit torch with them at night in addition to a pass from their owner or face being locked up for the night. Slaves were also required to have a pass from their owner specifying what they might sell in the markets (Mathews 1793). This was to prevent slaves from stealing from their owners and selling the items on to others. Slaves, free blacks, and whites were all said to be guilty of selling stolen sugar according to a law passed in 1793 (Schiltkamp and Smidt 1973, SE #90). Apparently, slaves were clandestinely topping sugar cane crops at night and making their way into town to sell this illicitly acquired product. The damage to plantation output was so great that the plantation owners were "not able to provide the amount that they had planned for." Slaves were not the only guilty parties here, as there was obviously a market for stolen sugarcane. The law stipulated punishments for both sellers and purchasers of the cane. Sugar and molasses were added to commonly stolen items by 1811.

Woodwork and ironwork, furniture, gold and silver, and other household effects were all also said to have been illegally sold by slaves. With the arrival of the French in 1795, a precipitous economic decline began on St Eustatius (Schiltkamp and Smidt 1973, SE #109). Trade was regulated to the strangulation point. Consequently, homes and warehouses were being abandoned across the island. People took advantage of this situation by pilfering what they could from these structures and offering them for sale in town. Slaves were apparently active participants in this trade. Another proclamation from 1811 shows that slaves who were merchants were apparently purchasing stolen property from both other slaves and free people (Schiltkamp and Smidt 1973). By 1812, uninhabited houses were being illicitly torn apart to sell the wood in the island's market (Schiltkamp and Smidt 1973, SE #193). Also in 1812, cattle were being stolen by "runaway slaves" according to a proclamation (Schiltkamp and Smidt 1973, SE #195).

As Statia settled into economic despair, slaves took to selling rum and other alcoholic beverages to soldiers stationed on the island. A regulation passed in 1810 forbade this activity (Schiltkamp and Smidt 1973, SE #179). By 1811, yams were being illegally sold in the public market by slaves, either from fields, or from those allotted to them in their weekly allowance (Schiltkamp and Smidt 1973, SE #189). Some people purchased large quantities in order to raise their price or to sell them abroad. This was deemed to be both harmful to the poor and detrimental to slave owners. At the time this proclamation was implemented, the island was in the possession of the British during the Napoleonic Wars. In 1811, Britain and the USA were about to go to war as well. In this proclamation there was also concern expressed that supplies from the USA that typically came to the island would cease and that the Statian people ought to be more conservative with their resources.

These proclamations reflect the economic and social trials that engulfed the island and the slaves that lived there. The strife they were suffering at this point was just a precursor to the wholesale economic collapse that would overcome the island within the decade. Prior to this, slaves and free blacks were integral elements in trading activities on St Eustatius. The trade on St Eustatius was probably similar to those found in other much larger urban centers such as Charleston, South Carolina (Morgan 1998: 250–252). However, conditions were likely easier for enslaved merchants on Statia. Under such conditions many slaves were able to earn money to purchase their freedom in less time than it took in other colonies. It is also evident that few freed slaves left the island to seek their fortune elsewhere during Statia's economic boom. The social and economic advantages to continue living on Statia were clearly evident to them.

Laws regulating slave housing

Two regulations passed on St Eustatius make reference to the slave housing on the island. The first of these was passed in 1803 and forbade the leasing of slave housing (Schiltkamp and Smidt 1973, SE #138). Some property owners may have had a surplus of housing and wanted to make some extra income. Manumitted slaves at the bottom of the economic spectrum would not have been able to afford more permanent accommodation, and were the likely tenants. Indeed, auction records for Statia indicate relatively high prices for housing in town in comparison to those found in other Caribbean colonies (Vendumeester 1794). Therefore, archaeological evidence for particular structures on Statian properties should be interpreted in the light that some "slave houses" were not occupied by slaves at all.

The second regulation found in legal records, enacted in 1806, indicates that some slave houses were thatched with straw and built entirely of straw (Schiltkamp and Smidt 1973, SE #167). The law addresses the issue that these dwellings were a fire hazard within the city. The existing homes were required to be pulled down and rebuilt outside the town. There are three significant points to be made that have a bearing on the archaeological record with regard to this edict. First, it will be difficult to locate homes principally built of straw. Second, not all homes were built from these impermanent materials and therefore should be archaeologically detectable via either stone foundations or the remains of more substantive wooden supports. Third, as I have stated previously (Gilmore 2002), slave dwellings were concentrated around the perimeter of Oranjestad.

Laws governing slave behavior

Laws that attempted to regulate the lives of slaves provide some of the most interesting insights into the dynamics of slave life on St Eustatius. In many colonies, slaves were perceived as always being up to no good if out at night without permission. St Eustatius was no exception. Interestingly, British implemented the first curfew on the island in March 1781 (Schiltkamp and Smidt 1973, SE #36.38). However, this eight o'clock curfew applied to both slaves and white inhabitants. A 1784 proclamation, passed when the island was in Dutch hands, moved the curfew for both races back to nine o'clock (Schiltkamp and Smidt 1973, SE #57).

Another apparent frequent leisure-time activity of Statian slaves was using fireworks and other noisemakers including drums (Schiltkamp and Smidt 1973, SE #50).

The first law dealing with this perceived problem was instituted in March 1782 when Statia was under French control. "Negro children" were especially singled out as being troublesome in this regard and were answerable to their parents. A further illustration of alleged delinquent behavior is indicated in a proclamation implemented in 1806 (Schiltkamp and Smidt 1973, SE #171). Apparently some slaves were "casting stones against houses"—to what purpose is not indicated.

Several proclamations were enacted to regulate slaves' use of knives, swords, and firearms. The first regulation of these weapons was enacted under French occupation in October 1783 (Schiltkamp and Smidt 1973, SE #55). Slaves were prohibited from being out in public with these items. Later, in December 1802, this regulation was amended and supplemented with additional details (Schiltkamp and Smidt 1973, SE #134). No slave was to possess or use shotguns on the island—even if it was under the "pretext of watching plantations or other properties." Although the specific "bad consequences" are not stated, the proclamation does state that the armed slaves were a threat to the "peace and security of the island." A further proclamation in 1810 may indicate the nature of the problem of armed slaves on Statia (Schiltkamp and Smidt 1973, SE #183). The government noted that previous proclamations were "issued for the purpose of preventing accidents and injuries." Further to this, an age limit for firearms use was set at 20 years old and people were not to "discharge firearms in and about town." The proclamation alludes to "serious accidents that have happened as of late." Also, people were not to pursue game across another's property without permission. Horse riding was a particularly fond pastime on Statia. A 1783 proclamation forbade slaves from riding horses and especially galloping wildly through town or even at a walk in the countryside (Schiltkamp and Smidt 1973, SE #55). In 1785, slaves were prohibited from riding horses unless they were holding the reins for someone else (Schiltkamp and Smidt 1973, SE #66). Slaves apparently paid no heed to these stipulations as they continued to ride on horseback "in the streets in improper ways with a danger for accidents" in 1802 (Schiltkamp and Smidt 1973, SE #124). This proclamation was specifically addressed to "negro and mulatto children."

In some slaveholding areas in the Americas (Charleston is one famous example), it was customary to have slaves going about an independent occupation identified by wearing "slave tags" (Packard 1999). Freed slaves were also generally required to carry their manumission papers with them at all times. Statia presents an interesting and significant variation on such practices. On St Eustatius, in 1785, it was the *free* Africans who had to wear an outward sign of their freedom in the form of a red ribbon on their breast (Schiltkamp and Smidt 1973, SE #66). Tellingly, the proclamation also forbade slaves from wearing red ribbons on their day off. This legislation was instigated due to the "insults and licentiousness given by negroes and coloureds" towards whites. Statia is described as "a land of evil"; probably due to the ruthless trading atmosphere that was more akin to a pirates din such as Port Royal, Jamaica than a refined market town such as Yorktown, Virginia. Two points regarding the slaves' perceptions of their freedom can be deduced from this law. First, some slaves clearly felt they had the leeway to be able to address Europeans in a less than respectful manner. In other slave-holding societies, this sort of behavior was not tolerated and could even result in death. Second, some slaves felt that on their days off, they were truly "free" and could act and behave as free men could—including wearing a red ribbon to signify this freedom. This, in combination with the other points, indicates a social situation where both whites and slaves tolerated certain uncommon behaviors. A unique inter-racial dynamic on Statia was a result.

A further illustration of this freer society on Statia is given in regulations implemented in 1797 under French occupation (Schiltkamp and Smidt 1973, SE #104). Slaves were apparently gambling and gaming with dice and cards to the detriment of their work. Not only that, but free people and whites were also encouraging them to do this and providing them places to gamble in their houses and yards, both in town and in the countryside. This regulation was an attempt to prohibit this practice. Unlike other regulations, the punishment is not specified which may indicate a half-hearted attempt at enforcement.

Laws governing slave labor on public works
Statian slaves, as in other colonies, were required from time to time to provide labor on public property and military sites. In fact in 1721, the first regulation passed on Statia regarding slaves required them to help repair the fort on the island—presumably Fort Oranje (Schiltkamp and Smidt 1973, SE #19). Additional proclamations requiring slaves to work on military sites were passed in 1781 and 1795. The island's topography also required a carefully designed drainage system to prevent soil erosion. Stone walls built between and within plantations, along public roads, and the cliff-side drain system in Oranjestad, all needed periodic maintenance. Slaves provided the labor for these activities as is evident in proclamations enacted in 1781 (Schiltkamp and Smidt 1973, SE #36.8 and 36.11) and 1786 (Schiltkamp and Smidt 1973). Slaves were also used to maintain government land and church properties (Schiltkamp and Smidt 1973, SE #182) and were appointed as executioners on the island (Schiltkamp and Smidt 1973). A decree passed in 1814 stipulated that the slave Andries, owned by a doctor William de Niefeld, be the new island executioner. It may have been that Dr De Niefeld was the person appointed to see to it that the person executed was dead. An interesting aspect in this law recognizes the stigma attached to the job of executioner as it expressly forbids others "[whites as well as coloureds] from making use of any improper or injurious language to the said negroman Andries."

Laws governing the slave trade, manumission, and treatment of slaves
The trade in slaves on the island was an integral part of the economy through much of the eighteenth century and there were laws passed to regulate it. In order to maximize profits for the Dutch West Indies Company, before the era of free trade on the island, a ban was placed on the buying and selling of slaves from foreign nations in 1755 (Schiltkamp and Smidt 1973, SE #26). The 1755 proclamation was again reiterated in 1802 (Schiltkamp and Smidt 1973, SE #129). Foreign "negroes" were again being imported to the consternation of the governing council. The French were specifically cited, probably for two reasons. First, Statia was under English rule at the time and thus recently at war with the French. Second, the situation for the British Army at Santo Domingue was dire—the former slave, Toussaint le'Oveture, had established Haiti at that point. It was cause for concern that such "revolutionary" activities might spread to St Eustatius.

As the trading atmosphere on Statia became more and more intense toward the end of the eighteenth century, additional regulations were implemented to govern the leasing of slaves. One regulation in 1783 stipulated that only the owners of slaves could hire them out to others (Schiltkamp and Smidt 1973, SE #55). This indicates that some lessees were sub-leasing slaves to others without the slave owners' permission—presumably to the profit of the sublessor. One can imagine that the regulation was passed after the governing Council heard endless arguments between lessees and lessors over such practices. The leasing of slaves was banned outright in 1812 (Schiltkamp and Smidt 1973, SE #194).

In 1790, an ordinance enacted on the island required a census of all residents, both slave and free (Schiltkamp and Smidt 1973, SE #81). The objective, at least in part, was to identify maroons or runaway slaves from other islands that were living on St Eustatius. Residents were supposed to swear under oath the accuracy of their returns or be fined. Any unregistered slaves found later to be owned by them would be confiscated. This implies two things regarding the ownership of slaves on Statia. First, slave owners wanted to conceal how many slaves they owned—presumably to evade taxes. Second, St Eustatius seems to have served as a haven for escaped slaves from other islands.

As the Statian economy declined, it seems that many slave owners began to neglect their slaves, sometimes freeing them without any financial support to avoid the extra expense of their upkeep. A proclamation enacted in 1806 established that slave owners were required to make a guarantee that they would support their freed slaves if they were not able to provide for themselves (Schiltkamp and Smidt 1973, SE #168). Otherwise, the slave owners would not be permitted to manumit slaves. Another act passed later that year prohibited the abuse or maltreatment of slaves by people other than the slaves' owner (Schiltkamp and Smidt 1973, SE #169). In 1814, an act implemented during British occupation, protested the mistreatment of slaves by planters and other proprietors (Schiltkamp and Smidt 1973, SE #197). It required all slave owners not to exceed the punishments proscribed in police regulations. In a similar vein, a few proclamations relate to the treatment of sick or maimed slaves. For example, in 1798, a proclamation was instituted that required owners to take care of their crippled, leprous, and otherwise infected slaves or face their confiscation (Schiltkamp and Smidt 1973, SE #110). They would then be charged for the further upkeep of these slaves by the government. Prior to this, such individuals were frequently seen wandering the streets and begging or stealing items to support themselves. Again, in 1801, an act was passed that required slave owners to keep infected slaves from public areas in order to prevent the spread of such diseases as leprosy (Schiltkamp and Smidt 1973, SE #118).

Newspaper accounts

Newspapers advertised the sale of slaves and notices of runaways. Both can be found in the few editions of the *St. Eustatius Gazette* that are still in existence (Hartog 1948). Edward Luther Low published the *Gazette* between 1790 and 1794. He initially had a printing office on St Kitts where he printed the *St. Christopher Gazette* before moving to Statia. The runaway slave advertisements are interesting, as they are not worded in

Figure 8.1   Advertisement for the runaway slave "Nonche."

the typical manner. One such advertisement was printed in the *Gazette* dated July 3, 1793 (Figure 8.1).

In regard to his slave "Nonche" that had apparently run away, Thomas Wintfield the subscriber says, "if she will return of her own accord she will be forgiven." This is different from what most runaway advertisements say. Although similar runaway slave advertisements have been noted for South Carolina, they are exceedingly rare (Mullin 1992). This implies two things. One, that the owner and slave had a personal relationship, and two, that the slave may have been literate or at least in communication with someone (most likely another person of African descent) who could read the advertisement. The advertisements imply that at least some St Eustatius slaves were perceived and treated differently by their owners than those in North American colonies or the rest of the Caribbean.

The Pleasures Estate Plantation in documents

The Pleasures Estate Plantation is one of the primary archaeological sites that I have investigated over the past few years. I present its document trail as an example of the breadth of written evidence available for an average Statian plantation (Figure 8.2).

The first mention of the Pleasures Estate Plantation is on a map drawn and engraved by Reiner Ottens in 1742 (Ottens 1742). On this map, Joan Z. Donker owns the Plantation. By this date plantations already covered the island. When a revised Ottens map was published in 1775, the plantation was co-owned by Judith Z. Donker and Robert Stuart [Stewart] (Ottens 1775). In 1781, when P. F. Martin drew up his survey of Statian landowners for the English occupiers, Martin Du Boise Godet, Jr owned Pleasures. He likely acquired the property through marriage to Elizabeth Z. Doncker (daughter of Judith). Sometime after he died, Elizabeth married Abraham Ahman, becoming Elizabeth Z. Ahman in the documentary records. Around 1820, the plantation is depicted on a map drawn by Lt. W. Blanken (Blanken 1820 ca.), with Elizabeth Ahman still as owner. In the same year, Elizabeth drew up her last will and testament directing that her estate go to the merchant John Martins upon her death. Between 1821 and 1826, Elizabeth had to mortgage the Pleasures Estate in order to raise funds to live on. Conditions for her grew so dire that John Martins had to cover

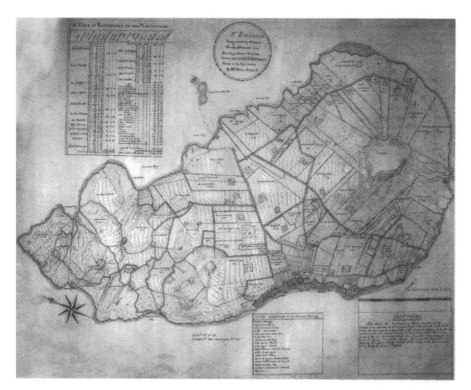

Figure 8.2 1781 Survey plan with the Pleasures Estate Plantation, St Eustatius, by P. F. Martin

some of the mortgage payments. She died in 1826 and Pleasures passed on to John Martins. When Teenstra visited Statia in 1829, the estate was still owned by John Martins but had become derelict and was serving as a sheep fold (Teenstra 1836). Pleasures then shows up on a map drawn by Bischop Grevelink in 1839 as a cattle farm (Grevelink 1839–1846). No documentary evidence regarding the plantation's owners has been located for the years between 1829 and 1876. Landowners between 1876 and the present can easily be traced through documents in the Cadastral Office on St Eustatius.

I will now provide an example of one of the inventories that I was able to locate for the Pleasures Estate Plantation (Groebe 1826). My translation of it follows:

> On this day in 1826
>
> Inventory of all such goods, so done as if through the will of the Mrs. Elizabeth Z. Doncker, who was the First Widow of the Gentleman Martin du Boise Godet Senior and last widow of the Gentleman Aaron Ahman, who on the fourteenth of August, here died.
>
> Done by the Good Noble Testator Mr John Martins, and these are valid as *Executor Testatmenter* and this, the deceased's estate of Mrs. Elizabeth Z. Ahman, follows:
>
> Permanent Goods
> The Estate called Pleasure, with the buildings standing upon it and in addition situated in this Island, between the Land of the Gentleman Richard Hassel, and that belonging to the heirs in the same and deceased's estate, of the Gentleman Johannes the Graaff,
>
> A House and Land situated here by the foot of the Old Land.,
>
> Some Land with stone walls standing on it.
>
> Some Land with a warehouse standing on it, including a strong room last mentioned. Land and that according to the property Commissioner. Land named in this and the deceased's estate in the will of the Gentleman Johannes the Graaff.
>
> Some Land standing in between the previously mentioned Land and that belonging to the same and deceased's estate, of the Gentleman John Williams.
>
> Silverware
> A silver bowl
>
> Furniture
> A clothing chest
> A watertable with a marble Top
> Five different mahogany tables
> Two card tables
> A mahogany, wooden bedstead

A Bed
A Sofa (broken)
Five old mirrors

Porcelain and Glassware
A porcelain display bowl
One porcelain bowl and dishes
One piece of glassware

Slaves
A negress called Jinny
A negress called Sophina
A young Negro called Sampson
A young Negro called Caesar
A young Negro called John
A young Negro called Jim
A negress called Sally

Animals
A cow, and
A calf

A storage room

On this day, the eighteenth of August the year, one-thousand-eight-hundred-six and twenty.

Appeared before me, Theophilus George Groebe, Secretary, in service of his Majesty the King Of the Netherlands residing on the Island St. Eustatius in the presence of the below named witnesses.

The humble Noble Master Gentleman John Martins residing here.

A valid declaration, as if *Epacutut Testamentair* in this, the will of the deceased's estate of Lady Elizabeth Z. Ahman, in the handing over of this Inventory, itself a true and candid accounting, this account is binding for these reasons at all times with solemnity. This oath shall be established. Thus inventoried at St. Eustatius *datum zit supra* in the presence of the Gentlemen David Viera and Alexander Beagins as witnesses.

David Viera
A. Beagins

Jno Martins,
Quod Attestor

T. G. Groebe,
Secretary

The range of possessions that is listed for Mrs Ahman does not imply prosperous circumstances either. This when combined with the account provided by Teenstra (1836) of Pleasures' formal glory provides even more evidence that the plantation was well on its way out by the 1820s.

Elizabeth Zimmons Doncker Ahman was a member of one of the most influential families in St Eustatius history. Several family members were governors of the island at one point or other and many were wealthy landowners and merchants. Elizabeth had outlasted two husbands, Martin Du Boise Godet, J and Aaron Ahman. Her last husband was likely Jewish and her marriage to him illustrates that on St Eustatius nothing, not even religion, came between making economically sound marriage contracts. She represents a class of women that is common in the St Eustatius documentary record. Unusually, women seem to have outlived one or more husbands in many cases. They then became wealthy landowners and the proprietors of successful merchant houses. Although they were not permitted to be Burghers, they were undoubtedly powerful members of Statia's ruling elite.

Conclusions

Documentary evidence for St Eustatius can be viewed in light of the three themes I set forth at the beginning of this chapter. I have shown that the economy on Statia was unique. It was based on unabated commerce. I have examined how slaves on St Eustatius were an integral part of the free trade environment on the island. Within such an economic context the freedom to conduct business was greater than in other colonies. In addition, the drive and opportunity to obtain and save money to purchase their freedom was high. The degree to which slaves participated in the international commercial trade on the island was unparalleled.

Also, within this economic context, the physical and cognitive landscapes or environment in which slaves lived and worked was different to that found within other colonies. Statian slaves were not tied to the land to the degree to which they were within the agrarian economies commonly found in much of the slave-holding colonial world. In fact, restricting physical freedom would have reduced the profits of owners who used them in commerce. Thus, they were able to wander about the island conducting business and even undertake expeditions off the island on behalf of their owners with relative ease.

Although the Euro-ethnic milieu that engulfed Statia was a veritable cornucopia, it was the fact that the island was Dutch for most of its history and that they permitted such an economic environment to exist in the first place. *Free-trade* was a core tenet of Dutch colonial policy. Thus, traders, Dutch and non-Dutch, slave and free, were able to thrive economically on the island.

According to documentary and cartographic evidence fewer than 1,000 slaves lived on Statia's plantations. However, in 1789, near Statia's economic peak, there were 4,944 enslaved Africans living on the island (Goslinga 1985:152). There were less than 90 plantations on the island at this time with most having fewer than 10 slaves. The largest landowner, the former Governor Johannes de Graff, owned 90 slaves distributed across nine different plantations consisting of 253 hectares (Barka 1996). It is thus clear that the vast majority of slaves were employed in the commercial trade on the island and living in Oranjestad itself (Klooster 1998). The documentary evidence related to slavery on St Eustatius that I have examined here provides many interesting insights into the unique nature of slave life on this Caribbean island. These sources are manifestly helpful in interpreting excavated slave material culture on St Eustatius.

References

Barka, N. F. (1996) "Citizens of St. Eustatius, 1781: a historical and archaeological study," in R. P. a. S. Engerman (ed.) *The Lesser Antilles in the Age of European Expansion*, 223–238, Gainesville, FL: University Press of Florida.

Bijlsma, R., and Lee, T. v. d. (1924) "Inventaris van het oud archief St. Eustatius, St. Martin, en Saba," in *Verslagen omtrent's Rijks oude archieven*, vol. 45. Gravenhage: Algemeen Rijksarchief Eerste Afdeling.

Blanken, L. W. (ca.1820) *Kaart van het Eiland St. Eustatius*, Leiden: Leiden University.

Chabert, C., and P. Ouckama (1782) "Monsterrol Gehounden aan boord van de Schooner Gennant De Cathron gemonteerd met," in *Algemeen Rijksarchief: St. Eustatius, St. Maarten en Saba, Oude Archieven tot 1828, 1709–1851, Call Number: 1 05.13.01:123–1782*, pp. 308, Oranjestad, St Fustatius.

Craton, M., and Walvin, J. (1970) *A Jamaican Plantation: The History of Worthy Park, 1670–1970*, London: W. H. Allen.

Departement van Kolonien, K. o. t. N. (1857) *Publicatien voor het eiland St. Eustatius, 1809–1844*, Gravenhage: Departement van Kolonien.

Du Sart, G. (1788) "Inventaris Gedaan Maaken (for Heer John Bailen)," in *Algemeen Rijksarchief: St. Eustatius, St. Maarten en Saba, Oude Archieven tot 1828, 1709–1851. Call Number: 1.05.13.01: 129–1788*, pp. 527–529, Oranjestad, St Eustatius.

Du Sart, G. (1790a) "Inventaris Gedaan Maaken (for Heer Jan L. Swartz)," in *Algemeen Rijksarchief: St. Eustatius, St. Maarten en Saba, Oude Archieven tot 1828, 1709–1851. Call Number: 1.05.13.01: 131–1790*, pp. 252–255, Oranjestad, St Eustatius.

Du Sart, G. (1790b) "Last Will and Testament (for Abraham Heyliger)," in *Algemeen Rijksarchief: St. Eustatius, St. Maarten en Saba, Oude Archieven tot 1828, 1709–1851, Call Number: 1.05.13.01: 133–1792*, pp. 358–360, Oranjestad, St Eustatius.

Du Sart, G. (1791a) "Deposition (for Benjamin Fox)," in *Algemeen Rijksarchief: St. Eustatius, St. Maarten en Saba, Oude Archieven tot 1828, 1709–1851, Call Number: 1.05.13.01: 132–1791*, pp. 325–326, Oranjestad, St Eustatius.

Du Sart, G. (1791b) "Inventaris en Prisatie gedan maken van het navolgende bevonden op een behoorente tot de Plantagei de Goudsteen geleegen in het Quartier genaamd Concordia op dit Eiland St. Eustatius toebehoooorende aan den Heer William Moore Burger," in *Algemeen Rijksarchief: St. Eustatius, St. Maarten en Saba, Oude Archieven tot 1828, 1709–1851, Call Number: 1.05.13.01: 132–1791*, pp. 400–410, Oranjestad, St Eustatius.

Du Sart, G. (1791c) "Inventaris Gedaan maaken Vaste Goederen en Toebehooren (for Jacobus Seys, Senior)," in *Algemeen Rijksarchief: St. Eustatius, St. Maarten en Saba, Oude Archieven tot 1828, 1709–1851, Call Number: 1.05.13.01: 132–1791*, pp. 490–501, Oranjestad, St Eustatius.

Du Sart, G. (1791d) "Inventaris Gedaan maaken Vaste Goederen en Toebehooren (Heer Hendrick Schroder and free mulatto Sarah Dixon)," in *Algemeen Rijksarchief: St. Eustatius, St. Maarten en Saba, Oude Archieven tot 1828, 1709–1851, Call Number: 1.05.13.01: 132–1791*, pp. 533–535, Oranjestad, St Eustatius.

Du Sart, G. (1791e) "Prisatie Gedaan maaken Heer Richard Owen, Coopman (Cooper)," in *Algemeen Rijksarchief: St. Eustatius, St. Maarten en Saba, Oude Archieven tot 1828, 1709–1851, Call Number: 1.05.13.01: 132–1791*, pp. 418–420, Oranjestad, St Eustatius.

Du Sart, G. (1791f) "Prisatie Gedaan maaken Vaste Goederen en Toebehooren (for Jacobus Seys, Senior)," in *Algemeen Rijksarchief: St. Eustatius, St. Maarten en Saba, Oude Archieven tot 1828, 1709–1851, Call Number: 1.05.13.01: 132–1791*, pp. 627–642, Oranjestad, St Eustatius.

Du Sart, G. (1792a) "Indenture of Adam de Windt to Henry Bastiaans (carpenter and joiner)," in *Algemeen Rijksarchief: St. Eustatius, St. Maarten en Saba, Oude Archieven tot 1828, 1709–1851, Call Number: 1.05.13.01: 133–1792*, pp. 257–258, Oranjestad, St Eustatius.

Du Sart, G. (1792b) "Inventaris van het Navolgende, aankoomen de den Boedel (John Marlton)," in *Algemeen Rijksarchief: St. Eustatius, St. Maarten en Saba, Oude Archieven tot 1828, 1709–1851, Call Number: 1.05.13.01: 133–1792*, pp. 686–697, Oranjestad, St Eustatius.

Du Veer, A. (1818) "Deed (for Glassbottle Fort Plantation)," in *Algemeen Rijksarchief: St. Eustatius, St. Maarten en Saba, Oude Archieven tot 1828, 1709–1851, Call Number: 1.05.13.01: 151–1818*, pp. 153, Oranjestad, St Eustatius.

Equiano, O. [1789] (1999) "The Interesting Narrative of the Life of Olaudah Equiano, or Gustavaus Vassa, The African," in Y. Taylor (ed.) *I Was Born a Slave: An Anthology of Classic Slave Narratives*, 29–180, Chicago, IL: Lawrence Hill Books.

Gilmore, R. G. (2002) "Urban transformation and upheaval in the West Indies: the case of Oranjestad, St. Eustatius, Netherlands Antilles," paper presented to the *Society for Post-Medieval Archaeology*, Southampton University, Southampton.

Goslinga, C. C. (1985) *The Dutch in the Caribbean and the Guianas 1680–1791*, Assen/Maastricht: Uitg. in samenwerking met het Prins Bernhardfonds Nederlandse Antillen door Van Gorcum.

Grevelink, A. H. B. (ca.1839–1846) *Topographische kaart van het Eiland St. Eustatius*, Amsterdam.

Grvelink, A. H. B. (1876) *Kaart van het Eiland St. Eustathius*, Amsterdam: Uitgegeven bij C. F. Stemler.

Groebe, T. G. (1826) "Inventaris van alle zodanige Goederen, zo neerende als onszeerende door wylen vrouwe Elizabeth Z. Doncker," in *Algemeen Rijksarchief: St. Eustatius, St. Maarten en Saba, Oude Archieven tot 1828, 1709–1851, Call Number: 1.05.13.01: 163–1826*, un-numbered, Oranjestad, St Eustatius.

Hamelberg, J. H. J. (1889) *Aantekenigen Hamelberg*, The Hague: Alegemeen Rijksarchief (ARA).

Hartog, J. (1948) "Oud nunvu van de 'St. Eustatius Gazette'," *West-Indische Gids I*, 29: 161–174.

Hartog, J. (1976) *History of St. Eustatius*, Aruba: Central U.S.A. Bicentennial Committee of the Netherlands Antilles: distributors De Witt Stores N.V.

Heyliger, A., Doncker, J. S., and Runnels, J. (1786) "Prisatie gedaan maaken ten behoeve van Heer Abraham Heyliger, Governeur," in *Algemeen Rijksarchief: St. Eustatius, St. Maarten en Saba, Oude Archieven tot 1828, 1709–1851, Call Number: 1.05.13.01: 127–1786*, pp. 110–125, Oranjestad, St Eustatius.

Hurst, R. (1996) *The Golden Rock: An Episode of the American War of Independence, 1775–1783*, Annapolis, MD: Naval Institute Press.

Jameson, J. F. (1903) "St. Eustatius in the American Revolution," *American Historical Review*, 8: 683–708.

Klooster, W. (1998) *Illicit Riches: Dutch Trade in the Caribbean, 1648–1795*, Leiden: KITLV Press.

Le Fer, P. (1788) "Inventaris gedan maken van het navolgende aan koomende, en besonden in de Boedel van Wylen de Heer Daniel Moniero," in *Algemeen Rijksarchief: St. Eustatius, St. Maarten en Saba, Oude Archieven tot 1828, 1709–1851, Call Number: 1.05.13.01: 129–1788*, pp. 3–5, Oranjestad, St Eustatius.

Mathews, S. A. (1793) *The Lying Hero; or, An answer to J. B. Moreton's Manners and Customs in the West Indies*, St Eustatius: E. L. Low, for the author.

Meilink Roelofsz, M. A. P. (1954–1955) "A survey of archives in the Netherlands pertaining to the history of the Netherlands Antilles," *West-Indische Gids I*, 35:1–37.

Mintz, S. (1985) *Sweetness and Power: The Place of Sugar in Modern History*, New York: Viking.

Morgan, P. D. (1998) *Slave Counterpoint: Black Culture in the Eighteenth-century Chesapeake and Lowcountry*, Chapel Hill, NC: The University of North Carolina Press for the Omohundro Institute of Early American History and Culture.

Mullin, M. (1992) *Africa in America: Slave Acculturation and Resistence in the American South and the British Caribbean, 1736–1831. Blacks in the New World*, Chicago, IL: University of Illinois Press.

Nationaal Archiefs [Dutch National Archives] .(1797) "Inventaris van Zodanige goederen (for May Harvis)," in *Algemeen Rijksarchief: St. Eustatius, St. Maarten en Saba, Oude Archieven tot 1828, 1709–1851, Call Number: 1.05.13.01: 147–1797*, pp. 358–360, Oranjestad, St Eustatius.

Ottens, R. (1742) *Plaan van St. Eustatius*, Den Haag: Algemeen Rijksarchief, Call number: 4 MIKO 5.5.1 339.

Otters, R. (1775) *Nieuve kaart van het eyland St. Eustatius in derzelver ligging & plantagien met de naamen der bezitteren, op order van de generaale geoctroojeeroe West-Indische Compagnie gemeeten en getekeno*, Amsterdam: Konst. Kaart en Boekverkoper.

Ouckama, P. (1782a) "Contra Inventaris gedan maken ten behoeve van de boedel van Wylen Thomas Loe," in *Algemeen Rijksarchief: St. Eustatius, St. Maarten en Saba, Oude Archieven tot 1828, 1709–1851, Call Number: 1.05.13.01: 123–1782*, pp. 101–102, Oranjestad, St Eustatius.

Ouckama, P. (1782b) "Contra Inventaris gedan maken ten behoeve van de Steen Martin Dubrois Godet Senior," in *Algemeen Rijksarchief: St. Eustatius, St. Maarten en Saba, Oude Archieven tot 1828, 1709–1851, Call Number: 1.05.13.01: 123–1782*, pp. 53–54, Oranjestad, St Eustatius.

Ouckama, P. (1782c) "Last Will and Testament of Cloe, Free Negro Wench," in *Algemeen Rijksarchief: St. Eustatius, St. Maarten en Saba, Oude Archieven tot 1828, 1709–1851, Call Number: 1.05.13.01: 123–1782*, p. 373, Oranjestad, St Eustatius.

Ouckama, P. (1782d) "Monsterrol Gehounden aan boord va de Schooner Gennant Adventure gemonteerd met", in *Algemeen Rijksarchief: St. Eustatius, St. Maarten en Saba, Oude Archieven tot 1828, 1709–1851, Call Number: 1.05.13.01: 123–1782*, p. 98, Oranjestad, St Eustatius.

Ouckama, P. (1782e) "Prisatie gedaan maaken ten behoeve van Mejussrous Rachael Salomons Wedurve Thomas Loe," in *Algemeen Rijksarchief: St. Eustatius, St. Maarten en Saba, Oude Archieven tot 1828, 1709–1851, Call Number: 1.05.13.01: 123–1782*, pp. 280–281, Oranjestad, St Eustatius.

Ouckama, P. (1784) "Last will and Testament of Free Black Joseph Howe," in *Algemeen Rijksarchief: St. Eustatius, St. Maarten en Saba, Oude Archieven tot 1828, 1709–1851, Call Number: 1.05.13.01: 125–1784*, p. 811, Oranjestad, St Eustatius.

Packard, C. (1999) Slave Tags, *North South Trader's Civil War* 27: 38–45.

Schiltkamp, J. A., and Smidt, J. T. D. (1973) *West Indisch plakaatboek. Werken der Vereeninging tot Uitgaaf der Bronnen van het Oud-Vaderlandsche Recht; 3. reeks, nr. 24/1*, Amsterdam: Emering.

Secretariële. n. d. "Protocollen van secretariële akten," in *Archief van Sint Eustatius tot 1828*, The Hague.

Singleton, T. A. (ed.) (1985) *The Archaeology of Slavery and Plantation Life*, New York: Academic Press.

Singleton, T. A. (ed.) (1999) *"I, too, am America": Archaeological Studies of African-American Life*, Charlottesville, VA: University Press of Virginia.

Teenstra, M. D. (1836) *De Nederlandsche West-Indische eilanden in derzelver tegenwoordigen toestand*, Amsterdam: C. G. Sulpke.

Tuchman, B. W. (1988) *The First Salute*, New York: Knopf, distributed by Random House.

Vendumeester (1794) "Venduboeken," in *Algemeen Rijksarchief: St. Eustatius, St. Maarten en Saba, Oude Archieven tot 1828, 1709–1851, Call Number:1.05.13:01*, pp. 231–239, Oranjestad, St Eustatius.

9   Identity and the mirage of ethnicity
Mahommah Gardo Baquaqua's journey in the Americas

PAUL E. LOVEJOY

The "interesting narrative" of Mahommah Gardo Baquaqua is one of the longest and most detailed accounts of someone enslaved in Western Africa and transported to the Americas under slavery (Moore 1854). The account, first published in 1854 in Detroit, runs to 65 printed pages. A poem by James Whitfield, the black abolitionist poet from Buffalo was appended (Sherman 1972). "Prayer of the Oppressed" (Whitfield 1853) was almost certainly chosen because it captured Baquaqua's thoughts that "when the bright sun of liberty/shall shine o'er each despotic land, And all mankind from bondage free, adore the wonders of thy hand." Baquaqua's quest for "freedom," the first word that he says that he learned in English, takes us along a road of multiple identities in which ethnicity informs the discussion of Baquaqua's situation but nonetheless does not explain the increasing individualization of his identity and the corresponding alienation that this implies. Ethnicity turns out to be a series of hats that he is assigned to wear. As a mechanism of self-identification, ethnicity appears as a mirage that disguises the individual under the hats.

At the time of his book's publication, Baquaqua was perhaps thirty, still a young man with a range of experiences that were unusual for most people of any time (Figure 9.1). Indeed, it is almost unimaginable that a man of thirty who had experienced enslavement and forced migration to the Americas has left such a vivid autobiographical account. Baquaqua first went to Brazil, before seeking freedom in New York City, and then refuge in Haiti, where he remained for two years (Figure 9.2). He converted to Christianity in 1848. For three years (1850–1853) he attended Central College at McGrawville, New York, whereafter he moved to Chatham, Ontario, then known as Canada West, and made arrangements to publish his story in Detroit in 1854. We last hear of him in Britain in 1857, awaiting the results of the efforts of his missionary friends to raise funds to send him back to Africa.

His surviving correspondence, as well as his biography, reflects his overriding aim to return to his "native land."[1] In 1857 he approached his previous benefactors, the American Baptist Free Mission, for their assistance: "Mahommah, the African educated in this country [United States], now in England, expressing his desire to return and labor among his countrymen" (*Free Mission Record* [New York], February 1857, 13). But, the decision to establish a mission was delayed a year, and apparently no such mission was ever sent. Baquaqua dropped out of sight after that.

Figure 9.1 Mahommah G. Baquaqua (1850)—frontispiece, A.T. Foss and Edward Mathews, *Facts for Baptist Churches* (Utica, 1850).

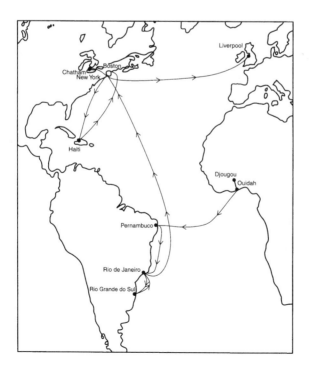

Figure 9.2 Published itinerary of Mohammah G. Baquaqua, ca. 1845–1857.

Baquaqua's account serves as an example of how biography can inform our understanding of the African Diaspora and how individuals fitted into the history of Trans-Atlantic slavery (Lovejoy 1997). In this chapter, I examine identity along the slave route from Africa to the Americas, using the personal profile of Baquaqua as a means of penetrating the often impenetrable silence of the enslaved. The details of biography allow the possibility of subjecting ethnic stereotypes, ascribed signs of identity, and the historicism of tradition and memory to the scrutiny of rigorous methodology. To what extent was ethnicity essentialist, existing independently of individuals and resisting the changes of circumstance and situation? What was the relationship between the individual and the collectivity under racialized slavery? Conducting such biographical research is difficult because data are widely dispersed, but in the case of Baquaqua there is considerable information available.

Many of the voices of enslavement from this era are those of males, and Baquaqua's account is no exception. In fact, there was a predominance of males among slaves, and especially so among enslaved Muslims (Eltis and Engerman 1993). Although Baquaqua is not included in Philip Curtin's collection of voices from the slavery era, his story conforms to the dominant theme of Curtin's collection (1967), which is entirely male and heavily Muslim. Similarly, Allan Austin's biographical material (1984) on enslaved Muslims in the Americas consists entirely of males. Michael Gomez (1998: 59–87) discusses examples of Muslim women in North America, but also notes that almost all of the enslaved Muslims were men. Sylviane Diouf (1998: 42–45, 53, 203) too has noted that most of the enslaved Africans who came from Muslim areas were males. These studies confirm my own conclusion that the overwhelming majority of enslaved Africans from Sudanic West Africa, including Borgu, were males, most of who went to Bahia in the early nineteenth century (Lovejoy 1994). Baquaqua's journey fitted this broader pattern, although he went to Pernambuco, not Bahia, and followed a route to the coast that was further west than that followed by most enslaved Muslims from the central Sudan (e.g. Lake Chad Basin) who ended up in Brazil. The more usual route was through Oyo to Porto Novo or Lagos (Law and Lovejoy 2001).

Baquaqua's life

Baquaqua was born in Djougou, apparently in the mid-1820s, into a Muslim family of local prominence. His date of birth is not known, but he was certainly born before 1830, possibly as early as 1824. As a child in Djougou, he attended Quranic school, probably starting when he was young. As a boy he was apprenticed to his uncle in needle-making, and otherwise seems to have been prepared for a life in commerce.

In the late 1820s and 1830s, when Baquaqua was growing up, Djougou was one of the most important towns between Asante and the Sokoto Caliphate, and his account attests to its role. During the long dry season, large caravans of 1,000 or more merchants and porters, and comparable numbers of donkeys, passed through Djougou, often staying for a short period (Lovejoy 1980, 1982; Brégand 1998). They carried kola nuts and gold from Asante, and European imports from the Gold Coast, eastward and returned with salt, natron, textiles, spices, leather products, livestock, slaves, and other goods. Baquaqua's family was heavily involved in this trade, his mother's brother owned a compound in Salaga, the most important market in northern Asante. His mother's family lived in Katsina and probably was involved in trade through Djougou to Salaga as well. His father was also well-placed commercially, apparently connected with the Wangara community in Nikki, and perhaps *shurfa*, that is North African, claiming descent from the Prophet, in origin (Lovejoy 1980: 58–59, 68–69, 70–71, 73). The details on trade, geography, and Islamic society are credible. Baquaqua's family is to be identified with the Muslim community of Djougou.

When he was a teenager, apparently in the early 1840s, he joined a group of porters carrying grain to the warfront near Daboya, in central Gonja to the west of Djougou. Baquaqua followed his older brother to Daboya, where the faction loyal to Kongwura Sa'id Nyantakyi in the prolonged succession dispute was based. His brother was serving as a diviner to the "king" at Daboya, perhaps a reference to Nyantakyi, who was contesting the paramountcy. Baquaqua and "many others" who had brought grain to the front were captured in what appears to have been an assault of the Asante army, confirmed by references to the importance of firearms in the engagement. Fortunately for Baquaqua, his brother was able to ransom him. Nyantakyi had become the *yagbum* on the death of Tuluwewura Kali in the early 1830s but an alliance of Gbuipe, Bole, and Wa forced him to retreat to Daboya, which he used as his base until his death in 1844. Asante sent an army into central Gonja in 1841 but without results. Further expeditions were launched in 1842–1844. In the final stages of the dispute, the resistance at Daboya took on characteristics of an anti-Asante revolt, but Nyantakyi was captured and executed by the Asante army in 1844 (Wilks 1975: 276).

Back in Djougou, he entered the service of a local official, apparently the chief of Soubroukou, located a few kilometers from Djougou on the caravan route westward to the Volta. The title of the chief of Soubroukou was *massasawa*; Baquaqua refers to the "massa-sa-ba" and hence the identification of the court where Baquaqua was tricked into enslavement. He appears to have been a palace servant (*tkiriku*), a position normally reserved for slaves and sometimes criminals seeking protection. Baquaqua's identification with this term raises questions about his status at the time. Indeed, in the earliest but perhaps discrepant account of his origins, it is mentioned that he had been a slave, which may refer to this period in his life. The earlier account (Foss and Mathews 1850: 392) says that Baquaqua was "clandestinely seized upon, and reduced to slavery" at an "early age," and "for some time he was held in this condition in Western Africa" prior to being transported to Brazil. Maybe this can be understood as a garbled version of the truth; after all he had been "seized upon" in Daboya, although then redeemed, and if *tkiriku* were technically servile in status (even if not necessarily slaves in origin) he had indeed spent "some time" in slavery.

Baquaqua was apparently enslaved at Yarakeou ("Zaracho"), a village to the west of Soubroukou, for reasons that he himself confesses were his own indiscretions in stealing from local peasants and his fondness for drink (Moore 1854: 35). Unlike his earlier experience in Gonja, he was not ransomed this time but instead was traded southward along an obscure route to Dahomey and its port Ouidah (Whydah). Baquaqua says that he traveled south during the dry season, remaining in Dahomey for a short period, suggesting that he may have reached the coast by late January or early February 1845 (Moore 1854: 36–37). The British anti-slave trade blockade made it impossible to load slaves at Ouidah, and therefore they were moved along the lagoons either eastward to Porto Novo or Badagry, or westward to Agoué, where the lagoons opened into the sea (Law 2003). Considering the seasonal fluctuations in the level of the lagoons, it is likely that he was shipped west through Agoué because the lagoon east of Ouidah was not usually navigable during the dry season. Instead, slaves being moved eastward would have been sent overland to Godomey, to be loaded on canoes to cross Lake Nokué. Baquaqua states that he traveled by water, which suggests that he did not travel via Godomey. Allowing for his stay at "Efau" for several weeks, as well as his traveling time, this chronology is consistent with him being shipped around the end of February, to arrive in Pernambuco on March 30.[2]

In Brazil, he was first sold to a baker who lived outside of Recife. According to his own testimony, Baquaqua worked under harsh conditions for almost two years. Because of drunkenness and absenteeism, he was eventually traded south to Rio de Janeiro and sold to Clemente José da Costa, a ship captain and part owner of the bark, Lembrança ("Remembrance"). Baquaqua then served on board the ship, along with another slave, José da Rocha, who belonged to da Costa's partner, Antonio José Rocha Pereira.[3] On April 24, the Lembrança, with a consignment of coffee, sailed for New York, arriving 66 days later on June 27.[4]

At the urging of local abolitionists and prompted by severe beatings, Baquaqua, along with his compatriot, jumped ship and sought the "freedom" that he describes so poignantly in his autobiographical account. The case of the two men, now identified as "Brazilians," came to the attention of the local press in New York. A third slave, Maria da Costa, who looked after the captain's wife and baby, was initially involved in the bid for freedom but either decided to return to the ship of her own volition or was otherwise intimidated into returning. Baquaqua and Rocha were put in jail; they did not have an easy time keeping their freedom (National Anti-Slavery Standard, July 29, 1847). Their abolitionist friends filed a writ of habeas corpus, and on July 22 the case was brought before Judge Charles P. Daly of the New York District Court. Unfortunately, for the two men, Daly ruled that they were members of the ship's crew and therefore should be returned under the terms of a treaty of reciprocity between Brazil and the USA governing the desertion of ship crew (National Anti-Slavery Standard, July 22, 1847). The status of slavery was not a factor in the decision. Their identity as crew was confirmed in a second legal decision (National Anti-Slavery Standard, July 29, 1847). In the opinion of Judge Henry P. Edwards, Daly was correct in his judgment, and therefore remanded the two men to the custody of the captain of the ship. In turn, this decision was to be appealed, but before yet another judge could hear the case, Baquaqua and Rocha miraculously disappeared from the jail on Eldridge Street on the night of August 9. The jailer admitted that he had fallen asleep and left the keys to the cell on his desk (Daily Tribune, August 10, 1847; National Anti-Slavery Standard, August 12, 1847). Whether or not the warden sympathized with Baquaqua and his fellow fugitive is not clear, but the two men were able to reach Boston, passing through Springfield. Four weeks later, Baquaqua left for Haiti, the land where blacks were "free" (Daily Tribune, August 23, 1847). José da Roche may also have gone to Haiti (Moore 1854: 59).

Because Baquaqua did not speak Haitian creole, he was not able to find many people with whom he could talk in Port-au-Prince (Moore 1854: 57–58). Hence he experienced some difficulty in maintaining himself, working at one time for an African American who did not treat him very well, or at least Baquaqua did not think so (Foss and Mathews 1850: 389–393; Moore 1854: 57–60). Moreover, it was not a period of political stability in Haiti; Faustin Soulouque came to power in 1847, crushed his opposition with much bloodshed in 1848, declared himself emperor in 1849, and relied on a force of secret police to run the country (Leyburn 1966: 91–93). The Rev William L. Judd of the American Baptist Free Mission Society took an interest in him, and in early 1849, Baquaqua experienced conversion and was baptized (Law and Lovejoy 2001). In late 1849, he returned to New York with the Rev. Judd's wife, and accompanied her to upstate New York, enrolling in New York Central College in McGrawville, an abolitionist institution founded in 1848 by the American Baptist Free Mission Society (Dunn 1957). While he was there, Central College had about 200 students, including ten blacks, among whom was someone with the surname "Senegal" and also the sons of prominent black families from Philadelphia (Hanchett 1997).

Baquaqua's days in McGrawville were not entirely pleasant. Upstate New York was a mixture, with reform-minded people like the Free Will Baptists with whom he associated, yet there was also an ugly racist side to local society. In one scandal, William Allen, a mulatto professor at Central College, became involved, and then married, one of the students, Mary King, a white girl from Fulton whose father was a minister (Law and Lovejoy 2001). Like Allen, Baquaqua also become close friends with the daughter of a minister, although how close is not clear. But because of Allen's marriage, Baquaqua was probably intimidated into distancing himself from his friend, while Prof and Mrs Allen fled upstate New York for England (Allen 1853; Woodson 1969: 282–290; Mabee 1979: 85–92). In late January 1854, he was still in McGrawville, but apparently shortly thereafter he moved to Chatham. Somehow he made contact with Samuel Downing Moore in Detroit, had an engraving made by J. G. Darby from a daguerreotype by Sutton, and published the book by August. The book was filed in the office of the clerk of the District Court, US District of Michigan, on August 21, 1854.[5]

Baquaqua had an overriding ambition to return to his "native land" and tried repeatedly to find ways to achieve his ambition. He applied to the Mendi Mission, which had returned the surviving members of the *Amistad* to Sierra Leone in 1851.[6] The struggling mission, a child of the American Mission Association, was reinforced in the early 1850s, but apparently did not include Baquaqua (Fyfe 1962: 222–223, 246, 285). He applied to the American Baptist Free Mission Society in 1857, as noted above, but apparently no mission was approved for lack of funds (*Free Mission Record*, February 1857, 13). There is no known record of Baquaqua after 1857.

Ethnicity and identity along the slave routes

References to ethnicity are frequent in the study of enslaved Africans in the Americas, but how the concept is used is the subject of considerable debate and disagreement. I argue that reconstructions of conceptualizations of ethnicity offer the possibility of bridging a methodological gap in the study of slavery. The gap is the lack of data on what slaves thought and believed. Baquaqua, for example, says nothing explicitly about how he identified himself in ethnic terms or by place of origin. Nonetheless, biographical materials implicitly track individuals, thereby, in theory, telling us how each person interacted in the social sphere and therefore how each was identified and how each perceived of him/herself in different situations. Hence, for me, ethnicity is not important in and of itself, but because it provides a methodological key to. the reconstruction of broader patterns of history than the single history of one person allows.

When examining issues of ethnicity as reflected in the life of Mahommah Gardo Baquaqua, it becomes clear that his identity was intertwined with the personal details of his life but otherwise ethnicity was little more than a 'mirage' that disguised the factors that led to his enslavement and sale. Baquaqua's middle name, Gardo, or more accurately Gado in both Dendi and Hausa, is the name given to the next child born after twins. Without explaining the meaning of the name, Baquaqua does state that he was born after his mother had given birth to twins, who died in infancy (Law and Lovejoy 2001). The retention of this name reveals the importance of kinship in Baquaqua's life history, confirming the memory of relationships that had once existed. Just as his first name reveals his ongoing association with the memory of his Islamic upbringing, his second name connects him with his family, and especially his mother, who is mentioned several times in fond memory.

His surname is a mystery, however. As Baquaqua notes in his vocabulary, *ba-* is a common prefix in Borgu, as in the title, *Ba-Parakpe*, an official at Djougou and Parakou, at least, who served as intermediary between the courts in these towns and the Wangara community. There was also a Borgu title, *'yan kwakwa*, who was the official responsible for overseeing the caravanserai, and this may be a possible derivation, but it is not known if this title was used at Djougou. The name he gives for his title at Soubroukou was "Che-re-coo," that is, *tkiriku*, which was normally a servile position in Borgu but also could include criminals attempting to escape justice by enlisting as palace servants (Lombard 1965: 112). If indeed Baquaqua was a *tkiriku*, therefore, this probably means that he had either been enslaved and failed to explain this condition in his text or was otherwise taken on in this capacity for reasons that are also not explained. In any event, the use of the term does not seem to be in accord with his claim to being free, and certainly raises the possibility that there are further details which he may have chosen to suppress.

The name Baquaqua also sounds Hausa, the language of his mother and uncle. The prefix *ba-* is common for the singular forms of many terms that denote place of origin, such as *Bakano, Bakatsini, Bazazzau,* or *Bazamfara* (someone from Kano, Katsina, Zaria, or Zamfara, respectively), or ethnically, such as *Bahaushe, Bayaraba,* or *Ba'agali* (for Hausa, Yoruba, or Agalawa), but "kwakwa" or "k'wak'wa" does not refer to a place or a known ethnic designation. There remains a hidden meaning in Baquaqua's name, which in itself indicates the difficulty of assessing identities.

Baquaqua's life story reveals much about how this one man, at least, was assigned a series of identities that related to his status in the course of staying alive. In one decade, he managed to stumble into enslavement in Borgu, to survive the forced march to the coast and the terrible Middle Passage, to experience brutal incarceration in Pernambuco and harsh treatment at sea, but he survived. Even the isolation of his Haitian days and the racism of upstate New York did not break him. There can be no stronger evidence that this man maintained an image of himself that could withstand violence, humiliation, and efforts at deracination. His identity in the context of enslavement kept changing, presenting the man in different guises in different situations.

Admittedly, his odyssey was unusual, taking him from Borgu, in the interior of West Africa, through Dahomey to Pernambuco, Rio de Janeiro, New York City, Haiti, upstate New York, Canada West, and England. Not very many enslaved Africans reached the Americas from Borgu, and the route that Baquaqua followed southward to Dahomey was not well traveled even for the relatively few who did find themselves on board ships for the Americas. What emerges from an examination of Baquaqua's life is an image of ethnicity that seems to have been of little importance in his self-identification or at least his personal experience. Yet, despite this, a sense of ethnic origins almost certainly remained fixed in his memory. His religious convictions appear to have become blurred, as suggested by his conversion to Christianity with the retention of his Muslim name. There is nothing incompatible with the establishment and maintenance of a double personality in matters of religion, and Baquaqua had earlier demonstrated his failure to appreciate the requirements of orthodoxy. He had not been a good student, not only because he had to study under the stern rule of his older brother but also because he liked to imbibe, the cause of his downfall and enslavement.

Baquaqua's father was from "Bergu," which almost certainly refers to Nikki, the most important city in Borgu, whose king was recognized by various other towns, including Djougou, as the capital of a loose confederation. He was "of Arabian descent," and once a prosperous merchant. He thereby must have identified with the Muslim community of Borgu, which was known as Wangara, and sometimes Dendi, speaking as their first language the Dendi dialect of Songhay, but also being able to speak, in many cases, Hausa, the principal trading language along the caravan routes between the Central Sudan and the middle Volta basin, which by this time was dominated by Hausa merchants from Kano, Katsina, and other parts of the Sokoto Caliphate. Mahommah's mother was from Katsina, a commercial center of considerable importance at the time. Her brother was a prosperous smith, indeed the blacksmith of the king of Djougou, who owned a house in Salaga, the most important market town in northern Asante, where Asante merchants and producers sold kola nuts to the Hausa caravans. As I have shown elsewhere, the kola trade between Asante and the Sokoto Caliphate was one of the most important commercial networks in West Africa in the nineteenth century (Lovejoy 1980; Brégand 1998). Mahommah's maternal kin were very likely connected with one of the important merchant houses of Katsina, and as Heinrich Barth (1965) reported in the 1850s, most of those families were Wangarawa. It was reported that Baquaqua "talks much of Africa, and ... Dreams often of visiting Kachna [Katsina], accompanied by a good white man, as he calls a Missionary, and being kindly received by his mother" (*Christian Contributor* in Law and Lovejoy 2001) The family, and its marital connections with an equally prominent merchant family from Nikki and Djougou, reveals the history of this important trade route in new ways. The likelihood that his mother was from a

Wangarawa family is increased because of the connection with craft production, the fact that his uncle had a house in Salaga, and the marriage alliance with a family possessing strong Islamic credentials (Lovejoy 1978; Law 1995; Wilks 1995; Brégard 1998: 18–20).

The vocabulary provided by Baquaqua in his book is Dendi, which was the language of the Wangara community of Borgu, but he also would have known the language of the peasantry, Gurma, perhaps also Baatonu, the local language in central Borgu. Although he had not been a good student as a boy, he clearly learned some Arabic, although not well, if the three words in one of his surviving letters are any proof of his fluency. The words are not written in a practised hand. Baquaqua apparently was attempting to write "*bismi'llah al-rahman*," but managed only a garbled "*bismi'llah al-ra[hman]*," with the bracketed part omitted.[7] Nonetheless, he had some facility with languages, having started to learn Fon ("Efau") in Dahomey, and even acquiring some Portuguese on board ship.

So, let us consider the identity that would have become Baquaqua's if he had not been ransomed in Daboya when he was a teenager. If he had not subsequently been ransomed, enslavement almost certainly would have meant that Baquaqua would have been taken to Asante. It was unlikely that he would have been sold into the Atlantic trade, although in the late 1840s some male slaves were bought on the Gold Coast by the Dutch for recruitment into the colonial army in Indonesia (La Torre 1978: 415). If Baquaqua had not been ransomed, the conquering Asante army probably would have taken him back to Asante, where he would have been identified as an *ndonko*, a slave of northern origin in Asante and greater Akan society, as distinct from a slave of Akan origin (Perbi 1997). Because Baquaqua was redeemed, this fate was avoided, but it was nonetheless a real possibility.

His enslavement outside of Djougou redefined his identity again. In the south, he would have been referred to as "Bariba," a term common in Dahomey. As his description makes clear, he might have been kept in Dahomey, along with his countryman, Woru, at Ouidah. There were other enslaved Muslims in Dahomey, such as those recruited by the French fort at Ouidah (Law and Lovejoy 2000). Muslims from this region were called "Malé," and if Baquaqua's religion was recognized, he might have also received that term as a description (Verger 1976). Such slaves were common in Bahia, the more usual destination for people from the Bight of Benin in the nineteenth century. However, since the Malé uprising in Bahia in 1835, Muslim slaves were not wanted (Reis 1993), and recognition as Malé was not desirable. Thus, Baquaqua's Muslim identity may well have been suppressed (Quiring-Zoche, 1995).

In Rio de Janeiro, Baquaqua's identity was tied to his master. His name, José da Costa, provided such a link, as it did for Maria da Costa, who was also on the ship, with his master, Clemente José da Costa. The other slave on the ship, José da Rocha, belonged to his partner Antonio José da Rocha Pereira. Baquaqua first learned Portuguese on the Atlantic crossing, clearly becoming more proficient in Pernambuco and Rio. A nominal understanding of Catholicism had been forced on these slaves, which is also implied in the names that were assigned to these individuals. At the time, Baquaqua was both a slave belonging to the master of the ship but also a member of the crew, and hence was identified in New York as a "Brazilian" (*National Anti-Slavery Standard*, September 2, 1847). He clearly still thought of himself as a Muslim, despite his forced introduction to Christian worship.

Baquaqua was assigned and assumed other identities after his escape from jail in New York. As a fugitive, he was spirited away to Haiti, but in the difficult times there he was clearly an outsider, someone who could not understand creole. He lived in Haiti for two years, this time openly converting to Christianity, and returning to the USA as a college student and abolitionist. He was listed in the US census of 1850 as a twenty-year old student at New York Central College. He confessed that "the English Language has been very hard for me to understand and speak," and the extent to which he mastered English is reflected in his letters.[8] The biography clearly belongs to the genre of abolitionist and missionary tracts, but he was apparently not successful in reaching Africa via missionary channels, at least by 1857(*Free Mission Record*, February 1857, 13). He did not accompany any of the missions to West Africa in the late 1850s and early 1860s.

Baquaqua's life story provides insights into the psychological impact of the journey along the slave routes upon a young adult male, whose changing consciousness of his predicament is documented to a degree that is rare. Baquaqua's sense of himself as a person and his relationship to a broader community can also be deciphered to some extent, as can the views others had of him. In this particular case, the factual details make it possible to situate ethnic identification in a specific historical context. Baquaqua's identity was indeed situational and particular. Whereas ethnic, religious, and other factors influenced his sense of identity and relationship with his community, he also came to identify with the diaspora and the quest to return home. This biography shows that ethnic and religious identification only make sense in a historical context and not in isolation.

Methodologically, the biographical approach revealed in the life history of Mahommah Gardo Baquaqua suggests that widely scattered information can be brought together to flesh out the bare bones of the identities of slavery's victims (Lovejoy 1997). Baquaqua's life history reveals many layers of identification that keep shifting as they were reinterpreted in different contexts. On one level, there are the languages that he knew, beginning with Dendi, Arabic, probably Hausa and Gurma, and a smattering of Fon. He certainly identified as a Muslim and as a resident of Borgu, and indeed specifically Djougou. But he also thought of Katsina as home because his mother and her family were from there. His merchant connections, with its guild structure and its class overtones, were reflected in his early, even abortive, education, and the opportunities that he was given through the connections of his parents. His identity, as revealed in the available source materials, was tied to his age, occupation, gender, family, class, religion, and language. His reduction to the status of slave did not initially alter his identity, although as his first captivity indicates, individuals might hide their identities in the hope of achieving freedom, as Baquaqua did when his brother pretended not to know him but nonetheless arranged his ransom.

When Baquaqua was enslaved a second time, he had no reason to believe that he would not again be ransomed. His account enables us to follow his changing view of his situation, and thereby his sense of identity. He records when he gave up hope of being redeemed. He reports the last countryman whom he recognizes. We follow him from one owner to another, along the slave routes of Africa, across the Atlantic, and from northeastern Brazil to Rio de Janeiro. During this sad journey, we see him stripped of his identity as a social being in ways that Orlando Patterson (1982) has emphasized. Yet in Pernambuco, he would have been quickly recognized as a Muslim, a Malé, in a country recently threatened by the 1835 uprising (Reis 1993; Lovejoy 2000). It may have been one of the reasons why he was treated so badly there.

Baquaqua underwent a transformation that reflected the slave condition in the Americas, in which self-identification and identification by the dominant class of slave owners is often blurred in the sources, and therefore it is not always easy to distinguish among stereotypes, self-perception, and bad reporting. Although the designations "Borgu," "Bariba," and "Barba" were known in the Americas, this was not a common ethnic label. It is possible that Baquaqua was at times recognized as such, but we have no proof. By the time he was in Rio, the principal tag that he wore was that of his master, which provided him with a nominal Portuguese, and indeed Christian, veneer, although he later says he was not a Christian then. José da Costa, alias Mahommah Gardo Baquaqua, was a name that denied his Muslim and African origins, identified him with his master, and implied conversion to Christianity.

As his Portuguese name suggests, José da Costa had been exposed to Christianity, but he did not convert until 1849. He dispensed with his Brazilian name, and we only know him as Mahommah Gardo Baquaqua after 1847. Even when he was presenting himself as a Christian, signing his letters "your Bro in Christ", he used his Muslim name.[9] When he first arrived in McGrawville, he was dressed in a white robe as a Muslim and was considered an "Arabian-speaking African" thought to have come from Egypt (*McGrawville Express*, March 28, 1850; Hanchett 1989). He actively campaigned to go to Sierra Leone, reflected on the advantages and disadvantages of moving to Haiti, Canada West, Britain, or of remaining in the USA. His principal concern was always his liberty, which increasingly was reflected in abolitionist sentiments. He went to Haiti because it was a country where blacks were free. His driving passion to return to Africa was tempered occasionally by the realism that he might not be successful in getting there and might have to remain in Upper Canada or the USA and eventually in Britain. In 1854, after publishing his autobiographical account in Detroit, he thereby acquired yet another identity as an abolitionist author.

This fascinating story of a young man enduring the horrors of the slave routes to the Americas, and yet escaping from slavery as a fugitive in the USA and Haiti, raises many questions about identity and ethnicity. Whereas the various identifications that inevitably arose can be conceptualized as forms of ethnicity, the overriding impression gained from Baquaqua's experiences is his emergent individualism and the malleability of his identity. Ethnic labels, class distinctions, religious convictions, and other means of self- and group-identification mattered, but they probably matter more to historians, as clues in the reconstruction of history, than to individuals such as Baquaqua enmeshed in racialized slavery in the Americas. In the 10 years that elapsed from his enslavement in a village outside of Djougou in 1845 to the publication of his autobiography in Detroit in 1854 this remarkable young man emerges as an individual with a unique personality that survived the experience of Trans-Atlantic slavery through perseverance and a considerable amount of luck.

Conclusion: the mirage of identity

The recent discovery that Olaudah Equiano may have been born in South Carolina in a strongly Igbo cultural setting, undoubtedly the child of Igbo parents, and not kidnapped as a boy in Africa, raises the question of authenticity and the difficulty of working with sources that are hard to verify. According to his baptismal certificate and his enlistment papers on the Arctic Expedition of 1773, recently discovered by Vincent Carretta (1999), the real life of this man may have begun in a quite different fashion than various versions of his published account seem to suggest (Walvin 1998: 3–15). Indeed, his childhood in Igboland may well have been an abolitionist invention.

The Equiano saga has long been used, indeed overused, as the quintessential example of the barbarities of enslavement and the horrors of the middle passage. But in fact, Gustavus Vassa, for he was not known by the name of Olaudah Equiano until the publication of his autobiography in 1789, was a Creole, that is, born in the Americas. Carretta suggests that Equiano may have successively "constructed" his own identity according to circumstances. His name was made up to enhance the abolitionist appeal of the book because it sounded more like an African name than the classical names often given to slaves. Was it also possible that someone reasoned that a kidnapped Equiano was more appealing for abolitionist purposes than a boy named Vassa from South Carolina? Minor discrepancies in the different editions that appeared in rapid succession after 1789 suggested to Carretta that there was perhaps more to the biography of this man than has been apparent until now. Carretta speculates that the discrepancies in the early editions arose because Vassa, alias Equiano, may have had trouble keeping the details of his childhood straight because the facts were changing along with his identity. If the documents are correct, an image was forced upon Vassa/Equiano that pictured a "tribal" origin in West Africa conforming to abolitionist strategies. The picture presented a poor boy, kidnapped from a modest but comfortable village setting, thrust into the evils of slave America. This interpretation would explain discrepancies in the several editions of the book, but are the documents themselves the whole story?

Baquaqua's origins are more believable than the African birth of Equiano because of the survival of verifying information. Whereas Equiano's description of the Igbo homeland has puzzled scholars for a long time, the various efforts at establishing his village of birth or even his region of origin have been fraught with controversy and speculation (e.g. Acholonu 1987). The discovery of two independent documents have thrown this emergent tradition of African birth into disarray, and some modified interpretation of his African birth seems warranted. If there should be further evidence for a connection with South Carolina, his story would then become, instead of a tale of the horrors of kidnapping, rather an account of the vibrancy and intensity of identity as Igbo in the diaspora. The account would take on a new meaning that is not any less important than the myth that it would displace. A South Carolina birth is consistent with the fact that Liverpool, Bristol, and London ships were responsible for shipping most slaves to Charleston, the principal port, either directly or indirectly through Jamaica or Barbados, and these ships dominated the trade in the Bight of Biafra, from where enslaved Africans speaking Igbo came. Indeed, they came almost exclusively from the ports of Bonny and Old Calabar in the period when Vassa/Equiano's parents would have arrived in the Carolinas. At least 2,100 enslaved Africans from the Bight of Biafra, most of whom probably Igbo, arrived in South Carolina in the 1740s and 1750s (Morgan 1998: 63). The Vassa/Equiano case, at least, forces us to be open to revision and reminds us of the importance of ongoing research.

Baquaqua's account, in comparison, contains verifiable information that confirms the Djougou origin and, moreover, places this individual in a broader historical and cultural context that enables a fuller appreciation of one young man's "social death" and "spiritual reawakening." His second name, Gardo, or more properly Gado, reflects an identity not apparent to others, one that tied him to the memory of his family, and hence maintained his sense of identity in terms of kinship. Yet there appears to be much that is hidden in Baquaqua's account, including further details of his enslavement or search for sanctuary, as suggested in his description of himself as *tkiriku*.

How did Baquaqua come to terms with his changing situation under slavery and his quest for freedom? What can be learned from the variety of sources, including his edited autobiography, about his image of himself and how that changed? One thing is clear. He wanted to return to Africa, where his identity was centered. He would have gone to Sierra Leone, but would he have stayed there as a missionary? The retention of his Muslim name raises the possibility that he would have absconded, using the assignment to Sierra Leone only as stepping stone. This is of course speculation, but not out of the realm of possibility considering the presence of a refugee Muslim population of liberated slaves in Sierra Leone, some of whom actually having come from Borgu, with many from Hausaland—perhaps even from Katsina, his mother's home. Yet, is it likely he would have known this? I suggest that it was possible, even probable, given his missionary connections, and the flow of information within those circles. A retention of his Muslim identity is less clear, but he retained his name, and a desire to return home. His single Arabic phrase of the *Bismi'llah* is a lonely cry, perhaps revealing of an identity that was confused with his Christian salvation. How he eventually resolved this apparent contradiction is not clear.

Acknowledgments

This chapter derives from collaborative research with Robin Law and was supported by the Social Sciences and Humanities Research Council of Canada and is part of the UNESCO/York University "Nigerian" Hinterland Project. I wish to thank Chery I. Lemaitre, Catherine Hanchett, Catherine Barber, Sylvia Hunold Lara, Manolo Florentino, Kwabena Akurang-Parry, and Ibrahim Hamza for their advice and assistance.

Notes

1 Baquaqua to George Whipple, McGrawville, October 8, 1853 (American Missionary Association Archives, No. 81362, Amistad Research Center, Tulane University, New Orleans).
2 The identification is tentative; see Consul H. Augustus Cowper to the Earl of Abderdeen, Pernambuco, March 2, 1846, in *Correspondence on the Slave Trade with Foreign Powers (Class B)*, January 1–December 31, 1845 (1846) 290; encl., 293. The ship is listed in the slave voyage database (No. 3592) in the "unspecified" category, not Bight of Benin (Eltis *et al.* 1999).
3 Clemente José da Costa is a common name and so far has not been further identified. Antonio José da Rocha Pereira has been identified through an 1871 postmortem inventory; see Law and Lovejoy (2001).
4 An advertisement for passengers was published in *Jornal do Commercio* (Rio de Janeiro), April 17, 1847, and for its arrival in New York, see *New York Daily Tribune*, June 28, 1847.
5 Moore was a Unitarian from Ireland who settled in Ypsilanti, Michigan; see "The Unitarian Ministers of Ireland and American Slavery," *The Liberator*, May 12, 1848; Samuel Moore, "A Protest," in *The Liberator*, February 29, 1856; and Samuel Moore to William Lloyd Garrison, *The Liberator*, December 4, 1857. The clerk was W. David King.
6 Baquaqua to George Whipple, McGrawville, October 8, 1853 and Baquaqua to Thomson, McGrawville, October 26, 1853 and January 29, 1854 (Amistad Collection).
7 Letters dated, McGrawville, October 28, 1853, and January 29, 1854 (AMA Archives).
8 Letter of October 8, 1853 (AMA Archives).
9 Letter of October 26, 1853 (AMA Archives).

References

Acholonu, Catherine O. (1987) "The home of Olaudah Equiano—a linguistic and anthropological survey," *Journal of Commonwealth Literature*, 22, 1: 5–16.

Allen, William G. [1853] (1969) *American Prejudice against Color: An Authentic Narrative, Showing How Easily the Nation Got into an Uproar*, New York: Arno.

Austin, Allan (ed.) (1984) *African Muslims in Ante-Bellum America: A Sourcebook*, London: Routledge.

Barth, Heinrich [1859] (1965) *Travels and Discoveries in North and Central Africa*, 3 Vols, London: Frank Cass.

Brégand, Denise (1998) *Commerce caravanier et relations sociales au Bénin: Les Wangara du Borgou*, Paris: l'Harmattan.

Carretta, Vincent (1999) "Olaudah Equiano or Gustavus Vassa? New light on an eighteenth century question of identity," *Slavery and Abolition*, 20: 96–105.

Curtin, Philip D. (ed.) (1967) *Africa Remembered: Narratives by West Africans from the Era of the Slave Trade*, Madison, WI: University of Wisconsin Press.

Diouf, Sylviane A. (1998) *Servants of Allah: African Muslims Enslaved in the Americas*, New York: New York University Press.

Dunn, Seymour B. (1957) "The early academies of Cortland county," *Cortland County Chronicles*, 1: 71–76.

Eltis, David, and Engerman, Stanley (1993) "Fluctuations in sex and age ratios in the Transatlantic slave trade, 1663–1864," *Economic History Review*, 46: 308–323.

Eltis, David, Behrendt, Stephen D., Richardson, David, and Klein, Herbert S. (1999) *The Trans-Atlantic Slave Trade: A Database on CD-ROM*, New York: Cambridge University Press.

Foss, A. T., and Mathews, E. (1850) *Facts for Baptist Churches*, Utica, NY.

Fyfe, Christopher (1962) *A History of Sierra Leone*, London: Oxford University Press.

Gomez, Michael (1998) *Exchanging Our Country Marks: The Transformation of African Identities in the Colonial and Antebellum South*, Chapel Hill, NC: University of North Carolina Press.

Hanchett, Catherine M. (1989) "New York College and its three Black Professors 1849–1857," Paper presented at the conference *A Heritage Uncovered: The Black Experience in New York State*, Elmira, NY, 22 April, 1989.

Hanchett, Catherine M. (1997) "New York Central College students," manuscript on file at Cortland County Historical Society, New York.

La Torre, Joseph R. (1978) *Wealth Surpasses Everything: An Economic History of Asante*, unpublished PhD thesis, University of California at Berkeley.

Law, Robin (1995) " 'Central, and Eastern Wangara': an indigenous West African perception of the political and economic geography of the Slave Coast as recorded by Joseph Dupuis in Kumasi, 1820," *History in Africa*, 22: 281–305.

Law, Robin (2003) *A Social History of Ouidah*, London: Heineman.

Law, Robin, and Lovejoy, Paul E. (2001). *The Biography of Mahommah Gardo Baquaqua: His Passage from Slavery to Freedom in Africa and America*, Princeton, NJ: Markus Wiener.

Leyburn, James G. (1966) *The Haitian People*, New Haven, CT: Yale University Press.

Lombard, Jacques (1965) *Structures de type "feudal" en Afrique noire. Etude des dynamismes internes et des relations sociales chez les Bariba du Dahomey*, Paris-LeHaye: E.P.H.E.

Lovejoy, Paul E. (1978) "The role of the Wangara in the economic transformation of the Central Sudan in the Fifteenth and Sixteenth Centuries," *Journal of African History*, 19: 173–193.

Lovejoy, Paul E. (1980) *Caravans of Kola: The Hausa Kola Trade, 1700–1900*, Zaria: Ahmadu Bello University Press.

Lovejoy, Paul E. (1982) "Polanyi's 'ports of trade': Salaga and Kano in the nineteenth century," *Canadian Journal of African Studies*, 16: 245–278.

Lovejoy, Paul E. (1994) "Background to Rebellion: The Origins of Muslim Slaves in Bahia," in Paul E. Lovejoy and Nicholas Rogers (eds) *Unfree Labour in the Development of the Atlantic World*, 151–180, London: Frank Cass.

Lovejoy, Paul E. (1997) "Biography as Source Material: Towards a Biographical Archive of Enslaved Africans," in Robin Law (ed.) *Source Material for Studying the Slave Trade and the African Diaspora*, 119–140, Stirling: Centre for Commonwealth Studies.

Mabee, Carleton (1979) *Black Education in New York State*, Syracuse, NY: Syracuse University Press.

Morgan, Philip (1998) *Slave Counterpoint: Black Culture in the Eighteenth-Century Chesapeake and Lowcountry*, Chapel Hill, NC: University of North Carolina Press.

Moore, Samuel (1854) *Biography of Mahommah G. Baquaqua. A Native of Zoogoo, in the Interior of Africa (A Convert to Christianity) with a Description of that Part of the World, Including the Manners and Customs of the Inhabitants*, Detroit, MI: Geo. E. Pomeroy & Co.

Patterson, Orlando (1982) *Slavery and Social Death: A Comparative Study*, Cambridge, MA: Harvard University Press.

Perbi, Akosua Adoma (1997) *A History of Indigenous Slavery in Ghana from the 15th to the 19th Centuries*, unpublished PhD thesis, University of Ghana.

Quiring-Zoche, Rosemairie (1995) "Glaubenskampf oder Machtkampf? Der Aufstand der Malé von Bahia nach einer islamischen Quelle," *Sudanic Africa*, 6: 115–124.

Reis, João José (1993) *Slave Rebellion in Brazil: The Muslim Uprising of 1835 in Bahia*, Arthur Brakel (ed. and trans.) Baltimore, MD: Johns Hopkins University Press.

Sherman, Joan R. (1972) "James Monroe Whitfield, Poet and Emigrationist: a voice of protest and despair," *Journal of Negro History*, 57: 169–176.

Verger, Pierre (1976) *Trade relations between the Bight of Benin and Bahia 17th–19th Century*, Ibadan: University of Ibadan Press.

Walvin, James (1998) *An African Life: The Life and Times of Olaudah Equiano, 1745–1797*, London: Continuum.

Whitfield, James (1853) *America, and Other Poems*, Buffalo, NY: Leavitt.

Wilks, Ivor (1975) *Asante in the Nineteenth Century*, Cambridge: Cambridge University Press.

Wilks, Ivor (1995) "Consul Dupuis and Wangara: a window on Islam in early nineteenth-century Asante," *Sudanic Africa*, 6: 55–72.

Woodson, Carter G. (ed.) [1926] (1969) *The Mind of the Negro as Reflected in Letters Written during the Crisis, 1800–1860*, New York: Russell & Russell.

10 Banya

A Suriname slave play that survived

G. M. Martinus-Guda

Three centuries of *banya*

Banya started as a pastime for the slaves in the coastal region of Suriname, where the majority of the plantations and the administrative center of the colony were situated. The first remarks about *banya* go back to the beginning of the eighteenth century. The writer J. D. Herlein (1718) observed that the slaves in Paramaribo used to go to a certain place on Sundays to enjoy a certain type of amusement *baaljaaren*, a form of dance and music which not only served as a distraction, but also as a means to pass around secret messages and information. Other eighteenth-century writers report the early existence of secular dances as well as religious dances called *watra-mama* dances or *winti* plays—as the religious ceremonies of the Suriname Creoles are still known today. Those religious dances were immediately prohibited because, obviously, possession by unknown gods, induced by music and dance in a crowd, meant an opportunity for rebellion (Labat 1725; Blom 1786, 1787). Secular dances like *banya* and *susa* were considered less risky. Yet they were only allowed to take place on certain occasions, required special permits, and the presence of overseers was required to guarantee safety and order. The secular slave plays usually took place around New Year, and about the first of July, when clothes and other rations were distributed, and sometimes also when a plantation owner wished to entertain visitors.

The fact that *banya* still exists today is due to the tenacity of the religious beliefs of the slaves, which were kept alive by their descendants in spite of massive efforts by church and state to wipe them out (Price 1983a, b). *Banya* in the coastal area is now part of the *winti* ceremonies and is used specifically as a way to communicate with ancestors who are enticed to take possession of their descendants during the presentation of the music and dances, which during their lifetime were their favorites. Usually an entire family organizes the event, when confronted with sickness and other types of misfortune. They are anxious to get in touch with their ancestors to receive information about unknown events or neglected rites, which need to be addressed in order to regain the well-being of the family. Certain *banya* plays, called *botobanya* or *banyiprey*, accentuate the journey of the slaves out of Africa. During these plays sometimes a small boat is wheeled into the dancing space. Songs, music, firework, and flintlock gunshots accompany it, creating a dramatic climax. It usually doesn't take long before some ancestral spirit manifests itself.

Social functions

Banya was a women's dance and *susa* was a dance for men, although members of the opposite sex always participated in both of the plays. *Susa* was a competition with winners and losers, a test of masculine agility, of which there were several variations. But although it became very popular and there existed several *susa* societies dedicated to this play, it never conquered the place *banya* acquired over time as a play accepted by the elites of society. The reason for the rise of the *banya* can probably be attributed to the fact that women played an important part in it.

Plantation owners often established relationships with female slaves, which were called "Surinamese marriages." These relationships presented a practical solution for several problems confronting single men. They were first of all of a sexual nature, although the women also acted as housekeepers. However, this arrangement did not change the women's social status. Even if these women were set free (manumitted), they were not accepted as equal by their "husbands," his peers, or by Europeans in the colony, in general. The children born out of such relationships sometimes served as slaves in their father's household. Yet when these women and their children were manumitted however, the children were sometimes sent to Holland to get an education or inherited land from their father. More and more concubines were recruited for "marriage" from this group of mixed racial descent. The housekeepers, respectfully called "Sisi" by the slaves, whose sphere of influence was confined to their own household, often loved the *banya* and started *banya* societies called *Doo*. The leaders of the *Doos* competed with each other, poking fun at some weak point of their opponents, and challenging them to react. But this seemingly innocent form of amusement could convert into bitter rivalry, and in play after counter-play the *Doo* members figuratively went out and slit each other's throats.

The existence of the *Doo* was resented by the European elite, particularly because their membership consisted of freemen and slaves. The slaves were fully accepted in the *Doo* for their beauty or for their artistic skills as singers, dancers, composers, musicians, designers, and organizers. These skills and qualities were essential for the success of their society, which was considered more important than the legal status of the participants. But socializing between the free and the enslaved was considered inappropriate and even dangerous because it could lead to disrespect for masters and for whites in general and would disrupt the elaborate body of regulations that kept slaves in check.

The artistic success of the *Doos* gradually led to their acceptance and appreciation by people in the highest ranks of society. In the nineteenth century it was socially acceptable for powerful men to become sponsors of *Doos*. Even governors are known to have become *Yobo* (sponsors) of a *Doo*. Often these *Yobo* used "their" *Doo* as a propaganda weapon against their enemies. In the second half of the nineteenth century however, when newspapers began to circulate on a regular basis the *Doo*, which as an oral art form was considered less effective than the written attacks, lost patronage. With this elite loss of interest the *Doos* gradually ceased to exist. *Banya* societies still remained popular however till the second half of the last century, but only among people of the lower social strata, who faithfully maintained the traditions of their ancestors.

Development of the *banya*

Suriname was a colony at one time so prosperous that the Dutch traded it for New York! The capital, Paramaribo, was a showcase of wealth at the end of the eighteenth century. No wonder then that in this climate the *banya* also became a thing of luxury. The leaders of the *Doos* often used their wealth (or that of their "spouses") to enhance their performances. Gradually the play was elaborated into a dramatic form, which had a fixed plot outline and fixed characters. The group of actors formed a reflection of slave society: a black governor, chief of police, prosecutors, judges, doctors, nurses, overseers, house slaves and field slaves and their great-great grandmothers and grandfathers were present in the background while female Masters of Ceremony, fragrance sprinklers, flower bearers, singers, dancers and musicians, participated in spirited attacks on the enemy of the occasion. The lead singers delivered their song phrases, which usually were composed and memorized beforehand, and were repeated by a chorus in a traditional pattern of speech and response ("troki" and "piki"). The ladies of the chorus swayed their bodies, while they constantly manipulated strings of dry seeds as musical instruments with which they accompanied the different types of *banya* drums.

The plot was always the same. One of the ladies, usually a beautiful young woman, represented the character of "Aflaw" (or, "she who looses consciousness"). She was the only such delicate character, who was affected by the attacks on the absentee opponent and who protested from time to time dutifully against the content of the songs. At the climax of the play Aflaw was so much affected that she lost consciousness. In a flurry of activities and with the appropriate songs and manipulations pharmacists, doctors, and nurses had to help Aflaw to get well again, much to the amusement of the public.

Often the *Doos* own beautifully carved objects called *kwakwa-banyi*, which as their symbol carried the name of the *Doo*. It had a small cupboard in which visitors could deposit a gift, some coins, or paper money. After the successful restoration of Aflaw's health the *kwakwa-banyi* often became the center of attention and the play ended with songs related to its name.

Banya is not an erotic type of dance. The women dance with their feet touching the ground so quickly that they gave the impression of floating, waving their handkerchiefs continuously and moving their shoulder, but scarcely moving their torso. Their male counterparts, who dance opposite them for just a few moments and then continue, make movements of a completely different nature, jumping and lifting their feet off the ground, as if imitating the mating dance of different kinds of birds. The women must master the art of "slenger"—moving gracefully and silently— sailing, barefoot across the clean dirt floor. This art, once mastered, is greatly admired by friend and foe, and often attracts money from admirers.

Continuity

Today, the religious *banya* is usually executed without the dramatic elements we just described. These modern plays have a more or less fixed structure in which other slave dances and plays such as *susa, laku, kanga,* and a form of *anasitori* are incorporated.

This is to ensure that as many ancestors as possible, with their varying different preferences, are attracted to the play.

In addition to local continuity, there is also a strong musical connection between the *banya* of the coastal area and the maroon dance called *ban(d)ya* which today is a popular social dance of one of the Suriname Maroon groups, the Matawai (De Beet and Sterman 1981). Considering the fact that all maroons fled from the coastal area where the *banya* was a general pastime, this conclusion doesn't seem far-fetched. The fact moreover that the Matawai refused to comply with the stipulation of a peace-treaty to send back runaway slaves who had sought refuge with them, makes it clear that there existed a bond between Suriname Maroons and those who remained in slavery.

The name of the Matawai dance is *ban(d)ya*, a creolization of the Spanish and Portuguese "bailar," old Dutch "baljaaren," and Creole "banya." The Matawai *ban(d)ya* is a social dance which is celebrated each New Year for several days and is also used by this group as general recreation. There still are famous Matawai *bandya* singers and there are still new *bandya* songs written, although younger generations now have come to prefer more popular Suriname dances. Matawai *bandya* also have religious aspects, but *bandya* at ceremonies for the recently deceased differ from the *banya* ancestor-ceremonies described above.

In Santigron, a village established in the coastal area by maroon elders and a veritable melting pot of disparate maroon groups, there is also a tradition of dancing *banya* around New Year. But here it is only one of many activities, given that different groups of the village, prefer their own traditional dances. The *banya* dancers of Santigron are related to coastal Creoles. The *banya* play of Santigron resembles a kind of *banya* called "kriorodron", known during slavery, which could best be described as a playful war between the sexes. Men and women take sides, teasing one another, with battles of love and jealousy publicly played out. There is also always someone, usually an older person, to remind the participants that this is only a game. Handkerchiefs whose names allude to certain well-known events or which carry the name of existing proverbs are used to communicate without words, while carefully chosen words constantly heighten the amusement, and dancers and musicians show off their skills.

The *banya* of today and their allied forms, based on analysis of the literature, recorded plays and observations of informants, seem to form a continuity with the eighteenth century slave plays. During their fieldwork in Suriname around the 1920s, the anthropologists Melville and Francis Herskovits (1936) taped and transcribed some *banya* songs. Some 80 years before, in 1858, the Suriname lawyer H. C. Focke (1858) published a few musical transcriptions of *banya* songs. He situated one of these almost 100 years earlier, around 1760, the time of the peace treaties with the maroons in the interior of Suriname. In considering the widespread survival of different forms of *banya*, one may hope to go further in reconstructing earlier *banya*—the slave play that survived.

Acknowledgments

This chapter is derived from work done in preparation for a publication by the Department of Culture of the Suriname Ministry of Education, by Hillary de Bruin, Christine van Russel and myself.

References

de Beet, Chris and Sterman, Miriam (1981) *People in Between: the Matawai Maroons of Suriname* Utrecht: Academisch Proefschrift.

Blom, Anthony (1786) *Verhandeling over den landbouw in de Colonie Surname*, Haarlem: Cornelis van der Aa.

Blom, Anthony (1787) *Verhandelingen van de Landbouw in de colonie Surname*, Amsterdam: J. W. Smit.

Focke, H. C. (1858) "De Surinaamsche Negermuziek," in *Bijdragen tot de bevordering van de kennis der Nederlandsch West-Indische kolonien*, Vol. 2, 93–107, Haarlem: A. C. Kruseman.

Herlein, J. D. (1718) *Beschrijving van de Volk-Plantinge Zuriname*, Leeuwarden: Meindert Injema.

Herskovits, M. J. and Herskovits, F. S. (1936) *Suriname Folklore*, New York: Columbia University Press.

Labat, Pere (1725) *Nieuwe Reizen na de Franse Eilanden van America*, Amsterdam: Balthasar Lakeman.

Price, Richard (1983a) *First Time, The Historical Vision of An Afro-American People*, Baltimore, MD: The Johns Hopkins University Press.

Price Richard (1983b) *To Slay the Hydra: Dutch Colonial Perspectives on the Saramaka Wars*, Ann Arbor, MI: Karoma.

11 Constructing identity through Inter-Caribbean interactions

The Curaçao–Cuban migration revisited

ROSE MARY ALLEN

In 1984 I interviewed "Peter," who had emigrated from Curaçao to Cuba in 1920 at the age of 18 to work in the cane fields. He told me the following:

> I learnt to play the bongo in Cuba ... Together with Wawa, another Curaçaoan who had lived in Cuba, we played the bongo here in Curaçao. The police used to stop us at first. We were not allowed to play. They thought it was the tambú. [The local drum] ... Well, first we went in the countryside and played, since nobody bothered us there. We afterwards went to the town. We continued till it became very popular and everywhere we would play the bongo ... Plakatampaban plakatampa (the sound he made while tapping on his chair).
>
> (Proj Cubag 35/1985)

Introduction

I have collected several life-stories like Peter's during my interviews held with older returnees from Cuba.[1] Their stories give evidence of the role migrations play in the transformation and construction of culture. In this chapter I will examine the relationship between migration and the process of regionalization of cultural identity by focusing on the labor migration from Curaçao to Cuba in the beginning of the twentieth century. I will consider how labor migration contributed to constructing the cultural identity of the Curaçaoan population and how this affected musical life in Curaçao.

Culture, identity and migration within the diaspora

In a theoretical sense my chapter attempts to place this past interregional Caribbean movement more closely within recent studies of transnationalism by looking at the cross-pollinating role of Afro-Cuban music in constructing and reconstructing a

Curaçaoan cultural identity. It is to contribute more knowledge on the diaspora experience of Caribbean people by showing it from another perspective. In most of the discourses on black diaspora, research on the experience of the Dutch islands in the Caribbean is excluded. It should not be left out, if we want to capture the complex and diversified histories of people of African descent.

Classically, Caribbean cultural identities are approached from the viewpoint that local dynamics within societies are the major contributors to their construction. Scholars look at particular groups within societies as autonomous ones that lived their lives without interconnecting with an exterior. Culture in this approach is localized with its transmission flowing within face-to-face relationships. The importance of interregional migration is neglected, especially the cultural impact of movements of groups within the Caribbean before and after the abolition of slavery.

Interregional migration in the Caribbean has long been a coping strategy for members of the poorer class of societies. Most of the time people leave their island in times of economic difficulties and seek a livelihood elsewhere. Hence, many researchers have studied this phenomenon from an economic functionalist perspective. This approach looks at how workers from several Caribbean islands participated actively in the capitalistic international labor system both in the Caribbean and outside. Their decision-making is mostly analyzed within the perspective of push factors present in the sending society and pull factors in the receiving one. Implicitly, their stay outside and return to their home country is mostly looked at in terms of economic ramifications, leaving out the implications of cultural interconnectedness.

What regional movements in the diaspora brought about local cultural identities thus needs further reflection. Recent studies, which look at contemporary population movements, principally those from the periphery to the center, may give a lead. Scholars argue that when people migrate they continue their cultural links with the society of departure and transport their cultural expressions to the host society. In the continuing contact with the society of departure the latter is also influenced by these migrations. Earlier migrations may by analogy be looked upon in a similar way. Chamberlain (1998) examined Caribbean migrations as continuing historical processes and events. Caribbean people have been migrants for over 500 years and this movement plays an important role in constructing cultural complexity in Caribbean societies (Chamberlain 1998: 5). The focus in some of the current literature on migration has thus shifted away from the causes of migration toward the nature and meaning of the migration experience. Migrants absorb and shape their new surroundings and are at the same time absorbed and shaped by them. Migration then, produces new forms of identity that transcend traditional notions of physical and cultural space. (Olwig 1995: 102). In this sense I will no longer look at the Curaçaoan identity as something statistic, rigid, and solely imbedded into the local society but will examine it within the concept of complexity as something fluid, flexible, and multi-scoped (Hannerz 1992).

The question of Curaçaoan migration to Cuba

How then did the movement to Cuba shape and define the cultural identity of African-Curaçaoans? And why did music play a part in this? In order to answer these questions, it is important first of all to explore the nature of the determinants of the social life of African-Curaçaoans during this migration. First of all, we should look at the demographic aspect of the group itself. The movement to Cuba from Curaçao started in 1917 and was at its highest peak in 1919, when some 1,900 left the country. It was mostly a working-class male event in which men left the island to work there as cane-cutters.[2] Even though the exact number of men leaving is not known, it is estimated that about 2,000 of them left Curaçao. Their number comprised about 50 percent of the labor population and thus sorely affected the labor situation at that time in their home country.

In the receiving country of Cuba, however, their number was relatively small in comparison with migrants from Haiti or Jamaica. Because of their small quantity they were hardly mentioned and remained for a long time virtually invisible in Cuban migration studies. Their small numbers, and the fact that some who had previously worked in Venezuela already knew some Spanish, made it sometimes easier for some of them to blend into Afro-Cuban cane-cutting culture.[3]

The age of migrants surely had an effect on how they absorbed the new culture. Even though improper record-keeping at that time makes it rather difficult for us to determine the average age of those migrating, according to the Cuban historian Moreno Fraginals (1978, 1983) the age range of the Caribbean migrants was about 18–45 years. This is further sustained by an author in a Curaçaoan newspaper of that time who claims that a large number of young boys were migrating to Cuba.[4] A large part of these migrants went during their formative years, which had consequences for their eventual settlement and integration into Cuba.

The level of cultural influence was further impacted by the fact that Curaçaoan–Cuban migration was circular. Many men would leave the island and return temporarily after the sugar-harvest finished and would make an impression on those remaining. Because of their renewed status as Cuban migrants, they were greatly respected by the Curaçaoan population of that time. As "Cubanos" (Cubans)—the way they identified themselves—they would speak Spanish, dance according to the newest dancing style, and display a new knowledge of music, which gave them a renewed social status and greater prestige in society.[5]

The returnee-stream intensified when Cuba was struck by the sugar crisis in 1921. After that year a large number of Curaçaoans returned each year. Documents fail to give exact figures regarding the returnees, who continued to flow out into the 1940s and even later. However, the newspaper La Union of April 23, 1925 mentioned that every parish on the island had made a list of names of workers who were still in Cuba at the time. Families were asked by the Catholic priests in their parishes to give the names and addresses of these men. The newspaper did not give precise figures, but calculated that about 500 to 600 Dutch workers were still in Cuba.

It is noticeable that returnees played an important role in the creation of a different culture in the Curaçaoan society. The cultural beliefs and practices they developed in Cuba were determined by the cultures of Cubans and fellow migrants from throughout the Caribbean. This interaction-process principally took place in the areas of work, recreation, and male–female relationship. Regarding the area of work, there seems to have been some relationship between Cuban migration and labor movements at that time. Most men who remained there until 1925 became members of the cane-cutting labor unions in Cuba. After that year Cuban labor unions were able to incorporate the labor migrants as members. Many were apprehensive of this influence on Curaçaoan returnees.[6] In the same article mentioned above (*La Union* April 23, 1925) this fear was apparent when it wrote that returnees were demanding better pay for their work. The article finished hoping that the government would soon do something for the Dutch workers stranded in Cuba, who were becoming "infected with the spirit of rebelliousness, which seems to be already bestowed in them." Most of the time returnees from Cuba were not favored as workers by the major companies on the island, as they were considered insolent or even immoral. Before some of these men were repatriated on government's account, their political records were checked (Paula 1973).

The migration had also some influence as to their spirituality. Here the interrelationship between traditional medical practices and religious beliefs and symbolism was very clear. When the migrants fell prey to mosquitoes and got ill, they were taken under the wings of local Cuban workers and visited traditional healers "kurandero," in whose powers they believed, more than those of the Western-trained medical doctors. Many developed their knowledge in this area as well. Until his death, one of the returnees cured people in Curaçao based on the knowledge of traditional medicine which he had acquired in Cuba.

Music, Cuban labor migration, and the reshaping of Curaçaoan identity

However, it was mostly in musical life that the Cuban migration was felt. In the interviews I had with the returnees from Cuba, parties and music-making were recurrent themes. They identified themselves as having been Cuban migrants through their music-making and dancing abilities. Those who had remained behind in Curaçao also emphasized these abilities as markers of identification of these men. People now in their fifties, who have heard about this migration from their elders hold the belief that most of these men had only migrated to Cuba to learn how to party and to make music. For the young, single, emigrant men in Cuba parties were a major leisure-time activity, sometimes even induced by the employers as a way to get those men to spend their hard-earned money.

"Raymundo" stated:

> Cuba is a place for people who like to party. That is why many left to Cuba and never returned. When you earn your salary you would go to a party. Two, three days of partying, because there are a lot of places to party. Uuuuuu! You will dance and dance.
>
> (Proj. Cubag. 55/1986)

Another interviewee said:

> There were many parties on Cuba. On the 24th of December the *noche buena* is the biggest. We would eat *lechón* (suckling pig). The Cubans

allowed you to go to their home-parties, if you were good. If you drank
and misbehaved, they would not. If you were serious, then they would.
There was also the color factor, but if you were good, they did not mind
and they treated you just as whites.

(Proj. Cubag. 4/1982)

The same interviewee emphasized segregation in those parties:

You know what I liked most, the dance of the whites. In Cuba there is
the dance of the colored and the dances of the whites. Colored, because
they don't say black. If there was a white dance you would go and
remain outside. What they served inside, what they ate and drank,
you would also get outside. Como no! Cuba is not the same as Curacao.
Very good.

(Proj. Cubag. 4/1982)

How then did these cane-cutters become involved in Cuban musical life? The answer
to this question becomes more urgent if we examine their position in the Cuba society
as "black migrant laborers." The main factor which determined the nature of their
absorption into the Cuban community was that of race. The massive migration of
African Curaçaoans to Cuba started 54 years after the abolition of slavery in the
Netherlands Antilles and about 35 years after large-scale slavery was abolished in Cuba.
It was during a period when both societies were adjusting from slave labor to free wage
labor but where socioeconomic relationships remained largely determined by racial
differences. Five years before they arrived in Cuba and under the presidency of
Gómez, African-Cubans revolted against the fact that members of the *Partido
Independiente de Color* (el PIC) were continually harassed and jailed as they were
believed to form a threat to the existing order, which denounced them as looking after
their own interest and not at that of the society. The revolt took place in the eastern
province where the Americans had a large part of their proprieties. The revolt went
along with a strike of some days, before the sugar harvest took place. Finally on June 27,
1912, the leader of the revolt, General Evaristo Estenoz was killed. In this uprising
3,000 Blacks died (Jenks 1970:115).

     The period of US military occupation of Cuba also complicated matters of race.
Even though Cuba had always favored the entry of solely white Europeans by law, as
a Caribbean country it knew a more fluid race relationship than the North American
typical bipolar racial order of Black/White. The Dutch emigrants entered Cuba in the
same year that the law barring Caribbean black laborers from entry in Cuba was
abolished. This decision was not the result of a more humanitarian attitude toward
people of African descent but a cynical strategy to oppress raging local labor conflicts
of the day. Cuban workers in the sugar industry were demanding better working
conditions and salaries to cope with the inflation of the First World War. The
Caribbean workers, on the other hand, coming from poorly developed countries,
were less demanding, and willing to work for less and in worse conditions than the
Cuban workers. As a result, the immigrants met with antagonism even from
Afro-Cubans. Middle-class Cubans also protested against such a large group of

Caribbean workers in Cuba, which according to them would mean the onset of re-Africanization of Cuba.

In Cuba, the Curaçaoan group thus became part of a large group of black emigrant workers in the eastern part of Cuba where at the turn of the twentieth century large sugar companies were established.[7] Many migrants when interviewed gave evidence of the hostility toward them as black migrants. One of them said in an interview how he bought a cup of coffee in a train, and when he had drunk the coffee the cup was broken openly so that the whites would know for sure that they would never have to drink from it.

The categorization of race based on skin color, hair texture, and facial features also manifested itself in the way the members of the Dutch migrants as a group were approached. Curaçaoans were called *holandeses negros* (black Dutch), the Arubans *holandeses blancos* (white Dutch), and the Bonairians *holandeses indio* (Indian Dutch). In that period due to their experience of slavery, African-Curaçaoans did not identify themselves by color and surely not as Africans. Any mention of the color black as identification was seen as an insult, something one could even take another person to court for. In their interaction with Cubans they would stress their identity as *Holandes*. The term "*Yo soy Holandes*" was utilized to distinguish oneself—especially from Haitian cane-cutters—who were most often victims of oppression in Cuba. By emphasizing this identity, they were able to gain a status apart from the Haitians, who were despised and severely discriminated against.

Given the panorama of racial discrimination mentioned above, the question of how Curaçaoans became involved in the musical life becomes more urgent. Some of them eventually mastered Cuban instruments so well that according to an informant even Cubans were astounded and respected them for that. Moore's (1997) book *Nationalizing Blackness. Afrocubanismo and Artistic Revolution in Havana, 1920–1940* might give us a lead.

Generally, he stated, the political repression of the African-Cubans had its effect on cultural life. After emancipation, African cultural expressions became more repressed, as they became more visible and hence more threatening (Moore 1997: 30). For example, the santeria ceremonies, ñáñigo and abakua ceremonies were criminalized and prohibited. However, in Cuba, music and dance have always been one of the democratic art forms accessible to people regardless of class and race. On the other hand art forms such as painting, literature, and poetry required more institutional training, school education, and a certain amount of literacy.[8]

Stories by the migrants also gave evidence of the easy accessibility to Cuban musical life in their work-sphere. Nicolaas Petrona explained that after work in their leisure time when they were sitting together, Curaçaoans and Cubans, a Cuban cane-cutter would start singing, for example, the *guaracha* transcribed below.[9] A characteristic of this type of song is improvisation, which was done by the Cuban, while the Curaçaoan, also familiar with improvising replied in a similar cunning way (Proj Cubag AAINA 6/1984).

The Cuban began:

> Esta mañana en la iglesia
> yo la vi una muchacha de Curazao
> Era una muchacha muy bonita

delegarita de cintura
Como me da gana enamorarla
le fui a preguntar a su madre
y su madre me lo dijo
que era chica todavía
yo dije a su madre
que la deja por si misma
porque era fea.

This morning in church/I saw a girl from Curaçao/Because I felt like making love to her/I went to her mother/The mother told me/That she was still young/I then told the mother/To keep her for herself/ As she was ugly
The Curaçaoan answered:

Sí, yo voy para Curazao
Yo no aguanto en Cuba mas
porque en Cuba se matan gente
porque en Cuba se comen gente

The Curaçaoan replied: I am returning to Curaçao/ I am not staying in Cuba/ Because in Cuba they kill people/ Because in Cuba they eat people

Most men recalled how Cubans taught them how to play instruments such as bongos,[10] tres,[11] and the marimbula.[12] The teaching of Cuban music was mostly done by Cubans who did not necessarily work in the same cane-field, but would pass by after work and play the guitar with the workers. Those who were interested would look and learn.

The genre of music learned was the *son*, which was popular in the eastern provinces, where most of the men stayed. Learning to play a musical instrument well and how to play Cuban music, the men were able to transcend certain barriers placed on them as black migrants and to acquire a new status. "Peter," in our interview with which we began, expressed this in the following manner:

> I also learnt to play the guitar in Cuba. One day we went to play at the home of a black driver. We were treated with great respect ... Hats were taken off. When I was playing they would throw money inside the guitar. While I played the coin would sound "poplok," poplok. I played the guitar so well that I was able to hold the guitar behind my neck and play. A man called Andres, a black man with a wooden leg, taught me how. I admired myself for that. When I left to Cuba I could not play anything. I also taught various Curaçaoans how to play.
>
> (Proj Cubag 10/1984)

Rethinking local identity

Returnees were instrumental in transmitting the knowledge of these musical forms and of dancing the Cuban *son* back in Curaçao. Their musical ability meant an important gain of status to them first in Cuba and later back home and it also aided their self-image. They transplanted their knowledge into different settings. It could occur, for instance, in the work-sphere. At the mining-company, which in the beginning of twentieth century was an important employer in Curaçao, and where many returnees worked and lived during the week, these men would play Cuban music after their shift. They would start playing the tres, and teach others how to dance.

Some men joined together and formed bands which played Cuban music when necessary at home-parties or at families in their neighborhood. In that way many local Curaçaoans were introduced to Cuban music and were taught to dance accordingly. Others played in public places, where especially those playing bongo were subjected to the same persecution that those who played the local drum (tambú) received.

Cuban music did indeed play an important role in Curaçaoan society during the twentieth century as is shown in an extensive survey done by Jappie Martijn (S. Martijn n.d.). In this period the "banda di bongo" (musical bands named after the bongo-drum) were very popular on the island. A large part of the musical repertoire of these band consisted of *son-montumo*,[13] and *guaguancó*.[14] These musical groups utilized African-derived instruments, before unknown in Curaçao, such as the marimba and the bongo.

"Juchi," for example, went to Cuba at the age of two in 1919 with his parents, where he learned how to play instruments such as the bongo and the marimbula. His father used to sing and his friends would pass by on Sundays and they would play the guitar and the bongo. Juchi returned at the age of 14 and formed a band and later a trio with Elkimo Candelaria and Sjaki de Windt. In particular they played songs of the Cuban trio Trio Matamoros (Proj. Cubag. 63/1991; see also Martijn n.d.: 38–39).

Thus, the impact of the returnees and the fact that Cuba globalized its culture in a very aggressive way led to an expansion of Cuban cultural influence in the Caribbean. The *son* was recorded on phonograph records in the early twentieth century and the radio soon broadcasted a variety of Cuban music, such as the *son*, guaguancó, rumba, mambo, and other types of music on the island. Even now, Cuban music is very popular in the weekly parties on the island, the so-called "fiesta di come-back." Thus, the significance of Cuban music in Curaçaoan society has by no means declined.

In conclusion, my chapter has examined inter-Caribbean migrations as an important factor in shaping a broader Caribbean cultural identity. In doing so, I hope that I have added another dimension to the discussions on the African Diaspora. In Cuba, migrants from Curaçao were reconnected both with people from other African Diaspora groups with cultural practices and beliefs they might have forgotten in the course of their history. Caribbean cultures thus are not solely shaped by their internal dynamics of a merging African, European, and sometimes Asian culture—but also by inter-Caribbean interactions, mostly as a result of migration.

Notes

1 This chapter is the result of an oral history project which I undertook in the 1980s (Allen 2001). I interviewed several Curaçaoan migrants who had gone to work in Cuba in the beginning of the twentieth century about their past experience. The interviews covered items such as the system of life before leaving Curaçao, their motives for leaving, their socio-cultural conditions in Cuba with reference to their working and living condition, contact

with Cubans and other emigrants, leisure time, health and spiritual life. Their testimonies helped to shed a different light on official documents. That said, for the study on Cuban migration, I also did extensive archival research both here in Curaçao as well as in Cuba. During my two field trips, each of one month, to Cuba, I was able to do archival research and interview some older "Hollandeses," as people from the Dutch Caribbean are still called in Cuba.

2 Some women had also migrated to Cuba. They went either alone or to accompany their spouses.

3 The two interviewees, Angel Martina and Nicolaas Petrona, knew some Spanish before they left to Cuba. Angel Martina could communicate easily with Cuban workers, as he had learned Spanish at school in the town of Curaçao. Nicolaas Petrona also knew some Spanish and based on his knowledge he was put at the head of a group of Curaçaoans much older than he at the time. He too knew quite a large repertoire of Cuban songs when I interviewed him.

4 *La Cruz*, April 3, 1919. The author pitied these boys who according to him were attracted to Cuba by all kinds of stories, but many of whom became disillusioned, disappointed, and trapped in their new home.

5 These stories of rapid economic self-betterment by men who had left earlier, during the sugar-boom in Cuba, inspired many to leave. An informant metaphorically said: "Those returning reported that in Cuba even lizards carried American dollars. Or they saw young boys who never wore leather shoes before walking around now wearing boots, suits of the latest fashion and sometimes even with dollar bills as handkerchiefs in their pockets."

6 Many interviews show that the workers from Cuba were less docile, more articulate, and no longer adhered to the existing pattern of respect toward landowners and others in power.

7 According to Moreno Fraginals in 1920 around 174,000 people from Haiti and Jamaica were brought into the newly developed sugar areas in the less populated provinces of Camaguey and Oriente in the eastern part of Cuba (Moreno Fraginals 1983: 101).

8 This was applicable to the Curaçaoan migrants as well. During my research I was able to find the name of only one returnee painter, Enrique Olario, who lived in Cuba for 51 years. He is known for his "naive style."

9 This type of song contained a special brand of humor and became popular in colonial times. It was forbidden in the press of the time because of the critical tone it adopted toward the oppressive policies of the Spanish government.

10 Two small drums joined by a piece of wood, it is held on the lap to play. It is played with the finger and palms (Fernández 1995: 181).

11 Three stringed guitar, typical of Cuba, mainly used in *son* and *punto guajiro*. (Fernández 1995: 184).

12 Many call this an African instrument (Fernández 1995: 184). It is bigger, but is similar in principle to the African one—the finger-piano. Its pitch and function have changed. In Africa the finger-piano normally supplies melo-rhythmic counterpoint, often to the singer, whereas in the Caribbean marimbula is used to provide a bass line.

13 A short repeating four- or eight-measure phrase based on a simple chord progression that contains the call and response portion of a piece (Charley Gerard 2001: 147).

14 A form of rumba in a mid- to fast-pace. If danced by a couple, these dances pantomime a man's efforts to seduce a woman and her repulsion of the man. The texts of the guaguancó are often comments on everyday life (Charley Gerard 2001: 146).

References

Allen, R. M. (2001) *Ta Cuba mi ke bai. Testimonio di trahadónan ku a emigrá for di Kòrsou bai Cuba na kuminsamentu di siglo XX*, Curaçao: Uitgeverij ICS Nederland/Curaçao.

Chamberlain, M. (ed.) (1998) *Caribbean Migration, Globalised Identities*, London: Routledge.

Fernandez, O. (1995) *Strings and Hide* (trans. Ester Mosak) Havana: ed. Jose Martí.

Gerard, Charley (2001) *Music from Cuba: Mongo Santamaría, Chocolate Armenteros and Cuban Musicians in the United States*, Westport, CT: Praeger Publishers.

Hannerz, U. (1992) *Cultural Complexity. Studies in the Social Organization of Meaning*, New York: Columbia University Press.

Jenks, Leeland Hamilton (1970) *Our Cuban Colony, A Study in Sugar*, New York: Arno Press and The New York Times.

Martijn, S. (n.d.) *Kòrsou Musikal. Un dokumentashon di nos historia musikal popular entre 1930 i 1989*, Curaçao: Promúsika.

Moore, R. (1997) *Nationalizing Blackness. Afrocubanismo and Artistic Revolution in Havana, 1920–1940*, Pittsburgh, PA: University of Pittsburgh Press.

Moreno Fraginals, Manuel (1978) *El ingenio, complejo económico social cubano del azúcar*, Havana: Editorial de Ciencias Sociales.

Moreno Fraginals, Mannel (1983) *La historia como arma y otros estudios sobre esclavos, ingenios y plantaciones*, Barcelona: Editorial Crítica.

Olwig, Karen Fog (1995) *Global Culture, Island Identity. Continuity and Change in the Afro-Caribbean Community of Nevi*, Reading, MA: Harwood Academic Publishers.

Paula, A. F. (1973) *Problemen rondom de emigratie van arbeiders uit de kolonie Curaçao naar Cuba, 1917–1937*, Curaçao: Centraal Historisch Archief.

Proj. Cubag. (1982–1991) An oral history project regarding Curaçaoans who migrated to Cuba, stored at the National Archives of the Netherlands Antilles.

Part III   Archaeology and living communities

12 The Cane River African Diaspora Archaeological Project

Prospectus and initial results

KEVIN C. MACDONALD, DAVID W. MORGAN,
AND FIONA J. L. HANDLEY

What remained was a core essence expressed in a walk, a gesture, a cadence, a blues song, or for food, an appreciation of a salty taste, a heated flavor, a leafy green sauce.

(Yentsch 1994: 210)

Introduction

For Americanist archaeologists, one of the key ways of engaging with the material culture of the African Diaspora has been through the search for retentions of African culture in the New World. While this has been somewhat successful in studies of contemporary music, language, and food, attempts to find "Africa" in the archaeological record have been insufficiently critical and at times under-informed (DeCorse 1999; Posnansky 1999; Hauser and DeCorse 2003). Indeed, up until recently, in almost any archaeological paper or book on the subject a recurring theme has been pinning the "smoking gun" of monolithic "African culture" on anything from pottery to clay pipes to chipped bottle glass. Today, these initial growing pains are dissipating, and the complexity of recognizing Diaspora material culture is being confronted (cf. Mouer *et al.* 1999; Singleton and Bograd 2000). Undoubtedly, the mission of African Diaspora archaeology is still evolving (see Jay B. Haviser and Kevin C. MacDonald, Chapter 1, in this volume).

What can Diaspora archaeology contribute? In our opinion, a key issue that realistically can be assessed is the comparative regional pacing of African cultural retention and syncretism, and eventual acculturation among the enslaved (cf. Herskovits 1958; Lovejoy 2000). Although Diaspora archaeology should, of course, take African culture as a central interest, a greater concern should be the understanding of new hybrid identities created in the New World. Thus the general thrust of this kind of archaeology is toward relationships *between* different groups at specific times, and the effects of these interactions as made evident in material culture. *De facto* this involves a broader agenda which may take the form of comparative studies

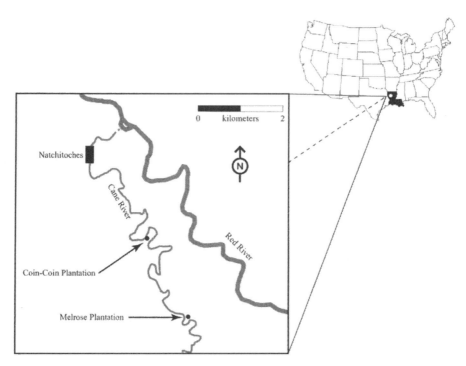

Figure 12.1 Map of the Cane River region with plantation locations.

of regional developments. For instance, one may pose questions concerning the comparative archaeological signatures of sites having slave populations of differing degrees of ethnic mixture (i.e. randomization—a practice adopted by slaveowners of purchasing slaves of diverse origins in order to discourage African affiliations and thus encourage the adoption of European language). This more complex understanding of identity involves a move away from essentialising notions of pure cultural transmission to the idea of ongoing responses to multivariate social circumstances.

Diaspora archaeology is an important witness to the inevitable and inexorable transformations that confronted culturally distinct African individuals and their descendants. African material culture retentions appear to have often been brief first-generation phenomenon, rapidly syncretised or assimilated. We are thus obliged to look for the evolution of cultural signals as those of African origin grow weak, or are reused in a new way, or are replaced over time. These issues lead us to consider a research agenda aimed at looking for gradations in "retention" or "syncretism" as being linked to a varied array of causal factors. Research questions become dependent on factors such as the ethnic mix of the enslaved at a particular plantation or regional group of plantations; their generational removal from Africa; their gender balance; their contact with indigenous groups; and of course the restrictions placed upon them by their regime of enslavement. These elements are the constants without which we cannot comparatively measure responses archaeologically. Without them we lack sufficient control to make sense of subtle dynamics within and between small communities in an archaeologically brief time frame.

In 2001, one of us (Kevin C. MacDonald) began to seek a region that would be suited to this sort of research agenda. Criteria included the presence of ethnically varied regimes of enslavement and temporally discrete sites where predominantly "first-generation" colonial contexts could be contrasted against "multi-generational" antebellum plantations. Other criteria included the presence of good documentation on the ethnicity of slaves and the organization of plantations to provide a comparative basis for archaeological fieldwork. With these considerations in mind, the Cane River region of northwestern Louisiana was chosen (Figure 12.1) and a varied team of researchers assembled (including both a West Africanist and a North Americanist).

The Cane River region

Cane River seems an ideal location to undertake Diaspora archaeology. Not only does it feature prominently in New World histories of colonialism and slavery, but it also has excellent documentary resources. Although there is by no means perfect archival preservation, in most instances it is comparatively easy to research the history of any of the eighteenth- and nineteenth-century plantations and houses that are the subject of the project, whether standing or destroyed. One may find the ethnic origin of sites' owners (French, African, Creole-of-Color, or Anglo-American), the demographic composition of their slaves (including ethnicity-region of birth in Africa, or place of birth in the New World), and sometimes even probate inventories of their grounds and houses. This means that we can compare diverse slave regimes and temporally discrete sites, for example, to contrast predominantly "first-generation" colonial contexts with antebellum mid-nineteenth-century plantations.

For these rich documentary resources we must thank the colonial officials of French Louisiana, who were especially meticulous in noting the ethnic origins of African slaves (Hall 1992). The buying and selling of slaves were recorded in detail and filed with notaries, who often noted the place of origin and ethnicity of the individuals sold. As a result of this record-keeping Gwendolyn Midlo Hall (2000) has recently released a CD-ROM containing the ethnic affinities of over 100,000 Louisiana slaves. There remain yet more records to be discovered in parish archives, and the existence of such a resource facilitates the sort of controlled Diaspora research we wish to undertake.

One subject that has been widely researched using these archives is the history of the Cane River "Creoles-of-Color." This ethnic group included both free and enslaved peoples of mixed French, Spanish, African-American, and Native American ancestry. More than any other area in continental America, antebellum Louisiana had a strong tradition of manumission for African and "mixed-race" slaves. Approximately 7,585 (one-sixth of the African-American population of Louisiana) were free by 1810, and this number increased to over 25,000 "Free People of Color" in the state by 1840 (Berlin 1974). Interestingly, some of these freed slaves went on to own slaves themselves. This adds another potential element to our research: was the survival or syncretism of African culture different at New World plantations owned by "Free People of Color" than at those owned by those of purely European descent?

Our research priorities have taken into consideration a variety of factors. First, one of our initial interests was investigating how people of different ethnic groups approached slave owning. Second, we were interested in sites where the ethnic affiliation of the slaves present was known. Finally, we also wanted to make an immediate contribution to the interests of the inhabitants of Cane River and to the research goals of the Cane River National Heritage Area. Out of a number of sites that we possibly could have covered, we chose to look in-depth at two sites in the first two years of the Cane River African Diaspora Archaeological Project that met these requirements. These are the *Maison de Marie Thérèse*, also known as the Whittington site (16NA241), and *Yucca Plantation*, now known as Melrose (16NA591).

Marie-Thérèse Coincoin

Fieldwork at the *Maison de Marie-Thérèse* began in 2001 with a program of field-walking and geophysical survey and was continued with test excavations in 2002. This property, though not open to the public, is on the National Register of Historic Places (NRHP) and is featured in *African American Historic Places* (Savage 1994). It is reputed to be the home of Marie-Thérèse Coincoin, a free African woman who received this land in 1786 and acquired at least 16 African slaves with whom she developed and expanded this 68-acre plantation.

Marie-Thérèse is today considered the matriarch of the Cane River "Creoles-of-Color," and most of the community's members can trace their ancestry back to her. Her story is legendary. Coincoin's descendants eventually became one of the wealthiest lineages on Cane River (Figure 12.2). They have been the subject of much historical research (Woods 1972; Mills and Mills 1973; Mills 1977) and continuing public and media interest (e.g., Tademy 2001). Unfortunately, the ancestry of Marie-Thérèse herself remains to be satisfactorily resolved.

According to Gary Mills (1977: 2–3) Marie-Thérèse, called Coincoin (or Coin-Coin), was born in 1742, the fourth child of a first generation slave couple baptised Francois and Marie-Francoise. However, the evidence leaves room for doubt. The putative Marie-Thérèse baptismal record in the Catholic Church archives of Natchitoches is dated August 24, 1742 and identifies the subject as "Marie-Therese, negritte." No parents are named, nor is the native name "Coincoin" mentioned (cf. E. Mills 1977). Given that Marie-Thérèse (or Marie-Thereze) was a common slave name in the Natchitoches colony, and that the stated owners—the St Denis family— were the largest slaveowners in the colony, this record is hardly definitive. Furthermore, in her 1972 book on the oral traditions and sociology of the Creole Coincoin/Metoyer family (to whom she gave the pseudonym of Letoyant), Sister Frances Jerome Woods quotes an informant as placing Marie-Thérèse's birthplace in "Guinea" (Woods 1972: 32). To add to the confusion, the Gwendolyn Midlo Hall's (2000) African-American ethnic origins database opts inexplicably for "Nago, Yoruba" as the cultural point of origin for Marie-Thérèse Coincoin.

Figure 12.2 Painting of an unidentified granddaughter of Marie-Thérèse Coincoin. (Courtesy of Northwestern State University, Watson Memorial Library, Cammie G. Henry Research Center, oil portrait on display).

Scholars and descendants are also divided as to the significance of the word Coincoin. Mills asserts that the etymology of Coincoin may be connected with "Ko Kwé" in Ewe (Togo), meaning second daughter. People also have suggested it refers to an African forename, an African family name, the sound a duck makes (implying a youthful tendency to prattle), and others. Here it is instructive to explore colonial era naming patterns among Christians from Kongo (both in Kongo and Brazil). Heywood (2002: 103) notes that,

> Africans incorporated in Angola's mixed Afro-Catholic culture had names that reflected the interpenetration of Christian and African customs … [Such names] combined African titles and names with full Portuguese names, or contained two Christian names (a common practice among African converts) … Here again, enslaved Africans carried to the Americas brought these Creole naming patterns with them.

This citation is not meant to add yet another possible point of origin (Kongo/Angola) to the Coincoin mystery, but to illustrate that the retention of African names (often clan/family names rather than forenames) was common in the early Diaspora, and that with "Coincoin" we are unlikely to be dealing with onomatopoeia. Indeed,

Hall (1992: 407–412) contains an entire appendix on "Evidence of Widespread Survival of African Names in Colonial Louisiana." What remains to be undertaken is a sweeping linguistic search through the hundreds of ethnies known to have been brought into Colonial Louisiana.

So, at present there is no consensus as to the birthplace or ethnic origin of Marie-Thérèse Coincoin. Her date of birth also remains uncertain though documents from her later life indicate that she was born around 1740, give or take five years (Mills 1977).

The history of Marie-Thérèse becomes more apparent as we reach her more mature years. It is known that she originally was owned by Louis Juchereau de St Denis, founder of Natchitoches. She remained a slave until 1778 when she was purchased and freed by Claude Pierre Metoyer, a French bourgeois by whom she had borne several children. He ended their alliance in 1786 with a gift of 68 acres of land astride the Cane River on which she built a house, which is clearly indicated on a 1794 property map, and began to cultivate tobacco. The last documentary record of Coincoin was long thought to be the settlement of her estate via property transfers to her children in 1816. However, during the course of the 2001 season of fieldwork a close examination of the 1820 census records by Rolonda Teal (of Northwestern State University of Louisiana) revealed that Marie-Thérèse remained on or not far from her original property between 1816 and 1820. The 1820 census account is important first because it demonstrates that we can still learn more about Marie-Thérèse from documentary sources, and second because it refutes one of the "legends" of the area. The latter recounts how, after selling her house in 1816, Marie-Thérèse immediately moved to her son Louis' property at what is now Melrose Plantation. While it is still conceivable that she relocated in her last years to Louis' home, this would have been in the early 1820s and Coincoin would have been in her eighties.

Marie-Thérèse's attitude to slavery seems contradictory: she worked hard in the first years after manumission to buy the freedom of all of her children who remained in bondage. Despite this, when her means allowed in later life, she purchased and kept slaves. A 1790 church tax list indicates that she owned no slaves at that time, but by the time of the settlement of her estate in 1816, we know that she had 14 slaves and had previously owned at least two more according to earlier church baptismal records. The Notorial Records for the spring of 1816 state that, of Marie-Thérèse's known 16 slaves: three were of the "Congo nation," one was of the "Quissay [or Kissy] nation" (of modern Sierra Leone) and the remainder were Louisiana born. It seems likely that the Louisiana-born individuals were the first-generation offspring of the four Africa-born individuals. Indeed, only four slave purchases are recorded for Marie-Thérèse Coincoin in the index of French records: two in 1794 and two in 1800. One well documented slave is Marguerite, noted in the sale record of 1816 as being 45 years of age and of the Congo nation. Her African origin is also supported by her baptism as an adult on December 20, 1809. She must have been one of the first slaves Marie-Thérèse bought as Marguerite was recorded in parish records as belonging to Coincoin at the baptism of her son Joseph in 1797.

To summarize, Marie-Thérèse and her slaves were probably only one generation removed from Africa at the most. The African families of her plantation would have shared Congo and Kissy cultural elements, some of which would have been passed to their children. Additionally, there also would have been input from the African ancestry of Marie-Thérèse herself, and the effect of French culture, represented by Marie-Thérèse's half-French children. This knowledge enhances our possibilities for detecting elements of these discrete identities in our excavations. The mixed African and French make-up of this family raises important perspectives on the nature of slave ownership and in particular, the extent to which their African ancestry had a bearing on the way they interacted with their slaves.

Yucca/Melrose Plantation

The second property we investigated is Melrose Plantation, formerly known as Yucca Plantation. It is registered as a National Historic Landmark, is open to the public, and receives the highest number of visitors to a plantation site in the area. As was mentioned above, the *Maison de Marie-Thérèse* is not open to the public, but because of Melrose's connections with Marie-Thérèse, her story is one of the site's main interpretative themes. The plot on which the present day antebellum home is built was purchased by Louis Metoyer, second son of Marie-Thérèse, in 1796. Louis was one of three highly successful plantation-owning descendents of Marie-Thérèse and Pierre Metoyer. Interestingly, two of these chose to employ their father's surname of Metoyer (Augustine and Louis) while the third (Dominique) for many years retained the surname of his mother and was styled "Dominique Coin-Coin." That this might also have implied certain cultural choices is a seductive notion.

The big house, which forms the focus of the current property, was not built by Louis Metoyer until 1833 (Figure 12.3). Other structures are reputed to be earlier in date. This was a large plantation, eventually utilizing more than 50 slaves, and it remained in the Metoyer family until the 1840s. Henry and Hypolite Hertzog, wealthy local Anglo-French planters, then owned the property for the remainder of the antebellum period, selling it to Francis Roman Cauranneau in 1881. The Henry family, Anglo-Americans, were the last private owners of the property, and for a time it functioned as an artist colony under the guidance of Cammie Henry.

Using archival data we can plot the rise and decline of the Metoyer's Yucca Plantation. By 1810, 15 slaves labored on this land. This number increased to 23 in 1820, and rose to 54 in 1830 in the final decade of Louis Metoyer's life. The slave population at Yucca peaked in 1838 at 65 individuals. By 1843 Louis's grandson Theophile had 33 slaves. The plantation never again attained its former size, and in 1850, by which time it had passed into the hands of the Hertzog family, only 35 slaves were present.

As might be expected with a proportionally larger plantation system, construction of slave genealogies has been more difficult at Yucca than at the Coincoin property. Initial indications are for a greater mix of birthplaces and ethnic origins at this property. Some slaves were brought from elsewhere in the USA, such as those purchased in 1811 from Robert Bell, a slave trader from Tennessee. While slaves imported from other regions in the USA are not always clear in the records, this

Figure 12.3   The second Big House of Melrose (aka Yucca) Plantation, the earliest elements of which were constructed in 1833 (photo: Jack Boucher, Historic American Buildings Survey, US National Park Service).

pattern of buying is demonstrated remarkably through the name of one of the slaves—"Tennessee." Additionally, we do have a number of sales records from 1816 when Louis Metoyer acquired Charlotte, a 30-year-old of the Caukau nation (presumably Kaka from the area of modern Nigeria), Babette, a 45-year-old from "Guinée," and Marie, a 20-year-old from the Congo nation. There are still other records that indicate the purchase of native Africans without specifying their ethnic origin, and others specifying purchased slaves as "creoles of this place" (i.e. Louisiana born).

One important document available to us is the 1838 succession file of Jean-Baptiste Louis Metoyer, which inventories all of his property, and records that 65 slaves were then present at the site. Some were owned by Jean-Baptiste Louis with his wife, with others being owned by his father's widow and by his son. This would suggest that a large percentage of the slaves there were originally owned by Louis Metoyer, and indeed, our research has supported this. Charlotte and Marie were both present in the inventory, but Babette was not recorded. Marianne, noted in the inventory as aged 60, was first recorded as Louis' slave in the baptism record of her daughter Marie Jeanne, who also appears in the inventory, now as the mother of two young children. Accompanying the succession document are a series of invoices that suggest some of the activities in which slaves were involved. For instance, Zenon was hired out with a plough for 98 days to Mr. St. Geoffrey for $13.61 in September 1838. In October of that year we know that the occupants of Yucca ordered goods from town and other plantations that were collected by Cesaire, Hilaire, and Marie. On one day alone, slaves from Melrose collected goods worth $62.25—a substantial amount of money in 1838. Since these slaves were running errands they were probably not field hands. This, and their high value (Cesaire was priced at $1,600, Hilaire at $1,700), would indicate they had a special status. The inventory of objects reveals not only much of what would be expected on a working farm—ox carts, spades, mill stones—but also clues to more specific activities: there was a forge, valued at $25, and a slave blacksmith, Frederick, valued at $1,400.

Documentary research undertaken on these two properties has provided valuable context against which to evaluate results from our excavations. Although our fieldwork is still ongoing, we will attempt below to draw some patterns from initial results of the 2001 and 2002 field seasons.

Results from the 2001/2002 field seasons

In August of 2001 we began our field investigations at the plantation Marie-Thérèse established along Cane River in 1786 and at Yucca/Melrose Plantation, the 1796–1847 plantation of Louis Metoyer, Coincoin's second son, and his descendents. At both sites the standing structures, steeped in folklore, served as an initial spatial framework for our inquiries. Our immediate goals were to re-establish the historical layout of the original plantation's out-buildings, most of which were no longer standing, in order to target dependencies such as slave cabins and kitchens for more extensive excavation. Our initial work, using both resistivity and magnetometry, identified promising subsurface anomalies at both sites that we then tested in summer 2002.

Fieldwork at the Maison de Marie-Thérèse
Some three decades ago, when historical research into the original property of Marie-Thérèse Coincoin began, her plantation had already been divided into several separate properties. However, it had been "generally accepted that the Whittington house site [was] the original and only house of Marie Therese" (Shaw 1983: 6) (Figure 12.4). This conclusion remained academically unchallenged until immediately prior to our fieldwork in 2001, when work by the Historic American Buildings Survey cast doubt on the age of the standing structure. They dated this Creole cottage to no earlier than the 1830s on the basis of nail chronology and a few stylistic features (Wilson 2001). Thus, in addition to our original research questions, we had unwittingly entered into a debate on the authenticity of the "Maison de Marie-Thérèse."

The Whittington site, as the locality surrounding the Creole cottage is officially known, was first tested in 1978–1979 by H. F. Gregory, B. Shaw, and J. H. Mathews (Mathews 1983; Shaw 1983). Today, the limits of this locality conform to the modern Henry Earl Metoyer property. The goal of the original test excavations was primarily to confirm the age of the standing structure for the purposes of having it placed on the NRHP. An extensive subsurface investigation of the area surrounding this dwelling included ca.19 m^2 of excavations and 29 shovel tests. The results were disappointing. No subsurface features were encountered, save a putative brick walkway and extensive

Figure 12.4   The Whittington/Metoyer House (photo: David Morgan).

sheet middens with only a handful of French faience sherds (diagnostic of eighteenth-century occupation) amidst a mass of whitewares (diagnostic of mid-nineteenth century and subsequent occupation) (Mathews 1983: 23–31, table 5). Likewise their work yielded no Native American or Afro-colonoware potsherds—common accompaniments to European wares at many American Colonial sites. However, finds subsequently made in a flowerbed being dug near the house, and surface collections made around the property, produced additional faience sherds. These were used in 1979 to support the listing of the property in the NRHP as the original dwelling place of Marie-Thérèse Coincoin. The feeling was that somehow the main eighteenth-century middens and dependencies had been barely missed by the original test excavation programme.

Our initial geophysical survey concentrated on the area tested by the 1970s excavations. We encountered three anomalies southwest of the standing structure that we tested in 2002. The results of our excavations produced similar findings to the excavations of the 1970s. Our anomalies proved to be either twentieth-century trash-burning areas or mid-nineteenth-century sheet middens. Only a single small eighteenth-century sherd was found among hundreds from the nineteenth and twentieth centuries. We were mystified. The idea that the standing structure was at least on the footprint of the historic Maison de Marie-Thérèse seemed reasonable. So, even if we had not located any outbuildings, should we not find at least some scatter of artifacts associated with her household? Puzzled, we returned to the master's theses of Billy Shaw (1983) and James Matthews (1983) that reported the results of the original 1978–1979 fieldwork.

In Shaw's (1983: 14–16, 22) thesis we discovered that the pottery consisted of 1,421 sherds collected from the ground surface over a four-year period with little to no contextual control, with the exception of 308 that came from the "south side of the house." An unspecified amount was obtained through "contract testing" of the site carried out by Gregory (Shaw 1983: 16), and 219 had no provenience at all. Shaw and his fellow students excavated an additional six test pits and fourteen shovel tests to recover a further 312 sherds. Shaw (1983: 40–41, table 3) concluded that 4.4 percent of the collection was faience that might date around 1760, and that 33 percent of the collection dated 1760–1830. The latter included sherds identified as undecorated pearlwares, undecorated creamwares, shell-edged wares, and Dutch Goudy handpainted wares. The faience and creamwares, noted the author (Shaw 1983: 40–41), "came almost exclusively from the surface collection south of the house or from features five and six [the flowerbed]," and elsewhere Shaw (1983: 21) stated that "all but two of the eighteenth century artifacts … were discovered in feature five and six by the owner of the property."

Matthews (1983: 30–31) clarifies the picture. He states that the garden features were located after the main excavations. Prior to their discovery of the garden feature, "artifacts from the excavations had suggested that the site was not settled before 1820 or 1830." Matthews (1983: 30–31) continues, stating, "Only four faience sherds had been found," and that "All of the other faience, creamware, and Rouen sherds in the Coincoin artifact counts … were removed by either Dr Whittington while digging the [flower]bed or by the author sometime later."

To summarize, two to four faience sherds were excavated somewhere on the property during the 1978 and 1979 fieldwork, and the only other provenanced eighteenth-century sherds were discovered by the property owner in a garden after the formal field season ended. Excavation of this enigmatic and undocumented pair of features apparently yielded the 86 sherds that Shaw assessed as eighteenth-century pottery.

Our three units, like those placed systematically around the property and even under the house in the 1970s, yielded nothing like that which came from the garden. The eighteenth-century material apparently was restricted to this tiny, specialized pair (?) of features. We therefore overlaid the Matthews (1983: 28, figure 7)/Shaw (1983: figure 1) site sketch map on our own transit-derived map to determine where the garden features were located, and H. F. Gregory confirmed we were in the correct general area. Then we excavated Unit W, a 0.5 × 2 m trench, across the estimated area of Feature 5/6, and again discovered nothing but mid-nineteenth-century and twentieth-century artefacts.

Subsequently, we created overlay maps of the original 1794 land survey and modern property maps, and eyed with increasing suspicion the mismatch between the placement of the Marie-Thérèse house on the 1794 survey and the emplacement of the current standing structure (Figure 12.5). What we originally had thought to have been acceptable surveyor error, given the epoch and its methods, now seemed significant: the 1794 map showed the Marie-Thérèse house 50–100 m northeast of the current structure, outside of the bounds of the current Metoyer property, on land currently owned by the Bouser family. Consequently, with the Bouser's kind permission, we undertook field-walking, shovel-testing, and test excavations in the area indicated by the 1794 survey. We found that the original 1794 surveyor, Pierre Maes, had been very accurate indeed.

The dearth of eighteenth-century finds from south of the modern Metoyer/Bouser property line became a veritable flood to the north of it (Figure 12.6). Indeed, on the

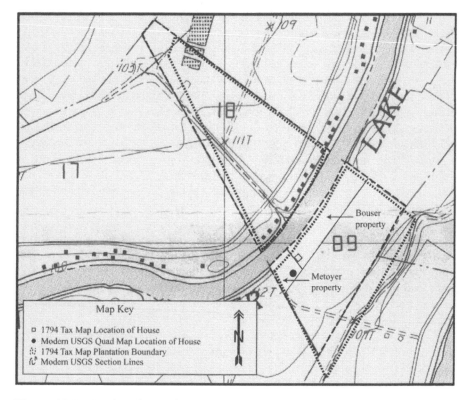

Figure 12.5 Overlay of original 1796 survey map (Northwestern State University, Watson Memorial Library, Cammie G. Henry Research Center, Map Collection, number 120) with modern topography and property boundaries.

modern Metoyer property (which surrounds the standing structure) the mean ceramic date given using South's (1977) method was 1883, while that of the modern Bouser property (site of the 1794 surveyed structure) yielded a mean ceramic date of 1797. Here we found three major categories of eighteenth-century diagnostic artefacts: French faience wares (*faience brune* in the Rouen Plain style being dominant, dating to ca. 1760–1800), low-fired coarse earthenwares, and hand-wrought nails (Figure 12.7). We also had other late eighteenth- to early nineteenth-century finds: handpainted polychrome pearlwares, plain pearlwares, and creamwares. In contrast we found virtually no mid-nineteenth-century or modern artefacts (only 3 percent of total surface and test excavation finds). Miraculously, it seems that the vicissitudes of time had left this area relatively untouched since its abandonment. Thus, only 50 m northeast of the current standing structure was a zone of ca. 40 × 60 m with a high density of finds indicating a late eighteenth to early nineteenth century homestead—the missing *Maison de Marie-Thérèse*.

Our test excavations indicate that this area still has a stratigraphy of at least 50 cm, including surviving subsurface features. In particular we found the edge of a shallow trash pit containing pig bones associated with low-fired earthenwares. Low-fired earthenwares such as these merit extensive investigation. Were they made by the

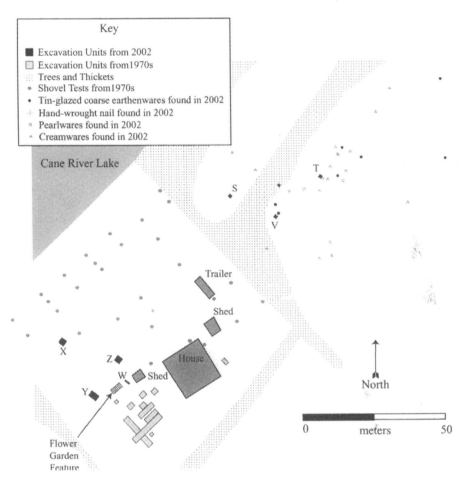

Figure 12.6 Plan of the Whittington (Marie-Thérèse Coincoin) site, showing archaeological investigations between 1978 and 2002, including the cluster of eighteenth-century artifacts found northeast of the present house.

Kongo or Kissy slaves of Marie-Thérèse—or do they reflect trade with neighbouring Caddoan Indian groups? Alternatively, do they reflect a variety of manufacturers with potential shared technological expertise between groups? Initial work has been able to place these ceramics in at least three broad categories:

1 undecorated shell tempered sherds (n = 67);

2 incised, combed, and plain reduced (black) sherds tempered with bone (n = 5);

3 plain and incised sand and/or grog tempered (n = 19).

Some of the sherds in these categories have immediate parallels with Native American traditions extant during the Colonial era. The first category is often described in Americanist literature as varieties of "Bell Plain" and "Mississippi Plain"

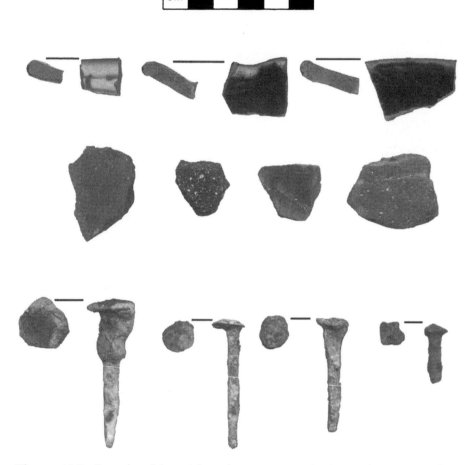

Figure 12.7 Example of late eighteenth-century to early-nineteenth-century artifacts recovered northeast at what is now thought to be the original Marie-Thérèse Coincoin house site (left to right).

Top row: Indeterminate blue on white tin-glazed earthenware (shovel test #32, level 2); Rouen Plain (surface collection #27; Unit S, context 3);

Middle row: Mississippi Plain *variety Unspecified* (shovel test #32, level 2; Unit V, context 5; Unit T, context 3; Unit T, context 5);

Bottom row: Hand-wrought nails (shovel Test #4, level1; shovel test #54, level 1 and 2; shovel test #6, level 2 Unit S, context 2).

(Phillips 1970: 58–59, 130–131). Compared to the early 1700s Caddoan Indian site of Lambre Point (16NA544), located about 3 km from Whittington, they are similar in terms of temper, firing techniques, and thickness (Morgan and MacDonald, in press). Other historic period Caddoan ceramic assemblages in Natchitoches Parish also are characterized by high frequencies of shell temper and low frequencies of decoration, so hypothesizing a Native American affiliation for the majority at this juncture seems reasonable.

The second category appears to represent Chickache Combed, a type attributed to Choctaw potters (Collins 1927; Voss and Blitz 1988; Galloway 1995). The presence of Choctaw wares at local sites of the late 1700s and early 1800s is not unexpected, considering the Choctaw began moving into Louisiana after the mid-eighteenth century and were particularly numerous after the first quarter of the nineteenth century, so much so that they overwhelmed other native ethnic groups demographically by the mid-1800s (Kniffen *et al.* 1987: 84–85). Chickache Combed has been found at other historic American Indian sites in the area, as well as among the Caddoan-related pottery present in great quantities at the Spanish border fort Los Adaes (16NA16) (H. F. Gregory personal communication).

The third category of pottery, while possessing a fabric common to Native American assemblages in southern USA in late *prehistory*, is scarce or absent at local *historic* period Native American sites (Morgan and MacDonald, in press). Although our sample size is a limiting factor, this third category of plain sand- and grog-tempered pottery—forming 21 percent of the Whittington site collection—may be of African-American manufacture.

These initial results indicate that Marie Thérèse was interacting with native populations, and may also indicate that her slaves were producing a limited quantity of their own pottery. Future planned excavations will investigate both this phenomenon and spatial patterning at the site with a mind to documenting the nature of inter-ethnic relations at this locality. The potential implications of our preliminary findings will be discussed after our presentation of results from the 2001 and 2002 seasons at Yucca/Melrose.

Fieldwork at Yucca/Melrose Plantation

In 2001 we faced at Melrose Plantation a similar situation to that at the Whittington site: how to determine where we might find slave quarters and outbuildings at which slaves worked? Unlike the Coincoin Plantation, at Melrose we had an idea of what to expect in terms of architecture. We knew 65 slaves worked Melrose during its 1830s economic peak, suggesting we might be searching for a number of slave dwellings, perhaps 10 or more. The documents also attest to the presence of at least one forge worked by an African-American blacksmith. Lastly, two original structures dated to 1796 still stand on the plantation, as do three more built in the early 1800s, providing us a working set of landmarks. These have been moved over time, but an aerial photograph from 1957 and a property map from 1877 have helped us document the past locations of these and other structures (Figure 12.8).

The land, reportedly granted to Louis Metoyer in 1796, spanned the north and south sides of Red River, the waterway that today is Cane River Lake (Mills 1977). However, the majority of Metoyer's land lay north of the river. The 1877 map, 1957 photograph, and oral traditions indicate that most post-emancipation plantation buildings were located on the north side. These buildings include the five remaining structures, along with a now destroyed overseer's house, gin, mill, and sharecroppers' cabins. An additional gin, a stable, and a house are shown south of the river on the

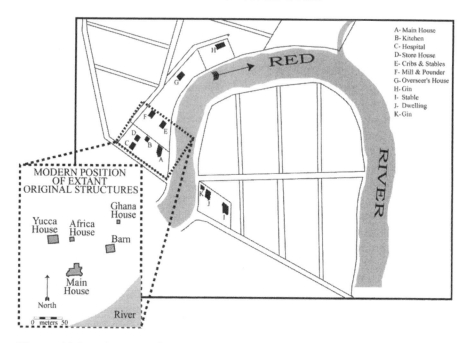

Figure 12.8 Adaptation of 1877 Hertzog map of Melrose Plantation showing modern building locations inset.

1877 map. Because most of the buildings were north of the river, and because recent housing developments have probably destroyed the integrity of the plantation area south of the river, we focused our search on the north side.

The five structural landmarks on the northern portion of the property consist of Yucca House, reputed to have been built as Louis Metoyer's first Big House in 1796; Africa House, also built ca.1796 for storage; Ghana House, a slave cabin of the early 1800s; a barn built in the early 1800s; and the current Big House, a two-story residence constructed for Louis Metoyer in 1833 and modified extensively by later residents. These five form what we refer to as the "core plantation."

All are visible on the 1957 aerial photograph, and all but Ghana House are marked clearly on the plan of the property drawn in 1877 when the land passed into the hands of the Hertzog family. In Ghana's place stood a "Mill & Pounder," agreeing with local tradition that Ghana House was a local slave cabin moved to the property by Cammie Henry in the early twentieth century. Judging from the map and photo, there were no structures in the fields and groves surrounding the plantation core, an observation that matches traditional verbal descriptions of the plantation layout. The one exception was the area east of the core along the historic road paralleling Cane River Lake. The 1877 and subsequent maps depict the overseer's house and agricultural labourers' cabins in this particular location.

Based on this information we targeted our efforts in two vicinities. First, we surveyed the entire historic core of the property, reasoning that dependencies would be located within a kilometer of the original main house, south of the backswamp, and north of the historic river-road. Second, we surveyed adjacent to the river-road east of the core, where the overseers' house was featured on the 1877 plan, and where a line of sharecropper's cabins stood until the 1960s. We speculated that the placement of these cabins might echo an older plantation layout in which the dwellings of the enslaved were situated outside the main cluster of work buildings and main house, along the high ground of the natural levee, and adjacent to the overseer's house.

At Melrose we used the same geophysical survey techniques as we did at the Whittington site. To rule out anomalies caused by modern debris we compared our results with our field observations, discussed our findings with local informants, and compared our results with an engineer's map of the modern utility lines, drain fields, and other features. In the historic core we identified three anomalies that warranted further investigation and that are discussed in detail below.

Along the historic road east of the core we augmented geophysical survey with pedestrian survey. We visually inspected the ground surface of a roughly 250 hectare area north of the road by walking 50 transects spaced 5 m apart. We pin-flagged and mapped the locations of 135 artefacts. When the locations were displayed as a plot map they formed four discrete clusters (Figure 12.9). That nearest the historic core corresponds to the location of the overseer's house shown on the 1877 map. That farthest from the core probably corresponds to the location of the cotton gin shown on the same document. The two clusters between them probably represent individual sharecroppers' cabins documented in the twentieth century by photographs. All four clusters were associated primarily with pottery types manufactured between the early nineteenth and twentieth centuries (e.g. whiteware, ironstone, Fiestaware, Albany-glazed stoneware, and polychrome transfer printed wares), along with some whose earliest production began in the last decades of the eighteenth century (e.g. creamware, pearlware).

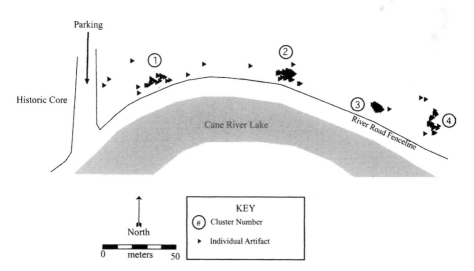

Figure 12.9   Finds distribution from surface survey east of the historic core of Melrose. These clusters are thought to represent the sites of late-nineteenth-century sharecroppers' cabins, and potentially, also the sites of earlier slave cabins.

In 2002 we began our work by targeting one major anomaly from the historic core identified in the previous year (Figure 12.10). North of the ca.1800 barn was an intense gradiometer signal spanning about 9 m², a reading we thought might represent the furnace and metal debris associated with the forge. To ground-truth the intense gradiometer signal we excavated four 2×2 m units arranged as a single block with 50 cm balks between units (Units A1–A4). Initial finds were promising, as we recovered several pieces of slag from the upper levels of the units. Our hopes lifted even higher when we found photographs showing the barn and an adjacent structure identified in the caption as 'the smithy' in Cammie Henry's scrapbooks (held in the Cammie G. Henry Research Center, Watson Memorial Library, Northwestern State University of Louisiana). It soon became apparent, however, that our four units were centered over a large depression filled with early-to-mid-twentieth-century debris, including rolls of baling wire, heaps of paint cans, a large pipe, and the leaf spring of an early automobile. Informants later told us that one of the Henry's may have used the area behind the barn in the 1920s as a mechanic's workshop. It certainly would explain our finds and the intense magnetometry signal. The feature unfortunately filled three-quarters of our units and presumably destroyed whatever was once located north of the barn, including the smithy.

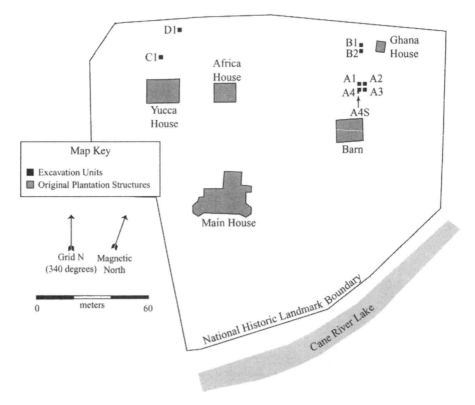

Figuer 12.10   Locations of the summer 2002 excavations in the historic core of Melrose Plantation.

Other anomalies—one behind Yucca house and another near Ghana house—also were found to be disturbances from the Henry era. That behind Yucca proved to be a sundial foundation, while the one near Ghana was the base of a water tower. A final anomaly situated 20 m north of Yucca house was tested and proved to be a gravel road that our informants later recalled as having lain at the boundary between the yard and cultivated fields.

We were unsatisfied with our excavation results. Thus, in December 2002 (in cooperation with Aubra Lee of Coastal Environments, Inc.) we made use of restoration work at Yucca House—thought to be the plantation's first Big House and the earliest structure north of the river—to conduct additional excavations around its perimeter, under its sills, and beneath its floors. We found evidence of the house's construction sequence and ample midden debris. Our findings and the dating of this structure will be discussed more fully elsewhere (Morgan et al. 2003; MacDonald et al. 2006). For this chapter it is sufficient to point out that, as elsewhere on the property, we found no certain evidence of African material culture or subfloor caches, nor any spatial patternings sometimes associated with Africa-derived spiritual practices. Thus, even when compared with local French Colonial plantations (see below) Yucca/Melrose is curiously lacking in obvious African cultural manifestations despite its reputation as a center of Afro-American heritage (e.g. Jones 1985: 201–204; Savage 1994) and despite its partially African-American ownership.

Discussion and conclusions

Our initial archaeological findings, primarily ceramic analyses, indicate an interesting pattern regarding the cultural choices made by African-American slaveowners in the Cane River region. The coarse earthenware at the Coincoin plantation comprises 47.5 percent of the excavated assemblage (n = 95 of 202 sherds). We believe these earthenware sherds represent vessels manufactured by American Indians and/or enslaved Africans and their descendants. The inhabitants of Yucca, in contrast, used refined earthenwares manufactured commercially in Europe and in America almost exclusively (99.9 percent of the assemblage). Such single-mindedness regarding ceramic usage is unusual even for contemporary French plantations. For example, low-fired earthenwares or "colonowares" comprise 7 percent (n = 75 of 1,071 sherds) of the old kitchen assemblage (ca. 1766–1808) at the Prudhomme-Roquier house (16NA240) in nearby Natchitoches (Matthews 1983). As another example, they form 21 percent (n = 1,733) of the circa 1790 to 1840s Robleau (16DS380) homestead in the Bayou Na Bonchasse community located north of Natchitoches (Girard 2002: 14–51).

This is not, as we intimated in the introduction, the "smoking gun" of an overt Africanism, but rather a subtle indication of the way in which African culture was negotiated by Coincoin's descendants or at least by her son Louis Metoyer. The virtual absence of African cultural evidence in Louis Metoyer's plantation debris, while so appreciably evident at his mother's plantation, may reflect Metoyer's effort to distance himself from his African heritage by controlling the kinds of vessels used in his residence and by his slaves. In her controversial study of the Metoyer family, Sister Frances Jerome Woods (1972: 33) observed that,

> [The Metoyers] were motivated to acquire the same status symbols as their prestigious white contemporaries: large plantations with spacious homes, exceptionally large slaveholdings, speculation in investments of capital, and a reputation as devout and loyal adherents to the church of the original French settlers.

The implication is that marginalized Creoles-of-Color, so as to protect their tenuous social position, had to be "more French than the French." In the case of Marie-Thérèse Coincoin's plantation we are dealing with both a slightly earlier time period and a woman of unmixed race, perhaps from the continent of Africa itself. During the eighteenth century, Cane River's Creoles-of-Color had neared a social par with French Creoles. However, after the 1803 Louisiana Purchase and its associated influx of Americans to Cane River, Creoles-of-Color and more recently freed slaves suffered a gradual decline in social standing. "Black" and "white" became rigid, mutually exclusive cultural constructs, and were no longer potentially ambiguous or even permeable social categories.

Other circumstantial evidence also may pertain. For instance, Coincoin's male children who assumed their father's French surname, such as Augustin Metoyer, are considered important founding members of the Cane River Creole community, whereas those who did not, such as Dominique Coincoin, have remained relatively obscure historical figures. Also, Marie-Thérèse Coincoin's burial site is unknown, while Augustin's is prominently marked by a large mausoleum outside of the Catholic church he founded. Lastly, Augustin and other descendants are celebrated in nearly life-size oil portraits, whereas no recorded images of Coincoin are known. To this end, Woods (1972: 45) noted of the Metoyer family that, "The affectional ties between Marie [-Thérèse] and her children must not have been sufficiently strong to counteract her children's desire to obliterate her memory."

In short, by 1820 it may have become socially, politically, and economically expedient to divorce oneself from vestiges of African heritage. One way in which this milieu may have manifested itself archaeologically was through the rapid disappearance of low-fired earthenwares from "Creole-of-Color" plantations. This chapter is only a first effort at unravelling archaeologically the ethnically and socially complex antebellum Cane River region, but it already shows that material culture has the potential to make a real contribution to understanding the evolution of human relations in the time of American slavery.

Acknowledgments

Our work along Cane River has been funded by grants from the British Academy, The Institute of Archaeology (University College London), the US National Park Service's Delta Initiative, and the Cane River National Heritage Area.

References

Berlin, I. (1974) *Slaves without Masters: The Free Negro in the Antebellum South*, New York: The New Press.

Collins, H. B. (1927) "Potsherds from Choctaw village sites in Mississippi," *Journal of the Washington Academy of Sciences*, 17: 10.

DeCorse, C. R. (1999) "Oceans Apart: Africanist Perspectives on Diaspora Archaeology," in T. A. Singleton (ed.) *"I Too Am America": Archaeological Studies of African-American Life*, 132–155, Charlottesville, VA: University of Virginia Press.

Galloway, P. K. (1995) *Choctaw Genesis 1500–1700*, Lincoln, NE: University of Nebraska Press.

Girard, Jeffrey S. (2002) *Regional Archaeology Program Management Unit 1: Thirteenth Annual Report*, Natchitokes: Report submitted to the Louisiana Division of Archaeology, Baton Rouge, on file at Northwestern State University of Louisiana.

Hall, G. M. (1992) *Africans in Colonial Louisiana: The Development of Afro-Creole Culture in the Eighteenth Century*, Baton Rouge, LA: Louisiana State University Press.

Hall, G. M. (ed.) (2000) *Databases for the Study of Afro-Louisiana History and Genealogy 1699–1860: Computerized Information from Original Manuscript Sources*, CD-ROM, Baton Rouge, LA: Louisiana State University Press.

Hauser, M. W., and DeCorse, C. R. (2003) "Low fired earthenwares in the African Diaspora: problems and prospects," *International Journal of Historical Archaeology*, 7: 67–98.

Herskovits, Melville J. (1958) *The Myth of the Negro Past*, Boston, MA: Beacon Press.

Heywood, L. M. (2002) "Portuguese into African: The Eighteenth-Century Central African Background to Atlantic Creole Cultures," in L. M. Heywood (ed.) *Central Africans and Cultural Transformations in the American Diaspora*, 91–113, Cambridge: Cambridge University Press.

Jones, S. L. (1985) "The African-American Tradition in Vernacular Architecture," in T. A. Singleton (ed.) *The Archaeology of Slavery and Plantation Life*, 195–213, Orlando, FL: Academic Press.

Kniffen, F. B., Gregory, H. F. Jr, and Stokes, G. A. (1987) *The Historic Indian Tribes of Louisiana: From 1542 to the Present*, Baton Rouge, LA: Louisiana State University Press.

Lovejoy, Paul E. (2000) "Identifying Enslaved Africans in the African Diaspora," in P. E. Lovejoy (ed.) *Identity in the Shadow of Slavery*, 1–29, London: Continuum.

Mathews, J. H. (1983) *Analysis of Ceramics from Three Eighteenth and Nineteenth-Century Sites in the Locale of Natchitoches, Louisiana*, unpublished Master's thesis, Department of History, Social Sciences, and Social Work, Natchitoches, Louisiana: Northwestern State University.

Mills, Elizabeth Shown (1977) *Natchitoches 1729–1803: Abstracts of the Catholic Church Registers of the French and Spanish Post of St. Jean Baptiste des Natchitoches in Louisiana*, New Orleans, LA: Polyanthos.

Mills, G. B. (1977) *The Forgotten People: Cane River's Creoles of Color*, Baton Rouge, LA: Louisiana State University Press.

Mills, G. B., and Mills, E. S. (1973) *Melrose*, Natchitoches, LA: The Association for the Preservation of Historic Natchitoches.

Morgan, D. W., and MacDonald, K. C. (in press) "Colonoware in Western Colonial Louisiana: Makers and Meaning," in K. Kelly and M. Hardy (eds) *The Archaeology of the French New World: Louisiana and the Caribbean*, Tallahassee, FL: Florida University Press.

Morgan, D. W., MacDonald, K. C., and Lee, A. (2003) *Interim Summary Report of Excavations at Yucca House, Melrose Plantation, December 2002*, Natchitoches, Louisiana: Report submitted to the Cane River National Heritage Area.

MacDonald, Kevin. C., Morgan, David W., Handley, Fiona J. L., Lee, Aubra L., and Morley, Emma (2006) "The Archaeology of Local Myths and Heritage Tourism: The Case of Cane River's Melrose Plantation" in R. Layton, S. Shennan, and P. Stone (eds.) *A Future for Archaeology*, pp. 127–142, London: UCL Press.

Mouer, L. D., Hodges, M. E. N., Potter, S. R., Renaud, S. L. H., Hume, I. N., Pogue, D. J., McCartney, M. W., and Davidson, T. E. (1999) "Colonoware Pottery, Chesapeake

Pipes, and 'Uncritical Assumptions'," in T. A. Singleton (ed.) *"I Too Am America":
Archaeological Studies of African-American Life*, 83–115, Charlottesville, VA: University of
Virginia Press.

Phillips, Philip (1970) *Archaeological Survey in the Lower Yazoo Basin, Mississippi, 1949–1955*, 2
Vols, Peabody Museum Papers no. 60, Cambridge, MA: The Peabody Museum.

Posnansky, Merrick (1999) "West Africanist Reflections on African-American Archaeology," in
T. A. Singleton (ed.) *"I Too Am America": Archaeological Studies of African-American Life*,
21–37, Charlottesville, VA: University of Virginia Press.

Savage, B. L. (1994) *African American Historic Places*, New York: The Preservation Press.

Shaw, B. W. (1983) *A Ceramic Chronology for the Whittington House Site: 1780–Present*,
unpublished Master's Thesis, Northwestern State University of Louisiana, Natchitoches.

Singleton, T. A. and Bograd, M. D. (2000) "Breaking Typological Barriers: Looking for the
Colono in Colonoware," in J. Delle, S. Mrozowski, and R. Paynter (eds) *Lines that Divide:
Historical Archaeologies of Race, Class, and Gender*, 3–21, Knoxville, TN: University of
Tennessee Press.

South, S. (1977) *Method and Theory in Historical Archaeology*, New York: Academic Press.

Tademy, L. (2001) *Cane River*, New York: Warner Books, Inc.

Voss, Jerome A., and Blitz, John H. (1988) "Archaeological investigations in the Choctaw
homeland," *American Antiquity*, 53, 1: 125–145.

Wilson, Jon Lamar (2001) *Historic American Buildings Survey: Coincoin-Prudhomme House*, Historic
American Buildings Survey/Historic American Engineering Record, Washington, DC:
National Park Service, US Department of the Interior.

Woods, Sister Frances J. (1972) *Marginality and Identity: A Colored Creole Family through Ten
Generations*, Baton Rouge, LA: Louisiana State University Press.

Yentsch, A. E. (1994) *A Chesapeake Family and Their Slaves: A Study in Historical Archaeology*,
Cambridge: Cambridge University Press.

13   East End maritime traders

The emergence of a Creole community on St John, Danish West Indies

Douglas V. Armstrong

Introduction

In 1844, four years prior to emancipation in the Danish West Indies, a group of travelers sailed from St Thomas to Tortola. They wrote:

> Being ready to pursue our journey, we concluded to go first to Tortola, and engaged a colored man to take us to that island, in a small vessel not much larger than the long boat of a merchantman. We made arrangements to leave early in the morning, hoping we could reach Road Town before night.
>
> (Truman, Jackson, and Longstreth 1844: 21)[1]

This account describes a vessel departing from St Thomas. It depicts a Creole boat captain, perhaps an East Ender and a vessel that was probably a Tortolan sloop. Who was the sloop captain and how did he attain this position in the pre-emancipation era in the Danish West Indies? The story of the Creole community on St John's East End provides a setting that explains such maritime autonomy for people of color in the early nineteenth century.

The East End community of St John began in the late eighteenth century and continued into the early twentieth century (Figure 13.1). It provides an excellent venue for the study of diversity in the African Diaspora. Between 1995 and 2000 archaeological and historical research was conducted on the ruins of nearly 50 East End house sites. This study sheds light on the significant role that Caribbean maritime life played in creating and maintaining relatively favorable circumstances for people of color in the periods prior to and immediately following emancipation.

Small maritime enclaves, like the East End, fed upon the region's constant need of a wide range of goods from fresh fish to supplement plantation and urban diets, to the stone used in the construction of buildings, and from the transport of replacement parts for the carts and industrial works of plantations to the thread and buttons needed for local cottage industries. As such, even as the maritime activities of the East End community turned the regional economy inside out, the East Enders' *petit* scale trade

Figure 13.1   East End sloops ca. 1900 (postcard, a Knight collection).

was necessary and tolerated, if not tacitly supported. These small-scale maritime networks were dependent on knowledge and skill and less dependent upon rigid definitions of race, ethnicity, or class, than the broader superstructure of the region's plantation economy. This is not to say that the people of the East End community did not face restrictions in their existence within what Elsa Goveia has defined as a "slave society." In fact, the East End community rested squarely within a broader community, which was as, Goveia observed, "based on slavery," and that "included masters and freemen as well as slaves" (Goveia 1965: vii).

The livelihood of East End settlement was dependent on their ability to produce, exchange, and trade goods and services with neighboring islands and settlements. Maritime trade and exchange was intensely skill-based and, as such, provided open doors to people that otherwise might have had restricted access based on their phenotypic "racial" identity (Bolster 1990, 1997; see also Horton and Horton 1997: 111). In the eighteenth and nineteenth centuries, fishing and maritime life involved a suite of activities that required interaction within a group as well as individually.

In this chapter I will concentrate on the significance of these maritime activities in shaping a community of small-scale maritime traders. Their households, now archaeological sites, provided a critically important home base with security and relative economic stability. Three interwoven threads of evidence are examined: (1) maritime trade and exchange as a mechanism to transcend stereotypical roles; (2) the social security provided by a home base of community owned lands; and (3) the need for cooperative social networking to participate in and maintain a maritime economy.[2]

Background—the East End setting

The East End of St John was dry and its hillsides steep and rocky. The area was not well suited for the production of regional cash crops like sugar (Figure 13.2). Though

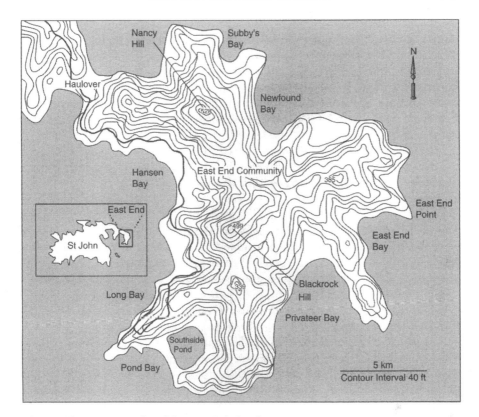

Figure 13.2 Topography of the East End, St John.

a donkey path straddled the steep slopes and ridge tops linking the East End to the settlement at Coral Bay, travel by water was much faster and provided a more versatile means of transportation. The geography of the East End, with its many small bays and beachheads, was well adapted to an economy with strong maritime ties. Towns on Tortola and Virgin Gorda were only a short sail away and the rapidly growing harbor and mercantile trading center of Charlotte Amalie (St Thomas) was only a morning or afternoon's travel away by sloop. The isthmus at Haulover could be negotiated to ease travel if wind conditions were inopportune. Good weather anchorage was available on both the north side of the East End peninsula, at Newfound Bay and Sibbys Bay, and at several beachheads at Long Bay and Hansen Bay on the southern coast. Furthermore, Hurricane Hole offered safe anchorage and protection from even the strongest of storms. These factors facilitated a settlement that operated at variance to the expectations and assumptions that governed the world around the East End.[3]

In the years following the formal settlement of St John by the Danish, in 1718, the East End settlement was comprised of provisioning plantations that were owned by absentee planters. Provisions, including both foodstuffs and natural resources, were produced by slaves of African descent laboring with little or no supervision.

By the mid-eighteenth century, a shift occurred with acquisition by a group of related families from the British Virgin Islands, who came to St John along with their slaves. The George and Sewer (later Ashton) families acquired the lands communally and lived and worked in close proximity with their laborers. They brought with them an in-depth knowledge of the sea, the result of decades of living on the margins of the region's plantation economy. The collective ownership of East End lands marks the beginning of what would become the East End community.

Maritime trade and exchange—foundation of an interactive autonomy

The social organization of a community involved in maritime activities fostered personal liberties and the need for crew cooperation. It is exactly these qualities that we see in the historical reconstruction of the East End community. It is likely that the cooperative skills required in fishing played a key role facilitating the East Ender's maritime trade (Figure 13.3).

Fishing and maritime trade undoubtedly constituted a mechanism at the core of the East End transformation and tied directly to their ultimate freedom and autonomy. Fishing provided the training needed to pilot boats in the waters of the Virgin Islands. Young men learned the lessons of maritime life first in the local harbors and bays and then on the more open ocean. Richard Price (1966a, b) has argued that the unique socioeconomic role of enslaved fishermen permitted a particularly smooth transformation to a life as a free fisherman (Price 1966a: 1363). Based on his research in Martinique, Price noted that "fishermen feel themselves to be very different from

Figure 13.3 Mending fish pots, St John (postcard, Knight collection).

their inland neighbors, and their individualism, pride, entrepreneurial values, and even their family organization seem objectively as well as in their own minds, to set them apart somehow" (Price 1966b).[4]

The fish and shellfish caught and gathered by East End fishermen provided a constant source of nutrition. Throughout the history of the community the archaeological record shows the presence of considerable quantities of fish bone, indicating the importance of fish in their diet. The regular supply of fresh fish also served as a commodity to sell or trade with the neighboring plantations, urban areas, the military, and the merchants and mariners at the port city of Charlotte Amalie in St Thomas. Not only did Charlotte Amalie's expanding population need a continual supply of fish and other provisions, but the harbor also hosted a large and continual flow of vessels that were in constant need of fresh goods. Moreover, construction in Charlotte Amalie made possible a fairly lucrative trade in ballast.[5] Limestone blocks were a readily available and renewable resource at places like Privateer Bay in the East End. The stone could be harvested from the shore and shallows and each new storm brought a fresh supply to the shoreline. Ballast made up the bulk of the formally recorded cargoes transported by East End Captains sailing under the Tortolan flag.[6]

By the turn of the nineteenth century much of the East End population had shifted its focus from land-based provisioning to fishing and maritime trades (Armstrong 2001, 2003) (Figure 13.4). Divisions between planter and slave were replaced by skill-based maritime trades. This shift coincided with an amalgamation of black and white residents and new generations of interrelated Creoles who had an in-depth knowledge of the sea. Rather than being enslaved or servile crewmen, the sailors of the small rural community on St John's East End built their own craft and made seinage for catching and trapping fish. The utilitarian boats made and used by the East Enders were generally sloops that were kept at anchor in East End harbors and fishing and seine boats that could be pulled ashore. The sailors also manufactured and used small seine boats (or dingys) to go from shore to sloop. The rowing craft, and small sailing vessels, were a regular part of wharf life at ports throughout the Caribbean from at least the early eighteenth century into the twentieth century.[7] They remain in limited use as a means of moving provisions from selected islands like Dominica and St Vincent. However, the patterns of trade have changed dramatically in the twentieth century with new boat-building patterns (including the use of fiberglass) having all but replaced traditional forms.

East Enders used these craft to travel freely between islands held by different colonial powers. In the days prior to the abolition of slavery, East Enders were able to do this because they were persons of good standing in the relatively open society of the Danish Islands. The Danish established Charlotte Amalie as a free port and encouraged a wide range of trade and mercantile traders. As such, there was great latitude in what was considered legitimate trade and in who could carry out that trade (Tyson 1977).[8]

East Enders played a significant role in local and inter-island trade throughout the nineteenth century. One measure of the success of this trade is found in an island-wide survey of watercraft and horses compiled in 1865 (SJLUC 1860–1870 #22). This survey shows the importance of the East End's small craft. While the East End population of 113 accounted for only 7.4 percent of the island population they owned

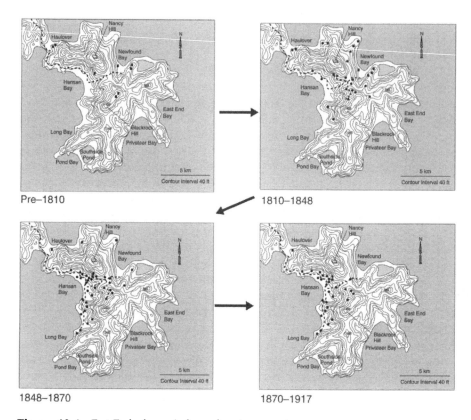

Pre–1810

1810–1848

1848–1870

1870–1917

Figure 13.4   East End: change in house location over time.

22 of 89 watercraft, or about 25 percent of the boats on the island. When broken down by type of boat, the East End had the highest representation of "deck and half deck" boats (7 of 20, or 35 percent) and row boats (13 of 49, or 26.9 percent). They also accounted for more than 10 percent of the island's sail boats (2 of 18).

The Harbor Master's record books for St Thomas are filled with entries documenting the movement of cargoes. Personal record books found among East End probates tell of voyages that took the East Enders throughout the region, including trips to St Croix, Dominica, and Puerto Rico. These records document trips made in their own boats and those that they captained for boat owners in the British Virgin Islands. The accounts are full of references to East End sailors, captains, and boat owners (like Timothy George and John Ashton) along with the names of their boats (like the *Kitty* and the *Harmony*). Maritime trade provided a steady income to support one's extended family and household, to secure the long-term ownership of one's family lands, and to facilitate the regional network of exchange that was necessary to maintain one's household.

Though much of the material culture associated with boats and boat-building for the East End was housed on the boat or in sheds on the beach, all of the excavated sites contained evidence of the importance of maritime activities. All of the sites contain a wide range of fish bones and shell indicating the importance of marine resources in the diet. We also found archaeological evidence of fishing activities at all households in the East End community (Armstrong 2003). In addition to fishhooks, one of the sites contained elements of a boat's block-and-tackle (found in a storage shed at a residential site known as Pleasant Lookout). These were perhaps salvaged from a lost vessel, or, were spare parts being stored in the household shed until they were needed. In any case, their storage represents an effort to plan ahead against potential adversity.

For the East End community, the emphasis on small craft and regional trade began to change in the late nineteenth century with the emergence of fleets of steamships like the Hamburg-America Line that took on local sailors including a regular flow of East Enders who departed from the port at Charlotte Amalie (SJR 1870–1911). Ultimately, in the twentieth century, the demand for larger vessels to carry bigger cargo, including the shipping containers and automobiles, brought a rather precipitous end to both the local boat-making industries and the associated maritime trade.

Community owned lands—a secure home base

From at least the mid-eighteenth century, the families of the East End acted in a cooperative fashion. This is reflected in the collective ownership of land among the many interrelated families of early planters beginning in 1755, and through time, in the maintenance of cooperative traditions in the entire community. There is no doubt that the formation of this community was distinctly different from those that were based on cash crop plantation production. The tax records for the East End document only the provisions and products of the land, because taxes were based on the products of the land, and were not designated to assess the products of the sea. Thus, even though tax records indicate land-based provision grounds, there can be no doubt that a basic element of provisioning within the settlement from the earliest days of cooperative ownership was, in fact, fishing and increasingly maritime trade. Moreover, though the land was used to produce provisions, and may have initially had somewhat of a balance in land- and sea-based provisioning activities, the community appears to have been reorganized to facilitate the infrastructure of fishing rather than traditional land-based products.

Archaeological evidence indicates that by the 1790s, the East End began to express evidence of transformation (Armstrong 2003). By their second generation in residence, and with ever-increasing reliance on the sea and maritime trade, social and ethnic divisions between owner and slave began to break down. This change is expressed in shifts in the layout, placement, and number of house sites, and would later be documented in the written records. This shift marks the union of black and white residents, who were joined by additional free blacks arriving from the British and Dutch Virgin Islands. Archaeological evidence indicates that, as early as 1790, houses were constructed on parcels within the collectively owned family lands. Later records indicate that these sites were given to mulatto and black sons and daughters of the community. Though well-established within the reconstructed spatial and social landscape by 1790, these parcels were not formally recorded in deeds until the second decade of the nineteenth century (Figure 13.4).

By the early nineteenth century dozens of East Enders had been manumitted and the majority of people of color in the community were free. When formal censuses were begun in the 1830s, this generation would show up in the records as established seamen, seamstresses, and planters. The maritime trades were gender specific, with males often beginning as fishermen and seamen and becoming boat-captains, carpenters, and boat-owners. While men engaged directly with maritime activities, women, along with children and the aged (males and females), worked within the household and associated provision grounds. On-site activities, within the community, included sewing, laundry, along with boat-building, net repair, provisioning, and schooling for boys and girls, the latter being a particularly valued enterprise that united the community.[9]

Through the early decades of the nineteenth century dozens of free households were established within the family lands and a gradual shift occurred in the location and distribution of house sites throughout the community. First, a few "planter"-based households were dispersed across the landscape to accommodate the needs of provision planting and cotton (Figure 13.4). Then, small freeholding households were established. As the maritime economy and associated social networking became more fully established, the location of house sites shifted and began to congregate on the flanks of Hansen Bay. The result was an aggregate community of interrelated households linked to an expertise in maritime trade and bound together by the security of a home base. The community provided a network of supporting family and interactive relatives, friends, as well as a few enslaved laborers. By the time of emancipation in 1848 all but nine of the community's 115 residents were free. Those who were enslaved were owned by "free-coloreds" and most of these were skilled men who lived within the households and served as mates on East End vessels or worked the family provision grounds. While maritime trades were reliant on skill, knowledge, and cooperation, and tended to blur racial and ethnic distinctions, they were not without stratified divisions based on status, rank, and economic position.

The East End community sustained itself through the island's transition to freedom as well as the hardships and stress caused by disease, storms, and earthquakes that had devastating effects on the island in the second half of the nineteenth century. Even with a series of hardships in the post emancipation era, including cholera epidemics, hurricanes, and the severe earthquake of 1867, the East End community continually renewed and stabilized itself while the population of the island as a whole dropped precipitously. The success of the community through the late nineteenth century and initial decades of the twentieth century, was due to a combination of maritime trade, a secure home base, and networked kinship and social relationships within and between households and with trading partners.

Free colored persons of the East End were able to parley their position as free landowners and skilled mariners to provide services necessary to the broader plantation and mercantile economies of the region. They continued on in the advantageous role as seamen even after slavery ended because they already possessed the skills and knowledge to sail the seas. Mariners could serve as distributors of goods in their small, locally made, craft. In these maritime trades, they had an advantage over recently freed persons in that the East End seamen already had a base of operations, a network of trading partners, and skills based on generations of maritime knowledge. They were thus able to shift with the times and serve as brokers and traders of the goods produced by the newly freed, but economically dependent, island peasantry (see Olwig 1994). Later, many were to utilize their knowledge of the sea to serve as crew for long haul steamships that were expanding their share of Caribbean and Trans-Atlantic trade.

Social networking

Cooperation and networking is an essential ingredient of fishing and maritime life. Price notes that the use of the seine required "a number of hands for effective use" (Price 1966a: 1371). The probate inventories of the East End community leave little doubt about the importance of seine boats and seinage in the personal inventories of the late-eighteenth-century East End "planters" and in the personal effects of free colored East Enders after 1800. Early on this cooperation was between master and slave or among fellow enslaved fishermen. As time passed, this cooperation would be taken up by the free colored descendants of all of these people. Ultimately, the cooperative interaction of fishing and maritime activities permeated the social relationships expressed throughout the community and took shape in cooperative ownership of land by extended families, households bound together by multiple generations of extended family, and a network of closely related households where residence shifted and overlapped to form a tight knit community.

In referring to fishing in plantation settings, Price suggests that fishermen were on the "periphery of slave culture," and that "these fishermen played a role that was perhaps more social than economic" (Price 1966a:1370). As played out in the East End community, the economic and social roles merged as fishing and ultimately maritime trade became an essential core to the local economy, and the way of life led to an inter-reliant community whose social relationships and family structures were intertwined with life on and from the sea.

The social structure of the East End community was built upon complex social interactions that shaped the cultural landscape of individual households, the community as a whole, and relations with neighboring communities and trading partners (Figure 13.5). Households themselves came to reflect the complex networks of social interaction of the community with each house site serving as home for at least three generations of extended families and support laborers. Registers of the unfree and free colored, as well as the censuses that began in the 1830s, show that by the third decade of the nineteenth century each East End household held multiple generations of the same family. In addition, two households still had slaves, even though the head of these households were free coloreds. After emancipation, most of the formally emancipated persons stayed on as laborers and house servants and eventually merged within extended East End families.

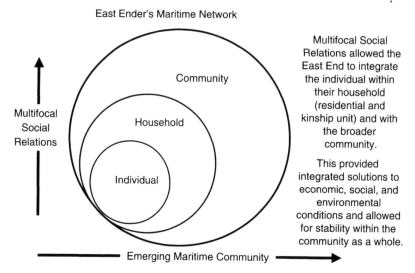

Figure 13.5   East Ender's multifocal social network.

A clear paradox in this story was the presence of a few slaves and their ownership by free people of color right up until emancipation. One could argue that the few remaining slaves had mobility and were involved in a constant movement back-and-forth with Tortola and so could at any moment have declared themselves "free." Some sailors were even documented as members of the British [Anglican] Church located on Tortola. In either case there is reason to believe that they frequently touched British soil in the British Virgin Islands and technically could have declared their freedom. However, the reality is that a few individuals remained enslaved until the formal day of emancipation. They remained on as a residual under-class of laborers long after the technical date marking the change in their status to "free."

The maritime way of life created a situation in which significant numbers of persons, mostly male, were away from the household and community for significant periods of time. The way of life of the East Enders was thus dependent on strong community bonds and multifocal family and household structures.[10] Whereas the more formal networks of the East Enders' economy were linked to maritime trade carried out primarily by men, women were active participants in cottage industries in households situated on lands that they, and their respective extended families, owned.

Throughout the history of the East End, community production of crafts allowed women the freedom to remain in their homes while the men pursued maritime trades. Needlepoint and sewing were key trades for women. The fact that the women of the East End were so fully involved in these cottage-based trades should not be overlooked or trivialized. It tells us about their abilities, and that they worked for themselves to produce goods for the market. Moreover, the sheer fact that they were able to carry out these trades tells us that they had the capital and/or reputation to acquire the materials and tools to sustain production. The regularity of the community's maritime trade facilitated marketing and distribution. Moreover, the integrated social and economic situation of the East End community gave women the opportunity to choose to participate in both childrearing and skilled craft production in the home at a time in which most women of color were enslaved and simply did not have these options.

Conclusions

The East End community projects a distinct variation in African Caribbean living experience facilitated by access to a maritime way of life. Maritime activities provided a means by which people of color in the East End gained freedom and a degree of autonomy during an era dominated by the institution of slavery. The East End setting provided a secure and insulated home base of operations for a predominantly free black community within an encompassing plantation economy. From this relatively remote setting, East Enders traveled from island-to-island carrying cargoes in their distinctive sloops. They distributed and traded goods, and sold the products of their community's provision and craft industries. The continued demand for their services and the stability provided by their home base sustained them through traumatic storms, earthquakes, and sweeping social change.

Upon reflection, it would appear that the social conditions of the East End community were ripe for independence associated with maritime life. The setting was conducive to the emergence of a fishing community involving both free and enslaved people, followed by a transition to a more complex maritime community which encompassed not only fishing, but the array of boat-building, maritime skills, and local cottage industries. Their maritime way of life was, as Price suggested in 1966, a "way out of the fearfully oppressive plantation system" (Price 1966a: 1378). The transformations that took place in this community broke away from the dominant plantation economy and its associated oppressive social infrastructure. In the process, productive skills were learned by women and by men in a small community located at a little island. These skills developed in an environment that was unencumbered, or kept in check, by the dominant power structure. Fishing and small-scale maritime trade did not really compete with the broader slave-based economy and society; rather, it produced needed goods and services, at an economical cost, for consumers in the expanding port city of Charlotte Amalie on St Thomas and at plantations throughout the region. By gaining a land-based foothold, even if in a remote location, the East End Creole community established a model for access to freedom that, although almost forgotten today, was well-recognized within the island in the eighteenth and nineteenth centuries.

The study of the East End community shows that people of color in the Caribbean were not simply, or only, enslaved; rather, in particular situations, such as in urban settings and in some rural context, they forged new paths and emerged as free and interactive participants in the broader regional community. The point is not to discount the human tragedy of slavery but to recognize that under certain conditions people of color were able to negotiate and gradually gain a degree of freedom and autonomy. Moreover, the study highlights the evidence that the history of the region is varied and textured, and that people, black, white, and in-between, the spectrum that makes up the Creole population, were able to overcome adversity through the application of creative diversity.

With the data from archaeological survey and excavations compiled and the details of the history of the East End reconstructed, one can begin to understand the point of origin of the Creole Captain described in the 1844 account of the sloop setting out from St Thomas. This captain had a home, a family, and friends. He, like the people of the East End community, of which he very well might have been a part, was the product of a complex set of social relations that provided him with greater access to mobility and goods associated with freedom than the majority of people of color in the region. In the case of the East End, archaeological inquiry used in conjunction with detailed historical analysis, has allowed us to add perspective and diversity to the African Diaspora.

The East End setting evoked a peculiar, if not unique, combination of opportunities. The East End Creole community fulfilled the wider society's need for small-scale maritime trade to redistribute goods on, and between, islands. The settlement ultimately supplied planters, merchants, and other free and nonfree persons alike, with goods and services that were critical to the broader economic system. However, in time, and through social intercourse, the East End community established an economy and identity based on skills and productivity associated with maritime life that transcended traditional boundaries of race and class. The productive skills of these people led to a reputation of the community as a place where women and men were acknowledged for their skills. The men of the East End became known as good seamen, fishermen, and craftspeople, and the women were acknowledged for their needlepoint, sewing, and later, fine basketry. Through skill, diligence, and earned reputation, the East End community thus attained the stature of a free and independent people.

Notes

1 The authors of this note were Quaker abolitionists and noted the short distance between the Danish islands and the British islands, making light of the possibilities of freedom via transporting oneself from the Danish to the British islands.

2 In the broader East End study (Armstrong 2003), I deal with a series of findings with respect to the community: it's networked multifocal social organization, dynamic gender- and age-based roles within society, shifting land tenure patterns, and spatial layout in and between households, as well as issues relating to the expression of community ethos in education and religion.

3 The East End was a community that functioned in a different manner than the encompassing plantation society. Consequently, the findings of this study are in sharp contrast to the initial archaeological descriptions found in the *St. John's Site Report of 1981–1982* (Ausherman 1982: 145–147). That study had examined the scattered remains on the ridge top between Hansen and Newfound Bays and found that the area did not possess the significant architecture of the type found in association with sugar estates on the island. Unfortunately, that study did not have the benefit of either local informants or detailed historical documentation. Therefore, they simply grouped everything they saw and found very little in the way of formal structure

or order to what they encountered. In fact, what they had encountered were parts of at least three free holdings, including about half of the ruins of Pleasant Lookout. The interpretations of the 1981–1982 report were predicated on economic and social assumptions that viewed this area as within the domain of the dominant plantation economy of the region. In this light, the types of sites found were not very impressive, and the significance of what was seen was minimized as a small plantation of little significance. This was perhaps a logical conclusion from the perspective of an island-wide survey aimed at documenting the island's plantations. They saw no need to look beyond what they had seen because almost all of the evidence from other plantation sites, with which they were comparing the East End, reflected a distinct pattern of nucleated planter residences, industrial works, and quarters for enslaved laborers. The East End yielded no massive planter's great house or sugar works. Thus, most of the less obvious ruins were missed and those that were found were considered insignificant. Consequently, the complexity and integrity of the East End was almost missed. They simply could not see the scattered ruins as part of a community of interrelated households, an example of cultural diversity, and an important yet poorly understood aspect of the African (and European) Diaspora.

4 Seine boats used by East Enders were small craft that were used for casting fishing nets and setting traps. The seine boats would work in teams to set out the nets and capture schools of small fish (Henningsen 1967: 55; Pyle 1981: 53).

5 A significant finding of this study was that a notable proportion of the trade engaged in by the East End seafarers was the cargo of ballast as a commodity. A detailed examination of the harbormaster's records for Charlotte Amalie for the first half of the nineteenth century showed that a majority of the formally reported cargoes for those vessels entering the harbor was ballast, which was used in construction in St Thomas.

6 An examination of the free black populations of the British Virgin Islands is found in Harrigan and Varlack (1991: 18–29). Prior to 1815, free blacks in the British Virgin islands had a degree of freedom and were permitted to own up to "eight acres of land and a maximum of fifteen slaves" (Harrigan and Varlack 1991: 19). Restricted in formal ownership of larger-scale plantation lands, many free blacks became well-off by pursuing maritime activities including boat building. The distinctive "Tortola boat" became a well-known craft used for rapid travel and trade within regional water. Self-employed Tortola boat-builders constructed these boats or worked as carpenters in small boatyards near Road Town and on small bayside plots throughout the island. East Enders are recorded as serving as captains on several of the Tortola craft and undoubtedly their own boat-building was influenced by the Tortola boat construction and vice-versa. In 1815, the free blacks of Tortola were granted rights as British West Indian citizens. At the time their holdings accounted for approximately 20 percent of the total value of property and by 1823 that proportion had more than doubled to 41 percent. It is possible that the increase relates to their investment in maritime industry and trade, which remained on the upswing, whereas land-based plantation production and associated land values dropped precipitously (Stobo 1834, as cited in Harrigan and Varlack 1991: 22).

7 While the forms used in the East End varied, they may be summed up in descriptions of the "Tortola" sloop. The Tortola sloop falls between the cracks of most maritime definitions, as did the similar ships of East End production. Pyle notes that the Tortola sloop is not gaff-rigged, also, that the Tortola sloop is a little large to be defined as a boat, since it is too big to be regularly pulled ashore. The only vessel of the twentieth century similar to the Tortola sloop is the Antigua fishing sloop, a vessel that claims to be modeled after the Tortolan vessel (Pyle 1981: 267).

8 The Danish system allowed diversity in the ownership of property by persons of many nationalities. Slave codes remained in place well into the nineteenth century, but by the second decade of the nineteenth century "Free Colored" persons could become "first class" citizens through the mastery of skills, accumulation of possessions through their own labors, through inheritance, and perhaps most distinctly, through intermarriage within the established Creole society. In establishing the "first class" citizen category, the Danish formally recognized what already existed in the form of a large free black population. It

allowed these people to formally acquire land and property; thus, not insignificantly, their success would increase the payment of taxes to the crown.

9 The importance given to education led to the construction of an East End school saving considerable travel time to Coral Bay and avoiding the problem of restricted travel during periods of epidemic.

10 I use the term multifocal to reflect the complex networks of persons that cohabited a household through its period of occupation. I feel that this term is more appropriate for the East End than the term matrifocal, which has often been applied to St John (Olwig 1985) and the Caribbean (Smith 1956, 1996). The term multifocal is intended as an inclusive term that recognizes the contribution of persons of all ages, genders, kinship, and friendship relations, that play a cooperative role to the long-term functioning of a household.

References

Armstrong, Douglas V. (2001) "A Venue for Autonomy: Archaeology of a Changing Cultural Landscape, the East End Community, St. John," in P. Farnsworth (ed.) *Virgin Islands, Island Lives: Plantation Archaeology in the Caribbean*, 142–164. Tuscaloosa, AL: University of Alabama Press.

Armstrong, Douglas V. (2003) *Creole Transformation from Slavery to Freedom: Historical Archaeology of the East End Community of St. John, Virgin Islands*, Gainesville, FL: The University Press of Florida.

Ausherman, Betty (ed.) (1982) *St. John Sites Report 1981–1982*, United States Virgin Islands, Charlotte Amalie, St Thomas: Division of Archaeology and Historic Preservation.

Bolster, J. (1990) "To feel like a man: black seamen in the Northern States, 1800–1860," *Journal of American History*, 76: 1173–1199.

Bolster, J. (1997) *Black Jacks: African American Seamen in the Age of the Sail*, Cambridge, MA: Harvard University Press.

Goveia, E. (1965) *Slave Society in the British Leeward Islands at the End of the Eighteenth Century*, New Haven, CT: Yale University Press.

Harrigan, N., and Varlack, P. (1991) "The Emergence of a Black Small-Holders Society in the British Virgin Islands," in J. Lisowski (ed.) *Caribbean Perspectives: The Social Structure of a Region*, 18–29, Somerset, NJ: Transaction Publishers.

Henningsen, Henning (1967) *The Danish West Indies in Old Picture*, St Thomas: American Danish Festival.

Horton, J., and Horton, L. (1997) *In Hope of Liberty: Culture, Community and Protest among Northern Free Blacks, 1700–1860*, New York: Oxford University Press.

Olwig, Karen (1985) *Cultural Adaptation and Resistance on St. John: Three Centuries of Afro-Caribbean Life*, Gainesville, FL: The University Press of Florida.

Olwig, Karen (1994) *The Land is the Heritage: Land and Community on St. John*, St John Oral History Association Monograph Number 1. Reproduction Center of the Division of Social Sciences. Copenhagen: University of Copenhagen.

Price, Richard (1966a) "Caribbean fishing and fisherman: a historical sketch," *American Anthropologist*, 68: 1363–1383.

Price, Richard (1966b) "Fishing rites and recipes in a Martiniquan village," *Caribbean Studies*, 6, 1: 3–24.

Pyle, Douglas C. (1981) *Clean Sweet Wind: Sailing Craft of the Lesser Antilles*, Preston, MD: East Reach Press.

Smith, R. T. (1956) *The Negro Family in British Guiana: Family Structure and Social Status in the Villages*, London: Routledge and Kegan Paul.

Smith, R. T. (1996) *The Matrifocal Family: Power, Pluralism, and Politics*, New York: Routledge.

Truman, George, Jackson, John, and Longstreth, Thomas R. (1844) *Narrative of a Visit to the West Indies in 1840 and 1841*, Philadelphia, PA: Merrihew and Thompson Printers.

Tyson, George F. Jr (1977) *Power, Profits, and Privateers: A Documentary History of the Virgin Islands During the Era of the American Revolution*, St Thomas, VI: Virgin Islands Bureau of Libraries, Museums and Archaeological Services.

Archival citations

Knight Collection, St Thomas, United States Virgin Islands:
ca. 1900   Mending Fish Pots, St John (postcard) ca. 1900.
ca. 1900   East End Sloops (postcard; also in Kongelige Bibliotek, The Royal Library, Copenhagen).

Rigsarkivit (Danish Archives), Copenhagen:
OM1799   Oxholm Map of St John (Rigsarkivet, OM 1799).
SJLUC   West Indies Local Archives, St John Landfoged, Unarranged Correspondence, 1851–1875, Rigsarkivet, Copenhagen.
SJR   Central Management Archives, Registers for St John, 1835–1911, Rigsarkivet, Copenhagen. Censuses of 1835, 1841, 1846, 1850, 1855, 1857, 1860, 1870, 1880, 1901, 1911 [data tabulated from microfilm copies at the Baa Library, St Thomas].

14 Hawking your wares

Determining the scale of informal economy through the distribution of local coarse earthenware in eighteenth-century Jamaica

MARK W. HAUSER

Introduction

Archaeological sites from eighteenth-century Jamaica contain significant quantities of locally produced coarse earthenware. Historical accounts are replete with references to street markets through which enslaved and freed African Jamaicans bought and sold goods, including such earthenwares, and products contained within them. This study attempts to understand the significance of these markets and determine the scale of the informal economic sector in which enslaved and free African Jamaicans operated. The primary subject of my research is the petrographic analysis of the local pottery traded in this internal market system. What I have found is that while there were many sites of pottery manufacture in Jamaica, pottery was traded across the island, indicating an island-wide scale of economy in contrast to the localized economy of the planters.

Exchange is becoming a powerful unifying activity in African Diaspora studies. Marketing systems have been discussed by scholars interested in the economic existence of the enslaved in South Carolina (Campell 1991; Olwell 1996), Virginia (Schlotterboeck 1991), Louisiana (McDonald 1991, 1993), Martinique (Tomich 1991), St John (Olwig 1977, 1985; Hauser and Armstrong 1999), Barbados (Beckles 1989, 1999, 2003), and Jamaica (Mintz 1955, 1960, 1974, 1983; Armstrong 1990; Bush 1990; Mint and Hall 1991; Turner 1991, 1995; Higman 1996; Reeves 1997). This study builds upon this previous work.

Global economic systems reorganized and expanded due to burgeoning European industries and explorations at the beginning in the fifteenth century. Rather than being a process of inevitable economic incorporation, many have argued that this expansion was a process of negotiated relationships at the local level (Stern 1988; Roseberry 1989; Spyer 2000; Stahl 2002). Thus, one must take into account local logics through which the global colonial economic system was configured. The internal economy of Jamaica can be seen as one such local logic. Much has been made of the seemingly contradictory Jamaican internal market system. This system, on the one hand, supported the plantations and their export-oriented economy, while on the other hand, it was a contradiction to the slave regime. If, as some scholars contend (Higman 1996), there were multiple internal economic systems in existence in Jamaica during the eighteenth century, then a comparison of local logics and how they intersect would prove useful.

World systems theory is a mechanism through which to understand empires within a context of emergent economic and social systems (Williams, E. 1970, 1994; Wallerstein 1974, 1980; Frank 1978, 1999; Wolf 1982). In archaeology, Earle (1987) sought to use it to describe the underlying organizational structures of economic systems. Inevitably, commodities figure highly in the archaeological understanding of world systems theory. The production, distribution, and control of commodities can be viewed as the stuff that allows polities to expand or consolidate. In studies of the emergent global economy, commodities are important because they allow researchers to focus on the relative permeability of seemingly isolated communities in the period of modernity (Orser 1996). This relative permeability extends to ideologies based in capitalism that affected the every day lives of peoples responsible for staple production, which in the case of the West Indies were the enslaved (Delle 1998). Steven Stern has said of the Caribbean,

> What better example could one hope to find of a capitalist world system whose global impact undermines the validity of local units of analysis and whose characteristic pattern combines in a single interlocked structure, free labor in the core and forced labor in the periphery?
>
> (Stern 1988: 858)

European nations in their race to meet the growing demands for prestige value goods such as sugar and gold created a periphery by the partial destruction of indigenous peoples, transplantation of peoples from West Africa, and the imposition of rigid structures that defined social relationships through the plantation economy (Mintz 1985). In such a macro-sociological approach, it is evident that the structure and processes that shaped the Caribbean revolved around the slavery (Best and Levitt 1967; Best 1998).

By the eighteenth century the sugar industry was the cornerstone of Jamaica's economy (Sheridan 1973: 215) and slavery was the primary means of labor (Williams, E. 1970: 136). The reason for this was quite simple. It was economically expedient to use slaves instead of wage labor (Williams, E. 1994: 6). The slave trade became a central mercantile activity in the seventeenth century (Dunn 1972: 336). In part, because of the high mortality rates of the slaves, and because planters felt it was cheaper to purchase more slaves than to ameliorate their lives, the slave trade exploded in the eighteenth century (Williams, E. 1970: 137). Through this slave trade, over twelve million people were taken from West Africa and brought to plantations in Brazil, the West Indies, and southeast USA (Lovejoy 1981: 45). These slaves were required to feed an economic system whose backers attempted to minimize the input costs.

This slave regime has been discussed from various perspectives, not least of which is economic. Lloyd Best, writing in the 1960s, posited the plantation model as a way of describing the series of relationships that existed between colony and colonizer, owner and laborer, planter and slave. At the center of this economy is a plantation, which Best claims "is a globally integrated peripheral economy." The plantation is peripheral to industrialized metropoles such as London to which they export commodities such as sugar and rum. In return, the plantations receive manufactured goods and processed foods. The plantation itself has peripheries that service the commodity-exporting plantation by providing provisions, labor, and energy. Best states, "It is a loosely knit but tightly managed joint stock corporation, of which the business is overseas investment in trade, carriage and production" (Best 1998: 27), "where the hinterland is called on to adjust ... or ... substitute home production for imports" (Best and Levitt 1967: 26).

Given the constraints of this system, a shortfall in the supply of imports from creditors would be met by local production and or exchange. Some have argued that the internal market system is one such set of relationships. In this setup, a series of local economic relationships develop to support a global external market.

Dale Tomich warns of, "treating the world economy as a completed totality whose parts related functionally to one another" (Tomich 1994: 344). Tomich argues that local social structure in which free and enslaved peoples of the Caribbean are involved go beyond mere functional support of the slave system and the global markets that system feeds. The functional nature of local systems of economy might more closely mirror the logic of planters rather than the nature of the relationship between these economic systems. One can gain access to the mindset of the local planters through what they said and what others said about them. Indeed, planters felt such a rigid plantation system avoided debt scandal and dependency on unscrupulous people. According to an eighteenth-century planter, Edward Long:

> These unhappy circumstances will justify the planters in ceasing to contract debts in Jamaica, and remitting their produce to the British merchants, in whose hands it will have all the value of money; upon such a certain foundation, as may relieve them from many of the present embarrassments to which they are subjected by the scarcity of money, and by advantages which this scarcity affords malicious, crafty, and knavish men an opportunity of making, to the very great detriment of the planting interest.
>
> (Long 1774, 1: 564)

The solution was obvious to planters: to maintain control of the plantation capital and production in London.

The manner in which planters adhered to the system was the cause for some complaint. In 1731 Governor Hunter complained, "but the inhabitants are so intent on the making of Sugars which it seems turn to better Account, that they Chuse rather to Purchase those Commoditys from their own neighbors than to employ their slaves in that work" (cited in Sheridan 1973: 220). The planters simply relied or wanted to rely on the machinery of the London markets to ensure steady income of cash and supplies.

Plantation Economy from the Ground Up

While the world system did create the demand for labor that precipitated the slave trade, the degree to which the daily lives of the enslaved and freed African Jamaican was dictated by markets in London is in question. The problem with relying on metropoles for the organization and provisioning of peripheral communities was that these plantations were rigidly fixed to market fluctuations in London and did not have the flexibility to adapt to local demands. But, this is an overly determined approach to understanding the integration of local and global economies. Rather than being simply functional reactions to shortfalls in supplies from metropoles, local economies must be understood as independent responses. The internal economies of the planter and the slave prove to be, taken as a partially articulated whole, a local logic. This logic is how the nexus of the global and the local is negotiated. The internal economies of the planter and the slave prove to be, taken as a partially articulated whole, a local logic. This logic, in which we centre enslaved economic agency within patterns of exchange and consumption, can be examined archaeologically. In short, the contradictions and ironies implicit in the material and archival record expose the social relations of the island's economy. These social relations can be envisioned through concomitant ideologies reflected in ceramic choice (Wilkie and Farnsworth 1999). By comparing the scale of economic activities undertaken by planters within Jamaica with those activities of enslaved and free African Jamaicans, I will demonstrate how African Jamaicans reconstituted their material world in light of the constraints placed on them by the slave regime.'

The exchange system in Jamaica has traditionally been framed in terms of an informal and internal economy. The internal marketing system actually consisted of several partially articulated systems. One system consisted primarily of planters, barter, and credit (Higman 1996: 228). Another system, more commonly discussed in the literature, was dominated by black women and depended on verbal negotiation and payment in coin. It operated on the margins of legality and was the subject of constant proscription.

While this chapter concentrates on the latter of the two systems, I would like to briefly mention the former system. This internal system entailed the exchange of livestock, commodities, and slaves. It usually operated on a local level in part because of geographic constraints (Higman 1996: 226). This exchange network was also local because it tended to focus on support industries for urban centers and plantations. Pens around Spanishtown and Kingston would provide fodder for horses within the cities (Higman 1996: 221). Livestock was primarily exchanged in agriculturally diversified areas instead of forming a strong flow from areas dominated by cattle pens to areas dominated by sugar or coffee cultivation. Instead cattle, old and lean from years of serving as draft animals were sold to pens. These pens then fattened up the animals and sold them to butchers in town (Higman 1996: 217).

The internal marketing system which is the focus of this study was dominated by black women and depended on verbal negotiation and payment in coin. This system is generally conceived of as linking the enslaved's provision ground to a broader world of commodities, both imported and local. Robert Olwell (1996: 106) has said that the Charleston market was the scene of a battle for control between slaves and masters where relationships were constantly negotiated. In Jamaica, the documentation of the markets includes anecdotal evidence from visitors to the islands (Sloane 1707; Edwards 1972; Anonymous 1976), local planters (Long 1774; Phillipo 1843; Lewis 1929), and laws attempting to control these markets. However, evidence from legal documents and descriptive accounts indicate little about the flow of commodities through the street markets. This is hardly surprising since the markets were operating on the margins of a formal economy. Because of the lack of information on commodity flow in the eighteenth-century Jamaican street markets, a comparison of the scales of economy between the planters' internal economy and the slaves' internal economy is difficult. Even more difficult is the way in which these economies intersect. Therefore, in this article I determine the scale of the internal market system by tracking one commodity's movement, local coarse earthenware.

Pottery and exchange

Phillip Mayes (1972) and Duncan Mathewson (1972a, b, 1973) were the first archaeologists to identify the local seventeenth through nineteenth-century production of low-fired ceramics in Jamaica. Both researchers classified these ceramics as "Yabbas," employing a traditional Jamaican term. The term itself was conjectured by Mathewson to be derived from the Twi word "ayawa" meaning "earthenware dish" (Mathewson 1972a: 55). Its use implies a link between a twentieth-century African Jamaican *Yabba* pottery tradition practised in Spanish Town by potter Maa Lou and her daughter, Munchie, and archaeologically recovered low-fired earthenwares. Jamaican local pottery has been described by a cohort of people including Mathewson (1972a), Mayes (1972), Ebanks (1984), Armstrong (1990), Pasquariello (1995), Reeves (1997), Meyers (1999), Higman (1998), and Hauser (2000).

The earliest documentary evidence of local pottery manufacture occurs in the seventeenth century. Hans Sloane makes brief reference to the use of earthen jars as musical instruments, but goes on to record:

> Pots for refining sugar were made at the Liguanea, and though more brittle and dearer than when bought from England, they were made here to supply the present needs of the planters, the clay of which they are made is dug up near the place.
>
> (Sloane 1707)

Speaking of the local clay sources on the island, Edward Long states:

> The first is used in claying muscavado Sugars as well as for a better sort of earthenware, manufactured by the Negroes.
>
> The second is more frequent, and supplies the inhabitants with water jars, and other convenient vessels for domestic use. It is likewise most proper for tiles, and drips.
>
> (Long 1774, 3: 851)

Edward Long also describes a source of clay for local potters around the area of "sixteen mile walk" (Long, 3: 851). Finally James Phillippo (1843: 72) described another potential source, "Particles of golden mica have been found in districts near the source of the Rio Cobre, and sometimes, near Spanish Town, it has been incorporated with the potter's clay." However, while African Jamaican manufacture of locally produced pottery is fairly well accepted (Mayes 1972; Mathewson 1972a, b, 1973; Armstrong 1990; Bratten n.d.), the location of manufacturing sites and the pottery's distribution remains fairly conjectural (Reeves 1997).

As I stated earlier, the markets were a meeting place of people and commodities. It was the point where imported and local goods met and were sold. The documentary record enables a great deal of inference in pottery manufacture and consumption. The same evidence more directly addresses the sale of local pottery on the Sunday street markets and through *hagglers*—itinerant free and enslaved traders. A 1711 legal code stated in reference to a prohibition against slaves selling goods: "This restraint is construed to extend only to beef, veal, mutton and saltfish; and to manufactures, except baskets, ropes of bark, earthen pots and such like" (Long 1774, 2: 487).

Bryan Edwards (1972: 125) recorded that,

> Some of them find time on these days to make a few coarse
> manufactures, besides raising provisions, such as mats for beds, bark ropes
> of strong and durable texture, wicker chairs and baskets, earthen jars and
> pans ready for sale.

The markets continued into the nineteenth century. In 1843 James Phillipo goes on
to say that *yabbas* and earthen jars were sold on the Sunday markets along with mats,
baskets, and other products of African Jamaican manufacture (Phillippo 1843: 72).

Sloane, Edwards, and Long describe a whole list of goods that were sold on the
market. Many of these goods were imported from Great Britain, North America, or
neighboring colonies. Writers make mention of staples like yams (Mintz 1960, 1974;
Mintz and Hall 1991; Higman 1996, 1998). We know that such goods were consumed
by the urban and rural freed and enslaved. Many more goods were either grown or
manufactured locally. Most of these materials, however, leave little to no
archaeologically recoverable residue. This leaves us with the durable goods produced
on the island of Jamaica. Local coarse earthenware as an item of exchange can be
viewed as a residue of the internal marketing system.

One can view historic local coarse earthenwares as commodities in networks of
market systems. Commodities here are defined simply as items of exchange and can be
residues of a local economic system. The term commodity is enmeshed in a historical,
disciplinary dichotomy with gift in which arbitrary distinctions are made between the
sacred and the everyday. In the period of modernity, this dichotomy has been poorly
translated into the local good and the imported good (Spyer 2000: 143). In this light,
gift is necessarily culturally imbued with reciprocity and underlying meanings. A
commodity, however, is seen somehow as outside culture penetrating various realms
and requiring a theory of context for its interpretation (Appadurai 1986: 184). Value,
then, becomes the key distinction. Where one's value is *a priori* and immutable, the
other's is locally constituted and transformable (Thomas 1991: 29).

For commodities, value is locally and temporally constituted (Spyer 2000). A
commodity is therefore a social reality whose meaning and exchange is negotiated on
many levels. Commodity in this sense, places the local and imported good on the same
level enabling an examination "of cases where different systems of commoditization of
different societies interact" (Kopytoff 1986: 88). Local coarse earthenwares represent
tangible residues of such processes. The distribution of low-fired ceramics is a partial, but
traceable, indicator of exchange settings where socioeconomic relationships can be
created and transformed (Hauser 1997; Hauser and Armstrong 1999). In turn, the
distribution of local coarse earthenwares provides a manner through which to determine
the extent of local systems and compare that to broader economic frameworks.

A majority of scholars who work with local ceramics in the Caribbean have suggested
that the market system was the means of ceramic distribution. Handler has said of
Antiguan pottery, "the female potter usually transports her wares to the St Johns market
place on Saturday ... Potters usually remain in the market place, but occasionally, I was
told, they will walk about hawking their wares" (Handler 1964: 151). Duncan
Mathewson (1973: 28) more clearly delineated a course of study centered around market
systems, "What is more important than defining the precise African origin of this type

of ceramic traditions is determining its structure and role within the socio-cultural subsystems of eighteenth century Jamaica." Armstrong (1990: 158), Heath (1988, 1990, 1999), Watters (1988, 1997), Petersen *et al.* (1999), and Crane (1993) have all suggested similar approaches to highlight the mechanisms of ceramic distribution.

Focusing on the eighteenth century, I have attempted to determine the extent to which local ceramics were distributed through the market systems of Jamaica. Adopting an approach in which ceramics are items of exchange in a network of market systems requires a focus on distribution and provenience. Archaeological and historical evidence suggest one of two mechanisms for the distribution of Jamaican earthenwares in the study collection. One mechanism revolves around the local production and distribution of these earthenwares. A second mechanism is a centralized production and an island-wide distribution of the earthenwares. Both mechanisms are hypothesized to represent different strategies of ceramic production and distribution.

At rural sites in Jamaica, locally manufactured forms are usually excavated from domestic contexts related to the houses of enslaved Africans. In urban settings, however, low-fired ceramics have been recovered from contexts associated both with palatial structures, as in the case of King's House, (Mathewson 1972a) and much smaller tenements in Port Royal (Mayes 1972). The simplicity of the forms and the crudeness of the manufacture would support a mechanism of localized manufacture and distribution system. According to this hypothesis, free and enslaved persons in urban and rural contexts would obtain their ceramics from a potter in the area of their residence. It would follow that ceramics in the study collection reflected local articulations, structurally and compositionally.

Then there is the scenario of centralized manufacture of pottery and an island-wide distribution. The similarity of the ceramics' matrix, form, and decorative inventory, suggest that a similar group of potters produced them. There is evidence suggesting that one such group of potters was located along the Rio Cobre River near Spanish Town, Jamaica. Currently, one of the few surviving pottery traditions with ceramics similar to those found in the archaeological record is produced in Spanish Town.

Both scenarios remain plausible given our current state of knowledge on ceramic manufacture and distribution in the eighteenth century. While ideally distinct, archaeological evidence could suggest that these two strategies are not mutually exclusive mechanisms of ceramic distribution. It is possible, for example, to find evidence of both scenarios at a specific site; where one group of ceramics is produced and distributed locally and another group of ceramics is produced centrally and distributed island-wide. In the following section archaeological data will be examined in the light of these hypotheses.

Testing the limits

Focusing on the eighteenth century, this study attempted to determine the extent to which local ceramics were distributed through the market systems of Jamaica. Adopting an approach in which ceramics are items of exchange in a network of market systems requires an emphasis on distribution patterns. Accordingly, my methodology applies ceramic petrography to ceramics recovered from seven sites. With this technique the aim has been to describe the variability of the ceramic population in space and whether that variation was somehow meaningful in the distribution of the pottery.

Seven sites that have been systematically excavated provide excellent spatial and chronological control for this study. These sites include Seville, Drax Hall, Juan De Bollas, Thetford, Spanishtown, St. Peter's Church, and Old Naval Dockyard (Figure 14.1). From these sites there were 6,427 sherds recovered from eighteenth-century contexts. Coarse earthenwares excavated from eighteenth-century contexts include both imported as well as locally produced varieties. All of these were primarily utilitarian in function. An examination of the turn of a late nineteenth-century photograph gives a good indication of these ceramics and their variability (Figure 14.2). The study population included both glazed and slipped *yabbas* (or restricted bowls), Spanish Jars, Chimney Pots, as well as Water Pots (or inverted pots). In addition, the assemblage also contained distinctive imported coarse earthenware, including Spanish jars, red filmed micaceous ware, and Iberian glazed earthenware. I examined a stratified random sample of 164 rim sherds petrographically, 150 of which were from the historic period. The balance of 14 sherds were from the prehistoric period and acted as a control.

Jamaica is a geologically diverse island and the alluvial sediments from which the potters would have extracted their clays reflect this diversity. The island is divided into two blocks: the Cornwall–Middlesex Block and the Blue Mountain block separated by the Wagwater trough in the area of Mona Heights (Robinson *et al.* 1970: 2). There are nine inliers composed of Cretaceous volcanic, metamorphic, and plutonic rocks. These inliers extend from Negril to St Thomas in an east–west direction (Robinson *et al.* 1970: 5).

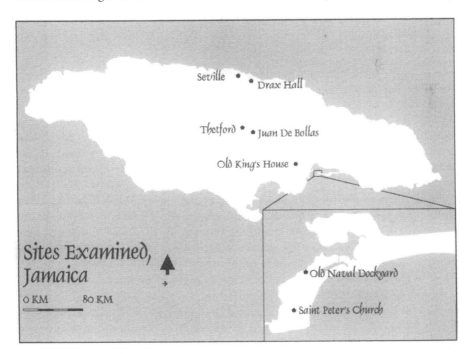

Figure 14.1 Location of sites used in this study, Jamaica.

Figure 14.2 Pot sellers in late-nineteenth-century Kingston (courtesy of the National Anthropology Archives, Smithsonian).

Superimposing these inliers are two limestone groups: the yellow limestone group and the white limestone group. These groups dominate the geology of alluvial sediments. Clays from Jamaica have been examined mineralogically by Green and Black (1970; Black *et al.* 1972), Bailey (1970), Blaise and Fenton (1976). Potential sources for clays include St Catherines' Rio Cobre alluvium (Phillipo 1843; Reeves 1997: 184), Hope River sediment in St Andrews (Sloane 1707), and riverine deposits in St Anne's. These potential clay sources are diverse in the composition of included minerals and the maturity of the soils.

Examination of detrital inclusions found in archaeological samples can be used to establish the heterogeneity of sources employed by potters. The textures of quartz and potassium feldspar, which are relatively resistant to chemical and mechanical weathering, can indicate the type of source rocks from which clay sediments were derived. These inclusions, as components of sediments used to construct pots, can be found in the fabric of archaeological ceramics through petrographic analysis.

Petrographic studies of locally produced ceramics in colonial settings have generally focused on the characterization of ceramic collections from a limited number of sites. Crane (1993), for example, examined 30 sherds from the Heyward-Washington house, hoping to add insight into the process of colonoware manufacture. Heath (1988) examined several St Eustatius collections petrographically, but not within definable exchange networks. Davidson (1995) analyzed sherds from sites associated with ceramic manufacture in Virginia.

Yet, ceramic petrography provides a robust mechanism to determine heterogeneity or homogeneity of clay sources in a geographically varied sample of ceramics (cf. Bishop et al. 1982; Rice 1988; Middleton and Freestone 1991; Orton et al. 1993). Ceramics, viewed as metamorphosed sedimentary rocks (Williams, D. F. 1994: 302), can be described and classified using methods similar to those employed in sedimentary petrography. Standard techniques of thin section petrography, employing a polarizing light microscope, can be used to identify minerals, their textural properties, and their relationship to the matrix (see Orton et al. 1993; Rice 1988). By recording granulometric data on detrital inclusions, including size, shape, sorting, alteration, and orientation, it is possible to determine the source materials, and maturity of the sediment from which the clay was sourced. This information can be turned into semi-quantitative data in order to segregate samples on the basis of composition statistically (Peacock 1970: 381; Gibson and Woods 1990: 225).

A point of complication stemming from petrographic analysis lies in the fact that ceramic manufacture can be a diagenic process. It has been demonstrated that clastic inclusions can go through phase equilibrium changes due to firing (Philpotts and Wilson 1994: 612). Actual clastic inclusions can also be problematic. The addition of sand and shell temper introduces foreign aplastic inclusions into the matrix of the sherd (Orton et al. 1993: 70). Careful examination of textural properties can reduce such complications. It is claimed that foreign and residual clasts can be differentiated on the basis of a bimodal distribution of size and angularity (Hodges 1963: 105; Barnett 1991; Philpotts and Wilson 1994: 611). Mature beach sand, added in the production of ceramics for example, can be differentiated from more immature river sediments where clay was mined. The quartz from the beach sand would be heavily rounded, whereas the immature sediment would have quartz that is more angular. This impact should be minimal and therefore clastic addition should not be difficult to determine.

Results from my petrographic examination of Jamaican samples are quite interesting. Following Stoltman (1999), percentages of clay-sized particles, silt-sized particles, and sand-sized particles were plotted against each other (Figure 14.3). This data indicate that there is considerable variation in the materials used to manufacture the pottery. In the case of the prehistoric pottery, the variation is somewhat concordant with the situation of sites from which the ceramics were excavated. With the historic ceramics, the variation in inclusion size does not correlate easily to the localities from which the ceramics were excavated.

The principal mineral components of the ceramic samples are a fine clay matrix, potassium feldspar, plagioclase feldspar, and quartz. To assess the compositional variability in the parent rocks of the source material, I plotted the relative abundances of the three minerals normalized to percentage on ternary diagrams (Figure 14.4). I first examined the prehistoric pottery to see if there would be significant variation in the composition based on location. What is interesting is that samples from both White Marl and Chancery Hall are heterogeneous and the source material used to make all nine ceramics is incredibly varied. The five ceramics recovered from Maima seem to be relatively homogenous and distinct from the White Marl and Chancery

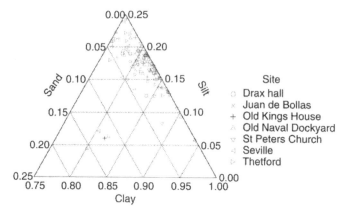

Figure 14.3 Ternary diagram demonstrating variation in the size of included minerals in the clay matrix of the samples examined.

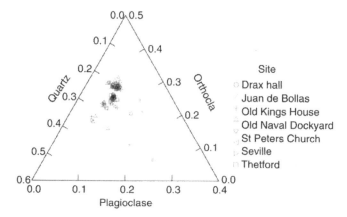

Figure 14.4 Ternary diagram demonstrating variation in the kind of included major minerals in the clay matrix of the samples examined. The three axis are quartz, plagioclase feldspar, and orthoclase feldspar.

Hall ceramics. This illustrates that this particular analysis is sensitive to variation in the sediments used to produce pottery. Turning to the historic ceramics, it is apparent that there are several distinct clusters. It is the assumption of this author that members of these clusters are samples of ceramics that were produced using the same clay source and manufacturing techniques.

For this analysis, I needed to establish two things: (1) the relative homogeneity or heterogeneity of detrital inclusions in the ceramic paste of the samples examined; and (2) whether that heterogeneity is linked to a specific geographic region. If the samples were relatively heterogeneous, and the variation seemed to be correlated with the specific region in which the pottery was recovered, then, I would argue that the pottery distribution is local in scale. If, however, the materials were homogenous, or there was no correlation between variation and site of recovery, then I would argue for more regional distribution.

Table 14.1 Membership table of ceramic population in eighteenth-century Jamaica

Cluster	Drax Hall(%)	Jjan de Bollas(%)	Old Kings House(%)	Old Naval Dockyard(%)	Saint Peters(%)	Seville (%)	Tethford (%)
1	0.0	0.0	25.0	50.0	0.0	25.0	0.0
2	5.6	7.4	31.5	22.2	18.5	3.7	13.0
3	9.8	3.9	21.6	33.3	21.6	9.8	2.0
4	5.9	23.5	5.9	23.5	29.4	5.9	17.6
5	0.0	0.0	14.3	7.1	7.1	7.1	14.3
6	20.0	0.0	20.0	20.0	20.0	40.0	0.0

The composition of the ceramic matrixes indicates that the population, as a whole, is varied. However, by plotting the types of minerals included in the matrix and their sizes, distinct clusters emerge. These clusters indicate that its members were produced within the same relative provenience. This means the same clay source and manufacturing techniques were employed. There are two potential reasons for variation between the clusters. The first reason is that the clay used to make the different ceramics come from different sources. The second is that those different ceramic groups represent different traditions of ceramic manufacture resulting in different textural properties. One can only speculate as to which of these possibilities is correct.

The scope of the analysis, however, was to simply assess the compositional similarity between pots located on the north coast and pots located on the south coast. Within each of the compositional groups there is evidence to indicate that ceramics did originate from the same source (Table 14.1). I found that certain pots recovered from Seville and Drax Hall on the north coast are compositionally identical to pots recovered from Old King's House, Old Naval Dockyard, and Saint Peter's Church on the south coast. This suggests that pots found in Drax Hall, Seville, Juan de Bollas, Thetford, Old King's House, Old Naval Dockyard, and Saint Peter's Church were made by the same people, or in a single locality. The people who lived on these sites and used these pots were of varied economic and social backgrounds with one common denominator: their access to the street markets and *higglers* of eighteenth-century Jamaica.

Conclusions

A combination of historical and archaeological analyses indicates the existence of an economic system in eighteenth-century Jamaica that was at least island-wide in scale. Petrographic analysis of local earthenware shows that these ceramics flowed between the north and south coasts and were involved in a network of commodity trade. The scale of this network suggests that this economy, though in part supporting the plantation economy, also extended beyond it. This is in contrast to the planters' internal marketing system that was both localized and global in scale. The internal market economy, rather than being a functionary of the global economic system, was a partially articulated local economy with its own rules. This chapter has offered one lens through which we might explore how people in a locality create and change their own social relationships. By looking at the interplay between archaeological evidence and the documentary record we can better understand the significance of the markets within the context of eighteenth-century Jamaica.

The informal economy has always been considered a vital institution through which to understand the shaping of everyday life. In a sense, Jamaica in the eighteenth century was a created locality where the colonizers did not have to negotiate with preexisting realms of power. Administrators could ostensibly create and control the institutions through which the enslaved operated. The local in Jamaica should thus be a near perfect articulation of the global, but the internal market system was hardly a perfect nexus between these spheres. Although there is relatively little information on commodity flow, through petrographic analysis of the distribution of local pottery, we can see traces of an economic system through which slaves were able to negotiate their existences.

References

Anonymous [1797] (1976) *Characteristic Traits of the Creolian and African Negroes in Jamaica, &c. &c.*, reprinted from *The Columbian Magazine*, Kingston, Jamaica, April–October, B. Higman (ed.) Mona: Caldwell Press.

Appadurai, Arjun (ed.) (1986) *The Social Life of Things: Commodities in Cultural Perspective*, Washington, DC: Smithsonian Institution Press.

Armstrong, Douglas (1990) *Old Village and the Great House*, Urbana-Champaign, IL: University of Illinois Press.

Bailey, B. V. (1970) *Jamaican Clay Deposits*, Economic Geology Department Report No. 3, Kingston, Jamaica: Economic Geology Department.

Barnett, W. K. (1991) "The identification of clay collection and modification in prehistoric potting at the early neolithic site of Balma Margineda, Andorra," in A. Middleton and I. Freestone (eds) *Recent Developments in Ceramic Petrology, British Occasional Paper No. 81*: 17–38, London: British Museum.

Beckles, Hillary (1989) "Slaves and the internal market economy of Barbados," *Historia Y Sociedad*, 2: 9–31.

Beckles, Hillary (1999) *Centering Women: Gendered Discourses in Caribbean Slave Society*, Kingston: Ian Randle Publishers.

Beckles, Hillary (2003) "An Economic Life of Their Own: Slaves as Commodity Producers and Distributors in Barbados," in G. Heuman (ed.) *The Slavery Reader*, 507–520, Routledge: London.

Best, Lloyd (1998) "Outlines of a model of pure plantation economy (after twenty-five years)," *Marronage*, 1: 27–40.

Best, Lloyd, and Levitt, K. (1967) *Externally Propelled Growth in the Caribbean: Selected Essays*, mimeo. McGill Centre for Developing Area Studies, Montreal: McGill University.

Bishop, R. L., Rands, R. L., and Holey, G. R. (1982) "Ceramic compositional analysis in archaeological perspective," *Advances in Archaeological Method and Theory*, 5: 275–330.

Black, C. D. G., Green, G. W., and Nawrocki, P. E. (1972) *Preliminary Investigation of the Castleton Copper Prospect, Economic Geology Report No. 4*, Kingston, Jamaica: Geological Survey Department, Division of Geology and Mines.

Blaise, Jean, and Fenton, Allison (1976) *Preliminary Investigation of the Mavis Bank Copper Prospect, Economic Geology Report No. 5*, Kingston, Jamaica: Geological Survey Department, Division of Geology and Mines.

Bratten, John R. (n.d.) "Yabba Ware, The African Presence at Port Royal," paper presented for the Society of Historical Archaeology and Underwater Archaeology, January 9, Kingston, Jamaica.

Bush, Barbara (1990) *Slave Women in Caribbean Society: 1650–1838*, Kingston: Ian Randle Publishers.

Campell, John (1991) "As 'A Kind of Freeman'?: Slaves' Market-related Activities in the South Carolina Upcountry, 1800–1860," in Ira Berlin and Philip Morgan (eds) *Cultivation and Culture: Labor and the Shaping of Slave Life in the Americas*, 243–274, London: Taylor & Francis.

Crane, Brian (1993) *Colono Ware and Criollo Ware Pottery from Charleston, South Carolina and San Juan, Puerto Rico in Comparative Perspective*, unpublished PhD dissertation, Department of Anthropology, University of Pennsylvania.

Davidson, T.E. (1995) "The Virginia Earthenware project: characterizing 17th century earthenware by electronic image analysis," *Northeast Historical Archaeology*, 24: 51–64.

Delle, James (1998) *An Archaeology of Social Space: Analyzing Coffee Plantations in Jamaica's Blue Mountains*, New York: Plenum Press.

Dunn, Richard (1972) *Sugar and Slaves: The Rise of the Planter Class in the English West Indies, 1624–1713*, New York: Norton and Company.

Earle, Timothy (1987) "Specialization and the Production of Wealth: Hawaiin Chiefdoms and the Inka Empire," in E. Brumfiel and T. Earle (eds) *Specialization, Distribution and Exchange in Complex Societies*, 64–75. Cambridge: Cambridge University Press.

Ebanks, Roderick (1984) "Ma Lou, an Afro Jamaican pottery tradition," *Jamaica Journal*, 17: 31–37.

Edwards, Bryan [1801] (1972) *The History, Civil and Commercial, of the British Colonies in the West Indies 1793–1794s*, 3 vols, New York: Ayer Company.

Frank, Gunder (1978) *World Accumulation, 1492–1789*, New York: Monthly Review Press.

Frank, Gunder (1999) "Abuses and Uses of World Systems Theory in Archaeology," in Nick Kardulias (ed.) *World-Systems Theory in Practice: Leadership, Production and Exchange*, 275–296, London: Rowman Littlefield.

Gibson, A., and Woods, A. (1990) *Prehistoric Pottery for the Archaeologist*, Leicester: Leicester University Press.

Green, G. W., and Black, C. D. G. (eds) (1970) *The Geology of the Hellshire Hills Quadrangle*, *Geological Survey, Bulletin No. 7*, Kingston, Jamaica: Geological Survey Department, Division of Geology and Mines.

Handler, Jerome (1964) "Notes on Pottery Making in Antigua," *Man*, 64: 184–185.

Hauser, Mark W. (1997) *Embedded Identities: Seeking Economic and Social Relations through Compositional Analysis of Low-Fired Earthenware*, unpublished MA thesis, Department of Anthropology, Syracuse University.

Hauser, Mark, W.(2000) *Distribution of Local Ceramics in Eighteenth Century Jamaica*, Report on file with Jamaica National Heritage Trust, Kingston, Jamaica.

Hauser, Mark W., and Armstrong, Douglas (1999) "Embedded Identities: Seeking Economic and Social Relations through Compositional Analysis of Low-Fired Earthenware," in Jay Haviser (ed.) *African Sites Archaeology in the Caribbean*, 65–93, Kingston, Jamaica: Ian Randle Publishers.

Heath, Barbara (1988) *Afro Caribbean Ware: A Study of Ethnicity on St. Eustatius*, unpublished PhD dissertation, Department of Anthropology, University of Pennsylvania.

Heath, Barbara (1990) " 'Pots of earth': forms and functions of Afro-caribbean ceramics," *Florida Journal of Anthropology*, 16, 7: 33–50.

Heath, Barbara (1999) "Yabbas, Monkeys, Jugs, and Jars: A Historical Context for African Caribbean Potterys on St Eustatius," in Jay Haviser (ed.) *African Sites Archaeology in the Caribbean*, 196–220, Kingston: Ian Randle Publishers.

Higman, Barry (1996) "Patterns of Exchange within a Plantation Economy: Jamaica at the Time of Emancipation," in Roderick McDonald (ed.) *West Indies Accounts: Essays on the History of the British Caribbean and the Atlantic Economy*, 211–231, Kingston: University of the West Indies Press.

Higman, Barry (1998) *Montpelier, Jamaica*, Kingston: University of the West Indies Press.

Hodges, H. M. W. (1963) "The Examination of Ceramic Materials in Thin Section," in E. Pyddoke (ed.) *The Scientist and Archaeology*, 101–110, New York: Roy Publishers.

Kopytoff, I. (1986) "The Cultural Biography of Things: Commoditization as Process," in A. Appadurai (ed.) *The Social Life of Things: Commodities in Cultural Perspective*, 131–148, Washington, DC: Smithsonian Institution Press.

Lewis, M. G. (1929) *M.G.:A Journal of a West Indian Proprieter 1815–17*, Boston, MA: Houghton Mifflin Company.

Long, Edward (1774) *A History of Jamaica*, 3 Vol, London: Longman.

Lovejoy, Paul (1981) *Transformations in Slavery: A History of Slavery in Africa*, Cambridge: Cambridge University Press.

McDonald, Roderick (1991) "Independent Economic Production by Slaves on Antebellum Louisiana Sugar Plantations," in Ira Berlin and Philip Morgan (eds) *The Slaves' Economy: Independent Production by Slaves in the Americas*, 182–208, London: Taylor & Francis.

McDonald, Roderick (1993) *The Economy and Material Culture of Slaves*, Baton Rouge, LA: Louisiana State University Press.

Mathewson, R. D. (1972a) "History from the Earth: Archaeological Excavations at Old King's House," *Jamaica Journal*, 6: 3–11.

Mathewson, R. D. (1972b) "Jamaican Ceramics: An introduction to 18th century folk pottery in West African tradition," *Jamaica Journal*, 6: 54–56.

Mathewson, R. D. (1973) "Archaeological analysis of material culture as a reflection of sub-cultural differentiation in 18th century Jamaica," *Jamaica Journal* 7: 25–29.

Mayes, Phillip (1972) *Port Royal, Jamaica: Excavations 1969–70*, Kingston: Jamaican National Heritage Trust.

Meyers, Allan D. (1999) "West African tradition in the decoration of colonial Jamaican folk pottery," *Journal of Historical Archaeology*, 3, 4: 201–224.

Middleton, A., and I. C. Freestone (eds) (1991) *Recent Developments in Ceramic Petrology, British Occasional Paper No. 81*, London: British Museum.

Mintz, Sidney (1955) "The Jamaican internal marketing pattern," *Social and Economic Studies*, 4: 95–103.

Mintz, Sidney (1960) "Peasant Markets," *American Scientific*, 203, 2: 112–122.

Mintz, Sidney (1974) *Caribbean Transformations*, Chicago, IL: Aldine Publishing.

Mintz, Sidney (1983) "Caribbean Marketplaces and Caribbean History," *Radical History Review*, 27:110–120.

Mintz, Sidney (1985) *Sweetness and Power*, New York: Penguin Books.

Mintz, Sidney, and Douglas Hall (1991) "The origin of the Jamaican internal market system," in Hillary Beckles and Verene Shepberd (eds) *Caribbean Slave Society and Economy A Student Reader*, Kingston: Ian Randle Publishers.

Olwell, Robert (1996) " 'Loose, Idle and Disorderly': Slave Women in the Eigteenth-Century Charleston Marketplace," in David Barry Gaspar and Darlene Clark Hine (eds) *More than Chattel: Black Women and Slavery in the Americas*, Bloomington, IN: Indiana University Press.

Olwig, Karen (1977) *Households, Exchange and Social Reproduction: The Development of a Caribbean Society*, unpublished PhD dissertation, Anthropology, University of Minnesota, Minneapolis.

Olwig, Karen (1985) *Cultural Adaptation and Resistance on St. John: Three Centuries of Afro-Caribbean Life*. Gainesville, FL: University of Florida Press.

Orser, Charles (1996) *A Historical Archaeology of the Modern World*, New York: Plenum.

Orton, C., Tyers, P., and Vince, A. (1993) *Pottery in Archaeology*, Cambridge: Cambridge University Press.

Pasquariello, Raymond (1995) *An Analysis of Non-European, Coarse Earthenware from Port Royal, Jamaica*, MA thesis, Department of Anthropology, Syracuse University.

Patterson, Orlando (1969) *The Sociology of Slavery*, Rutherford, NJ: Farliegh Dickinson University Press.

Peacock, D. P. S. (1970) "The scientific analysis of ancient ceramics: a review," *World Archaeology*, 1: 375–389.

Petersen, J., Watters, D., and Nicholson, D. (1999) "Continuity and Syncretism in Afro-Caribbean Ceramics from the Northern Lesser Antilles," in Jay Haviser (ed.) *African Sites Archaeology in the Caribbean*, 157–220, Kingston: Ian Randle Publishers.

Phillippo, James (1843) *Jamaica, Its Past and Present*, London: Dawson.

Philpotts, A. R. and Wilson, Nancy (1994) "Application of petrofabric and phase equilibria analysis to the study of a potsherd," *Journal of Archaeological Science*, 21: 607–618.

Pitman, Frank (1917) *The Development of the British West Indies, 1700–1763*, New Haven, CT: Yale University Press.

Reeves, Matthew (1997) *By Their Own Labour: Enslaved Africans' Survival Strategies on Two Jamaican Plantations*, unpublished PhD dissertation, Department of Anthropology, Syracuse University.

Rice, Prudence (1988) *Pottery Analysis: A Sourcebook*, Chicago: University of Chicago Press.

Robinson, E., Lewus, J., and Cant, R. (1970) *Field Guide to Aspects of the Geology of Jamaica. Guidebook to the Caribbean Island Arc System*, Washington, DC: American Geological Institute.

Roseberry, William (1989) "Peasants and the World," in Stuart Plattner (ed.) *Economic Anthropology*, 108–127, Stanford, CA: Stanford University Press.

Schlotterboeck, John (1991) "The Internal Economy of Slavery in Rural Piedmont Virginia," in Ira Berlin and Philip Morgan (eds) *The Slaves' Economy: Independent Production by Slaves in the Americas*, London: Taylor & Francis.

Sheridan, Richard (1973) *Sugar and Slavery: An Economic History of the British West Indies, 1623–1775*, Baltimore, MD: Johns Hopkins University Press.

Sloane, Hans (1707) *A Voyage to the Islands Madera, Barbados, Nieves, S. Christophers, and Jamaica: With the Natural History of the Herbs and Trees, Four-footed Beasts, Fishes, Birds, Insects, Reptiles, &c. of the Last of Those Islands to Which is Prefix'd an Introduction, Wherein is an Account of the Inhabitants, Air, Waters, Diseases, Trade, &c. of that Place, with Some Relations Concerning the Neighbouring Continent, and Islands of America. Illustrated with Figures of the Things Described, Which Have not been Heretofore Engraved in Large Copper-plates as Big as the Life*, London: Published by Author.

Spyer, Patricia (2000) *Memory of Trade: Modernity's Entanglements on an Eastern Indonesian Island*, Durham, NC: Duke University Press.

Stahl, Ann Bower (2002) "Colonial entanglements and the practices of taste: an alternative to logocentric approaches," *American Anthropologist*, 104, 3: 827–845.

Stern, Steven (1988) "Feudalism, capitalism and the world system in the perspective of Latin America and the Caribbean," *American Historical Review*, 93: 829–872.

Stoltman, James (1999) "The Chaco-Chuska Connection: In Defense of Anna Shephard," in James Skibo and Gary Feinman (eds) *Pottery and People: A Dynamic Interaction*, 9–24, Salt Lake, UT: University of Utah Press.

Thomas, Nicholas (1991) *Entangled Objects: Exchange, Material Culture and Colonialism in the Pacific*, Cambridge, MA: Harvard University Press.

Tomich, Dale (1991) "*Une Petite* Guinee: Provision Ground and Plantation in Martinique, 1830–1848," in Ira Berlin and Philip Morgan (eds) *Cultivation and Culture: Labor and the Shaping of Slave Life in the Americas*, 221–242, London: Taylor & Francis.

Tomich, Dale (1994) "Small Islands, Large Comparisons," *Social Science History*, 18, 3: 339–358.

Turner, Mary (1991) "Slave workers, Subsistence and Labour Bargaining: Amity Hall, Jamaica, 1805–1832," in Ira Berlin and Philip Morgan (eds) *The Slaves' Economy: Independent Production by Slaves in the Americas*, 92–105, London: Taylor & Francis.

Turner, Mary (1995) "Chattle Slaves into Wage Slaves," in Mary Turner (ed.) *From Chattle Slaves to Wage Slaves*, 33–47, Kingston: Ian Randle Press.

Wallerstein, Immanuel (1974) "The rise and future demise of the world capitalist system: Concepts for comparative analysis," *Comparative Studies in Social History*, 16: 387–415.

Wellerstein, Immanuel (1980) *The Modern World System II: Mercantilism and the Consolidation of the European World Economy*, New York: Academic Press.

Watters, David (1988) "Afro-Montserratian ceramics from the Harney Site cemetary, Montserrat, West Indies," *Annals of the Carnegie Museum*, 57: 167–187.

Watters, David (1997) "Historical Documentation and Archaeological Investigation of Codrington Castle Barbuda, West Indies," *Annals of the Carnegie Museum*, 66: 229–288.

Wilkie, Laurie, and Paul Farnsworth (1999) "Trade and the Construction of Bahamian Identity: A Multiscalar Exploration," *International Journal of Historical Archaeology*, 3: 283–320.

Williams, D. F. (1983) "The Petrology of Ceramics," in D. R. C. Kempe and Anthony P. Harvey (eds) *The Petrology of Archaeological Artefacts*, 301–329, Oxford: Clarendon Press.

Williams, E. [1944] (1994) *Capitalism and Slavery*, Chapel Hill, NC: University of North Carolina Press.

Williams, E. (1970) *From Columbus to Castro: The History of the Caribbean*, New York: Vintage Books.

Wolf, Eric (1982) *Europe and the Peoples Without History*, Berkeley, CA: University of California Press.

15 African community identity at the cemetery

JOHN P. McCARTHY

Introduction

The archaeology of cemeteries is concerned both with burial practices and the wealth of information available from the osteological record. As I have argued previously, this information must be properly contextualized to give it meaning (McCarthy 1997). Thus it is important to know whose grave and bodily remains we are studying.

Mortuary archaeology considers the graves of individuals whose identities included, but were not limited to, membership in the communities in which they lived and worked. The graves of the working people of the past, and of African-Americans in particular, are often anonymous in that we do not know the specific identity of the individual in the grave. Grave markers from such cemeteries, if ever present, may have been of natural materials, such as fieldstone boulders. They may have been of impermanent materials, which did not survive the elements, such as wooden crosses. Or, they may have been removed through lack of respect for the dead coupled with a desire to put the land to "productive use." It is often the case that we only know that the deceased was a member of a particular congregation or community.

This chapter discusses some theoretical issues pertaining to death and social identity and then presents a summary of my ongoing research on African-influenced burial practices in Antebellum Philadelphia to illustrate the expression of African community identity in the context of burial. I will argue that European objects were given new, African-influenced, and socially charged meanings reflecting a uniquely African-American sociocultural identity. Further, the considerably *greater* occurrence of what appear to be creolized burial practices, in the *later* of the two cemeteries associated with the First African Baptist Church (FABC), suggests the maintenance, or revival, of African identity was an active expression of resistance to domination in a context of in-migration, economic stress, and growing racism in the first half of the nineteenth century.

Death and identity

In the last decade or so there has emerged a literature in the social sciences concerned with theories of the body, and the body's central place in the formation and expression of social identity. Such studies have been influenced to a considerable degree by Foucault's (e.g. 1973, 1977) work demonstrating that our understanding of such apparently natural things as the mind and the body are, in fact, socially constructed through a series of historically and culturally specific discourses in which social power is expressed. Additionally, increasing importance has been attached to a phenomenological perspective that emphasizes a materiality in which the human subject is the primary site for all perceptions and social action. Shilling (1993: 1) crystallized this position in stating that "there is a tendency for the body to become increasingly central to ... a person's sense of self-identity." Thus, for many people it may be considered that BODY = SELF.

A subset of this writing is concerned specifically with death, dying, and identity. These are bodies in a state of crisis or transformation (e.g. Hallam et al. 1999). In this context, looking cross-culturally, one finds that the relationship between the body and the self is not so straightforward. There are live bodies without effective self-identity: the "brain dead" of intensive care wards; zombies that are not exactly dead and that may or may not have self; and finally, there are "selves" without corporal presence—ancestors, ghosts, and various god/godess-figures (Hallam et al. 1999: 1–2).

The anthropological literature has long recognized that death and its attendant rituals are important events in which key values and beliefs are represented, often in over-determined forms (e.g. Levi-Strauss 1973). For example, a Durkheimian perspective would see transformative effects through participation in rituals—taking the personal and individual and making it social. In this vein, Giddens (1991: 54) has suggested that through death's liminal quality personal identity may be gathered, sifted, and recast. That which is left unsaid or unexpressed, those identities that are lost, result in disturbing silences that resonate powerfully—particularly in societies that afford the continuity of individual biography a high priority.

Bodies have individual personal histories that are part of dynamic sociocultural relations and particular historical processes. Religious beliefs, morals, and value systems, themselves temporally dynamic, construe various relationships between individual bodies, communities, and broader social contexts.

In the context of ritual burial practices then, what we as archaeologists encounter is not the body as self-identified or a site for individual agency but, rather, the individual as understood, imagined, and constructed by surviving family and community members (Hallam et al. 1999: 19). Self-identity then, in this sense, is inter-subjective and collective, much like Barth's (1969) notion of ethnicity. It is not enough that one identifies one's self as a member of a particular group; one must also be recognized by others as a member of that group. Identity then, in the context of burial, does not rely solely on the self as an agent. In fact it cannot. In death, the self becomes truly powerless and must rely on others for identity and action. Thus, individual and community identities are reconciled in the graveside, if nowhere else. The cemetery, then, is a special venue for the expression of identity.

Burial practices at the First African Baptist Church cemeteries

The two cemeteries associated with the FABC were excavated preceding the construction of the Vine Street Expressway, a six-lane, depressed grade highway running through central Philadelphia. In 1983 and 1984, a cemetery located near 8th and Vine Streets was excavated. This cemetery had been in use from 1824 to at least 1841, and contained the remains of approximately 140 individuals (Parrington and Roberts 1990). In 1990, a second cemetery was excavated near 10th and Vine Street. This site had been used from 1810 to 1822, and the remains of approximately 85 individuals were recovered (McCarthy 1997).

In the course of the excavation of these cemeteries, a number of what appear to be non-Christian, African-influenced burial practices were observed. However, the positioning and orientation of the burials in both cemeteries followed Christian convention widely found in North America; that is, the deceased were laid supine on their backs with hands together on the abdomen or to the sides of the body with the head of the deceased to the west. The head was placed toward the west so that the deceased would be facing east so as to view Christ's Second Coming.

Both sites had been affected by redevelopment activities after their abandonment as cemeteries. No grave markers or surface deposited decorations were found at either site. All evidence of African-influenced customs was found at the level of the actual burial, either in or immediately outside the coffin. These practices included: (1) placement of a single coin in the coffin, usually near the head of the deceased; (2) burial of a shoe on the top of the coffin; and (3) burial of a plate on the stomach of the deceased.

The practice of placing coins on each of the eyes of the deceased is widely documented in many cultures (Puckle 1926: 50–51), but this was observed in only two instances at the FABC cemeteries. In both of these cases, the burials had been disturbed during the redevelopment of the property, and I believe that the coins were placed at that point in time (inasmuch as the coins were found deeply set into the eye sockets of the individuals skulls). More commonly, a single coin was found inside the coffin, nearly always near the head. This monetary offering may represent an association of death with a journey, perhaps back to an African homeland, with the coin being provided to pay for passage. The placement of similar monetary offerings is documented in some areas of West Africa, where it is generally associated with passage over the river of death to an afterlife (Parrinder 1961: 107).

Single coins have been recovered from at least 11 other African-American burials in the American South (Cabak and Wilson n.d.), and there is a report of a coinlike metal disk recovered from an African grave in Montserrat (Waters 1994). A total of 48 coins were recovered from the graves of 28 individuals at the Freedmans' Cemetery in Dallas, Texas (Peter et al. 2000: 429). Twenty-one of these were drilled or pierced (Peter et al.: 430). Pierced coins were often worn by African-Americans around the neck or ankle for spiritual and bodily protection (Puckett 1968: 288, 314). Such coins are commonly recovered at African-American habitation sites in the South, such as the slave quarters at President Andrew Jackson's home, the Hermitage, outside Nashville, Tennessee (Russell 1997). However, none of the coins from the FABC burials had been pierced.

In six cases the remains of a shoe were found placed on top of the coffin. Shoes can be seen as being required for a journey. While we may take shoes for granted in our post-industrial, disposable economy, in the past shoes were costly items of apparel, especially for the rural poor. The receipt of one's first pair of shoes, regardless of race, was often a special event that marked a stage in the passage from child to adult, and as such, was especially remembered. Shoes are also associated with African-American folk beliefs concerning power over spirits or good luck. It is said that burial of a shoe under a full moon will keep the devil away (Puckett 1968: 555). The association of shoes with spiritual protection may have originated in Europe, for in southern England and parts of northern continental Europe shoes were used as house charms from medieval times into the nineteenth century (Merrifield 1988). There are apparently well over 1,000 documented cases of such charms (Eastop 2001).

Over the course of their use shoes take on the shape of the wearer's foot, and it is probably no coincidence that the bottom of the shoe is the sole (a metaphor as pun?). Shoe house charms misdirected the devil and protected the inhabitants. Burial of a shoe under a full moon to keep the devil away suggests a similar effort to misdirect evil. Burial of a shoe with the deceased may represent putting the soul to rest with the body. Archaeological documentation of this practice seems to be limited to the FABC and the Freedmans' Cemetery, where the remains of a shoe were recovered from the lid of one coffin (Peter et al. 2000: 428).

Finally, a ceramic plate had been placed on the stomach of the deceased inside the coffin of two burials at the 8th Street cemetery: the first was of blue edge-decorated pearlware, a widely popular earthenware of English manufacture, and the second was of handpainted Chinese porcelain. The Old World and Native American archaeological literatures are replete with examples of ceramic vessels as "grave goods" in burials, and the placement of pottery grave goods is extremely common throughout much of West and Central Africa (Handler and Lange 1978: 200). Ceramic grave goods have been documented in colonial period graves in Ghana, for example (DeCorse 1992: 183). Such offerings were apparently provided for use by the deceased in the afterlife and perhaps also served as a form of social display of wealth and power.

The recovery of ceramic vessels from historic period burials in North America is *not*, however, common at all, although a number of examples have been documented in the South and the Caribbean. Cabak and Wilson (n.d.) documented five examples of the recovery of ceramic vessels from nineteenth-century African-American burials in the South. Four of these were saucers found either on the chest or pelvis of the deceased, and in the fifth case a flower pot found at the foot of the coffin. A shallow red earthenware bowl was found in the grave of an African at the Newton Plantation Cemetery in Barbados (Handler and Lange 1978: 136), and a white salt-glazed stoneware saucer and a feather-edged creamware plate, both of eighteenth-century English manufacture, were recovered from two English graves in Jamaica (Fremmer 1973). Finally, an ironstone plate was recovered from the grave of a poorly preserved female of indeterminate race at the nineteenth-century Quaker Cemetery in Alexandria, Virginia (Shepard and Bromberg n.d.).

Fremmer (1973) concluded that the inclusion of the ceramic vessels in the two Jamaican cases was likely due to oversight, rather than the result of an intentional act. However, he also noted that in isolated parts of Jamaica it is traditional to place a dish containing a mixture of coffee and salt on the stomach of the deceased throughout the wake and burial. I've been told by African-Jamaicans that this practice and other uses of salt during a funeral are meant to keep the devil away. Several authors writing on rituals of death have also reported that plates of salt were traditionally used in parts of Ireland and England to control odor and/or the bloating of the deceased. This practice is also reported in Appalachia during the nineteenth century (Crissman 1994: 32). However, the practice does not seem to have been widespread, or at least, not to have often resulted in the burial of the ceramic vessel. With the exception of the 8th Street FABC cemetery, there are no known examples of the recovery of plates from burial contexts anywhere in the northern United States or Canada.

It is possible that these plates were deliberately placed in the graves for use in the afterlife, or the plate last used by the deceased may have been buried in an effort to prevent the deceased's spirit from harming the living. In parts of the American South and Africa it was believed that the "energy" or "essence" of the dead was embodied in objects last used (Thompson 1969: 151–152). Barley's (1994) analysis of African pottery traditions asserts the importance of pots in Africa deriving from concerns with "non-material forces" that can act only through localization in a material object. These pots then serve to contain or direct the force. Pots are often ritually smashed in order to destroy these forces. If the plates had been deliberately broken, then that would lend support to the notion that their placement in the grave was to "ground" the energy of the deceased. However, excavation photographs indicate that the plates were probably broken *in situ* by the weight of earth pressing down upon them.

The practices described above appear to reflect African-influenced, creolized adaptations of European material culture and perhaps European folk practices as well. John Vlach (1991) documented the survival and maintenance of African traditions in a wide range of folk arts and crafts, and noted that various art forms possess a cultural unity. Indeed, stylistic consistency in design and the process of creation (style and performance) appear to be major aspects of ethnic integrity in African-American culture. Whereas some artifacts represent the uninterrupted survival of African traditions, such as coiled grass baskets produced in the Carolina Low Country, others (such as quilts) incorporate *African* themes and meanings into *European* objects. Leland Ferguson's (1992) analysis of Colonoware pottery suggests a similar adaptation of European forms into an African craft tradition.

Historian Sterling Stuckey (1987: 43) observed that being on good terms with the spirits of the ancestors was an overarching concern of enslaved Africans throughout the New World. Various songs, rhythms, movements, and belief in the curative powers of roots and the efficacy of a world of spirits and ancestors appear to have survived well into the nineteenth century and even beyond. These were then combined in creative ways with the various evangelical denominations of Christianity to which Africans on the North American mainland were introduced. Enthusiastic singing, clapping, dancing, and even spirit-possession were and remain common, in the context of African-American Christian liturgy. The concept of syncretism, the synthesis of cultural forms, is helpful here. Once a disparaging ethnocentric label for traditions that were seen as impure, or inauthentic, due to incorporation of local ideas and/ or practices, this concept is now recognized as a force that can support resistance to cultural dominance, provide links to a lost history, and/or provide a means of establishing identity.

Discussion and conclusions

It is particularly interesting that there is greater occurrence of African or creolized burial practices at the *later* of the two cemeteries. Only two burials in the *earlier* 10th Street cemetery exhibited clear evidence of African burial practices. In those instances, a single coin was recovered from the interior of the coffin. In contrast, the later 8th Street cemetery included eight coffins each containing a single coin. In six cases the remains of a single shoe were found on the coffin lid, and the two burials containing ceramic plates were both found in the later cemetery as well. The relative occurrence of African-influenced burial practices in the 1810–1822 cemetery is between 2.5 and 6.0 percent, depending upon how one interprets the evidence, with the lower number being, in my mind, the more likely. In the 1824–1841 cemetery, the relative occurrence is nearly 11.5 percent. In absolute terms, clear examples of these African-influenced burial practices are eight times more common in the later of the two cemeteries.

At the end of the eighteenth century, people of African ancestry comprised just 10 percent of Philadelphia's population. Earlier, in 1780, when slavery was abolished in Pennsylvania, the proportion may have been as low as about 4 percent (Nash 1988:143). In Philadelphia, enslaved Africans lived in close proximity to their masters, who often held only one or two slaves and seldom more than four (Nash 1988:13). While new slave arrivals helped to renew African-based cultural practices, the preponderant pressure on enslaved Africans in Philadelphia was to outwardly adapt to the culture of the European-descended majority with whom they lived in close contact.

In the first half of the nineteenth century, Philadelphia was transformed from a colonial port into the most important industrial center in the United States (Cochran 1982). Population growth, ethnic diversification, and social distinction were part and parcel of the economic changes transforming the city at this time (Laurie 1974). Philadelphia became the largest and most important center of free African-American life in the USA (Curry 1981). At this time, most of the city's new African-American residents were freed slaves who migrated from the South.

The growth of both immigrant and African-American populations caused increasing competition for the same unskilled jobs. In the economically difficult years surrounding the Panic of 1838, many workers were reduced to part-time employment and as many as one-third are estimated to have fled the city to seek work elsewhere (Laurie 1980: 108). While Pennsylvania in 1780 became the first state to abolish slavery, late eighteenth-century Enlightenment ideals of the universal equality of humankind gave way to nativist and racist sentiments by the 1830s and the voting rights of African-Americans were rescinded in 1837 (Nash 1988: 10–4). Between 1838 and 1847, Philadelphia African-Americans are estimated to have suffered a 10 percent decrease in per capita wealth (Hershberg 1973: 114). In the first half of the nineteenth century, free African-Americans in Philadelphia, and throughout the urban north, became what historian Leonard Curry (1981: 82) has termed "a wholly-distinct and outcast class."

Despite these conditions, the African-American community of Philadelphia continued to grow, developing its own means of dealing with a hostile social environment. The success of African-Americans in Philadelphia prompted Frederick Douglas to write in 1848, that Philadelphia "more than any other (city) in our land, holds the destiny of our people" (quoted in Nash 1988: 6). In fact, in 1845 six African-Americans were among the city's several dozen wealthiest people (Lapsansky 1980: 57). The African-American community formed separate institutional structures including not only churches, but also mutual aid societies and chapters of the masons and other fraternal organizations (Curry 1981; Nash 1988).

Accordingly, in-migration of former slaves from the South, and the growing resentment and racism of the larger society, may have served to revitalize certain signs and symbols of African identity within Philadelphia's increasingly autonomous African-American community, and particularly within that community's own newly formed institutions. The maintenance, or revival, of African-influenced burial customs in the 8th Street FABC (1824–1841), then, fits into this overall pattern of in-migration and socioeconomic stress, evidencing the community members' active resistance to domination.

References

Barley, N. (1994) *Smashing Pots: Feats of Clay from Africa*, London: British Museum Press.

Barth, F. (1969) *Ethnic Groups and Boundaries*, Boston: Little Brown.

Cabak, M. A., and Wilson, K. (n.d.) "Gender differences among African-American interments in the American south," paper presented at the Annual Meeting of the Society for Historical Archaeology, Atlanta, Georgia, January 1998.

Cochran, T. C. (1982) "Philadelphia: the American industrial centre, 1750–1850," *The Pennsylvania Magazine of History and Biography*, 106, 3: 323–340.

Crissman, J. K. (1994) *Death and Dying in Central Appalachia: Changing Attitudes and Practices*, Urbana and Chicago, IL: University of Illinois Press.

Curry, L. P. (1981) *The Free Black in Urban America, 1800–1850: The Shadow of the Dream*, Chicago, IL: The University of Chicago Press.

DeCorse, C. (1992) "Culture contact, continuity, and change on the Gold Coast, A.D. 1400–1900," *African Archaeological Review*, 10: 163–196.

Eastop, D. (2001) "Garments deliberately concealed in buildings," in R. Wallis and K. Lymer (eds) *A Permeability of Boundaries? New Approaches to the Archaeology of Art, Religion, and Folklore*, BAR International Series S936, 79–84, Oxford: Archaeopress.

Ferguson, L. (1992) *Uncommon Ground: Archaeology and Early African America, 1650–1800*, Washington, DC: Smithsonian Institution Press.

Foucault, M. (1973) *The Birth of the Clinic: An Archaeology of Medical Perception*, London: Tavistock.

Foucault, M. (1977) *Discipline and Punish: Birth of the Prison*, London: Tavistock.

Fremmer, R. (1973) "Dishes in colonial graves: evidence from Jamaica," *Historical Archaeology*, 7: 58–62.

Giddens, A. (1991) *Modernity and Self Identity: Self and Society in the Late Modern Age*, Stanford, CA: Stanford University Press.

Hallam, E., Hockey, J., and Howarth, G. (1999) *Beyond the Body: Death and Social Identity*, London: Routledge.

Handler, J. S., and Lange, F. W. (1978) *Plantation Slavery in Barbados: An Archaeological and Historical Investigation*, Cambridge, MA: Harvard University Press.

Hershberg, T. (1973) "Free Blacks in Antebellum Philadelphia," in A. F. Davis and M. H. Haller (eds) *The Peoples of Philadelphia: A History of Ethnic Groups and Lower-Class Life, 1790–1940*, 111–134, Philadelphia, PA: Temple University Press.

Lapsansky, E. J. (1980) " 'Since they got those separate churches': Afro-Americans and racism in Jacksonian Philadelphia," *American Quarterly*, 32, 1: 54–78.

Laurie, B. (1974) " 'Nothing on compulsion': lifestyles of Philadelphia artisans, 1820–1850," *Labor History*, 15, 3: 337–366.

Laurie, B. (1980) *Working People of Philadelphia, 1800–1850*, Philadelphia, PA: Temple University Press.

Levi-Strauss, C. (1973) *Tristes Tropiques*, London: Cape Publishers.

McCarthy, J. P. (1997) "Material culture and the performance of sociocultural identity: community, ethnicity, and agency in the burial practices at the First African Baptist Church cemeteries, Philadelphia, 1810–1841," in A. S. Martin and J. R. Garrison (eds) *American Material Culture, The Shape of the Field*, 359–379, Knoxville, TN: The University of Tennessee Press.

Merrifield, R. (1988) *Archaeology of Ritual and Magic*, New York: New Amsterdam Books.

Nash, G. B. (1988) *Forging Freedom: The Formation of Philadelphia's Black Community, 1720–1840*, Cambridge, MA: Harvard University Press.

Parrinder, G. [1949] (1961) *West African Religion: A Study of the Beliefs and Practices of Akan, Ewe, Yoruba, Ibo, and Kindred Peoples*, London: Epworth Press.

Parrington, M., and Roberts, D. G. (1990) "Demographic, Cultural, and Bioanthropological Aspects of a Nineteenth-century Free Black Population," in J. E. Buikstra (ed.) *A Life in Science: Papers in Honor of J. Lawrence Angel*, Scientific Papers 6, 138–170, Kampsville, IL: Center for American Archaeology.

Peter, D. E., Prior, M., Green, M. M., and Clow, V. G. (eds) (2000) *Freedman's Cemetery: A Legacy of a Pioneer Black Community in Dallas, Texas*, Plano, TX: Geo Marine, Inc.

Puckett, N. N. [1926] (1968) *Folk Beliefs of the Southern Negro*, Montclair, NJ: Patterson Smith.

Puckle, B. S. (1926) *Funeral Customs, Their Origin and Development*, London: T. Werner Laurie, Ltd.

Russell, A. E. (1997) Material Culture and African-American Spirituality at the Hermitage, *Historical Archaeology*, 31, 2: 63–80.

Shepard, S. J., and Blomberg, F. W. (n.d.) "The Quaker burying ground in Alexandria: archaeological evidence of eighteenth- and nineteenth-century burial practices," paper presented at the Annual Meeting of the Society for Historical Archaeology, Washington, DC, January 1995.

Shilling, C. (1993) *The Body and Social Theory*, London: Sage Publications.

Stuckey, Sterling (1987) *Slave Culture: Nationalist Theory and the Foundations of Black America*, New York: Oxford University Press.

Thompson, R. F. (1969) "African Influences on the Art of the United States," in A. L. Robinson, C. C. Foster, and D. H. Ogilvie (eds) *Black Studies in the University: A Symposium*, 122–170, New Haven, CT: Yale University Press.

Vlach, J. M. (1991) *By the Work of Their Hands: Studies in Afro-American Folklife*, Charlottesville, VA: The University Press of Virginia.

Waters, D. R. (1994) "Mortuary patterns at the Harney Site slave cemetery, Montserrat, a Caribbean perspective," *Historical Archaeology*, 28, 3: 56–73.

16   The archaeological study of the African Diaspora in Brazil

Some ethnic issues

PEDRO PAULO A. FUNARI

Introduction

What do we understand, when we speak of "Diaspora"? In its original usage, the Greek term referred to the dispersion of people (*John* vii, 35), or to "the scattered people" (*Peter* 1, 1). Such peoples were not necessarily forced to disperse, yet this is precisely the meaning associated with the forced transfer of millions of Africans to the New World.

Brazil has the largest number of people of African descent outside of Africa and archaeology plays a special role in the rescue of African values. For centuries, the vast majority of people in Brazil were Africans or people of African descent—even if they were neglected in the documentary record. Africans in Brazil were enslaved for several centuries and were ethnically mixed, so that they did not usually retain their own languages and customs. The best way to have access to their heritage is thus through the study of past material culture. Brazil today is a country with mixed origins: some 40 million people have Native American descent; another 40 million have African descent; and 80 million have a wide variety of origins (Portuguese, Arab, Jewish, Italian, but also Japanese, and more recently Korean, among many others).

In this chapter I try to address some issues relating to African ethnicity in Brazil through an archaeological case study: Palmares, the seventeenth-century rebel ("maroon") polity. I begin by dealing with the mixed features of Brazilian society, then show how archaeological theory and praxis is linked to politics, and finally turn my attention to Palmares and its ethnic identity.

Mixed features of Brazilian society

The two main features of Brazilian society are huge social inequalities and the seclusion of the so-called non-Europeans. It has been so since the inception of the colonization and is the result of the hierarchical character of the Brazilian social system (Da Matta 1991: 399), and as a consequence of the dominance of patronage. Considering the cultural diversity within the country's first four centuries, the historian Luis Carlos Soares (1991: 101) went so far as to deny the existence of a single socioeconomic structure within the area now known as the "Brazilian territory." He proposed instead that "there existed not one, but many pre-capitalist economic and social formations within the area that is today Brazil." Accepting the main contention that there were huge differences in the social organization of this Portuguese colony in the Americas, it is also clear that this system of patronage and its consequences were ubiquitous and pervasive. Inequality has been the main characteristic of social organization in Brazil. Nowadays, for instance, Brazil has one of the most uneven income distributions in the world, and as a result only some 20 million inhabitants can be considered as ordinary consumers, while 130 million people survive consuming very basic products such as staple food and cheap clothing. Despite the fact that Brazil has developed strong industries, producing almost everything from cars to aircraft, social imbalances are as strong today as centuries ago when the country only produced raw materials (brazilwood, sugar, gold, coffee).

Most of the ordinary excluded majority is considered by the elite as "non-European" (cf. Skidmore 1994: 13). Indeed, the culture of the elite has always been integrally European or "Western" (Hale 1989: 225). There should be no need to stress that notions of "subordinate races"—notably blacks, mulattoes, Indians, and their mixed results—do not refer to actual biological differences, but do constitute an ideological concept (Wade 1993: 32 et passim). The elite is white and European by definition, and there is thus no need to prove ethnic purity. David Babson (1990:22) links racism in modern society in general with the masking of economic and social gain. There has been however a false theory that in Brazil there was no real prejudice against dark-skinned people, but in fact this country is no exception to the overall rule stated by Babson (ibid.). It is true that there is no racial segregation as such, but ordinary people are labelled as dark-skinned, and the elite are white. Although it is not impossible to overcome the subtle line dividing the two groups, it is very difficult. The subtlety is however only skin-deep, as a striking remark written by Fernando Henrique Cardoso in the late 1960s, reminds us: "the fact that blacks were emancipated did not of course change their slave mind and habits, which were incompatible with free wage labor in industry" (1969: 196–197). As summed up recently by Thomas E. Skidmore (1993: 375), "Brazil's "racial democracy" does not exist." Cláudio Bojunga (1978: 177) emphasized, some time ago, that even if more than 80 percent of the population at Bahia State is non-White, the University there continues to be "a white institution." As there is no legal injunction against people of African descent, the exclusion of this large majority, at Bahia as elsewhere in the country, is carried out in a non-ethnic, "clean" way: poor people are uneducated and usually do not succeed in going to universities. Different authors refer to this appalling situation as a direct result of slavery, and as a consequence, to its disenfranchising character, to the subordination of ordinary people.

This has led to the acculturation and "whitening" of non-elite people's culture (Fernandes 1969: 282). The black scholar Eduardo de Oliveira e Oliveira (1984: 70) accepted the validity of the famous dictum by Fernando de Azevedo and emphasized that "culture in Brazil is for the elite and we, the blacks, in terms of both race and class, we do not belong to the elite." All other things being equal, skin color matters. While black cultural identity has become widely accepted and even celebrated in the form of music, dance, food, and sometimes religion, there is no equality (Lovell 1999: 414). The idea that Brazil is a color-blind society masks everyday racism and internalized racism in Brazil (Goldstein 1999: 573).

Archaeological theory and politics

It is in the context of a divided society that we must consider the role of archaeological theory in Brazil. Some archaeologists have chosen not to challenge current prejudices. There is still a strong tradition in Brazil to consider archaeology as a handmaiden to history, with no interpretive role whatsoever: "archaeology, by its very nature, is a handmaiden to history and is far from being a pursuit in itself" (Meneses 1965: 22). Archaeological theory is thus particularly important, if we aim at empowering subordinate groups, as Hodder (1991: 10) proposes. Archaeologists must work closer with related Humanities disciplines, such as history, anthropology, and semiotics to develop a wider interpretive perspective (D'Agostino 1995: 104).

We face two different problems which are to be addressed through theory: ethnicity and the political implications of our interpretive efforts. Ethnicity in the material record is a complex issue in itself. Michael Blakey (1990: 39) suggests that "American archaeologists exhibit an ethnic bias that 'whitens' national heritage and identity." In this way, it is impossible to dissociate ethnicity, archaeological interpretations, and present social and political contexts (Wood and Powell 1993: 407). If archaeology cannot be a neutral source-discipline, as Leo Klejn (Taylor 1993: 279) dreamed, and theory mediates data and vice-versa (Shanks and Tilley 1987: 1), we must study the connection between present and past as a source of power within society (Wilk 1985: 319). Personal views and class interests, as well as the elite social milieu, are at the root of interpretation (Trigger 1989: 777–778), which is inevitably subjective (Ucko 1989: xii). Traditionally, "archaeological work and interpretation has always reflected and contributed to the class relations of power and domination" (Handsman and Leone 1989: 134). I agree with Brian Durrans (1989: 67) when he proposes that "the most useful way in which archaeologists can contribute to a wider political movement is by exploring the ideological bias of archaeology, thereby encouraging people to recognize and therefore transcend ideology in their own lives." For example, Martin Bernal (1990: 128) was able to link Renfrew's archaeological interpretations with his active role in the British Conservative Party. We must acknowledge that usually "objective" interpretations of the archaeological record are in reality ideologically charged (Nassaney 1989: 76). It is not surprising to discover that positivist archaeologists in Brazil were in close contact with military and intelligence authorities during the dictatorship (1964–1985). During the heyday of the Cold War, a positivistic ("Archaeology as Science") outlook related well with the political aspirations of the United States Establishment (Rowlands 1982: 159).

It is in this context that Black material culture—or rather ordinary, mixed race, non-learned expressions—must be considered. Russel-Wood (1974: 573) was keen to emphasize that,

> ... all survivals in colonial Brazil of African traditions in dance, song, music, religion, or social mores were persecuted. An edict of 1719 instructed parish priests in Minas Gerais not to accept blacks or mulattoes as godparents at weddings or baptisms.

As a historian, the written information from the edict was considered by the scholar as a strong stance by the authorities, but how effective was it? Very recently, Charles E. Orser

(1994a: 34) has reviewed the current debate on the African character of cultural traits in the Americas and concluded that "Africans did not abandon or lose their cultures during enslavement ... [but] the cultures they forged in the New World were not exact duplications of those in Africa." Perhaps a case in point is the study, by Eliane Azevedo (1983: 113), of surnames of black people in the northeast of Brazil. She proposed that the surnames are chosen differently by different ethnic groups and that people of African descent sometimes choose specific Portuguese names of Saints on purpose. There is no way of disentangling African and European traits: they create an original American (Native American)—African—European ensemble.

Palmares, ethnic identity, and archaeology

Resistance against oppression has been studied as a way of avoiding the traditional disenfranchising role played by learned scholarship. The slave system was not benign (Conrad 1973: 50), racial slavery and oppression were not abnormalities (Higgins 1991: 25), and there was a continuous struggle against slavery (Schwartz 1977: 75). Runaway communities are the most clear evidence of this resistance (Reis 1992: 17), denying the once accepted view of Negro docility (Davidson 1979: 82), and challenging the delightfulness of the slave system (Aptheker 1979: 165). "The construction of distinctly African-American cultures and communities is eloquent testimony of the frequent success of the New World slave's struggle to build autonomous institutions of local social reproduction" (Glassman 1991: 278). Maroons were the strongest expression of non-conformity (Bakos 1990: 51) and the fact they were unable, up to the mid-nineteenth century, to change the dominant social structure does not diminish their importance in comparison with short-term, violent confrontations, like revolts, uprisings, and insurrections (Orser 1991: 40).

Palmares was a runaway settlement established at the beginning of the seventeenth century in the northeast of Brazil and was able to grow for almost a century. At its heyday, it comprised several villages and its largest site, at the *Serra da Barriga*, or Belly Hill, was a town with hundreds of houses. After many attacks, the pioneers from São Paulo, in the south, were able to destroy that polity in 1694 and to kill the last black ruler, Zumbi, on November 20, 1695 (Carneiro 1988). Centuries later, in the 1970s, Palmares would return to the forefront of public interest thanks to Afro-Brazilian institutions. The Hill was declared a National Heritage Monument in the 1980s and Palmares and Zumbi were considered as strong symbols against oppression:

> At Palmares, there was an organized slave uprising, and the result was a multiethnic society strongly anti-colonial in outlook. This was the first liberation movement in the Americas ... There is now the opportunity to re-enact the pluralistic experience carried out at Palmares. If you look at this most glorious page of Brazilian history, you will remember that at Palmares there were, not only Blacks, but also Indians, Jews, and all other people subjected to discrimination.
>
> (Serra 1984: 107–108)

Escalante (1979: 74) described maroons as "communities where they [i.e. Blacks] could keep their original cultures alive." At Palmares, however, some authors refer to the mix of African, Native American, and European elements (e.g. Genovese 1981: 53; Saraiva 1993: 46). This is the result of references in the written documents about different ethnic groups in this polity but it is also an ideological assumption. Serra's citation is clear on that matter: it was the first multi-ethnic state and we should recreate it. Other social activists would take a completely different stance, interpreting Palmares as overwhelmingly African and rejecting any racial interaction, in the past and in the present. In any case, the archaeologist must face a very strong symbolism when studying the subject.

In the early 1990s Charles E. Orser, Jr and the author decided to set up an archaeological project on Palmares. From its inception, we have been acting in close contact with the Afro-Brazilian Studies Center at the Federal University of Alagoas and its director, Zezito de Araüjo and through him also with the Black community at large. Archaeological theory has been at the heart of our concerns as we must deal with ethnicity at two levels: we face archaeological artefacts related to ethnic groups and we face modern perceptions, by social agents, of pure ethnicity and its contemporary consequences. Since 1990, several books and papers have been published on the archaeological study of Palmares by Charles Orser, Pedro Paulo Funari, Michael Rowlands, and Scott Allen (see Orser and Funari 1992; and references in Funari 1999). Allen (2001: 214) has summed up a decade of archaeological research at Palmares emphasizing that "combined archaeological research has unequivocally determined that there are multiple narratives to the Palmarino past ... Palmares is a site that requires a reflexive approach as only then can we reach a true multivocality." The fact that we found mostly Native American related pottery is meaningful in itself (Orser 1994b: 12–13). We should also not forget that the European and African societies were much more similar to each other than once thought (Thornton 1981: 186) and it is thus not surprising to find evidences of a mix of cultural traits at Palmares. Recently, Scott Allen (2001) has proposed that the archaeology of Palmares can use a model of ethnogenesis that places neither Africans nor Native Americans at center state in archaeological analysis, but rather the Palmarino themselves: a specific, freedom-fighting polity. Perhaps the main message of the archaeology of this extremely important free polity is to show that Africans fought not only for their own freedom as individuals or as an ethnicity. Africans contributed to the struggle for the freedom of all those oppressed, be they black, Indian, Jew, Moor, "witch," sodomite, or whatever. The fight for freedom and justice and archaeology has a special role in showing this to society at large.

Acknowledgments

I owe scholarly thanks to Scott Joseph Allen, Zezito de AraUjo, Margarete Bakos, Martin Bernal, Donna Goldstein, Brian Dunans, Jonathan Glassman, Peggy A. Lovell, Charles E. Orser, Jr, Michael Rowlands, Thomas Skidmore, John Thornton, Bruce G. Trigger, and Peter Ucko. The responsibility for the ideas in this chapter rests fully with the author.

References

Allen, S. J. (2001) " 'Zumbi nunca vai morrer': history, race politics, and the practice of archaeology in Brazil," unpublished PhD Dissertation, Brown University.

Aptheker, H. (1979) "Maroons within the Present Limits of the United States," in R. Price (ed.), Maroon societies, 151–167, Baltimore, MD: Johns Hopkins University Press.

Azevedo, E. S. (1983) "Sobrenomes no Nordeste e suas relaçoes com a heterogeneidade étnica," Estudos Econômicos, 13, 1: 103–116.

Babson, D. W. (1990) "The archaeology of racism and ethnicity on a Southern plantation," Historical Archaeology, 24, 4: 20–28.

Bakos, M. (1990) "Sobre a mulher escrava no Rio Grande do Sul," Estudos Ibero-Americanos, 16,1–2: 47–56.

Bernal, M. (1990) "Responses," Journal of Mediterranean Archaeology, 3, 1: 111–137.

Blakey, M. (1990) "American nationality and ethnicity in the depicted past," in P. G. Gathercole and D. Lowenthal (eds) The Politics of the Past, 38–48, London: Unwin Hyman.

Bojunga, C. (1978) "O negro brasileiro, 90 anos depois," Encontros da Civilização Brasileira, 1: 175–204.

Cardoso, F. H. (1969) "Condições sociais di industrialização: o caso de São Paulo," in F. H. Cardoso, Mudanças sociais na América Latina, 186–198, São Paulo: Difel.

Carneiro, E. (1988) O quilombo de Palmares, São Paulo: Editors Nacional.

Conrad, R. (1973) "Neither slave nor free: the emancipados of Brazil, 1818–1868," Hispanic American Historical Review, 53, 1: 50–70.

D'Agostino, M. E. (1995) "Review," Historical Archaeology, 29, 1: 103–104.

Da Matta, R. (1991) "Religion and modernity: three studies of Braziian religiosity," Journal of Social History, 25, 2: 389–406.

Davidson, D. (1979) "Negro slave control and resistance in Colonial Mexico, 1519–1650," in R. Price (ed.) Maroon Societies, 82–106, Baltimore, MD: Johns Hopkins University Press.

Durrans, B. (1989) "Theory, profession, and the political rôle of archaeology," in S. J. Shennan (ed.), Archaeological Approaches to Cultural Identity, 66–75, London: Unwin Hyman.

Escalante, A. (1979) "Palenques in Colombia," in R. Price (ed.) Maroon Societies, 74–81, Baltimore, MD: Johns Hopkins University Press.

Fernandes, F. (1969) A integração do negro na sociedade de classes. No limiar de uma nova era, São Paulo: Dominus.

Funari, P. P. A. (1999) "Maroon, race and gender: Palmares material culture and social relations in a runaway settlement," in P. P. A Funari, M. Hall, and S. Jones (eds) Historical Archaeology, Back from the Edge, 308–327, London: Routledge.

Genovese, E. D. (1981) From Rebellion to Revolution. Afro-American Slave Revolts in the Making of the Modern World, Baton Rouge, LA: Louisiana State University Press.

Glassman, J. (1991) "The bondsman's new clothes: the contradictory consciousness of slave resistance on the Swahili Coast," Journal of African History, 32: 277–312.

Goldstein, D. (1999) " 'Interracial' sex and racial democracy in Brazil: twin concepts?," American Anthropologist, 101, 3: 563–578.

Hale, C. A. (1989) "Political and Social Ideas," in L. Bethel (ed.) Latin America Economy and Society 1870–1930, 225–300, Cambridge: Cambridge University Press.

Handsman, R. G. and Leone, M. P. (1989) "Living History and Critical Archaeology in the Reconstruction of the Past," in V. Pinsky and A. Wylie (eds) Critical Traditions in Contemporary Archaeology, 117–135, Cambridge: Cambridge University Press.

Higgins, N. I. (1991) "The deforming mirror of truth: slavery and the master narrative of American History," Radical History Review, 49: 25–48.

Hodder, I. (1991) "Interpretive archaeology an its role," American Antiquity, 56, 1: 7–18.

Klejn, L. (1993) "Conversations with," Current Anthropology, 34, 5: 723–735.

Lovell, P. A. (1999) "Development and the persistence of racial inequality in Brazil: 1950–1991," The Journal of Developing Areas, 33: 395–418.

Meneses, U. T. B. (1965) "Sentido e funcao de urn Museu de Arqueologia," *Dédalo*, 1: 19–26.

Nassaney, M. (1989) "An epistemological enquiry into some archaeological and historical interpretations of 17th century Native American-European relations," in S. J. Shennan (ed.) *Archaeological Approaches to Cultural Identity*, 76–93, London: Unwin Hyman.

Oliveira e Oliveira, E. (1984) *Intervenção, in Trabalho escravo, economia e sociedade*, 69–72, Rio de Janeiro: Paz e Terra.

Orser, C. E. (1991) "The Continued Pattern of Dominance. Landlord and Tenant on the Postbellum Cotton Plantation," in R. H. McGuire and R. Paynter (eds) *The Archaeology of Inequality*, 40–54, Oxford: Blackwell.

Orser, C. E. (1994a) "The archaeology of African-American slave religion in the antebellum south," *Cambridge Archaeological Journal*, 4, 1: 33–45.

Orser, C. E. (1994b) "Toward a global historical archaeology: an example from Brazil," *Historical Archaeology*, 28, 1: 5–22.

Orser, C. E., and Funari, P. P. A. (1992) "Pesquisa arqueológica inicial em Palmares," *Estudos Ibero-Americanos*, 18, 2: 53–69.

Reis, J. J. (1992) "Differences et resistances: Les noirs a Bahia sons l'esclavage," *Cahiers d'Etudes Africaines*, 125: 15–34.

Rowlands, M. J. (1982) "Processual Archaeology as Historical Social Science," in C. Renfrew, M. Rowlands, and B. Seagraves (eds) *Theory and Explanation in Archaeology*, 155–174, New York: Academic Press.

Russel-Wood, A. J. R (1974) "Black and mulatto brotherhoods in Colonial Brazil: a study in collective behaviour," *Hispanic American Historical Review*, 54, 4, 567–602.

Saraiva, J. F. S. (1993) "Silencio y ambivalencia: el mundo de los negros en Brasil," *America Negra*, 6: 37–49.

Schwartz, S. B. (1977) "Resistance and accomodation in 18th century Brazil: the slaves' view of slavery," *Hispanic American Historical Review*, 57, 1: 69–81.

Serra, O. (1984) "Questões de identidade cultural," in A. A. Arantes (ed.) *Produzindo a Passado*, 97–123, São Paulo: Brasiliense.

Shanks, M., and Tilley, C. (1987) *Re-constructing Archaeology: Theory and Pratice*, Cambridge: Cambridge University Press.

Skidmore, T. E. (1993) "Bi-racial USA vs. Multi-racial Brazil: it the constrast still valid?," *Journal of Latin American Studies*, 25: 373–386.

Skidmore, T. E. (1994) *O Brasil visto de fora*, Rio de Janeiro: Paz e Terra.

Soares, L. C. (1991) "From Slavery to Dependence: a Historiografical Perspective," in R. Graham (ed.) *Brazil and the World System*, 89–108, Austin, TX: University of Texas Press.

Taylor, T. (1993) "Conversations with Leo Klejn," *Current Anthropology*, 34, 5: 723-735.

Thornton, J. (1981) "Early Kongo-Portuguese relations: a new interpretation," *History in Africa*, 8: 183–202.

Trigger, B. G. (1989) "Hyperrelativism, responsability and the social sciences," *Canadian Review of Sociology and Anthropology*, 26, 5: 776–797.

Ucko, P. (1989) "Forward," in S. Shennan (ed.) *Archaeological Approaches to Cultural Identity*, ix–xx, London: Unwin Hyman.

Wade, P. (1993) "Race, nature and culture," *Man* (NS), 28: 17–34.

Wilk, R. R. (1985) "The ancient Maya and the political present," *Journal of Anthropological Research*, 41: 307–326.

Wood, J. J. and Powell, S. (1993) "An ethos for archaeological practice," *Human Organization*, 52, 4: 405–413.

17 The other side of freedom

The Maroon trail in Suriname

E. Kofi Agorsah

Introduction: resistance culture and archaeology

The spring 1996 launch of the Maroon Heritage Research Project (MHRP) in Suriname, began the extension of an archaeological research program that had previously worked in Jamaica. The main objective was to investigate the locational distribution and spatial formation of settlements created by "runaway slaves" (Maroons) in Suriname. As is well known, these were groups of people who escaped from slavery into wild and difficult environments, formed independent communities, and pioneered the struggle against slavery. Archaeological studies of the heritage of freedom fighters, carried out in Northern Florida (Weisman 1989; Deagan 1995), Palmares in Brazil (Orser and Funari 1992; Orser 1994), Jamaica at the sites of Nanny Town, Seaman's Valley, and Old Accompong (Agorsah 1993, 1994, 1999, 2001; Carey 1997), and in Suriname at Kumako and Tuido (Agorsah 1997) are beginning to throw light on the formation and transformation of resistance culture in the African Diaspora. Research in all these areas is showing that Maroons became an almost ubiquitous, though politically variable, feature of the African Diaspora.

The MHRP uses oral, ethnographic, and historical documents to guide its archaeological surveys and test excavations in order to reconstruct the pattern of settlement development in the areas inhabited by the Maroons. Our project has been very fortunate to have available a large corpus of oral tradition, ethnographies, and historic maps as well as very enthusiastic and supportive Maroon Chiefs and guides (de Lavaux 1737; Wekker 1976; Mitrasingh 1979; Price 1983, 1996; Hoogbergen 1990). Several seasons of fieldwork have now been undertaken but each season has brought more questions than answers.

The approach

The archaeological extension of the study of Suriname Maroon Heritage, beyond oral traditions and ethnographic evidence, is important for both the explanation of the history of the formation of these settlements and to better understand the demise of slavery in Suriname. Place names of Maroon settlements in Suriname may be used to explain the cultural formation and transformation of the Saramaka and Matawai Maroons. Our work includes enumerating the geomorphological locations, distributions, geographical relationships, and connectivity between Maroon settlements. It is important that we understand the implications of geo-archaeological evidence for our understanding of *marronage*, and specifically, the military and social networking among Suriname Maroons. This chapter calls for a greater use of spatial evidence in the study of resistance culture.

The trail: place names and site identification

One of the preoccupations of the MHRP has been the compilation of place names derived from oral traditions, as they related to the founding and use of sites as they disengaged from the plantation system. Names were compiled with the help of local informants and from those already documented by J. B. Wekker (1976), F. E. M. Mitrasingh (1979) and Richard Price (1983), and in historical maps (de Lavaux 1737; Koeman 1973). Generally, names of Maroon villages have been shown to refer to nearby old burial grounds (Animbau, Mama–Ndjuka), or to geographical or physical features (Baakawata, Bakakun, Kumako, Tukumutu, Hansesipo, Tupi Kiiki and Asinkulogozo, Tutubuka, and Sabana), or related to personalities (Kwakugron, Dosu Kiiki, Kaasi (Class)), or events (Bakaafetihila, Kofijompo, and Waimakalafu). The place names have also provided information regarding circumstances of the founding and even the environmental conditions of the areas around the settlements. Those with names of founders or leaders provide yardsticks for chronological reconstruction and clues about family or clan relations. The significance of place names is not limited to one Maroon group.

   Linked to these place names are those of the specific groups who often took the names of the plantations from which they escaped. For example, one of the clans called Nasis is said to have escaped in the early 1690s from Suriname colonial plantations that belonged to the Nassys—the colony's most prominent Jewish family in the 1690s. The clan names identify not only the source or origin of the founders of the settlements but also the traditions and experiences by which the settlements were established. Their trails went through various sites or waypoints which they named.

   However, it should be noted that one danger in the use of these place names stems, first, from the fact that they are recorded in colonial documents and maps that were usually not obtained through actual visit and identification of the specific locations. Second, Maroons of Suriname, like those of Jamaica, in those days like today, traditionally used a great deal of name substitution and masking of information about locations and events surrounding sacred sites and life of important personalities, concealing secrets about them from outsiders (as has also been documented by Price 1983).

Tracing the trail

The escape routes of the Maroons appear to have some common features, such as establishment of several hiding places close to the plantation, moving away gradually as they became more and more self-supporting. The established settlements along the trail took on new characteristics as clans grouped together or separated into different political entities in the face of the constant military harassment. Using locational characteristics, the sites could be placed in different categories according to the time of the formation of a settlement. The earliest ones were mere hiding places not too far from the plantations of escape. The more permanent sites of the earlier period were mainly located inland and at headwaters and well-protected mountain or higher-ground locations. The later ones, particularly those after the post-peace treaty times, were closer to the waterways. A comparison of the distribution of sites illustrates this observation (Figures 17.1 and 17.2). The earlier phase of occupation required the

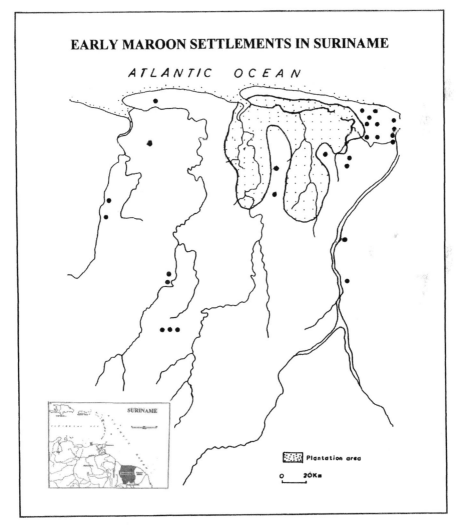

EARLY MAROON SETTLEMENTS IN SURINAME

ATLANTIC OCEAN

Plantation area

0   20Km

Figure 17.1   Location and distribution of early Maroon settlements. Note their locations in inaccessible areas (after W. Hoogbergen 1990: 83 with modifications).

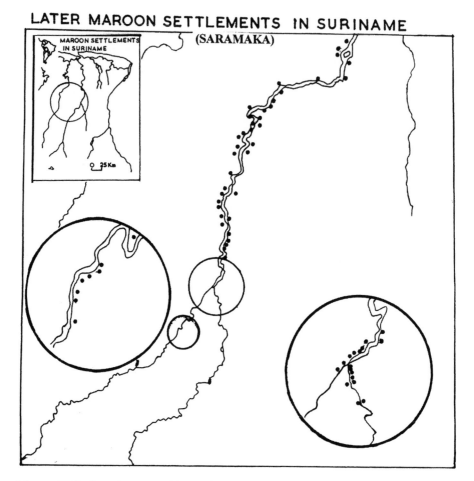

Figure 17.2   Later (post-treaty) Saramakan Maroon settlement. Note that the settlements are strung along the waterways (after Price 1983: 17).

Maroons to emplace their settlements based on their relative security and isolation, and the later phase requiring only a minimum of security but unfettered access to the waterways. The location and distribution of early Maroon sites clearly indicates that initially, the Maroons were a "forest people," only later becoming "river people." As one would expect, there was a consequent shift in their economic behavior and associated lifestyle between these two periods.

Tracing the Maroon trails is not a straightforward affair, owing to the complete absence of roadways as well as restricted and controlled waterways. The project has focused on relocating two of the four sites earmarked for study in previous seasons: Kumako in the Suriname River basin, and Tuido in the Saramacca River basin (Figure 17.3). The environment of each of these sites continues to hold an abundance

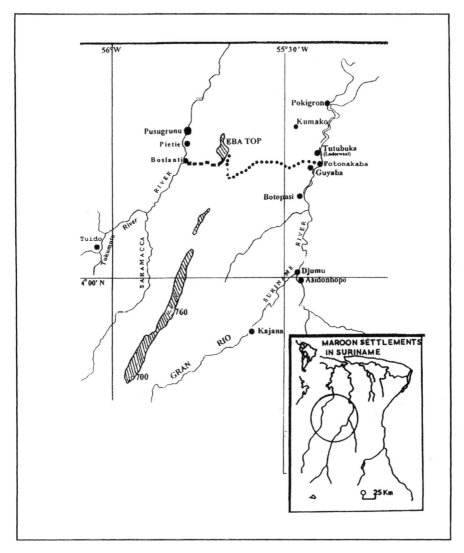

Figure 17.3 Map showing the relative locations of the Saramaka site(s) of Kumako, and the Matawai site of Tuido.

of wildlife within a deteriorating virgin forest. Archaeological survey and excavations included location and mapping of the distribution of sites, recording of physical features and artifacts, and observing surviving Maroon communities, who continue to exhibit vibrant cultural traditions, architecture, and artistic expressions.

The Kumako site

Background

Kumako (Kunakuum), also referred to as Kuna's Hill, was one of the earliest major settlements of the Saramaka. Oral traditions indicate that it was founded in the early 1700s under the leadership of one Kaasi and his runaway followers, who arrived there from a place called Kaasipumbu in the headwater areas of the Kleine Saramacca River, probably not too far from the northern end of the Eba Top range (Figure 17.3). By combining the evidence available to us, it seems that the foundation of Kumako dates to ca. 1717. Kumako would have been situated on a hilltop, as the name implies. The Maroons are mentioned to have later moved from Kumako, after it was attacked by colonial forces in 1743, to the Djibi and Yawe Creeks along with groups of Matawai.

The exact location of the Kumako site is still unclear. Saramakan elders indicated to us what they believe to be its locality. However, it is suspected that the actual location may be nearby, closer to the Eba Top range, at a second locality we discovered in the course of our study. Indeed, after a second field season it was realized that the first site excavated might be another village either contemporaneous with Kumako or founded by inhabitants of the original Kumako as recorded in the oral traditions. Test excavations indicate that the location remembered by the Saramaka elders was, by all accounts, a settlement of some significance. The site indicated by the elders is therefore referred to as Kumako I, the one we recently discovered closer to the Eba Top ridge being tentatively termed Kumako II.

Kumako I has also been linked with the history of the Nassi, one of the major clans of the Saramaka Maroons from their 1690 escape from the plantations near the coast, to Kaasi's (Class) village on the Suriname River. The site (or sites) of Kumako seem to have eventually attracted many Maroon clans. Kumako I may have been large enough to accommodate several groups, but the uncertainty about its location relative to historical records and oral descriptions makes a clear attribution difficult at this point.

The site

The site is one of the largest open areas in the thick forest to the northwest of Tutubuka and south of the stream which curves around the northern limits of the ridge. Dominating the site are many giant trees such as the *kankantri* that tradition prohibits any one to cut down. Although in the most open section of the forest, long and winding vines twist about the trunks of palm trees adding to the tangle of vegetation. One can sense the undergrowth foliage fighting for light and air. The surface was mainly sandy soil, but clayey underneath, particularly where mounds, probably formed by collapsed wooden huts or structures, were observed. Dry creek beds mark areas around the boundaries or streams, with dark brown to black clayey wet soil getting darker as one heads down the slope from the highest point of the ridge. Pinkish patches, probably decaying termite mounds, could also be observed in sections of the site. The numerous valleys of creeks and streams, as well as swampy sections in the general area, are part of a drainage complex that would be activated during the rainy seasons. A large and high boulder seems to have marked the center of the settlement. The site is flattish at the highest part, only gradually sloping away toward the valleys of the creeks that surround it.

Excavations at Kumako I

Excavation concentrated on two loci in the southern portion of the site—seven 2 × 2 m units in Locus 1, and four 2 × 1 m units in Locus 2. Artifacts recovered from Locus 1 consisted of ceramics (mainly body sherds), musket balls, cowry shells, and several pieces of green glass, some looking rather recent (Figure 17.4). The earthenware was generally undecorated, light brown to reddish in color (between Munsell 2.5YR 3/6 and 2.5YR 4/8), and ranging from approximately 0.4–1.0 cm in thickness.

While the ceramic finds indicate it was one of the few permanent settlements of the Maroons in the area, the musket balls represent the armed struggle that required that they hide away at this location. The presence of cowry shells in the same layer indicates an immediate African connection. Comparison of material from Kumako II, when recovered in subsequent field excavations should, hopefully, throw more light on the relationship between the two sites in the early stages of the Saramaka Maroon trail. The exact significance of Kumako I in the Maroon trail still needs to be determined.

The Tuido site

Background

Tuido, a Matawai settlement located on the Pikin Tukumutu Creek, a branch of the Saramacca River is described in oral traditions as a very large Matawai village consisting of many clan groups. It is said to have had several entry points, perhaps one for each group. Oral traditions indicate that after leaving the plantations, the Matawai groups moved along the bank of Saramacca River to Djibi Creek and to Yawe Creek. However, after separating from Saramaka, they went southwest along the Saramacca River to Tafelberg mountain area, and subsequently to the village of Hansesipo, and to the Tukumutu Creek (approximately around 1740), where the large village of Tuido was established on the Pikin Tukumutu. Tuido was considered a safe and secure cluster of Maroon settlements because of its defensive position and distance from the coast and the colonial authorities. It is mentioned that in 1747 a planned colonial expedition was to attack the stronghold of "Loangadorp" considered to be Tuido, but it is not certain whether or not it happened. Matawai oral traditions identify a spot on the Tukumutu Creek where their ancestors had established a camp while waiting to fight back that attack.

Tuido is located in a bend of the Pikin Tukumutu Creek approximately three or four kilometers westward from where it parts with the Tupi Creek. Tuido has been located on several maps of the Saramaka River just a few miles down on the Tukumutu River south of Djomasanga and is said to be specifically located off the Piki Tukumutu Creek. The Awana, another clan of the Saramaka Maroons, are considered to have escaped around 1715 to join settlements to southeast of Mindindeti Creek and

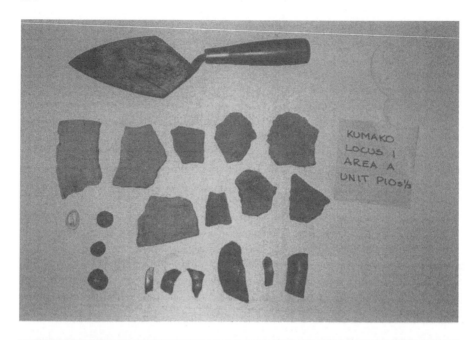

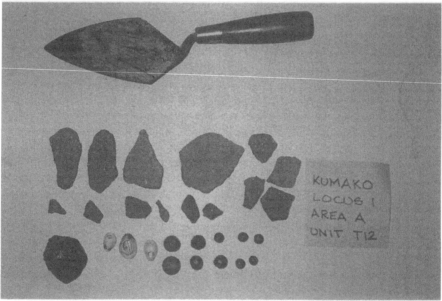

Figure 17.4 Examples of finds from the site of Kumako I—local low-fired ceramics, musket balls, and cowry shells.

then later continued, by way of the Tutu Creek, to Kumako from where they eventually also went to Tuido.

The location of Tuido has been confirmed by oral traditions and Maroon guides. Landmarks, as one approaches the site, include the protected area around Taawa Creek, which branches off the Pikin Tukumutu in a very wide bend, almost 70 m across to the westward. It is not clear in the Matawai traditions whether the journey was totally by footpaths or by river, though a combination of both is likely to have been the case. Tukumutu Creek marks the eastern and southern boundaries of the Tuido site, which extends westward into the area within the loop of the creek. A small stream that branches off the Tukumutu partially demarcates the northern limits. Although almost surrounded by the creek and swamps, the site appeared to have several access points, very untypical of Maroon sites which normally have restricted entry points. Within the open area of the site, several big trees including those locally referred to as *duumu, lokisi, kandeafuta* can be identified. Monkeys, deer, tapir, agouti, iguana, wild pig, a variety of spiders, snakes, birds, and insects, too numerous to list, have been the only inhabitants of the area around the Tuido site since it was abandoned some 250 years ago.

Field investigations and cultural material

The 2000 field season concentrated more on surveying the areas around the site than on excavating. It is hoped that more extensive excavations will take place in the seasons ahead. Two areas of the site were particularly productive although it is premature to make any conclusions on overall artifact distribution at the site. A test pit indicates that the stratigraphy at the site is comparatively deep. The site contains clusters of earthen mounds. The mounds are considered to represent collapsed wooden habitation structures or middens. Other surface features include clay hearths and stone circles. Several pieces of black to dark brown earthenware including large flat pieces, rim and body fragments, and several pieces of imported stoneware were surface collected. The coincidence of the hearths with the mound areas indicate settlement in family or clan quarters, the stone circles seem to mark out shrine or bath house areas, while the ceramics once again suggest that this was a rare "permanent" Maroon settlement. The stoneware and other imported ceramics (Figure 17.5) were obviously obtained through contact with plantations and brought along the escape trail. It is not possible to draw any firm conclusions about the Tuido site owing to the very limited excavation undertaken so far. There is also the need to examine other sites within the general area in order to be able to determine the spatial relationships between them. The geographical gap in the trail between the Saramaka site of Kumako I and the Matawai site of Tuido is a wide one. A few sites recently located and recorded by the MHRP such as Sabana, Kwakiki Paasi, Debabunu, Paaba, Djomasanga, and a few others, all yet to be mapped and investigated, might help fill some parts of this gap.

Some general observations

The archaeology of Maroon Heritage in other parts of the African Diaspora gives support to the conviction that with additional evidence, the cultural web of the

Figure 17.5   Imported stoneware collected from the site of Tuido.

Suriname Maroon trail could be reconstructed. For example, the excavation of the site of Nanny Town in Jamaica was particularly fruitful (Agorsah 2001). Terracotta figurines and the associated local, thin but highly fired, earthenware at the bottom of the lower cultural level appear to be typically Amerindian (Arawak). It is speculated that "Arawaks" may still have been inhabiting parts of the Blue Mountains at the time that the British took over the island and had, therefore, not been exterminated by the time of Maroon settlements as has often been asserted. If dates later support these speculations, then it would be a very clear archaeological evidence of the link between African and Amerindian societies in the Caribbean. In Brazil, ceramic types recovered at the site of Palmares, specifically at Serra da Barriga, also appear to support views that good relations existed between the enslaved Africans and the native people (Orser 1994: 13). These results hold hope for the project in Suriname.

The archaeology of Maroon Heritage is growing very slowly but has so far brought a new and a dynamic dimension to the evidence and interpretations of the culture of resistance in the African Diaspora. Meanwhile, many Maroon Heritage sites are being identified in other parts of the New World and in coming years should tell us much about the processes of the formation and transformation of resistance culture(s). Larger excavation and surveys in Suriname should help establish the layout of the sites and make it possible to speculate about social organization at and among the sites. It appears that the maintenance of the clan system, with mutual support between clans, and relationships with Native Americans may have enabled them to maintain the cohesiveness required to defend their territories. There are two key questions for future Maroon research in Suriname.

First, how did the Maroons adapt to the environmental circumstances of the rain forest and marshlands at the time of their struggle? The ecological circumstances exploited by the Maroons in the rainforests of Suriname were almost identical to those exploited by Maroons in the Jamaican Blue Mountains and Brazil. It appears that the Maroons developed almost a symbiotic system of mutual dependence with the native people of the forest. Some of the excavated ceramics appear to support this view. Versteeg and Bubberman (1992) have provided good background information on the native people of Suriname. Their ethnographic and historical evidence should help us to define the interdependence of the African runaways and the native people. Such a co-existence has been observed, though not clearly defined for Maroons in other areas of the African Diaspora (Weisman 1989; Pereira 1994; Agorsah 1994, 2001). The process probably began with barter and developed over time into a more symbiotic system.

Second, what was the impact of the physical/locational characteristics of their settlements on survival strategies, and what are the differences in observed spatial/artifactual patterns between archaeological sites and modern settlements? Cheryl White's ongoing research on the early "dwellings" of the Saramaka should open up the opportunities for discovering more essential evidence about the layout of the settlements (White n.d.).

As indicated at the outset, for the MHRP in Suriname, determining the locational and spatial transformations of Maroon settlement constitutes the main challenge of the project. The stage has now been set for larger field seasons that can excavate and examine larger portions of the sites. The expectation of this research is that the Maroon trail, when fully reconstructed, will provide a means of reconstructing the backbone of the heritage that the modern Maroon populations represent. At this time we are certain of one thing: the Maroon trail to freedom appears to have been very rough indeed. Tracing it archaeologically is even rougher. Only a concerted and collaborative effort can help us trace it to the end. Where are the historians? Where are the linguists? Where are the anthropologists? Where are the geomorphologists and the geologists? And where are the funding agencies on which we depend for resources and support?

Acknowledgments

I wish to express my sincere thanks to the Faculty Development Committee of Portland State University and the National Geographic Society for sponsoring these very fruitful seasons of the project. I wish to acknowledge the support and collaboration of the Suriname National Museum, particularly Drs Laddy van Putten and Hanna van Putten, and the Office of the Commissioner for Paramaribo, particularly Dr Hermes Libretto, Hugo Jabini, Stephen Petrusi and Christine Samsom. Mention must be made of the support of the Paramount chiefs,

Granman Songo Aboikono and Oscar Lafantie of the Saramaka and Matawai respectively. These chiefs enthusiastically supported the field teams through the help of their subchiefs, boatmen, hunters, and students. I wish to make specific mention of individuals who made the trip a great success going through the difficulties of the canoe journeys, bush and swamp walk, the rapids, and the rain. These include, for the trip in the Saramaka area Lane Justen, Tom Becker of Portland State University, and Cherryl White of University of Florida, Gainesville, who were my research and field assistants during the last expedition to Suriname.

References

Agorsah, E. Kofi (1993) "Nanny Town Excavations: Rewriting Jamaica's History?," *Jamaican Geographer (A Newsletter of the Jamaican Geographical Society)*, 8: 1, 6–8.

Agorsah, E. Kofi (1994) *Maroon Heritage: Archaeological, Ethnographic and Historical Perspectives*, Kingston: Canoe Press, and University of the West Indies.

Agorsah, E. Kofi (1997) "Locational and spatial transformation patterns of Maroon settlements in Suriname: a preliminary report," A Report submitted to and on file at the National Geographic Society, USA, Suriname National Museum, and Portland State University, March.

Agorsah, E. Kofi (1999) "Ethnoarchaeological consideration of Social Relationship and Settlement Patterning Among Africans in the Caribbean Diaspora," in Jay B. Haviser (ed.) *African Sites Archaeology in the Caribbean*, 38–64, Kingston: Ian Randle Publishers.

Agorsah, E. Kofi (2001) "The Secrets of Maroon Heroism, as Pioneer Freedom Fighters of the African Diaspora," E. Kofi Agorsah (ed.) *Freedom in Black History and Culture*, 1–25, Middletown: Arrow Point Press.

Carey, Beverly (1997) *The Maroon Story, the Authentic and Original History of the Maroons in the History of Jamaica 1490–1880*, Kingston: Agouti Press.

Deagan, K. (1995) *Fort Mose: Colonial Americas Black Fortress of Freedom*, Gainesville, FL: University of Florida Press.

Hoogbergen, W. (1990) "Resistance and Rebellion: Old and New," *Studies in Third World Societies*, 43: 65–102.

Koeman, C. (1973) *Bibliography of Printed Maps of Suriname, 1671–1971*, Amsterdam: Theatrum Orbis Terrarum.

Lavaux De, A. (1737) *Generale Caart van de Provintie Surname*, Amsterdam.

Mitrasingh, F. E. M. (1979) *Suriname Land of Seven Peoples: Social Mobility in a Plural Society— An Ethnohistorical Study*, Paramaribo: H. van den Boomen.

Orser, C. (1994) "Historical archaeology: an example from Brazil," *Historical Archaeology*, 28, 1: 5–22.

Orser, C. E., and Funari, P. P. A. (1992) "Pesquisa arqueológica inicial em Palmares," *Estudos Ibero-Americanos*, 18, 2: 53–69.

Pereira, J. A. (1994) "Maroon Heritage in Mexico," in E. Kofi Agorsah (ed.) *Maroon Heritage: Archaeological, Ethnographic and Historical Perspectives*, 94–108, Kingston: Canoe Press, and University of the West Indies.

Price, R. (1983) *First Time: The Historical Vision of an Afro-American People*, Baltimore, MD: Johns Hopkins University Press.

Price, R. (1996) *Maroon Societies, Rebel Slave Communities in the Americas*, Baltimore, MD: Johns Hopkins University Press.

Versteeg, A. H. and Bubberman, F.C. (1992) *Suriname Before Columbus* (Columbus Edition) Paramaribo: Stichting Surinaams Museum.

Weisman, B. (1989) *Like Beads on a String A Culture History of the Seminole Indians in North Peninsular Florida*, Tuscaloosa: University of Alabama Press.

Wekker, J. B. (1976) "Surinamese Toponyms," *Stichting Surinaams Museum*, 19/20: 24–48.

White, Cheryl (n.d.) "The dwellings of the Maroons of Suriname," paper presented at the IX Congress of the International Association For Caribbean Archaeology, Aruba, Netherlands Antilles, 2001.

18 Bantu elements in Palenque (Colombia)

Anthropological, archaeological, and linguistic evidence

ARMIN SCHWEGLER

Chi ma nkongo,	*From the Kongo (people) [we come],*
chi ma ri loango ...	*from those of Loango ...*

(Opening lines of Palenque's best-preserved
ancestral song; Schwegler 1996a: 524ff.)

Introduction

This chapter examines Bantu remnants found in the maroon village of El Palenque de San Basilio (Colombia). More specifically it concentrates on the special impact that Bakongo slaves[1]—speakers of Kikongo (Figure 18.1)—must have had in the formation of Palenquero culture and language. In the examination, I will assemble evidence from a variety of disciplines, including linguistics, oral literature, archaeology, and anthropology. In an effort to make the article accessible to scholars in different fields, technical jargon will be kept to a minimum. Space limitations will allow only for the presentation of a small number of Palenque's Kongo-derived traditions—many of which have never been investigated in detail or with sufficient scientific rigor.

My focus on Kongo (rather than, say, Mbundu or other Bantu) influences should not be interpreted narrowly. That is, in pointing to the highly specific westernmost regions of the lower Congo and its adjacent territories (where Kikongo is spoken), I am not at all implying that Bantu slaves from other territories did not also contribute to the formation of Palenque's creole language. As Huttar (1993) and others have recognized, it is generally misguided to dwell on some specific African language when a feature is shared by many of the African languages. Much the same could be said with respect to Palenque's cultural phenomena, parallels of which can be found throughout large sections of central West Africa (a case in point is Palenque's animist tradition). What I am claiming, however, is that the currently available evidence from Palenque strongly points to the Lower Congo Basin as the principal source of the phenomena described hereafter.

The evidence presented in this chapter rests primarily on fieldwork carried out by the author during his extended stays in Palenque. I first visited Palenque in the mid-1980s,

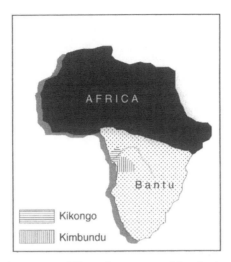

Figure 18.1 Approximate area of Bantu languages, and localization of approximately 400 Bantu languages (including Kikongo and Kimbundu).

that is, shortly before the village began to undergo fairly rapid modernization (installation of electricity, arrival of TV sets, replacement of palm-thatched roofs by "fancy" tin coverings, etc.). My many subsequent stays (usually lasting 1–2 months or more) in the community and, moreover, the fluency I acquired in the Palenquero creole (locally known simply as *lengua* "speech, tongue, language") have created a situation of mutual trust usually not afforded to outsiders. This social integration has made it possible to obtain insight into a number of behavioral patterns that are authentic specimens of recurring activities in the lives of Palenqueros (some of these activities are, however, now shunned by the younger generations; thus the *lumbulú* funeral chants and dances [described below] are held with ever-decreasing frequency).

From the outset of my fieldwork, I expressed a special interest in the early history of Palenque. Extended conversations with village elders about former linguistic and cultural practices provided fine-grained historical information extending all the way back to the late 1800s (Schwegler 1996a). It is this historical information, for instance, that has yielded insights into the burial practices described below. In this context it should be noted that the Palenqueros have no recollection of the period of slavery, nor of their ancestors' African homelands. To most if not all Palenqueros, "Africa" is a very vague concept at best, though the term itself continues to evoke feelings of socioethnic solidarity and pride.

A brief introduction to Palenque and a contextualization of the "African" evidence

Palenque is located some 80 km from Cartagena (Figure 18.2). The almost exclusively Black village of ca. 5,000 inhabitants commands an extraordinary position within Latin American social and linguistic history. Probably founded around 1650–1700, this former maroon settlement (Arrázola 1970) derives its name from the "palenques" (fences made of *palos* "sticks") that were driven into the ground to defend against possible military attacks.[2] Until recently (i.e. the late 1980s), the village has remained distinct from the surrounding coastal society with which it has always been in contact of varying intensity. Palenqueros frequented nearby villages and especially Cartagena; until recently, however, this contact with the outside world was unidirectional, that is, only very few outsiders ever visited their community. This relative isolation explains, in part, why the community has been able to preserve certain traditions that, perhaps only a century or two ago, might have also been celebrated in other Afro-American communities of the Atlantic Coast.

Palenque is well known for its creole "Palenquero," which is essentially unintelligible to Spanish speakers despite the fact that the two languages share 98 percent or more of their vocabulary (Schwegler 1998a; Schwegler and Morton 2003). The Palenqueros, all of whom speak Spanish with native fluency, are undeniably "Black," and being "Black" in Latin America has widely been considered antithetical to the concepts of social progress, "pureza de sangre" ("purity of [Spanish] blood") and *cultura* "eurocentric culture" (cf. Pérez Sarduy and Stubbs 1995: 6; Wade 1993, in press). Subject to social stigmatization and marginalization, these negative attitudes have also been extended to their "lengua" so that they have been made to feel ashamed of their local speech. Not surprisingly, today the younger generations avoid the creole altogether. And the same can be said of other, non-linguistic local traditions (several of which may have African origins) that in the eyes of many *Costeños* (Colombians from the Atlantic Coast) have a markedly "backwards flavor."

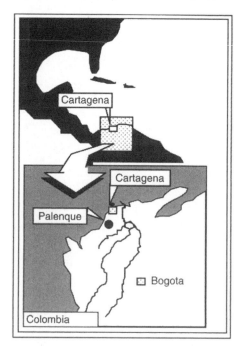

Figure 18.2 Cartagena and nearby Palenque.

The earliest conclusive documentary evidence of Palenque's existence dates from 1713, when a Cartagenero official traveled to the rebellious village to ratify a series of mutual concessions. This date and other considerations make it reasonable to infer that Palenque was founded between 1650 and 1700. At that time, nearby Cartagena was still Latin Americas' major slave trading port (Del Castillo 1982: 43; Böttcher 1995), and Blacks had become established as the numerically dominant element of coastal society. Indeed, by then, the local Indian population was already insignificant (Ruiz Rivera 1996)—Amerindian influence has not been a factor in Palenque.

The pioneers of Palenquero studies all correctly argued that the early Palenqueros came mainly from Angola and the Congo (see Bickerton and Escalante 1970; Granda 1978; Del Castillo 1982, 1984; Megenney 1986). This is the area of Central Africa from where the majority of slaves were exported during the early phase of the Cartagena slave trade (Del Castillo 1982). Subsequent anthropological and linguistic investigations have lent further support to the notion that a Bantu (rather than a West African) substrate must have played a crucial role in the formation of Palenquero (Schwegler 1996a, 1998a). But while we can be quite certain that Bakongo and other Bantu slaves (Mbundu included) were well represented among Cartagenero *Bozales* (African-born slaves with little knowledge of Spanish), we know relatively little about the exact demographic make-up of the seventeenth century African population of Cartagena. We know even less about how slaves of various ethnic and linguistic backgrounds of that city interacted with each other, both during the initial phases of their life in America as well as thereafter (Sandoval 1627; Bottcher 1995; Schwegler 1996a, 1998a). As a result, Palenque's early history and the African provenience of its inhabitants must be pieced together with fragmentary information, most of which has, until now, come from linguistic rather than other types of evidence.

Perhaps nothing in the history of Cartagenero slaves is more obscure than the psychological disposition that they held toward the language and culture of their oppressors. We do not know, for instance, if *Bozales* commonly adopted a mechanism of passive oral resistance, purposefully slowing down their acquisition of Spanish. The case of Palenque suggests, however, that this may not have been the case, since the community at large seems to have been fluent in both languages as early as 1772.[3] Similarly, we ignore whether slaves intentionally favored African or Africanizing speech patterns or cultural practices in order to symbolically manifest their ethnicity. And we mostly ignore whether Palenque's African cultural and linguistic survivals are (1) strictly the result of local (re-) creations; (2) generally reflective of once wider Afro-Colombian traditions;[4] and (3) perhaps "(re-)inventions" that took hold only decades *after* the community had formed, that is, at a time when Palenqueros may have felt a special need to (re)assert their ethnicity and special status as a (former) maroon society.[5]

Bantu (Kikongo) remnants in Palenque

Comparative evidence from the Congo region, some of which has been available to me only in the form of unpublished sources (often obtained through informal conversations or e-mail exchanges with Kikongo-speaking colleagues, including the native Kongo specialists Dr. Fu-Kiau Kia Bunseki and Jean Nsondé), has led me to believe that Bantu influence in Palenque is pronounced in many domains of past or current everyday life, including the following:

1 language (vocabulary, grammar, style, etc.)

2 music[6]

3 dance[7]

4 religion and cosmology in general[8]

5 superstition[9]

6 gestures and body language in general[10]

7 healing and magical practices[11]

8 aesthetics[12]

9 social organization[13]

10 color symbolism[14]

11 legal traditions[15]

12 dietary habits[16]

13 recreational practices[17]

14 deep reverence for certain plant life[18]

15 sexual practices and preferences[19] and

16 material life in general, including the layout of dwellings, the design of traditional furniture,[20] the fabrication of sleeping mats,[21] the construction of traditional animal traps,[22] and many more.

When assessing the examples of Bantu (Kikongo) influence examined below, readers should thus contextualize the evidence against this backdrop of potentially widespread African survivals.[23]

Linguistic evidence

Linguistic evidence for Palenque's Bantu and, more specifically, Kikongo heritage seems scant at first, which is why it has historically been underestimated. There are several reasons for this; first, even though the Palenqueros have preserved an ancestral ritual code (used in the aforementioned *lumbalú* funeral ceremony), this type of speech is not composed of one or several (mixed) African languages. Rather it consists of straightforward everyday Palenquero creole, albeit one that is at times peppered with Kikongo-derived and/or "African"-sounding stock expressions (one such formula is "*chi ma nkongo*," which is partially unintelligible even to initiates of Palenquero rituals

(Schwegler 1996a)). This is tantamount to saying that, contrary to what one finds, for instance, in Cuba where Yoruba, Ewe, Efik, and Kikongo are spoken to this day (Schwegler 1998b, 2000b, 2002 and relevant sources cited therein; Fuentes and Schwegler 2005), in Palenque one no longer encounters a (ritual) African language. Second, as far as the everyday lexicon is concerned, Palenquero and local Spanish, are remarkably devoid of African vestiges, totaling at best a dozen terms (for a sampling see Schwegler (1999a, 2000a), where the common *moná* "child," *majana* "children," and *ngombe* "steer" are all linked to Kikongo etyma). The third factor that contributes to this seemingly non-African character of Palenquero speech is found in its phonology and morphosyntax, neither of which offers abundant "obvious" signs of substrate African influence. Except for the sporadic addition of prenasals (underlined in the examples hereafter: *ndo* < Sp. *dos* "two"; *mbala* < Sp. *bala* "ball"; *nKongo* "Congo"), the sound patterns of Palenquero words never violate the rules of Spanish phonology.[24] There is, then, virtually nothing systematic in the sound system of Palenquero that would betray African influence.

Closer examinations (Moñino 1999, 2002; Schwegler 1999a, 2000a, 2002) of the Palenquero language have revealed that the African legacy is considerably stronger than had originally been assumed. Because Palenque's African lexicon had not been subject to systematic study, in 1995 I engaged in a methodical compilation of putative Afro-Palenquerisms. This search has yielded about 200 autochthonous lexical items of putative African origins, many of which are archaic and belong to specialized semantic domains (Schwegler 1999a, 2000a). Etymological research on these newly discovered Africanisms (Schwegler 1999a, 2000a) lends further credence to earlier claims that Kikongo played a dominant role in the formation of Palenquero. The following is a small random sampling of Kikongo-derived words:

Palenquero		Kikongo
chaku–chaku	"peccary; pig"	< **cáku-cáku** "onomat. for the liquid sound that when it eats makes the sound *cha-ku—cha-ku*"
mokuño	"type of small trap to catch certain wild animals"	< **mu[†] + kú + nyō**, literally "small prison"
mulumba	"sexual predator"	< **mu + ndúmba** literally "young woman, virgin"
mongolona	"vulva; a woman's private parts"	< **mu + ngúla > ngúl +** Span. suffix **-ona** (augmentative) literally "private part(s)"
kwâ	"not at all, in no way"	< **kuá** "idem"

†Note: In this and the two examples that follow, *mu* is a class prefix. Class prefixes of this sort are a characteristic feature of Bantu languages.

So overwhelming is the preponderance of lexical Kikongo material in this creole that scholars of Palenquero must face a puzzling question with which they are just beginning to grapple. Namely, how could Kikongo-speaking slaves—never numerically dominant[25]—play such a dominant linguistic role in a slaving area (Cartagena) known to have received thousands of Africans from throughout Central *and* Western Africa?

Scholars recognized early on, for instance, that two of its subject pronouns—*ané* "they" and *enú* "you (pl.)"—are almost certainly of Bantu stock. Yet, within the domain of grammar, African influence on Palenquero has traditionally been characterized as minimal at best (but see Moñino 1999, 2002). Scholars have generally assumed, or implied, that all other Palenquero subject pronouns (see Table 18.1) are derived from Spanish or Portuguese, so that the pronominal system is still said to be overwhelmingly "European" rather than African. To take just three examples: Pal. *i*— "I" and the variant *y'*— "I" in examples (1a–c) below have always been considered derivatives of Spanish *yo*. And *Pal. o*—"you (s.)" has invariably been etymologized on the basis of Port. *vós* and/or Span. *vos* both "you (s.)."[26] As it turns out, a detailed reexamination of Palenquero pronoun usage has revealed that Kikongo influence is pronounced in much of the Palenquero subject paradigm, and that the

Table 18.1 Origins of Palenquero subject pronouns (somewhat simplified from Schwegler in press). Although Kikongo is given as the source, other African languages may have also contributed. Under this revised analysis, half of all Palenquero subject pronouns have Kikongo roots. Scholars generally agree that Portuguese-derived grammatical elements in Palenquero reached the Cartagena area via an Afro-Portuguese contact vernacular. Etymologies such as Palenquero *bo* < Portuguese *vós* should, therefore, always be understood as Palenquero *bo* < Afro-Portuguese *vó(s)* < Portuguese *vós*.

		Palenquero Subject Pronouns (Origins)		
	European Origin	Euro-African Origin (convergence)	African Origin (Kikongo)	Etymology
1 s.	yo			< Span. **yo** (1s.)
		y-		< Kik. **y-** (1s.) **x** Span. **y'** < **yo** (1s.)
			i-	< Kik. **i-** (1s.)
2 s.	bo			< Port. **vós** (2s.).
		o-		< Kik. **o-** (2s.) **x** Port. **vós** (2s.)
	(u)té			< Span. **usted** (2s.)
3 s.	ele			< Port. **ele** (3s. masc.)
		e-		< Kik. **e-** (3s.)
1 pl.	(s)uto		(?) -to	< Span. **nosotros** (1pl. masc.) (perhaps with Kik. -to "we" as a contributing factor)
2 pl.	utere			< Span. **ustedes** (2pl.)
			enú	< Kik. **énu** (2pl., emph.; indep. pronoun)
3 pl.			ané	< Kik. **ane** "those (yonder)"
	ele (archaic)			< Port. **eles** (3pl. masc.)

Note: s. = singular; pl. = plural; masc. = masculine; Span. = Spanish; Kik. = Kikongo; Port. = Portuguese.

aforementioned forms are the result of either straight descent from Kikongo forms or admixture of European and Kikongo elements (Schwegler in 2002). Example 1 illustrates the multiple origins (European, African, and Euro-African) of Palenquero first-person markers.

(1)	(a)	**yo**	a	miná	María.	< Span.	yo
	(b)	**y'**	a	miná	María.	< Kik.	y- + **Span.** yo
	(c)	**i**	a	miná	María.	< Kik.	i

Span. yo ha   mirar María
Engl. I   have look   Maria

"I (have) looked at Maria."

What is particularly arresting—and especially telling as regards the *depth* of Kikongo influence—is the extent to which the African substrate has influenced not only the forms of the pronouns but also their morphosyntax.[27] Witness, for example, the patterning in Palenquero of the pronominal reiteration *yo y-* (essentially meaning "I" [emphatic]) in Example 2, where one notes a striking "one-to-one correspondence" with the Kikongo construction *mono y-* "I (emphatic)" (pronominal reiteration of this type is not found in Spanish).

		FREE 1. sing. "I"†	BOUND 1. sing. "I"	PAST Tense	VERB	TRANSLATION
(2)	Kik.	**(mòno)**	**y-**	a-	bazola.	"I (emph.) loved them."
	Pal.	**(yo)**	**y-**	a-	kelé-lo.	"I (emph.) loved them."

†Note: These three forms (Kik. *mòno*, Pal. *yo*) are not obligatory, that is, one finds Kik. *mono y-a bazula* as well as simply *y-a bazola* "I loved them," which corresponds to Pal. *yo y-a-kelé-lo* and *y-a kelé-lo* "idem" respectively.

In addition to language-internal evidence, Palenquero speech offers external proof that the roots of their community are to be found in Kongo territories. Most prominent among this evidence figure funeral chants called *lumbalú* (< Kikongo *lu-mbálu* "recollection, memory, melancholy") whose melodies, rhythm, and cosmovision are reminiscent of Kongo traditions (Schwegler 1996a). Typically celebrated during the nine-day wake, the best-known *lumbalú* explicitly locates the Palenqueros' origins in areas where Kikongo has always been spoken. In assessing the importance of the text, readers should keep in mind that, as indicated by Nsondé (1995: 31, 47), (1) Loango is a coastal city in northern Kikongo territory; and (2) that historically the territory extended further south than today, reaching all the way to the Dande river of northern Angola.

Chi ma **nkongo**	From the Congo people (I am)
Chi ma ri **luango**	From those of Luango
Chi ma di **Luango** *ri* **Angol'** *e!*	From the Loangos of Angola, eh![28]

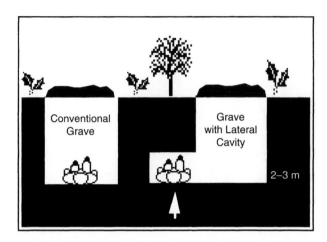

Figure 18.3   Early grave type with lateral cavity. By the early 1900s, Palenqueros had ceased to bury their dead in this fashion.

Archaeological evidence

Archaeological excavations have never been carried out in Palenque, even though this promises to be a particularly fruitful area for researching the Afro-American past. I previously reported (in Spanish) on former Palenquero burial practices that can be linked to central West-African traditions (Schwegler 1992). What follows is a brief summary of one of these burial traditions.

Palenquero elders revealed to me that "the dead used to be buried in very deep graves—from two to three meters deep—and the body was placed in the grave without a coffin." A traditional gravesite of this type is located just a few yards to the right of the church (the lot is currently unoccupied and shows no signs of ever having been a burial site). According to the Palenquera Inés Martinez, these traditional graves had a special feature, which consisted of a lateral shelf-like cavity, dug out on one side of the rectangular grave (Figure 18.3). When questioned about the rationale for this lateral cavity, the same informant responded that this was done to insert the body sideways "so that the dirt would not fall on to the face of the deceased."

Initially I had interpreted the informant's explanation as an interpretation *a posteriori*. Subsequent reading of Milheiros (1951), Parrinder (1954), Ardener (1956) and information from my Kongo informants (obtained after the publication of my aforementioned 1992 article) have, however, provided historical confirmation of the explanation offered by my Palenquero informants. In Ardener's *Coastal Bantu of the Cameroons* we read that "formerly a chamber used to be excavated in the side of the grave, into which the body was placed so that earth was not thrown directly on to it. This practice has now generally ceased" (1956: 87). And in *African Traditional Religion* Parrinder (1954: 99) notes that

> [g]reat attention is given to prevent the earth from falling directly on to
> the body. In some places a shelf is dug in the grave at the side, on which

the body is placed. Others place branches or grass over the body to protect it. Formerly winding-sheets and mats were used. Nowadays coffins are increasingly popular.

Information about Kongo-Angolese traditional burial practices is scant, though Hambly does note that "the depth of the grave is about six feet" (1932:569). More relevant is what Milheiros reports when he states that "at a depth of about a meter and a half they dig a type of horizontal shelf, where they place the deceased ..." (1951: 116, my translation). I have been unable to obtain similar written documentation for areas historically inhabited by the Bakongo. However, two of my older Kongo informants did confirm the former use of lateral burial shelves by their ancestors, though they were unable to provide information about the depth to which such shelves were normally dug.

Anthropological evidence

The placement of personal items on a tomb
Some Palenquero families customarily deposit a deceased's personal belongings (plates, forks, spoons, reading glasses, chamber pots, toothbrushes, shaving utensils, mats and mattresses, etc.) in a trench dug within the walled confines of the cemetery (Figure 18.4). Heavily overgrown by shrubs and trees, this "special" area has the outer appearance of a trash dump, and most of today's Palenqueros can no longer offer a rational explanation as to exactly why they hurry to that part of the cemetery to rid themselves of a deceased person's belongings. However, some still recall why they adhere to the custom. As one Palenquero explained in creole: *e pogke suto a-tené miero*

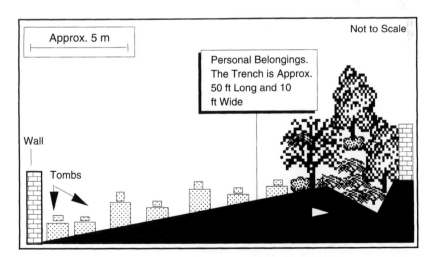

Figure 18.4 Palenque's cemetery and the trench where personal belongings are deposited. During the rainy season the terrain becomes muddy and many of the belongings gradually disappear in the dirt.

ri ma muetto—"it's because we are afraid of the dead [spirits]" (Palenqueros believe in
the afterlife of their ancestors, who watch over them and are said to revive at night).

As my Palenquero informant Inés Martínez (1901–1992) confirmed, Palenqueros
used to deposit these personal belongings directly on the grave. But with the early
nineteenth-century adoption of "modern" burial customs—customs that included the
construction of aboveground cement-tombs (see Figure 18.4) into which coffins are
tightly fitted—these personal belongings could no longer be buried with the dead.
The trench offered a ready solution, as it provided a common burial ground where the
old tradition could somehow be maintained, albeit admittedly in syncretic fashion.

There is good reason to believe that here too we are faced with a custom whose
origins ultimately go back to Kongo traditions (Schwegler 1992). In Wing's *Études
Bakongo: Sociologie—Religion et magie* (1959), which to this day constitutes one of the
best studies about religion and magic of central West Africa, we are informed that the
placement of personal objects on a tomb was a common tradition[29]:

> Elle [la tombe] est creusée en haut des collines, dans une terre sèche; elle
> est plus ou moins rectangulaire et profonde de deux ou trois mètres,
> d'après les dimensions du ballot qu'elle doit contenir. Son emplacement
> est marqué d'ordinaire par un petit tertre. Tout autour on plante des
> *mbota (Milletia versicolor; leg.)*, arbustes très vivaces d'un bois très dur.
> A leurs branches on fixe des objets dont le défunt s'est servi ou qu'il a
> achetés, pour être exhibés sur sa tombe, *particulièrement des objects de
> faïence, comme des assiettes et des cruches.*
>
> *Sur la tombe même et tout autour on dispose d'autres objets, comme des
> ustensiles, des instruments de pêche, des touques vides, etc., etc.*
>
> (249; my italics)

Similar reference to the removal of belongings from a dead person's house to the
gravesite is made by Laman:

> ... burial mounds are adorned with all sorts of articles, such as porcelain,
> figures, guns, umbrellas, powder-kegs and elephants-tusks. The porcelain
> articles may comprise mugs ... plates, cooking utensils, jugs, various
> porcelain figurines.
>
> (*The Kongo* 1957, Vol. 2: 95)

The (re)location of the cemetery

Now that we have made reference to Palenque's two burial sites—one where graves
were dug with lateral shelf-like cavities, and the other where *personaliae* are deposited
in a trench—we are in a better position to consider additional data that is suggestive of
Bantu (Kongo) influence. The historical existence of not one but two cemeteries begs
these two related questions: What may have motivated the Palenqueros to relocate their
traditional burial grounds away from the Central Plaza to the outskirts of their village?
And what criteria of selection did the Palenqueros follow in choosing the new site?

Particularly from a comparative African-American perspective, the placement of
both cemeteries is revealing in that they are each placed at cardinal points in the

sociogeographic layout of the community. As the map of Palenque (Figure 18.5) illustrates, the current cemetery is located at the very entrance of town, that is, where most Palenqueros pass by on a daily basis, either en route to another town, or to the *casimbas* "waterholes" at the *loyo* "creek." As concerns the old burial ground, one needs to contextualize its historical importance and cardinal placement vis-à-vis the community. Until about the middle of the twentieth century—that is, until the time when the road that now connects the village to the outside world was built—Palenque was oriented in the opposite direction, thus facing what is now the backside of town where the agricultural fields and the hamlet of La Bonga are located. At that time, the Central Plaza was the locale from which practically all pedestrian traffic flowed, and this placed the former cemetery at a much-frequented cross section.

I have highlighted the historical prominence of both cemeteries because, as Kimpianga notes in "Les fonctions religieuses et thérapeutiques du cimitière chez les Kongo du Zaïre" (1977: 56) and "La mort dans la pensée kongo" (1980: 42), to protect a village against evil spirits, Kongo cemeteries were traditionally placed at the entrance or exit of a town. The geographic proximity of the cemetery vis-à-vis the center of

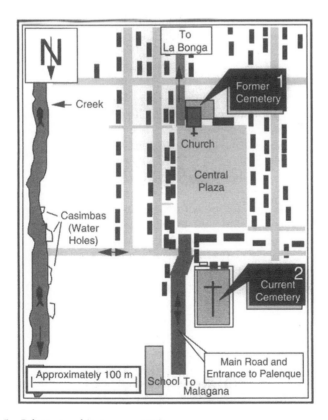

Figure 18.5 Palenque and its two cemeteries.

town is symptomatic of the spiritual proximity that West Central Bantu communities feel between themselves and the ancestors who "protect their clan."[30] One cannot help but suspect that the socioreligious behavior of nineteenth-century Palenqueros followed habits acquired from their Kongo-Angolan ancestors, and that, once the old cemetery had lost its geographic prominence because of the newly built road, the Palenqueros felt the need to bury their dead in a more prominent area, where they rest today.

The "Chakero" tradition

Also worth noting is the "Chakero" tradition. Described for the first time in a brief newspaper article by Simarra Torres (1998), *chakero* is the term used to designate those charged with announcing a recent death to the community by literally running from door to door to disperse the news (the action itself is known as *chakear*). The tradition and the term itself are both of Kongo origin. The root of *chakero* and *chakear* is Kikongo *nsáki* "haste, hurry" (Laman 1964:753), which in Kikongo is also found in *nsákila* "young person" and *ñsáakilà* "loud, energetic, alarming cry (e.g. to announce a victory, someone's death, etc.)" (Laman 1964: 753).[31] The suffixes *-ero* and *-ear* of *chakero* and *chakear* are, however, of Hispanic origins. My older Kongo informants had no trouble identifying this tradition, though they generally considered it antiquated.

Concluding remarks

The finding that Kongo influence appears to have been remarkably pronounced in Palenque naturally raises a series of questions that future studies will need to address. Were the maroons that settled Palenque predominantly of Kongo stock? Or were they perhaps an ethnically and linguistically diverse group in which Kongo slaves were "simply" more influential linguistically? Should one assume, as I have suggested in this article, that Kongo *linguistic* survivals were matched by similar Kongo *cultural* survivals? Or should we suppose that, for reasons not explored here, Kongo linguistic influence was paramount *without* constraining cultural transfers from other, ethnolinguistic diverse maroons, thereby allowing for the ready adoption (and adaptation) of Cokwe (Tshokwe), Yaka, Mbundu, and other Bantu traditions? And how do we explain that, contrary to Cuba's Paleros (Fuentes and Schwegler 2005), the (Ba)Kongo inhabitants of Palenque exerted strong linguistic influence, but apparently did so without managing to preserve their native Kikongo?

The Palenqueros have remained arguably the most culturally, linguistically, and genetically "African" of Colombia's *Costeños* (Schwegler and Morton 2003). Yet, I must reiterate that this has not been appreciated sufficiently by scholars in and outside of Colombia. Hopefully this study will encourage specialists in a variety of related disciplines (anthropology, archaeology, [art] history, linguistics, genetics, musicology, and so on) to document and trace, with the necessary academic rigor, the origins of this community.

Notes

1 As Thompson and Cornet explain, the

> Kongo people [= the Bakongo], several million strong, live in modern Bas-
> Zaire and neighboring Cabinda, Congo-Brazzaville, and Angola. The present
> division of their territory into these modern political entities masks the fact that
> the area was once united, under the suzerainty of the ancient kingdom of
> Kongo, as one of the most important civilizations ever to emerge in Africa.
>
> (1981: 27)

> For more recent studies of Kongo people, see Nsondé (1995) and relevant
> sources cited therein.

2 Friedemann (1993: 98) and I (Schwegler 1996a: 15) have suggested that Palenque may not
be the original place to where the maroons escaped, and that it is rather a residual palenque
initially composed of maroons that had settled in other palenques, some of them perhaps
located hundreds of miles inland on the banks of the Cauca River. This would explain why
a *lumbalú* chant uses the formulaic expression "o Kauka landá ri é" "oh, [the canoe = dead
person] is descending into the Cauca river" (the nonliteral meaning of the expression is "oh,
the recently deceased is entering the world of the dead").

3 A 1772 document mentions that "de que cortan con mucha expedición el castellano, de que
generalmente usan" "they are [also] fluent in Spanish, which they generally use" (Gutierrrez
Azopardo (1980, 34, my translation)).

4 It remains controversial, for instance, whether the Palenquero creole was once a more
widespread type of speech and could potentially have influenced the development of popular
Caribbean Spanish (Lipski 1994, chapter 4; Schwegler 1996b, 1999b).

5 Such "(re)inventions" can be observed even today. For instance, the youth band *Ané swing*
(literally "They swing"), some of whose members are from Palenque, has become famous
on the Coast for playing songs whose lyrics are presumably articulated in Palenquero (see
Bilby 2000). But in reality these musical texts are largely fanciful inventions not rooted in
true Palenquero speech.

6 Examples would include traditional instruments (drums, etc.), rhythmic clapping, and
communal rhythmic singing during field work (no longer practised today) (see Schwegler
1996a: xlii–xliii). Except for Cárdenas' brief article and Escalante's (1974: 86–91) summary
treatment (which includes interesting photos of antiquated instruments), and my
publications on the *lumbalú*, the musical tradition of Palenque has never been studied.
Although centered on Brazil, a good point of departure for tracing this aspect of Palenque's
culture may be Mukuna (2000).

7 Typical traditional dances were the *bullerengue, gaita, and cumbiamba* (Escalante 1974: 87–88),
which are no longer in vogue today.

8 See Schwegler (1996a, chapter 1), Escalante (1974: 42–57).

9 Two of the superstitious practices that were recognized at once by one of my older Kongo
informants are (1) a Palenquera insisted that during a full moon, chicken eggs must be
covered by a plate, hat, or other object, as they would otherwise rot and bring bad luck, and
(2) in the eyes of Palenqueros, infants must be protected from rain at all times, as even
the shortest exposure to it would do serious harm.

10 When relaxing informally on a chair, it is customary to lean the chair and body at a
45 percent angle against an adjacent object (wall, tree, etc.). For a photographic example,
see Friedemann and Cross (1979: 60). Also practised in other parts of (Black) America,
this leaning of the chair was immediately recognized by one of my Kongo informants as "the
way we love to sit when we hang out."

> Writing about negation strategies in *fiote* (Cabinda area, just north of the mouth of the
> Kongo river), Troesch noted two expressive "negative" gestures, both of which I repeatedly

observered in Palenque as well as other areas of the Caribbean and the Pacific Lowlands (Western Colombia):

> Le geste est aussi important et aussi expressif que la parole. Rien, c'est frapper une main dans l'autre puis les tourner largement ouvertes vers l'interlocuteur; battre les mains de haut en bas et de bas en haut, l'une effleurant légèrement l'autre.

> (1953: 136)

11 For a description of some of these practices, see Escalante (1974: 42–57) and Schwegler (1996a: 238–250). To cite just two examples: The *nganga* "medicine man, sorcerer" and *nkisi* "ritual objects endowed with magic powers or divine forces of nature with a specific function" are concepts shared by both Kongos and Palenqueros, though the latter now no longer use the terms except in funeral chants.

12 For instance female hair styling and the use of palm oil for that purpose.

13 Adolescent males are, for instance, only very occasionally obliged to participate in backbreaking agricultural activities. Girls, on the other hand, are asked to perform regular household and other duties (including the bartering of goods in nearby towns) already from an early age (5–6 years onward). According to several Kongo informants, this very much reflects traditional patterns of childrearing in their society. Moreover, Palenquero elders traditionally commanded deep respect from the rest of the village, and were placed at the top of the social hierarchy (not surprisingly, Palenquero elders used to hold most executive powers). In the section "Qui est aîné," Nsondé (1995: 119–121) describes a very similar situation for traditional Kongo society.

14 See Schwegler (1996a: 10–11), where women dressed in white (rather than black) are readying themselves for a funeral march. As in most of Africa, in Palenque white is associated with death.

15 Including the (former) sharing of land plots, or the special way in which dowries were arranged.

16 For instance the older Palenqueros' love for peanuts (a common and much appreciated staple in traditional Kongo society), or their high regard for certain types of peas or beans (including the *guandú*, which Del Castillo [1982: 209–211, 1984: 157] correctly relates to Kikongo *wandú* "peas" [see also Schwegler 1999a: 197]).

A good starting point for future comparative research on dietary practices will be chapter 8 "Permanences et évolutions dans l'alimentation du XVIIème au XVIIIème siècle" in Nsondè's *Langues, culture et histoire Koongo* ... (1995), where *wandú* is mentioned on page 155. Del Castillo's "Bantuismos en Cartagena de Indias: Vegetales, alimentos y bebidas" (1985) and Obenga's "Tradiciones y costumbres alimenticias Kongo en el siglo XVII: estructuras del sabor" (1992) will also prove useful.

17 For instance, the rearward smoking of cigars by older women who insert the burning portion of the tobacco in their mouth. When presented with this curious practice, my Kongo informant Fu-Kiau Kia Bunseki burst out into laughter, as he immediately recognized it as something typical from his homeland. The practice was also confirmed by Jean Nsondé:

> Je confirme personnellement le goût immodéré des Kôngo pour l'arachide, consommé sous toutes ses formes; fraîche, sèche, bouillie, grillée, en pâte, en sauce, etc. Idem pour les haricots appelés wandu. Je confirme aussi, pour l'avoir vu de mes propres yeux, l'habitude singulière qui consiste à fumer en mettant la partie allumée de la cigarette à l'intérieur de la bouche!

> (e-mail, April 2002)

18 Trees, shrubs and certain herbs are afforded special status. In this respect, Palenqueros embrace behavioral and attitudinal patterns similar to those found in the *Palo Monte* tradition of Cuba (Cabrera 1971 [1954], 1979, 1984a, 1984b; Castellanos 1977), whose (linguistic) Kongo origins are now firmly established (Schwegler 1998b, 2000b, 2002; and especially Fuentes and Schwegler 2005).

19 For instance, Palenquero men predictably prefer women with large (rather than small) buttocks. This preference is, of course, far from exclusive to the Kongo region, but may nonetheless serve as a noteworthy point of correspondence.

20 See for instance the bed (made of sticks) photographed in Schwegler (1996a: 580). According to one of my informants, its design is reflective of inherited Kongo traditions.

21 Shown in Friedemann and Cross (1979: 112) and Schwegler (1996a: 229).

22 Good illustrations of a typical trap can be found in Friedemann and Cross (1979: 110–111).

23 I wish to emphasize that my assessment of this presumably "copious" influence will need to be confirmed by more formal investigations, especially as nonlinguistic "evidence" is concerned. At the same time I wish to reiterate that even cursory examinations of some of the Palenquero data (which included some of the behavioral information mentioned above) by my Kongo colleagues produced such spontaneous reactions on their part that I cannot help but suspect a direct link between key Palenquero and Kongo phenomena. The most poignant example is found, perhaps, in how quickly Dr. Fu-Kiau Kia Bunseki recognized the melody of the funeral chant "Chi ma nkongo," cited at the beginning of this article. I had hardly initiated the first line of the song when he joined in and completed the tune with me, humming along as he was listening intently to the creole lyrics, whose meanings he naturally could not understand (I say "naturally" because Kikongo—the native language of my informant—and Palenquero are mutually unintelligible languages).

24 Prenasals are exceedingly common in Kikongo, and are also found in many other languages of Black Africa. Scholars concur that the feature in Palenquero has African roots (Schwegler 1998a: 264). Not surprisingly, prenasalization is also a common development in Afro-Hispanic language (Lipski 1992).

25 *Pace* Arends (2002), I recognize that the overall numerical distribution of ethnolinguistic groups provides an insufficient basis for identifying major substrate languages. Additional information relating to the timing and compactness of substrate input may help determine the relative importance of a given group of speakers in creole formation. Nevertheless, it is still perplexing that the Bakongo should have played such a predominant role among seventeenth-century maroons who escaped to the Cartagenero hinterland.

26 *Portuguese vós* "originally 2d plural; later 2d singular" is no longer in use today, having been replaced by *você*.

27 African morphosyntactic influence in Palenquero almost certainly extends beyond pronoun usage. For instance, embracing negation patterns of the type *nu* + VERB + ... *nu* (Schwegler 1991a) probably have substratal origins, as Dieck (2000: 159) has recently recognized. Virtually identical predicate negation patterns are also found in Brazil (Schwegler 1991b) and the Dominican Republic (Schwegler 1996c).

28 The interpretation offered for the chant is essentially that given in Schwegler (1996a: 525), where *chi* was derived from (Afro-)Portuguese *di ~ de* "from." Jean Nsondé rightly pointed out to me (personal communication, April 2002) that a slightly different interpretation is equally plausible since Palenquero *chi* could be derived from Kikongo *nsí* "area, region, place." The literal meaning of the first line would thus be "From the land of the Kongo (I am)."

29 In the Americas, this tradition is not exclusive to Palenque. In *The Four Moments of the Sun: Kongo Art in Two Worlds*, Thompson and Cornet report for the USA:

> Some objects which decorate a grave—a cup, a wheatherbeaten hat, a rusting pair of scissors—lack the flash which embeds the spirit. Often these are the kinds of things which arrest the being of the departed person in other ways. Because of their intimate relation to the deceased, the things last used by the dead person become especially important: "the last strength of a dead person is present within that sort of object ... Placing such objects on the grave safely grounds their awesome potentiality, keeps the dead from coming to the house to claim them back." To touch them is to receive, mystically, powerful messages from the dead, communicated in dreams ... .
>
> (1981: 200)

30 Readers interested in this and other traditional Kongo socioreligious practices should also consult *Religion and Society in Central Africa*. The *BaKongo of Lower Zaire* (1986) and *Art and Healing of the Bakongo Commented by Themselves* (1991) by MacGaffey. Although of a more general nature, Thornton's excellent *Africa and Africans in the Making of the Atlantic World, 1400–1800* will also be essential reading in any comparative examination of Palenquero/Kongo traditions.

31 Compare also Kikongo *(ba-) nsāki-nsaki* "person who is not old; someone neither young nor old" (Laman 1964: 753), literally "person capable of moving about with haste or speed." The etymology given here has not been presented elsewhere. In evaluating my etymological proposal it should be kept in mind that the palatalization of [ns-] > [tʃ] in *ṉsáki* > *＊ḏɦak[ero]* is an expected result, also found in other Palenquero words, including *cherre-cherre* "cob of corn whose kernels are ill-formed" < Kikongo *nzéle* "apoplexy" (Schwegler 1999a: 190).

References

Ardener, Edwin (1956) *Coastal Bantu of the Cameroons*, London: International African Institute.

Arends, Jacques (2002) "The Historical Study of Creoles and the Future of Creole Studies," in Glenn Gilbert (ed.) *Pidgin and Creole Linguistics in the 21st Century*, 49–61, Frankfurt and New York: Peter Lang.

Arrazola, Roberto (1970) *Palenque, primer pueblo libre de América: historia de las sublevaciones de los esclavos de Cartagena*, Cartagena, Ediciones Hernández.

Bickerton, Derek, and Escalante, Aquiles (1970) "Palenquero: A Spanish-based creole of northern Colombia," *Lingua*, 24: 254–267.

Bilby, Kenneth (2000) "Making modernity in the hinterlands: new Maroon musics in the Black Atlantic," *Popular Music*, 1: 265–292.

Böttcher, Nikolas (1995) *Aufstieg und Fall eines atlantischen Handelsimperiums. Portugiesische Kaufleute und Sklavenhändler in Cartagena de Indias von 1580 bis zur Mitte des 17. Jahrhunderts*, Frankfurt: Vervuert Verlag / Madrid: Iberoamericana.

Bunseki, Fu-Kiau Kia (1987) *Digging Up the Past. An approach to fundamental education and community development (case of Zaire)*, PhD dissertation, Ann Arbor: University Microfilms International.

Cabrera, Lydia [1954] (1971) *El monte, igbo finda, ewe orisha, vititi nfinda (notas sobre las religiones, la magia, las supersticiones y el folklore de los negros criollos y del pueblo de Cuba)*, Miami, FL: Colección del Chicherekú.

Cabrera, Lydia (1979) *Reglas de congo: palo monte mayombé*, Miami, FL: Ediciones CR.

Cabrera, Lydia (1984a) *Vocabulario congo. El bantú que se habla en Cuba*. Miami, FL: Colección del Chichereku.

Cabrera, Lydia (1984b) *La medicina popular de Cuba: médicos de antaño, curanderos, santeros y paleros de hogaño*. Miami, FL: Ultra Graphics Corp.

Castellanos, Isabel (1977) *The Use of Language in Afro-Cuban Religion*, unpublished PhD dissertation, University of Michigan, Ann Arbor.

Del Castillo, Nicolas (1982) *Esclavos negros en Cartagena y sus aportes léxicos*, Bogota: Instituto Caro y Cuervo.

Del Castillo, Nicolas (1984) "El léxico negro-africano de San Basilio de Palenque," *Thesaurus*, 39, 80–169.

Del Castillo, Nicolas (1985) "Bantuismos en Cartagena de Indias: Vegetales, alimentos y bebidas," *Muntu*, 2, 85–109.

Dieck, Marianne (2000) *La negación en palenquero. Análisis sincrónico, estudio comparativo y consecuencias teóricas*, Frankfurt: Vervuert / Madrid: Iberoamericana.

Escalante, Aquiles [1954] (1974) *El Palenque de San Basilio*, Barranquilla: Editorial Mejoras.

Friedemann, Nina S. de, and Cross, Richard (1979) *Ma ngombe. Guerreros y ganaderos en Palenque* Bogota: Carlos Valencia Editores.

Friedemann, Nina S. de, and Cross, Richard (1993) *La saga del negro*, Bogota: Universidad Javeriana, Instituto de Genética Humana.

Fuentes, Jesús, and Schwegler, Armin (2005) *Lengua y ritos del Palo Monte Mayombe: dioses cubanos y sus fuentes africanas*. Frankfurt: Vervuert Verlag/Madrid: Iberoamericana

Granda, German de (1978) *Estudios lingüísticos hispánicos, afrohispánicos y criollos*, Madrid: Gredos.

Gutierrez, Azopardo (1980) *Historia del negro en Colobmia. ¿Sumisión o rebeldía?* Bogota: Editorial ABC.

Hambly, Wilfred D. (1932) "Spiritual beliefs of the Ovimbundu of Angola," *The Open Court*, 46: 564–580.

Huttar, George (1993) "Identifying Africanisms in New World Languages: How Specific Can we Get?," in Salikoko Mufwene (ed.) *Africanisms in Afro-American Language Varieties*, 47–63, Athens, GA: The University of Georgia Press.

Kimpianga, Mahaniah (1977) "Les fonctions religieuses et thérapheutiques du cimitière chez les Kongo du Zaïre," *Psychopathologie Africaine*, 13: 47–70.

Kimpianga, Mahaniah (1980) *La mort dans la pensée Kongo*, Kinsantu: Centre de vulgarisation agricole.

Laman, Karl Eduard (1957) *The Kongo*, Vol. 2, Uppsala: Almquist and Wiksells.

Laman, Karl Eduard (1964) *Dictionnaire kikongo-français*, 2 Vols, Ridgewood, NJ: The Gregg Press. [1936]

Lipski, John M. (1992) "Spontaneous nasalization in the development of Afro-Hispanic language," *Journal of Pidgin and Creole Languages*, 7: 261–305.

Lipski, John M. (1994) *Latin American Spanish*, New York: Longman.

MacGaffey, Wyatt (1986) *Religion and Society in Central Africa. The BaKongo of Lower Zaire*, Chicago, IL: The University of Chicago Press.

MacGaffey, Wyatt (1991) *Art and Healing of the Bakongo Commented by Themselves*, Stockholm: Folkens museum-etnografiska.

Megenney, William W. (1986) *El palenquero. Un lenguaje post-criollo de Colombia*, Bogota: Instituto Caro y Cuervo.

Milheiros, Mario (1951) *Etnografia angolana: esboço para um estudio etnográfico das tribos Angola*, Angola: Mensário Administrativo.

Moñino, Yves (1999) 'L'aspect en palenquero: une sémantaxe africaine', *Actances*, 10, 177–190.

Moñino, Yves (2002) "Las construcciones de genitivo en palenquero: ¿una semantaxis africana?," in Y. Moñino and A. Schwegler (eds), *Palenque, Cartagena y Afro-Caribe: historia y lengua*, Tübingen: Max Niemeyer Verlag.

Moñino, Yves, and Schwegler, Armin (eds) (2002) *Palenque, Cartagena y Afro-Caribe: historia y lengua*, Tübingen: Max Niemeyer Verlag.

Mukuna, Kazadiwa (2000) *Contribução bantu na música popular brasileira: Perspectivas Etnomusicológicas*, 2nd ed., São Paulo: Terceira Margem.

Nsondé, Jean de Dieu (1995) *Langues, culture et histoire Koongo aux XVIIe et XVIIIe siècles*, Paris: Editions L'Harmattan.

Obenga, Theophile (1985) *Les Bantu: langues, peuples, civilisationss*, Paris: Présence africaine.

Obenga, Theophile (1992) "Tradiciones y costumbres alimenticias Kongo en el siglo XVII: estructuras del sabor," *América Negra*, 3: 71–87.

Parrinder, Geoffrey (1954) *African Traditional Religion*, London: Hutchinson's University Library.

Perez Sarduy, Pedro, and Stubbs, Jean (1995) "Introduction," in Minority Rights Group (ed.) *Afro-Latin Americans Today. No Longer Invisible*, 1–17, London: Minority Rights Publications.

Ruiz Rivera, Julian Bautista (1996) *Los indios de Cartagena bajo la administración española en el siglo XVII*, Bogota: Archivo General de la Nación.

Sandoval, Alonso de [1627] (1987) *De instauranda aethiopum salute. Un tratado sobre la esclavitud*, Introduction and transcription by Enriqueta Vila Vilar (ed.) Madrid: Alianza Editorial.

Schwegler, Armin (1991a) "Negation in Palenquero: synchrony," *Journal of Pidgin and Creole Languages*, 6: 165–214.

Schwegler, Armin (1991b) "Predicate negation in contemporary Brazilian Portuguese—a linguistic change in progress," *Orbis*, 34: 187–214.

Schwegler, Armin (1992) "Hacia una arqueología afrocolombiana: Restos de tradiciones religiosas bantúes en una comunidad negroamericana," *América Negra*, 4: 35–82.

Schwegler, Armin (1996a) *Chi ma nkongo: lengua y rito ancestrales en El Palenque de San Basilio (Colombia)*, 2 Vols, Frankfurt: Vervuert / Madrid: Iberoamericana.

Schwegler, Armin (1996b) "Lenguas criollas en Hispanoamérica y la contribución africana al español de América." *Contactos y transferencias lingüísticas en Hispanoamérica*, Special issue of *Signo y Seña*, 6: 295–346.

Schwegler, Armin (1996c) "La doble negación dominicana y la génesis del español caribeño," *Hispanic Linguistics*, 8: 246–315.

Schwegler, Armin (1998a) "Palenquero," in Matthias Perl and Armin Schwegler (eds) *América negra: panorámica actual de los estudios lingüísticos sobre variedades criollas y afrohispanas*, 220–291, Frankfurt: Vervuert / Madrid: Iberoamericana.

Schwegler, Armin (1998b) "El vocabulario (ritual) bantú de Cuba. Parte I: Acerca de la matriz africana de la 'lengua congo' en *El Monte* y *Vocabulario Congo* de Lydia Cabrera," *América Negra* 15, 137–185 [Also published, along with Part II, in Schwegler 2002].

Schwegler, Armin (1999a) "El vocabulario africano de Palenque (Colombia). Segunda Parte: compendio de palabras (con etimologías)," in Luis Ortiz (ed.) *El Caribe hispánico: perspectivas lingüísticas actuales (Homenaje a Manuel Álvarez Nazario)*, 171–253, Frankfurt: Vervuert/ Madrid: Iberoamericana.

Schwegler, Armin (2000a) "The African vocabulary of Palenque (Colombia). Part 1: introduction and corpus of previously undocumented Afro-Palenquerisms," *Journal of Pidgin and Creole Language*, 15: 241–312.

Schwegler, Armin (2000b) "On the (sensational) survival of Kikongo in 20th-century Cuba," *Journal of Pidgin and Creole Languages*, 15: 159–164.

Schwegler, Armin (2002) "El vocabulario (ritual) bantú de Cuba" (Part I and Part II). In Norma Díaz, Ralph Ludwig, and Stefan Pfänder (eds) *La Romania americana. Procesos lingüísticos en situaciones de contacto*, 97–194, Frankfurt: Vervuert / Madrid: Iberoamericana.

Schwegler, Armin (2002) "On the (African) origins of Palenquero subject pronouns," *Diachronica*, 19(2): 273–332.

Schwegler, Armin, and Morton, Thomas (2003) "Vernacular Spanish in a microcosm: *Kateyano* in El Palenque de San Basilio (Colombia)," *Revista Internacional de Lingüística Iberoamericana (RILI)*, 1: 97–159.

Simarra Torres, Nicolas (1998) "La costumbre del chakero en la sociedad palenquera," *El Universal*, April 26: 4–6.

Thompson, Robert Farris, and Cornet, Joseph (1981) *The Four Moments of the Sun: Kongo Art in Two Worlds*, Washington, DC: National Gallery of Art.

Wade, Peter (1993) *Blackness and Race Mixture: The Dynamics of Racial Identity in Colombia*, Baltimore, MD: Johns Hopkins University Press.

Wade, Peter (in press) "Understanding 'Africa' and 'Blackness' in Colombia: Music and the Politics of Culture," in Kevin Yelvington (ed.) *Afro-Atlantic Dialogues: Anthropology in the Diaspora*, Santa Fe, NM: School of American Research Press.

Wing, J. van [1922] (1959) *Études bakongo: Sociologie—religion—magie*, Brussels: Desclee de Brouwer.

19   Medium vessels and the Longue Dureé

The endurance of ritual ceramics and the archaeology of the African Diaspora

Kenneth G. Kelly and Neil L. Norman

As research into the dynamic social environment of the African Diaspora has expanded, archaeologists have frequently attempted to identify items or categories of material culture that could be used as "calling cards" to conclusively demonstrate the presence of persons of African heritage on historic-era sites. This admirable goal was spearheaded by researchers who became increasingly aware that historians, folklorists, cultural anthropologists, and others were identifying material culture that could be argued, and in some cases demonstrated, to have West African antecedents (Herskovits 1941; Vlach 1976; Joyner 1984; Thompson 1993; Rosengarten 1994; Goucher 1999). These items of African inspiration included basketry, carvings, textile traditions, aspects of foodways, and architecture, to name a few. Yet, from the perspective of an archaeologist, most of these artifacts are less than ideal for they will not survive except in extraordinary circumstances.

Vessels for food

It is on to this stage that research into "Colonowares," low-fired hand-built earthenwares, has stepped. In at least some circumstances they have been convincingly argued to have been produced by persons of African heritage, providing important tangible evidence of "Africaness" on archaeological sites in various regions of the Americas (Mathewson 1972, 1973; Handler and Lange 1978; Armstrong 1990; Ferguson 1992, 1999; Steen 1999; Hauser and Armstrong 1999; Health 1999; Peterson et al. 1999; Mouer et al. 1999; and others). Much debate has revolved around the formal characteristics of this pottery as an expression of African cultural aesthetics, including the ideas that these pots were an instrument of affirmation of African values through both cooking and cuisine techniques (slow, long-term stewing), and eating preferences (the use of small bowls for sauces and relishes that were shared communally by the group). What seems to be clear, however, is that in the context of cooking and eating practices, the fabric of the pot, although preferred for some foods, was not essential. This has been posited because in some contexts colonowares are absent, but iron cook pots and mass-produced bowls and earthenware pots are common, suggesting that they may have served as the functional equivalent for these low-fired earthenware vessels (Otto 1984, Armstrong 1990: 144–146). Current work in Guadeloupe (French West Indies) is demonstrating that pots produced for their own use by African-descended populations are apparently rare, as are iron cooking pots, but that glazed and unglazed culinary pottery mass-produced in France and possibly in the Caribbean was incorporated into daily practice by enslaved workers (Kelly n.d.). These functional equivalents may have been used in many cases because the ability, or desire, to make adequate pottery may not have been present in some African communities as a result of the demographics of the slave trade or owing to local social and environmental conditions.

Indeed, it has been argued that the generalized forms of colonowares, which often little resemble definitive African forms and rarely resemble European pottery, is due to the dearth of individuals well-acquainted with ceramic techniques in enslaved African communities (with one possible exception being the early Chesapeake where a different set of circumstances is believed to be relevant, cf. Deetz 1993: 160). This argument has been supported by the observations that in many parts of Africa, older women are the curators of pottery traditions (Dark 1973:63; Fagg and Picton 1978: 8–10; Beier 1980: 48; Fatunsin 1992: 7; Barley 1994: 64), and this is the segment of the population that is most underrepresented in transported Africans (Curtin 1969).

An ethnoarchaeological (for a review see Stark 2003) survey of the modern potters in the village of Sé in southern Bénin (Figure 19.1), indicated that all of the ceramic artisans were female (Norman 2000: 101). Female ceramicists explained that there were prohibitions both against men creating ceramic vessels and young boys receiving

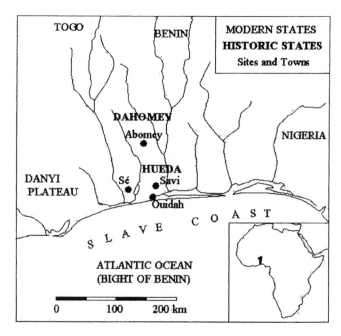

Figure 19.1 Map of modern and historic sites.

the restricted knowledge about pot-making acquired by young girls. It is understandable that this information is restricted, as controlling the transformative art of changing clay to ceramic is closely related to political and social prestige in southern Bénin (cf. Herbert 1993s discussion of male blacksmiths and LaViolettes 2000 discussion of blacksmiths, potters, and masons). Edna Bay notes a historic precedent for older women controlling ceramic industries in southern Bénin during the eighteenth and nineteenth centuries and using their monopoly of ceramic industries to secure profit and positions in the Dahomean court. These ceramic artisans were also charged with creating political insignias (Figure 19.2) and as late as in rule of King Guezo of Dahomey, ca. 1840, only the wives of the king were allowed to produce the small tobacco pipe bowls that were symbols of high rank in the Dahomean court (Bay 1998: 210).

Recent research (Norman 2000) in southern Bénin has demonstrated that among present-day potters there exists a high degree of specialization (cf. Etienne-Nugue 1984: 109; LaViolette 2000). Indeed, this specialization is so pronounced that a potter will only make a limited number of forms, and if that potter needs other forms for her family, she will buy or trade for them, rather than attempt to make them herself (see also Crossland and Posnansky 1978: 81; Igibami 1984: 107; Etienne-Nugue 1984: 109). Thus, even expert potters may not have the "competence" (in the linguistic

Figure 19.2 Statue of the "Unity Jar" at the Marché Zobé in Ouidah. The Unity Jar was first adopted as a political insignia during the rule of Guezo, King of Dahomey, ca. 1840

sense of the term, cf. Rickford 1980), experience, or willingness to manufacture anything approaching the full repertoire of a particular societies' vessel forms.

This suggests that if pottery competence were restricted historically in ways similar to those seen today, then, should an older woman who was a potter have been enslaved and transported, it is possible that certain categories of ceramics may have been outside her particular expertise. In spite of this, the requirement of satisfying basic culinary needs for cooking pots and eating bowls may well have resulted in potters being obliged to manufacture wares that lay outside of their repertoire or experience. Furthermore, it is possible that individuals who had never made a pot may have been compelled, by circumstances, into attempting basic pottery.

Norman's research in southern Bénin suggests that manufacturing competence for culinary pottery is narrowly restricted in at least some societies and may well have been equally restricted historically. However, while manufacturing competence may be restricted, we must remember that the competence for use is not. Thus, while not all individuals knew how to *make* pottery, nearly everyone knew how to *use* it. This opens up a range of possibilities for interpreting African American pot-making, including either the option outlined above, of potters operating outside their expertise and producing generalized forms, or the production of less-refined wares by amateurs according to a generalized set of rules (Ferguson 1992). Either way the result would be the creation of generalized colonowares. Alternatively, the substitution of industrially produced cooking and serving wares that otherwise conform to an African cultural aesthetic may be seen in some settings (Otto 1984; Armstrong 1990; Kelly n.d.). We must note, however, that while the argument may be very strong for the continued presence of an "African" aesthetic in culinary behavior, it may be that the widespread use of bowls and pots for potages is also an artifact of necessity in rural, farm-laboring settings where slow-cooking foods that do not need close attention may be advantageous. Therefore colonowares, and particularly European or American factory-produced hollow forms such as bowls, may not always exhibit an indexical relationship to African descendant populations. This point was made succinctly by Singleton and Bograd (2000: 4), who suggest that rather than attempting to identify the race or ethnicity of the creator or user of the colonoware, more effort should be placed on describing the political, social, economic, and religious contexts in which these artifacts were deployed. Here Martin Hall's (1987: 3–4) adaptation of "signification" is helpful in interpreting the active role that colonoware vessels played in the archaeological past, as items designed to *define social boundaries* and *naturalize or resist relations of power*. Contrary to culinary ceramics, we suggest that the dynamics that surround ceramics used in ritual and ceremonial settings in West Africa would make them resistant to the consolidating effects of trans-Atlantic transportation and the creation of African-American identities in the New World (Gomez 1998).

Vessels for health and healing

Leland Ferguson (1992, 1999) has noted that, in a few instances, colonoware pottery little different from culinary wares has been found in archaeological contexts suggestive of its use in ritual activities. Indeed, the study of ritual pottery use in Bénin has demonstrated some interesting parallels with culinary pottery. Ritual pottery is also made by specialists (Etienne-Nugue 1984: 109; Norman 2000: 101–102), who only manufacture a limited scope of forms out of the entire range of often elaborate ritual forms (cf. Savary 1970; David 1983). Thus, no single potter is the repository of knowledge for manufacture of the entire corpus of ritual ceramics. In southern Bénin, the female ceramic specialist is even further removed from the application of ceramics in ritual settings, as a ritual specialist is required to place ceramics in social settings (Norman 2000).

Even more relevant to questions concerning the transmission of knowledge of ritual ceramic manufacturing is the observation that older women, in many African societies, are the sole potters permitted to make ritual wares (Savary 1970; Norman 2000). The reasoning provided to Norman in southern Bénin was that threat of contamination by younger women would compromise the efficacy of the ritual pottery. However, again paralleling the circumstances that pertain to culinary ceramics, most adults in the community know how a majority of ritual ceramics are placed and used. Norman's work in Savi (Norman 2000) demonstrated that most individuals would have no problems identifying a cluster of ceramics as a shrine or other ritual space designed to secure relationships with certain members of the *Fon* (also known as *Fongbe*, the ethnolinguistic group, who reside throughout the southern regions of the modern political states of Togo, Bénin, and Nigeria) pantheon, mitigate life's sorrows, alleviate illness, and celebrate births and weddings. That is to say shrines of purposefully arranged clusters of ceramics are placed in and around the home and fields to mark those events that punctuate life. These shrines are maintained by ritual specialists, who organize communitywide ceremonies to recharge the efficacy of these shrines in mediating between the spiritual and earthly planes (Norman 2000). In her investigation of *boció* statuary among the Fon of southern Bénin and Togo, Susan Blier notes a similar connection between ceramics avatars, or ceramic representations of members of the Fon pantheon, and attempts to define and maintain social relations through religious practices. So much so that one of her collaborators suggested that "… pottery does the things of *vodun*" (Blier 1995: 302).

In such a social setting where ceramic objects mediate and signify relations in political, religious, economic, and social settings, it is important for lay Fon to be able to identify the particular deity (Figure 19.3), or circumstance, for which a shrine with ritual ceramics was constructed. Speaking to the widespread ability of people to "read" shrines, adults, and even children, have a similar knowledge of the formal characteristics and social import of the ritual ceramics created by their neighboring ethnic groups. However, only ritual specialists are charged with the restricted knowledge relating to shrine construction and maintenance (Norman 2000). Thus, we have the same issues of competence of construction versus competence of application for ritual pottery as we see for culinary wares, with the former being very restricted, but the latter being nearly universal.

Seeing ritual ceramics

The context of use is a consideration that further complicates the identification of colonoware as ritual ceramics in New World settings (Ferguson 1992, 1999).

Figure 19.3   A collection of ritual ceramics from the village of Sé.

Frequently, at least in Lowcountry South Carolina, certain classes of ritual ceramics were used in ways that limit their recovery by archaeologists. Ferguson has documented an association of whole or complete colonoware ceramics with riverine settings, where apparently they were cast adrift in bodies of water, ultimately sinking to the bottom. Hence, most of these whole vessels have been recovered by sport divers and not by archaeological investigations focused on living areas. Historic documents occasionally mention that enslaved Africans would meet under cover of night in the undeveloped bush lands of plantations to perform "country dances" accompanied by drumming and chanting. It is extremely likely that these were ritual events that may have necessitated particular kinds of material culture, yet the remote nature of their practice would make the identification of any archaeological sites specifically associated with such activities unlikely.

Another factor that may potentially hamper the archaeological identification of ritual ceramics is that, at least contemporarily, many ritual items are produced to a less durable standard of ceramic technology. Among the Fon and others in southern Bénin, ritual ceramics are often poorly shaped, with walls of uneven thickness. Many are poorly fired, scarcely making the transition from clay to ceramic (Norman 2000: 69). These are not very durable pots. Furthermore, archeological evidence suggests that this characteristic poor-firing of ritual vessels has been practised for some time. For an example of this we can refer to archaeological work at Savi, the capital of the seventeenth and early eighteenth-century Hueda kingdom, located near the coast in the modern nation of Bénin. At Savi, excavations of a 300-year-old structure in 1999 identified a ritual pot that had been placed in the foundation of a structure in the palace compound that appears to have been so poorly fired (or even unfired) that it was identifiable only as a stain in the soil (Figure 19.4)(Kelly *et al.* 1999). This barely visible pot would have defied interpretation were it not for the participation of Fon in the archaeological excavation crew. When they saw this unusual feature, they were quick to assert that, based upon the size, form, and consistency of the paste, this pot was part of a ritual activity relating to births and the burial of the placenta. It is further worth noting that in many archaeological settings, this ceramic vessel would not have been visible at all.

Beyond the identification of the paraphernalia of shrines, their organization can be nuanced as well. The discrepancy between competence of creation and competence of use seen in the construction of shrines or ritual spaces further complicates the identification of ritual spaces. While most adults can identify shrines with ease, their construction or assembly is restricted to specialists. If a person in southern Bénin today wishes to establish or consecrate a shrine for a particular reason, that individual will not do it themselves, but will call upon a specialist, who has normally been indoctrinated into ritual practices from a very early age. Social mores even restrict these ritual specialists from creating shrines for themselves or their families (Norman 2000: 103–105). Thus, while exposure to, and participation in, ceremonies associated with shrines is widespread, and a part of the life's experience of nearly every West African, the esoteric and often restricted knowledge required for the creation and maintenance of these ritual spaces is highly restricted. This being said, anecdotal accounts from our interviews suggest that if a non-ritual specialist from southern Bénin found himself or

Figure 19.4   Poorly fired "placenta pot" visible in excavation profile, Savi, Bénin.

herself in a strange land without the aid of a ritual specialist that lay person would be compelled to create these shrines to the best of their ability (Antoine Agomadje, interview, 1999).

Medium vessels in the African Diaspora

Given this topography of traditional knowledge in southern Bénin, and generalizing it into the African past, we should expect to see certain transformations or modifications in the expression of such beliefs among people of the African Diaspora in the Americas. With the demographic profile of the slave trade, the mature women most likely to possess specialized ceramic knowledge are those least likely to have been enslaved, and those mature men and women most likely to possess well-developed and complex knowledge of ritual activities would also have been less likely to be enslaved (Curtin 1969). The demographics of the trade, favoring young and middle-age adults, and older juveniles, militated against precisely those more senior members of society that were traditionally the bearers of the intricacies of the culture. Therefore, the efforts to seek anything approaching one-to-one correspondence between any African homeland (whether *Kongo, Igbo, Akan,* etc.) and the material expression of an African Diaspora aesthetic is flawed. Instead, we must develop a set of ideas for interpreting African expressions contextualized by these new circumstances.

The demographics of the slave trade also may have led to a more rapid reinterpretation of ritual activities and the appropriateness of particular aspects of material culture. Here Norman's (2000: 120–129) ethnoarchaeological work among the Fon on conservatism and openness to substitution of glass, iron, or aluminum vessels among ritual specialists is relevant. He found that while mass-produced metal and glass items are appropriate supplementary materials for shrines, it is the shrine's ceramic vessels that help define relationships with the Fon pantheon. For example, shrines dedicated to the memory of a particular family member might have modern items to express that person's personality or consumer preference, but it is the ceramic vessels that are considered necessary for the shrine to help a family communicate with ancestors (Figure 19.5).

Furthermore, interviews indicated that although it is not unheard of to create traditional medicines in mass-produced receptacles such as glass bottles or iron or enamel pots, tradition strongly recommends the use of hand-built earthenwares for these rites (Norman 2000: 70–71, 103–105; cf. Sargent and Friedel 1986: 189–193). These medicines take the form of salves and ingested treatments created by ritual specialists to prevent bio-medical and spiritual illnesses. These findings beg the question of how this conflict between conservatism and openness might have been differently expressed if the individuals trying to reconstruct their ritual life were not fully indoctrinated in the creation of the shrines but only in the recognition and use of them. In the Americas, glass bottle bases, or gourds, or calabashes, may have been pressed into service in ways that may not have been appropriate in West African homelands, but flexibility may have been required in these new settings (Brown and Cooper 1990; Leone and Fry 1999).

Figure 19.5 Ceramic vendor's stall from the Marché Zobé in Ouidah showing both ritual and utilitarian ceramics.

It stands to reason that if enslaved African communities of the Americas recognized the need to use ceramics to negotiate with their Africa-derived pantheons, and these communities lacked the specialists necessary to create and consecrate these items, inexact interpretations of ceramics inspired by memories and recollections would have been created. Undoubtedly, these impressionistic New World ritual ceramics of the African Diaspora would have been used in rites and ceremonies that held fast the tradition and fervor of African ritual practices; however, it is possible that these rites lost some of the intricate and idiomatic nuances that researchers often use to define ethnic and cultural affiliations on the African continent. African-descended potters who were encouraged, if not compelled, to create ritual ceramics in the New World might have been further constrained by social mores that precluded them from making certain ritual forms, or even servicing their own families. Thus, archaeologists should not expect to find the often elaborate and specialized forms associated with ritual use in Africa, in the Americas. Instead, in such an environment it is conceivable that there would be a greater openness to adopting new, or simply available, vessel forms to uphold and maintain the spirit of ceremonies traditionally used in West Africa to mitigate anxiety, alleviate sorrow, express thanksgiving, and celebrate life (cf. Thompson 1974, 1983).

Through this interpretation, we suggest that it would be difficult to identify one-to-one parallels between the potting traditions of Africa and those they inspired in the New World. That being said, we also strongly believe that the ideological importance of ritual ceramics on the African continent would promote the preservation of analogous vessels with similar functional, contextual, and stylistic characteristics in the Americas long after their utilitarian culinary counterparts had gone out of vogue. Although these New World interpretations of African exemplars most likely would have been created by those who did not posses the specialized knowledge held by their contemporary West African counterparts, we believe that African descendant communities in the New World would have possessed a corporate knowledge of the importance of ritual ceramics and competence in their applications. Such hypotheses may offer interesting (re?)interpretations of ceramics recovered from sites involved in the African Diaspora.

References

Armstrong, Douglas V. (1990) *The Old Village and the Great House: An Archaeological and Historical Examination of Drax Hall Plantation, St. Ann's Bay, Jamaica*, Urbana, IL: University of Illinois Press.

Barley, Nigel (1994) *Smashing Pots, Feats of Clay from Africa*, London: British Museum Press.

Bay, Edna G. (1998) *Wives of the Leopard: Gender, Politics and Culture in the Kingdom of Dahomey*, Charlottesville, VA: The University of Virginia Press.

Beier, Georgina (1980) "Yoruba pottery," *African Arts*, 13, 3: 48–53.

Blier, Susan Preston (1995) *African Vodun: Art, Psychology, and Power*, Chicago, IL: University of Chicago Press.

Brown, Kenneth, and Cooper, Doreen (1990) "Structural continuity in an African-American slave and tenant community," *Historical Archaeology*, 24, 4: 7–19.

Crossland, L. B., and Posnansky, Merrick (1978) " 'Pottery, People and Trade at Begho,' Ghana," in I. Hodder (ed.) *The Spatial Organization of Culture*, London: Duckworth.

Curtin, Philip D. (1969) *The Atlantic Slave Trade: A Census*, Madison, WI: University of Wisconsin Press.

Dark, Philip J. C. (1973) *An Introduction to Benin Art and Technology*, Oxford: Oxford University Press.

David, Mireille (1983) "Poterie Domestique et Rituelle du Sud-Bénin," *Archives Suisses D'Anthropologie Générale*, 47, 2: 121–184.

Deetz, James (1993) Flowerdew Hundred: the archaeology of a Virginia plantation, 1619–1864, Charlottesville, VA: University Press of Virginia.

Etienne-Nugue, Jocelyne (1984) *Traditional Handicrafts in Black Africa: Bénin*, Dakar: Institut Culturel Africain.

Fagg, William and Picton, John (1978) *The Potter's Art in Africa (2nd edition)*, London: British Museum Publications.

Fatunsin, Anthonia K. (1992) *Yoruba Pottery*, Lagos: National Commission for Museums and Monuments.

Ferguson, Leland (1992) *Uncommon Ground: Archaeology and Early African America, 1650–1800*, Washington, DC: Smithsonian Institution Press.

Ferguson, Leland (1999) " 'The Cross is a Magic Sign': Marks on Eighteenth-Century Bowls from South Carolina," in Theresa A. Singleton (ed.) *"I, Too, am America": Archaeological Studies of African-American Life*, 116–131, Charlottesville, VA: University Press of Virginia.

Gomez, Michael A. (1998) *Exchanging Our Country Marks: The Transformation of African Identities in the Colonial and Antebellum South*, Chapel Hill, NC: The University of North Carolina Press.

Goucher, Candice (1999) "African-Caribbean Metal Technology: Forging Cultural Survivals in the Atlantic World," in Jay B. Haviser (ed.) *African Sites Archaeology in the Caribbean*, 143–156, Princeton, NJ: Markus Wiener Publishers.

Hall, Martin (1987) "Archaeology and modes of production in pre-colonial Southern Africa," *Journal of Southern African Studies*, 14: 1–17.

Handler, J. S., and Lange, F. (1978) *Plantation Slavery in Barbados: An Archaeological and Historical Investigation*, Cambridge, MA: Harvard University Press.

Hauser, Mark, and Armstrong, Douglas V. (1999) "Embedded Identities: Piecing Together Relationships through Compositional Analysis of Low-Fired Earthenwares," in Jay B. Haviser (ed.) *African Sites Archaeology in the Caribbean*, 65–93, Princeton, NJ: Markus Wiener Publishers.

Heath, Barbara J. (1999) "Yabbas, Monkeys, Jugs, and Jars: An Historical Context for African-Caribbean Pottery on St. Eustatius," in Jay B. Haviser (ed.) *African Sites Archaeology in the Caribbean*, 196–220, Princeton, NJ: Markus Wiener Publishers.

Herbert, Eugenia W. (1993) *Iron, Gender, and Power: Rituals of Transformation in African Societies*, Bloomington, IN: Indiana University Press.

Herskovits, M. (1941) *The Myth of the Negro Past*, Boston, MA: Beacon.

Igibami, R. I. (1984) "Some socio-economic aspects of pottery among the Yoruba peoples of Nigeria," in J. Picton (ed.) *Earthenware in Asia and Africa*, Colloquies on Art and Archaeology in Asia No. 12, 106–117, London: Percival David Foundation of Chinese Art/School of Oriental and African Studies.

Joyner, Charles (1984) *Down by the Riverside: A South Carolina Slave Community*, Urbana, IL: University of Illinois Press.

Kelly, Kenneth G. (n.d.) "African Diaspora archaeology in Guadeloupe: initial excavations at two sugar plantation village sites," paper presented at the Society for Historical Archaeology Conference, Providence, RI, 2003.

Kelly, Kenneth G., Brunache, Peggy, and Norman, Neil L. (1999) "Archaeological fieldwork at Savi, Republic of Bénin: the 1999 season," *Nyame Akuma*, 52: 2–10.

LaViolette, Adria (2000) *Ethno-Archaeology in Jenné, Mali: Craft and Status Among Smiths, Potters and Masons*, British Archaeological Reports, International Series 838, Oxford: Archaeopress.

Leone, Mark P., and Fry, Gladys-Marie (1999) "Conjuring in the Big House Kitchen: an Interpretation of African American belief systems based on the uses of archaeology and folklore sources," *Journal of American Folklore*, 112, 445: 372–403.

Mathewson, R. Duncan (1972) "Jamaican ceramics: an introduction to 18th century folk pottery in West African tradition," *Jamaica Journal*, 6, 2:54–56.

Mathewson, R. Duncan (1973) "Archaeological analysis of material culture as a reflection of sub-cultural differentiation in 18th century Jamaica," *Jamaica Journal*, 7, 1–2: 25–29.

Mouer, L. D., Hodges, M. E. N., Potter, S. R., Renaud, S. L. H., Hume, I. N., Pogue, D. J., McCartney, M. W., and Davidson, T. E. (1999) "Colonoware Pottery, Chesapeake Pipes, and 'Uncritical Assumptions'," in T. A. Singleton (ed.) *"I Too Am America": Archaeological Studies of African-American Life*, 83–115, Charlottesville, VA: University of Virginia Press.

Norman, Neil (2000) *Through the Medium of the Vessel: An Ethnoarchaeological Investigation of Ritual Earthenwares in Southern Bénin, West Africa*, unpublished MA thesis, The University of South Carolina.

Otto, John Solomon (1984) *Cannon's Point Plantation, 1794–1860: Living Conditions and Status Patterns in the Old South*, New York: Academic Press.

Petersen, James B., Watters, David R., and Nicholson, Desmond V. (1999) "Continuity and Syncretism in Afro-Caribbean Ceramics from the Northern Lesser Antilles," Jay in Haviser (ed.) *African Sites Archaeology in the Caribbean*, 157–195, Princeton, NJ: Markus Wiener Publishers.

Rickford, John R. (1980) "Analyzing Variation in Creole Languages," in A. Valdman and Arnold Highfield (eds) *Theoretical Orientations in Creole Studies*, 165–184, New York: Academic Press.

Rosengarten, Dale (1994) *Row Upon Row: Sea Grass Baskets of the South Carolina Lowcountry*, Columbia, SC: McKissick Museum.

Sargent, Carolyn F., and Friedel, David A. (1986) "From Clay to Metal: Culture Change and Container Usage Among the Bariba of Northern Benin, West Africa," *The African Archaeological Review*, 4: 177–195.

Savary, Claude (1970) "Poteries Rituelles et Autres Objects Cultuels en Usage au Dahomey," *Bulletin Annuel*: Musée D'ethnographie de la Ville de Genève, 13: 33–57.

Singleton, T. A., and Bograd, M. D. (2000) "Breaking Typological Barriers: Looking for the Colono in Colonoware," in J. Delle, S. Mrozowski, and R. Paynter (eds) *Lines That Divide: Historical Archaeologies of Race, Class, and Gender*, 3–21, Knoxville, TN: University of Tennessee Press.

Stark, Miriam (2003) "Current Issues in Ceramic Ethnoarchaeology," *Journal of Archaeological Research*, 11, 3: 193–242.

Steen, Carl (1999) "Stirring the Ethnic Stew in the South Carolina Backcountry: John de la Howe and Lethe Farm," in Maria Franklin and Garrett Fesler (eds) *Historical Archaeology, Identity Formation, and the Interpretation of Ethnicity*, 93–120, Williamsburg, VA: Colonial Williamsburg Research Publications.

Thompson, Robert Farris (1993) *Face of the Gods: art and altars of Africa and the African Americans*, New York: The Museum for African Art.

Thompson, Robert Farris (1983) *Flash of the Spirit: African and Afro-American Art and Philosophy*, New York: Random House.

Thompson, Robert Farris (1974) *African Art in Motion: Icon and Act*, Los Angeles, CA: University of California Press.

Vlach, John Michael (1976) "Affecting Architecture of the Yoruba," *African Arts*, 10, 1: 48–53.

Part IV Slavery in Africa
Other Diasporas

20 The Trans-Atlantic slave trade and local traditions of slavery in the West African Hinterlands

The Tivland example

CALEB A. FOLORUNSO

Introduction

This study is a re-evaluation of a portion of a larger field research project undertaken on the Benue River Valley of Nigeria. In addition to historic Tiv settlements, this project also investigated the thesis that the Bantu-speaking peoples had their origins somewhere around the Nigerian–Cameroonian border. In the course of this work, sites of Late Stone Age, Early Iron Age, and the Historic period were identified and studied (Andah 1983, Folorunso 1989).

Of particular interest here are historic "refuge" sites, located on hilltops, for which there are accounts in Tiv oral traditions. These oral traditions are of particular importance since there has been little written historical reference to regional events during the occupation of the sites. The occurrence of hilltop settlements here and elsewhere in West Africa during the last few centuries calls for a rethink of their interpretation and broader implications. These sites, mostly located inland, have been understood from oral traditions to represent points of settlement built during periods of local conflict. The sources for the conflicts had not been adequately investigated and might be related to raids for captives to be sold into slavery. Studies of the relics of the slave trade period have been concentrated on the coastal regions of West Africa while the hinterlands have been virtually ignored. There is the need to re-evaluate the sites in the context of the global events of the slave trade period.

Tiv origins: a summary based on oral traditions

Tiv oral traditions state that "creation" took place somewhere to the southeast of their present location. They refer to their original homeland as Swem, which is said to be a hill located somewhere on the Nigerian–Cameroonian border. Swem is believed to be a sacred and spiritual place, which only specific elders visit in spirit. From Swem the Tiv first moved to Binda Hills and from there migrated northwestward into the Benue Valley in successive waves from one hilltop to the other until they reached the

Benue River. The settlements on the hills were necessitated by the incessant attacks they suffered at the hands of a group they called *Ugenyi*. The *Ugenyi* were dreaded, and traditions record that the *Ugenyi* had to be defeated before the Tiv could safely leave their defended hilltop settlements. To this end a decisive battle was fought around the Ushongo Hill from which the Tiv emerged victorious. Ushongo became one of the major hills on which the Tiv settled.

It has been suggested that the Tiv migration took place relatively recently because throughout Tivland, from the banks of the Benue up to the Obudu Hills in the southwest, the Tiv speak a common language with very few dialectal variations. The only groups speaking idioms close to the Tiv are located in the south, on the Nigeria–Cameroon border. It is suggested that the Obudu Hills might have constituted the penetration passage of the Tiv into the Benue Valley as the Utanga who inhabit the Obudu Hills are among the groups linguistically closest to the Tiv (Neyt and Désirant 1985: 17).

Historically, the Tiv were said to be newcomers who upset the population balance of the Benue Valley at the end of the seventeenth century. Before their arrival, the river had been a natural means of communication for the Igala and the Jukun in trade and cultural exchange. The Tiv movement into the Benue Valley created a buffer state and stopped the earlier migrations of the Idoma and the Igala who spread toward the west from Kwararafa in the northeast. The Idoma were particularly greatly affected by the Tiv invasions, which were said to have increased between 1685 and 1745, and were obliged to leave the Benue banks. The Tiv invasions are recorded in the oral traditions of the Idoma (Neyt and Désirant 1985: 161–164).

Slavery in Tivland

Ndera (n.d.) has undertaken a study of evidence for slavery among the Tiv from early times to the twentieth century. He is of the opinion that both oral and written information suggest that the Tiv practised domestic slavery long before the Trans-Atlantic slave trade. The Tiv refer to a slave as *kpan* (singular) or *ikpan* (plural). A *kpan* was a person of inferior status without independent social and economic freedom. In Tiv society, slaves were a source of cheap labor for food production and a man who had abundant food for his household was regarded as a *Shagbaor* (man of honor or substance). Slaves were also kept as trophies of warfare. Some trusted slaves ran errands, took care of the compound of their masters, and sometimes even came to exercise authority over the freeborn. Therefore, slaves in Tiv society enjoyed a degree of freedom—especially if they were obedient.

The Tiv obtained slaves through various means. First, wicked members of the *Mbatsav* society, who were considered a threat to life, were sold into slavery by their own kinsmen. *Mbatsav* is a secret society, its members possessing supernatural powers called *tsav* that can be used negatively or positively. People suspected to have negative *tsav* were sold into slavery to safeguard the community from their destructive acts. Second, miscreants in the society (thieves, etc.) were also sold into slavery if they did not reform. Crimes like incest and adultery were considered abomination, and the offenders were usually automatically sold into slavery. Third, some people became slaves through being given out to other lineages in exchange for food during severe famine periods. At such periods, women were given out in marriage in exchange for food, though they enjoyed all the privileges as wives but remained inferior to the women that were married through the traditional marriage exchange system. A fourth instance of people becoming enslaved was if they could not pay their debt. Such people were captured and held as pawns until their lineage could pay back the debts. They could be sold-on if the debts were not paid on time (Ndera, n.d.).

On a larger scale, people were also taken into slavery in Tivland due to internal rivalries between groups. Captives were sometimes freed after amicable settlement of a conflict, but if not, they remained slaves and were sold if the need arose. By the nineteenth century Tiv leaders, known as *tor agbande* (drum chiefs), and prominent individuals (*ashagbaior*), who once kept slaves only as a status symbol, or for domestic use, had gone into commercial slavery. Bands of warriors from different lineages or ethnic groups organized themselves to capture members of other lineages or ethnic groups so as to engage in the slave trade. The institution of the *tor agbande* developed in Tiv society probably in the late eighteenth century to contain the incessant attacks from the Tiv neighbors. Neighbors such as the Jukun captured Tiv as slaves during wars or raids. For instance, the Jukun paid annual tributes to the Emir of Muri in slaves mostly obtained from the Tiv ethnic group (Ndera n.d.).

From the above account summarized principally from the work of Ndera (n.d.) it is obvious that although the Benue Valley is far removed from the coast there was still intensive slave raiding in Tivland. The people of Tivland would have responded to these raids by seeking for refuge in safer places. The hilltop settlements scattered all over Tivland might have provided such refuge and there is therefore the need to look at these settlements from a new angle—rather than the traditional interpretation of Tiv migration from one hilltop to the other. In other words, the hilltop settlements could have been inhabited only during the time of the Trans-Atlantic slave trade.

The archaeology of the hilltop settlements

Hilltop settlements have been identified from a large part of Tivland, from the southeast to the Gboko area in central Tivland (Figure 20.1). The settlement's features include relics of stonewalls, clusters of circular hut bases made of granite stones, grinding stones, and potsherd scatters. In the Tse Dura–Ushongo area, rock shelters have been investigated and they show evidence of occupation during the Late Stone Age, Early Iron Age, and the Historic period. The materials from the upper levels in the rock shelters (Historic period) are characterized by the presence of smoking pipes, iron tools, iron slag, and pottery. They are very similar to the artifacts found at the open-air hilltop settlements. It should be added that the smoking pipes were of local manufacture.

Archaeological remains have also been identified at the foot of some hills and on the plains but they have been greatly disturbed by farming and construction activities. For the most part there are only scattered potsherds and grinding stones. However, around

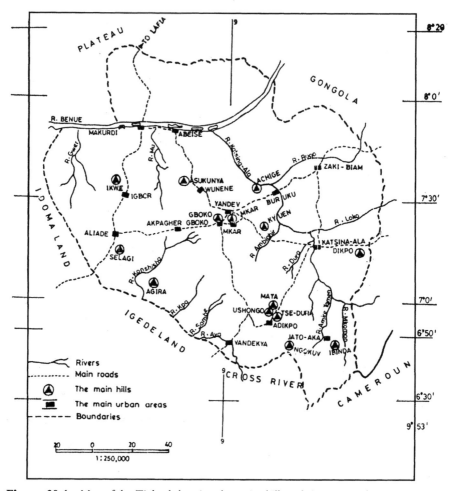

Figure 20.1   Map of the Tivland showing the major hills and river networks.

Ushongo Hill there are ditches and embankments, as well as circular bases of former huts at the foot of the Tse Dura Hills. There are also dye-pits on the road between Ushongo and Manor, and the remains of furnaces, iron slag, and potsherd scatters in the Mkar area. Because of the state of preservation of the sites in the valleys and plains they have not yet been properly investigated.

The sites located to the extreme southeast of the Tiv country are all well-preserved with the stonewalls standing at considerable heights of 60 cm and more. The stone circular bases of huts are very distinctive (Figure 20.2). The Akoo Hill presents a vivid picture of the hardship the people might have suffered in their quest for self-preservation during the time of slavery. The elevation of the hill is in the region of 1600 m above sea level and the slopes are quite steep, requiring roughly about one hour of climbing through rocky gullies to reach the summit. The difficult terrain of

Figure 20.2 Photographs of two circular stone structure bases typical of the historic hilltop Tiv settlements studied. (Photos: C. A. Folounso)

the hill would have been an important defensive factor influencing its occupation; the other three hills occupied near Akoo Hill do not have such a difficult access and their heights are considerably lower. The local people did not allow excavation at one of these three hills as it is said to be a sacred site.

On the Mata Hill in the Ushongo area where access is quite easy, farming activities had destroyed the circular bases of huts as the stones had been moved away into heaps. However, the stone boundary wall is still intact attaining a considerable height of about 60 cm and more at some points. Remains of iron smelting furnaces and potsherd scatters are found within this stone enclosure.

On the Tse Dura Hills, whose access is not very difficult, the site designated KA4S1 had been heavily farmed and disturbed. The stones forming the bases of the circular huts had been moved and only a few such circular bases were visible in the farms at the time of study in 1983. There was no trace of any stonewall. In another section of this hill, the site designated KA4S2 also had circular hut bases and traces of a stone boundary wall, but the site was destroyed by farmers shortly after it was mapped so that the land could be put under cultivation.

The Ushongo Hill has quite a difficult access and the settlement features are well protected from human factors. However, the bases of the circular huts are not very distinctive in some places because of natural factors causing the stones to disintegrate into the soil. The stone boundary wall is also considerably lower, hardly more than 15–20 cm high. The Mkar hill settlement is similar to what is obtained at Ushongo.

On Kyuen Hill, the site is well-preserved with the stone boundary wall being of considerable height. An additional feature on this hill is the presence of stonewall enclosures separating the different settlement units. Boulders were quite significant in the construction of the circular huts on the Kyuen Hill as opposed to the other hills where granite cobbles were piled up to make the circular base.

The common features of the hilltop settlements as we have seen are the stone boundary walls and the clusters of the circular bases of huts made with granite stones. Parts of the stone boundary walls, we were told, had been employed as missiles by rolling down the stones into the slopes of the hills against invaders. A similar explanation has been offered for stone boundary walls in Yorubaland on the Imofin Hill in the Ibarapa North Local Government Area of Oyo State.[1]

Today, the Tiv have a dispersed settlement pattern made of compounds that may consist of anywhere between three and 50 circular huts. From five compounds sampled, the size of the huts varies between 1.8 and 6.8 m in diameter, and the average diameter is 4.4 m. Chicken huts and granaries measure between 1.8 and 2.1 m in diameter, while sleeping huts, kitchen huts, store huts, and reception huts measure between 2.7 and 6.8 m. We have measured the distances between nearest neighbor huts to have an idea of the spacing between huts and to compare it with the situation at the hilltop settlement sites. These measurements vary from 0.6 to 8.4 m but most often fall between 2.6 and 4.0 m.

For the purpose of comparison, we have obtained measurements of huts bases and nearest neighbor distances from the archaeological sites. At the Tse Dura hilltop settlement designated KA4S2, 40 bases of stone circular structures were identified and their diameters vary between 2.3 and 5.8 m with an average of 3.9 m. At the Ushongo Hill, 138 bases of circular stone structures were identified and their diameters vary from 1.8 to 5.8 m with an average of 3.7 m.

At the site on Tse Dura Hill the nearest neighbor distance varies between 0.2 and 6.8 m while it is between 0.2 cm and 8.4 m for the Ushongo Hill. Most of the measurements fall within the range of 0.20–2 m.

It is evident from the above measurements that the ethnographic compounds generally have larger huts (4.4 m versus 3.7/3.8 m) and that the modern huts are better spaced (0.6–8.4 m versus 0.2–2 m). It should also be added that the most convenient spots for situating huts on the hilltops was in depressions between spurs where soil had developed, but that when such space was exhausted, huts were located on rock surfaces. While it was possible to use posts to support roofs in the depressions as shown in one excavation, this was not possible on the rock surfaces and alternative modes of construction had to be employed. This was probably in the form of a broad wooden frame covered with grass as has been noted in the construction of Tiv yam barns today (Folorunso 1989). Overall, one is given the impression of constrained circumstances at these hilltop settlements where large populations were forced for extended periods into dense defensive settlements, altering normal settlement patterns.

Broader implications of the hilltop settlements

Oral traditions have led to the expectation that the hills located to the southeast were the first to be occupied and might possess earlier and longer sequences than sites located to the north. However, excavations do not seem to support an earlier date for the sites located in southeast Tivland. For example, a radiocarbon date obtained for Akoo Hill located near River Moan on the Cameroonian border is fifteenth to sixteenth century, and is similar to one obtained for the Ushongo Hill located further to the north (Folorunso 1989). Also the occupational deposits at Akoo Hill, which are hardly 50 cm thick are far thinner than deposits at Ushongo, Tse Dura, and Mkar Hills where they sometimes exceed 100 cm in thickness.

Important evidence for interpreting the antiquity of the Tiv in parts of the Benue Valley, particularly the Katsina Ala River Valley, comes from excavations at the rock shelters of Tse Dura. There, a very definite break between the Late Stone Age and the Early Iron Age periods, coupled with radiocarbon dates, suggest the commencement of Iron Age occupation during the fourth century BC (Andah 1983). The Early Iron Age was marked by the appearance of distinctive pottery decoration achieved by impression with a woven mat. This pottery decorative motif is also dominant at all the hilltop settlements and other lowland sites. Ethnographically, this decorative motif continues to be widely spread in Tivland today and might be described as the most distinctive decorative motif on Tiv pottery (Folorunso 1998). The Early Iron Age pottery assemblage is therefore an important element to establish cultural continuity in the Benue Valley from the beginnings of the Iron Age to the present.

While further work demonstrating Tiv cultural continuity is needed, particularly for the first millennium AD, it seems that the Tiv gradually occupied the plains of the Benue Valley from the Early Iron Age onward. The earliest occupations may have been limited to the rock shelters in the area. As farmers, they would also have sought rich soils in the lowlands to cultivate. Relics found in the plains dating to this period include iron smelting furnaces, dye-pits, grinding stones, and potsherd scatters. The original settlers of the valley no doubt resisted their systematic advancement and this might have led to the conflicts as recorded in the oral traditions of the Tiv. However, these territorial conflicts alone could not have driven the Tiv to the hills, especially given the historically documented successes of the Tiv in such disputes.

What subsequently forced the Tiv to seek refuge in the hills were organized raids by their neighbors in search of victims to be captured and sold into slavery. The Tiv people themselves later joined in raiding their kinsmen as indicated earlier in this chapter. This present interpretation would explain why the occupational deposits are so thin on Akoo Hill in the far southeast, where the plains are well protected by the surrounding hills and are far from the contact point with the marauding neighbors. The populations located closer to the raiders at Tse Dura, Ushongo, Mata, Kyuen, and Mkar Hills would have been confined to the hills for a longer period of time, as is evident from the thicker occupational deposits there and the severely worn grinding stones.

The period of the Trans-Atlantic slave trade probably put a stop to or slowed down the migration of the Tiv people in their gradual occupation of the Benue Valley. The rise of commerce in slaves and the attendant raids organized by kingdoms such as the Jukun and the Chamba drove the Tiv to the hills and retarded their movement in the Benue Valley. Protection was sought on the hills, and settlements were located close to hills for easy retreat to those hills in case of raids. Since the Tiv are quite mobile, their movements during the period of the slave trade were also dictated by the presence of hills that provided them with protection. This late date of this period of re-settlement has not been clearly recorded in Tiv oral traditions, which depict these troubles as coeval with their initial migration into the area. Thus, this period of secondary migration, has somehow been recorded in oral traditions as the primary migration of the Tiv into the Benue Valley. However, given the nature of oral tradition, several temporally diverse events may easily have been telescoped into a single narrative.

The global events of the fifteenth and sixteenth centuries (the beginnings of the Atlantic slave trade) rather than the rapidity of the Tiv migration would seem to explain the contemporaneous dates of occupation of the hilltops. Bohanna and Bohanna (1953) were of the view that the Tiv were still taking refuge on the hills until the eighteenth century when the Jukun Empire, which had long menaced them, began to decline. This decline might have given the Tiv some reprieve to leave the hills for the plains in order to continue their expansion in the Benue Valley. In the early eighteenth century the Tiv had displaced some of the Idoma in the Benue Valley (Neyt and Désirant 1985). By the middle of the eighteenth century the Tiv themselves had become a threat in the valley, so much so that the Turu had to request for protection from the King of Jukun (Downes 1933). It is also recorded that the Tiv had turned the tables on the Jukun by the nineteenth century, invading the Jukun lands in their ceaseless expansion. By 1871, the Jukun had to employ Dankaro (a Fulani soldier of fortune) and his mercenaries to check the Tiv menace (Bohanna and Bohanna 1953).

A re-assessment of the interpretation of the oral traditions and archaeological evidence in the Benue Valley seems to suggest that the Tiv people may have entered the valley earlier than the sixteenth century, a traditionally accepted date provided via genealogies, linguistics, and radiocarbon dates obtained solely from hilltop settlement sites. Instead, the Tiv probably occupied the plains, as evidenced by archaeological remains, long before slave raiders in the sixteenth and seventeenth centuries forced them to the hills.

Conclusions

A re-assessment of the interpretation of the oral traditions and archaeological evidence in the Benue Valley seems to suggest that the Tiv people had probably entered the valley by the Early Iron Age (i.e. during the late first millennium BC). The Tiv then occupied the plains as shown by archaeological relics. Only much more recently, from the sixteenth to the eighteenth centuries, were they forced into hilltop settlements by raiding kingdoms attacking their territories to obtain captives to be sold into slavery. They continued to express their cultural identity in terms of settlement layout on the hilltops but labored under significant spatial constraints.

For a complete understanding of the African Diaspora, there is a need to link the archaeology of the Diaspora in the New World with evidence for impacts of the slave trade on the African continent. It would also be of tremendous interest to study archival materials that show the movement of peoples from specific locations on the African continent to their specific destinations. This could lead to important investigations of culture continuity and change by studying contemporary sixteenth to nineteenth century African and New World examples via Historical Archaeology. Of course, this will require much needed collaborative work between researchers on the different continents.

Note

1 According to traditions, groups of Yoruba people and migrant Nupe people occupied the hill when they were under incessant attacks by Dahomey apparently during the slave trade period. The site was only visited this year and it is yet to be surveyed. It is the most extensive hilltop settlement site I have yet seen, spanning over 1 km in one direction (length) and about 100 m across. Potsherds and grinding stones are scattered all over the site and the outline of possible rectangular houses were faintly visible in some places. The hill has very steep slopes and very difficult access. It is another archaeological evidence of the stress people of the West African hinterland were subjected to during the Trans-Atlantic slave trade.

References

Andah B. W. (1983) "The 'Bantu homeland' project: ethnoarchaeological investigations in parts of the Benue Valley region," *West African Journal of Archaeology*, 12/13: 23–60.

Bohanna, P., and Bohanna, L. (1953) *The Tiv of Central Nigeria*, London: Stone & Cox Ltd.

Downes R. M. (1933) *The Tiv Tribe*, Kaduna: The Government Printer.

Folorunso, C.A. (1989) *Recherches sur la continuité du peuplement Tiv dans la vallée de Katsina-Ala (bassin de la Bénué au Nigeria): Sondages sur le site ancien d'Ushongo et ethnoarchéologie de l'habitat actuel*, unpublished PhD thesis, Université Paris I, Sorbonne.

Folorunso C. A. (1998) "The Compound of the Tiv of Benue State of Nigeria: The Reality of Ethnoarchaeology," in B. W. Andah (ed.) *Africa: The Challenge of Archaeology*, 235–255, Ibadan: Heinemann Educational Books (Nigeria) Plc.

Ndera, J. (n.d.) "Evidence of Slavery among the Tiv from Early Times to the 20th Century," paper presented at the Workshop on Benue Arts, from the Field to the Museum, IFRA, Ibadan, November 2002.

Neyt, F. and Désirant, A. (1985) *The Arts of the Benue to the Roots of Tradition*, Tielt: Lanoo, Editions Hawaaiiab Agronomics.

21 Toward an archaeology of the other African diaspora

The slave trade and dispersed Africans in the western Indian Ocean

JONATHAN R. WALZ AND STEVEN A. BRANDT

No topic pervades historical African Studies more than slavery. Millions of Africans were extracted from local settings and forced to labor over much of the tropical and subtropical world. Research on this forced diaspora overwhelmingly focuses on the Atlantic slave trade and slavery in the USA, Brazil, and the Caribbean. Yet, another slave trade, oriented toward the Red Sea and Indian Ocean, thrust Africans abroad as early as Pharaonic times.[1] Reaching its height during the middle to late nineteenth century, the Indian Ocean trade scattered eastern, central, and southern Africans as far afield as Egypt, Persia, India, Indonesia, and Madagascar (Figures 21.1 and 21.2). Slaves served as soldiers, sailors, field laborers, domestic servants, concubines, and pearl divers, among other roles. The socioeconomic systems in which these Africans were entangled and the details of their lives at home and abroad are poorly understood, especially as one delves deeper into antiquity. As Harris (1989: 5) laments, "[U]ntil serious ... studies appear [on the African diaspora to the East] ... we will remain grossly uninformed about the scope and impact of the global dimension of the African diaspora."

While archaeological studies of the slave trade and African diaspora communities in the New World abound, similar projects in other regions of the world are few to nonexistent (Orser 1998: 63–66; Lilley 2004). The absence of such investigations in the western Indian Ocean leaves African and Afro-Asian pasts incompletely explored and, moreover, limits our understanding of events critical to the shaping of the modern world. Within an interdisciplinary framework, archaeology holds great potential for improving our knowledge of the slave trade, slaves, and their descendants primarily because it is uniquely capable of retrieving information about everyday life in both recent and ancient contexts. In some cases archaeology may provide the sole source of historical data on this subject. More than a mere "handmaiden to history," archaeology can bring the circumstances, lives, and actions of Africans, including those in the diaspora, into better relief by exploring the material correlates of trade, community formation, exploitation, and struggle on ever-changing Asian and African frontiers.

We begin our task by posing an essential question: Why have scholars, including archaeologists, paid comparatively little attention to the African diaspora in the East?

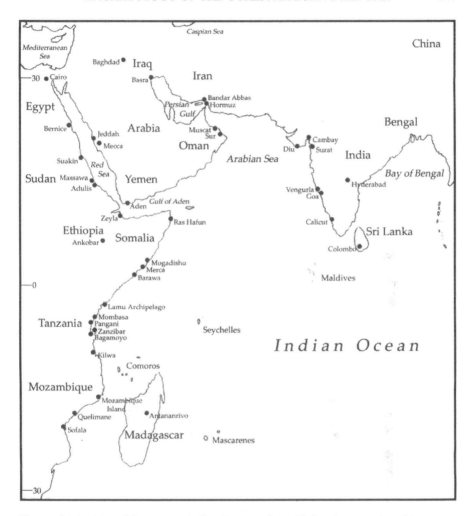

Figure 21.1 Map of the western Indian Ocean region with locations mentioned in text.

Next, we review the concept of *diaspora*, stressing the importance of temporality in diaspora studies. Subsequently, we present an abbreviated historical review of the African slave trade in the western Indian Ocean over the past two millennia. Demonstrating the potential of archaeology, we then introduce topics, approaches, questions, and research pertinent to investigating each component of the regional slave trade and wider diaspora system. We conclude by arguing for in-depth case studies at localities through time. Such studies will facilitate remaking African and regional histories and hopefully instigate comparative archaeological studies of diasporas, slave trades, and dispersed Africans across space and time.

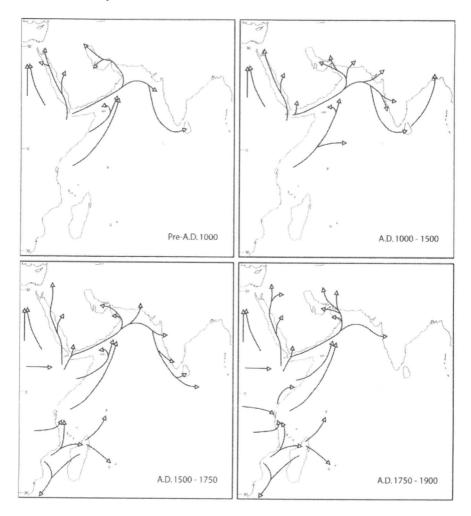

Figure 21.2   The African slave trade in the western Indian Ocean through the ages.

Why silences?

Why has the wider academic community comparatively neglected the African slave trade and Africans abroad in the Indian Ocean?[2] For starters, the expanse of space and time involved is daunting. Diverse communities were linked by systems of transport stretching tens of thousands of kilometers over maritime and terrestrial landscapes. Tracing individual slaves, traders, or families would oblige the historian or anthropologist to cast a wide intellectual net and visit archives as well as descendant communities in numerous countries. The examination of documents pertinent to a single locality might require, for example, literacy in Arabic, Swahili, Urdu, and Portuguese, and a sound knowledge of

Shi'ah Islam, Hinduism, and Roman Catholicism. In short, the diversity of the Indian Ocean forces scholars to make an enormous commitment.

To tackle the diaspora necessitates collaborative research. But, with few notable exceptions, African Studies and Asian Studies programs tend to reify rather than dissolve traditional academic and geographical boundaries; a problematic and alarming trend, especially considering the popular Africanist engagement with studying Arab and Indian settlers in Africa. Perhaps Asians in Africa had a greater lasting impact than Africans in Asia. Yet, should African settlement and influences on Asian societies receive less consideration? Does the imbalance result from comparatively copious source material on Asians in Africa or does western and eastern racism(s) play a role (Lewis 1990; Gupta 1991)?[3] Or, is it that African descendants in contemporary Asia tend to have depressed social statuses and poor education, making them less attractive to researchers and hindering Afro-Asian explications of history (Alpers 2000: 87–88)? Scholars in the Americas and Europe appear largely unconcerned with the diaspora to the East[4] due, at least in part, to Atlantic tunnel-vision, a lack of familiarity with eastern languages, literatures, and cultures, and a general absence of strong Pan-African sentiment in Afro-Asian communities. Disinterest combined with the underdevelopment of academia in Africa and parts of Asia clearly restricts research. Nation-states also present impediments, as they often are weary of allowing outsiders to delve into slave pasts, fearful of igniting societal debate and criticism. Even in African societies where memories of slavery continue to resonate, research is hampered by shame or desires not to stir-up social discord by reviving turbulent pasts (Klein 1989). As Hunwick (2002: xii) notes, "[For Africans] in the Muslim world a past in slavery indubitably points to a past in 'unbelief' … which is a particularly heavy burden to bear."

Exploring the history of slavery presents further problems. There are relatively few documents in which slaves are mentioned prior to AD 1000 and gaps in sources sometimes stretch for more than decades, for example between the *Christian Topography* of Cosmas Indicopleustes (McCrindle 1897) and later writings of Arab and Chinese scholars, traders and adventurers. When slaves are noted in early documents, it is usually left to the reader to determine whether these were Africans or peoples from other regions. But, did ancient travelers and traders even possess the contextual knowledge to identify slaves and their origins? Notwithstanding the relevance of such a critique, it is telling that for later periods scholars continue to neglect the topic despite the robust documentation for Islamic and Christian slavery and the significant expansion of the trade in Africans. Islamic slavery, usually accompanied by more humane treatment and represented by a diverse range of "slave" types, appears to be less attractive to the western academy, perhaps because slaves in these systems often were less visible, fewer in number, or absorbed into local communities through religious indoctrination.

For all these reasons and others, archaeologists largely have failed to broach the topic of slavery in the region. Yet, more than two decades ago Gerbeau (1979: 186, 203) prodded historians disappointed in the shortcomings of available documents to seek other perspectives and expand their evidentiary bases:

> The historian will have to be an archaeologist, an ethnologist, a specialist
> in oral traditions … even when there are no texts concerning a

slave-trade phenomenon, the historian can still proceed with his work. He will have to go to the spot himself, i.e. to the land whence the slaves departed and to the one where they arrived. It is essential for him to glean information from local inhabitants, to search their memories and their land. His archaeology should extend to the sites inhabited by the Maroons. Perhaps then we shall understand better how far the slaves ... have kept Africa alive in the "Indian Ocean" area.

More recently, Alpers (1997, 2000), among others, began tackling the ethnological component of Gerbeau's challenge to erase silences, documenting African cultural survivals in contemporary Asian communities by researching place names and folkways. While connecting the more recent past to contemporary communities is a laudable goal, why not also work in the other direction, extending cultural survivals deeper into the past or studying the transformations in survivals through time by applying archaeological methods to the *longue-durée*?[5]

Regrettably, much archaeology in eastern Africa and southern Asia remains in intellectual doldrums. For the most part, archaeologists in the wider region have yet to practice fully fledged historical and social archaeologies, these being arguably the most relevant to investigations of the African diaspora. Underwater archaeology, capable of retrieving critical data on the "middle passage," also remains poorly developed. Instead, archaeologists in the Middle East and South Asia are engrossed in art history or writing culture-historical reports unlikely to interest other social scientists (Insoll 1999: 4–5). For eastern Africa, archaeological funding and interests are skewed heavily toward "prehistory," impeding the investigation of processes crosscutting broad time frames, such as the diaspora. However, archaeologists hold the potential of making histories of Africans and Afro-Asians in the western Indian Ocean and other world regions to replace the daunting silences of the past (Agorsah 1996; DeCorse 2001).

A beginning: *diaspora*

Making histories of the slave trade and Africans abroad in the East requires that social scientists pay particular attention to the diaspora concept. This politicized term represents both a process and a condition of entanglement (Patterson and Kelley 2000). *Diaspora* derives from the Greek word for dispersal and refers most commonly to the scattering of Jews, Greeks, and Armenians across the globe. Since the 1950s, however, scholars have applied the term to Africans transplanted to the New World, principally as slaves. More recently, those invested in studying the "black Atlantic" have moved beyond merely identifying transplanted cultural survivals as evidence of identity linkages and have begun to explore diasporic identities and African consciousness(es) in the New World (e.g. Gilroy 1993). While "identity as inheritance" (surviving traditions) and "identity as politics" (group consciousness and action) (Clifford 1997: 46) are intertwined, does the use of the term *diaspora* require the existence of both?

A cadre of social scientists has proposed cross-contextual diaspora traits, the most important of which include (1) dispersal of a population to two or more destinations; (2) some relationship to a homeland, whether it be actual or imagined; (3) self-awareness of group distinctiveness; and (4) multi-generationality (Safran 1991; Clifford 1997; Cohen 1997; Butler 2001). Of his types of diaspora, Cohen (1997) labels the African diaspora in the Atlantic a "victim diaspora." The Atlantic case is both temporally compact (400 years) and massive in scale. The African diaspora in the Indian Ocean differs from its Atlantic counterpart because it includes a small-scale forced migration stretching into antiquity, a massive historic slave trade, and a modest tradition of labor migration and travel by free persons that continues to the present (Harris 1971; Alpers 2003a: 21–22). Further, the Indian Ocean diaspora injected Africans into a wide variety of societies and slave systems.[6] The variety of contexts and various degrees of separation, assimilation, and ethnogenesis displayed by Africans in response to host societies makes it difficult to define the Indian Ocean diaspora by a limited set of traits. Consequently, Alpers (2003a) suggests the following definition offered by Clifford: "[D]iaspora cultures ... mediate, in a lived fashion, the experiences of separation and entanglement, of living here and remembering/desiring another place" (Clifford 1997: 255). One manner of "mediating" is to preserve aspects of traditions and materialities connected to the homeland.

Scholars questioning whether *diaspora* applies to Africans dispersed in the Indian Ocean may well accept a stricter conceptualization of the term, employing the scattering of Jews as an archetype. While an "identity as politics" or "ethnonational consciousness as politics" unifying displaced Africans across the wider region largely is absent, there are, in cases, different consciousnesses or subconsciousnesses in specific subregions (e.g. Basu 2003). Thus, the Indian Ocean is perhaps best envisaged as a number of subdiasporas; in other words, multiple diasporas from certain homelands to certain hostlands, resulting in diasporan consciousnesses of proximity, for example amongst the *habshis* of India. There may not be a larger "black Indian Ocean" as there is a "black Atlantic," but there are many "black Indian Oceans."

As Clifford notes, "[A]t different times in their history, societies may wax and wane in diasporism." (Clifford 1997: 249). However, temporality plays a role that extends beyond mere chronology. Would a community displaced 200 years ago and another displaced 1000 years ago provide similar evidence of their diasporan roots and connections *in the present*? Safran (1999: 265) raises such a point, "If an expatriate community ... has remained abroad for so long that it has only an indistinct memory of its place of origin, no longer has links with its homeland, and is no longer capable of effectively perpetuating its culture, is it still a diaspora?" But, should social scientists make this characterization without considering whether a community itself *was* the result of the diaspora process?

Researchers must investigate diasporan communities and diaspora histories using all available sources and methods, particularly those that have the potential to explore societies not from present survivals or traditions—as important as these may be—but with data retrieved directly from the past. Locating material correlates of diasporan "separation and entanglement,"[7] including evidence of survivals and contestations over power with host societies, may be our best chance to identify and examine unique conditions and processes in the past. In short, expressions in the archaeological record offer an opportunity to assess struggles for identity as "inheritance" and as "politics" by displaced communities. An exploration of these and other topics relevant to the African diaspora and Africans abroad in the East must be attentive to the full range of material residues indicative of any stage of slave extraction, transport, existence, exploitation, or struggle over millennia.

Historic overview of the regional slave trade[8]

The slave trade and associated African diaspora in the western Indian Ocean began as a trickle from wider northeastern Africa to Egypt and the Red Sea as early as Pharaonic times. As attested by texts and antiquities, Egypt and the Graeco-Roman world exploited African slaves obtained from Nubia and Abyssinia (Ethiopia) as bi-products of military campaigns and trading expeditions (Snowden 1970; Kobishchonav 1979: 150–158). The *Periplus of the Erythrean Sea*, a first-century AD traveler's account, mentions markets at Malao and Opone (Ras Hafun) on the Gulf of Aden and Indian Ocean coasts of present-day Somalia that sold slaves "the greater number of which go to Egypt" (Casson 1989: 56, 59). If vessels sailing west eluded Nabataean pirates, their slave cargoes would have been disembarked at ports in the northern Red Sea, such as Berenice or Myos Hormos, for eventual overland transfer. The *Periplus* also records the importation of "slave musicians" and "beautiful girls for concubinage" into western India (Casson 1989: 71, 81). According to Pliny as well as the *Christian Topography*, the Aksumite Empire of the first to seventh century AD traded heavily in goods, including slaves, to Arabia, Persia, India, and Ceylon (Sri Lanka) from its Red Sea port of Adulis. Hundreds of northeastern Africans entered Arabia annually, fewer reached India.[9]

African slaves from the Horn also are known from later periods. Writing in the last centuries of the first millennium, Duan Chengshi (cited in Freeman-Grenville 1975: 8) mentions slave raids along the Somali coast while Al-Muqaddasi labels Yemen "the country of kerchiefs, cornelian, leather and slaves" (cited in Chaudhuri 1985: 190). In Egypt from AD 1036–1094, tens of thousands of black soldiers guarded the powerful Fatimid Caliphate as the center of Islam shifted from the Persian Gulf to the Red Sea. Pearl divers for Bahrain and Lingeh were in high demand during that same century, drawing Africans from ports in present-day Eritrea and Djibouti. As early as the twelfth century, many thousands of Ethiopian slaves reached western India, particularly Gujarat and Maharashtra. Called *habshis* or *sidis*, soldiering was often their duty; however, some, such as Malik Ambar, later rose to lead Muslim polities (Figure 21.3). Others were seafarers transporting food, minerals, and rare spices, or pirates plying monsoon winds in the Arabian Sea. In wider Arabia, the Persian Gulf, and Pakistan, Muslim elites sought eunuchs, concubines, and domestic servants from northeastern Africa. Slavery, officially recognized in Ethiopia by the *Fetha Nagast*, a traditional legal code, expanded on the mainland, as did slave raiding for export, through the early sixteenth century (Pankhurst 1968: 73). Of this period, the Portuguese traveler Pires writes, "[T]hey [peoples of Arabia] make raids on horseback, in the course of which they capture large numbers of Abyssinians whom they sell to the people of Asia" (cited in Freeman-Grenville 1975: 125).

Mathew (1966: 106) notes that the capture and export of "Zanj" (black) slaves along the East African coast was "probably a constant factor" before AD 1498. The launch of Islam in the wider region in the seventh century AD ushered in a period of enhanced regional contact and commerce. Muslim commercial towns, such as Aden and Basra, developed slave markets, and other cities, including Baghdad, Cairo, and Mecca, marketed African slaves and exploited them as heavy laborers during this period (Harris

Figure 21.3   Portrait of Malik Ambar (ca. 1620–1630), Museum of Fine Arts, Boston.

1971: 3–25). Intermediate staging areas for slave trafficking also burgeoned during the late first millennium AD. Kanbalu, thought to be an island locality off East Africa, and Unguja Ukuu on Zanzibar expanded to meet the commercial needs of Arabs and Chinese seeking Africans "who, being strong men, are able to stand heavy labour" (Hornell 1934: 307–308). Africans drawn from the periphery of nonbelievers, or *Dar al-Harb*, usually seized during raids, were absorbed regularly into the wider Arab world as their territories were incorporated into the land of believers, or *Dar al-Islam*. Alternatively, eastern Africans were lured to their capture, as Al-Idrisi (Jaubert 1975: 56) and Zhou Qufei (Duyvendak 1949: 22) inform us during the twelfth century. The *Kitab al-Ajaib al-Hind* (cited in Freeman-Grenville 1975: 9–13) as well as the *Hadrami Chronicles* (Serjeant 1963) also indicate an active slave trade from the African coast to Arabia.

During the early Islamic period, the dispersal of Zanj slaves widened, including to Egypt, the Persian Gulf, India, and even Java and China. The number of slaves exported likely fluctuated as it grew beyond a few hundred per year. As early as the eighth to ninth century East African slaves as well as others, particularly from wider Nubia and Sudan, formed a community of tens of thousands in lower Mesopotamia toiling as gang laborers draining salt marshes (Popovic 1999). Under horrendous circumstances of forced labor they rose up, most famously, from AD 869–883 during the Great Zanj Revolt. Some of those remaining after defeat chose to join other Africans in Bahrain during the tenth century to form an agricultural labor force estimated to be 30,000 strong (Hunwick 1978: 34). By the thirteenth century, date plantations in the Near East, for example at Bandar Abbas, continued to exploit Africans. And, in Bengal many of the thousands of Africans in Sultan Rukn al-Din's fifteenth-century army likely originated from present-day Tanzania (Mathew 1966: 121). Perhaps they and earlier Africans entered the western Indian Ocean slave system through one of the many Swahili city-states, including Kilwa, later reaching Aden, Cambay, or other ports in southern Asia up to AD 1500.

From the middle sixteenth to eighteenth century, Omani involvement in the slave trade intensified and European slaving began on a large scale, especially along Africa's southeastern coast (Barendse 1998). While the African slave trade to most Islamic lands remained steady, slave imports to Oman and Yemen grew significantly to stock armies and meet the demands of date and cotton production. Alternatively, Arabs in Muscat or Sur, aware of Ottoman influence in the Red Sea, transshipped Africans to the Persian Gulf or India. The fall of Portuguese-held Mombasa in 1698 further boosted the Omani-run slave trade out of ports such as Mogadishu and Zanzibar. The Portuguese, themselves, intermittently traded Africans and practiced military, domestic, or administrative slavery, especially in India and on the *prazos* (estates) along the Zambezi River (Isaacman 1972; Pescaletto 1977). Indigenous caravan routes, established by the Yao, among others, facilitated Portuguese and other slave trafficking to the coastal ports of Kilwa, Quilmane, and Mozambique Island (Alpers 1975). Northern and central Madagascar also suffered slave extractions while the Comoros provided ports for slave dhows and smugglers operating under European and Malagasy overlords. As early as 1614, the English East India Company sent ships, including one ironically named *Blessing*, to gather slaves off the southeastern coast (Beachey 1996: 6–7).

Dutch settlement in South Africa and Mauritius and burgeoning Dutch shipping activity increased the trade in Africans and Malagasies between Africa's south coast and the oceanic islands (Worden 1985; Ross 1988: 212–214). Not to be outdone, by 1770 the French, operating in Mozambique, the Seychelles, and Madagascar, began exporting slaves in the high thousands *per annum* to work on sugar and indigo plantations in the Mascarenes (Mauritius, Reunion, and Rodrigues) (Larson 2001). On Reunion alone 37,000 slaves toiled by 1788 (Hintjens 2003: 103).

The Arab trade in slaves from the Horn declined somewhat during the seventeenth century but remained substantial into the nineteenth century. Originally slave exports grew to meet the demands of the Mughal and Ottoman empires of Asia. However, by the middle nineteenth century thousands of slaves, including Gurage and Oromo, arrived at ports such as Suakin, Massawa, and Barawa to meet "luxury," military, and agricultural demands in Egypt, Turkey, Arabia, and Persia (Austen 1988). Pankhurst (2003: 217) suggests that approximately 10,000 slaves exited the Horn annually during the first two-thirds of that century, many passing through Jeddah. Others, African ex-slaves and migrants, moved across the northwestern Indian Ocean as crewmen, dockworkers, or pirates (Ewald 2000). In the early nineteenth century, thousands of Africans from as far away as present-day Malawi were transited to Somali ports for shipment to Asia or to service the expanding agricultural economies of Somalia's southern littoral. By the 1870s, as many as 10,000 Africans per year were marched overland into Somalia to avoid British antislaving vessels (Cassanelli 1982: 168). Many escaped or were manumitted, establishing large maroon communities along the Shabeele and Jubba rivers.

During the nineteenth century, eastern Africa and its offshore islands witnessed a growth in slave exports. The slave trade to the Mascarenes intensified into the middle 1830s as did the trade to the Persian Gulf, the latter absorbing at least 140,000 Africans from 1722–1872 to fuel the renaissance of Iran (Ricks 1988: 67). Omani dominance in coastal slave trafficking later in the century resulted, in part, from the disruption of European slaving by the Napoleonic Wars, the implementation of the Moresby Treaty in 1822 (outlawing the southern trade), and British antislavery campaigns. Although slave-based agriculture had origins centuries earlier (Vernet 2003), for the first time, plantations in the coastlands of present-day Kenya and Tanzania began to retain slaves *en masse* (Cooper 1977; Sheriff 1987). Retention increased following the relocation of the capital of Oman from Muscat to Zanzibar in 1840 by Sultan Seyyid Said. Shortly thereafter, slaves, arriving at the coast accompanied by Swahili middlemen, flooded the ranks of Zanzibar and coastal Kenya to tend cloves and sesame. By one account as many as 40,000 slaves labored in Kenya's Lamu Archipelago during the middle 1840s (Sheriff 1987: 71).

Along the eastern African coast, slave trading continued into the middle 1800s despite naval patrols and treaties outlawing the oceanic trade. For example, the Merina Kingdom of Madagascar increased its slaving activity following the Moresby Treaty; the Merina capital, Antananarivo, expanding fivefold in population between 1820 and 1833 to 50,000 inhabitants, two-thirds of which were Malagasy and Mozambiquan slaves (Newitt 2003: 90). According to the British explorer Richard Burton, slave exports from the southern Tanzanian coast reached their apogee after 1850 with more than 110,000 exiting the port of Kilwa Kivinje between 1862 and 1869, some eventually reaching the Caribbean (Alpers 1975: 238). Zanzibari trade, always central to the wider exchange of slaves, spices, and ivory, flourished until the late 1870s but succumbed to British protests shortly thereafter. By the middle nineteenth century, the demand for African slaves in India was greatly reduced, but elsewhere it remained high, especially in the Persian Gulf, Yemen, Mecca, and Egypt (Austen 1988; Clarence-Smith 1988). In some subregions prohibitive maritime laws caused an increase in accidents at sea as captains chose suspect vessels and more dangerous paths of navigation to elude patrols (Carter and Gerbeau 1988). Under increasing world scrutiny, slavers became more clandestine in order to negotiate an increasingly illicit activity, a task made easier by improved maritime technology. Nevertheless, by the last quarter of the nineteenth century, rising prices, declining demand, Omani subordination to British rule, antislaving and antislavery treaties and agreements, and slave resistance instigated a movement away from slavery and toward wage labor (Cooper 1997). However, slaving continued in Ethiopia into the 1930s and the practice of slavery was not officially outlawed in some countries until the latter half of the twentieth century, for example, Saudi Arabia in 1962.

The organized African slave trade in the western Indian Ocean and peripheral areas played a significant role in the economies, politics, and societies of Africa and southern Asia for more than two millennia. In the end, slaving conservatively transplanted more than three million Africans to Asia and the Indian Ocean islands. Many Africans died before reaching their final destinations. Millions more, both slaves and nonslaves, were displaced within Africa or negatively affected by the trade or the practice of slavery, resulting in instability and underdevelopment. Living communities in Asia and Africa, including Zinjibar in Yemen and those along the lower Jubba River in Somalia, as well as cultural practices, such as *goma* dances in western India, provide evidence of a once flourishing diaspora of African peoples, traditions, and ideas. Material remains of this lengthy history should provide further evidence of the regional diaspora, confirming, revising, and extending aspects of our knowledge.

Archaeological potential and pathways forward

Despite potential, Africa and southern Asia have received little attention in developing African diaspora and slave-associated archaeologies, with a few exceptions (e.g. Hall 2000; DeCorse 2001). The primary objective at this preliminary stage of research in eastern African and Asian lands should be to identify, record, and conserve material remains pertinent to the diaspora while posing explicit questions of the record in a scientific manner.[10] To meet these goals, both traditional and new technologies should be employed at various scales across landscapes and seascapes through time. Moreover, archaeologists should begin to develop regional historic artifact typologies, practice ethnoarchaeology in communities comprised of the descendants of dispersed Africans, and more skillfully integrate available cultural and historical resources. We advocate focusing on three components of the diaspora system and their material correlates spanning Africa, the Indian Ocean and its islands, and southern Asia, which are (1) extraction; (2) transit; and (3) existence, community formation, labor, and struggle.

Each component is likely to elicit shared signatures and questions across its extent. Below, we review available resources and opportunities for advancement and highlight recent archaeological studies of slave-associated pasts in the region.

Slave extraction (component 1)

Foreign demands for slaves often were met by collaboration with African leaders interested in expanding their authority often collaborated with foreigners to meet demands for slaves. New sources of social power based on foreign goods accessed through increased external trade, including that in slaves, had three potential consequences for African communities: collapse, fragmentation, or fluorescence. Such was the case throughout East Africa, for example in northeastern Tanzania where the Shambaa Kingdom collapsed, Pare states fragmented, and cooperative Zigua chiefdoms expanded. As political economies shifted, raiding and devastation of proximal communities increased, forcing flight to refuges or heightened defensive measures. Slave extraction areas, usually hinterlands of powerful entities or ports, offer tremendous potential for identifying, through material remains, the impacts of the slave trade on Africans. Archaeological traces of slave extraction are best recognized in rapid changes to settlement patterns, abandonment or depopulation due to raiding and out-migration, increased evidence of trade along routes penetrating frontiers, increased defenses at effected sites, and sudden transformations in technology and material culture (Hall 1993:185; DeCorse 2001; Kusimba 2004).

Sources attest that trade and warfare in eastern Africa were associated with slaving over the past 400 years. Recent archaeological projects have located material evidence likely resulting from heavy slaving. Working in southeastern Kenya, Kusimba (in press) discovered changes in settlement strategies among the Kasigau who shifted their habitation from plains and hill bases to fortified rockshelter enclosures beginning in the middle eighteenth century. Excavations also identified atypical structures at rockshelters with hidden exits and fewer indications of external interaction.

In northeastern Tanzania, evidence from field survey indicates abandonment of sectors of the lower Pangani Basin, the fluorescence of walled or stockaded villages, and the growth of trade along known slave routes during the eighteenth and nineteenth centuries. Additional clues demonstrate interaction along trade routes deeper into antiquity than previously thought (Walz, 2005), coinciding with periods of settlement change in the proximal highlands. The totality of recovered evidence suggests that substantial changes occurred in this corner of the Indian Ocean due to heightened interaction and that human exploitation may have been a prominent reason for hinterland penetration and material changes.

Further work in these and other areas, especially Ethiopia, Mozambique, Central Africa, and Madagascar, has the potential to identify similar materialities related to slave extraction. Attention to detail is key to differentiating slaving from other potential causes forcing material change, the *difaqane* of southern Africa being a case in point (Lane 2004). Vicinities with histories of slave raiding occurring along known trade routes may prove the best predictor of zones of intensive slave capture. Regional approaches to the archaeological record that sample a range of environments through survey and a range of site types through excavation are essential to identifying indications of both the human devastation caused by slaving and the resiliency of African populations.

Systemic transit (component 2)

Following capture, middlemen forced slaves toward their final destinations. The transit system of the western Indian Ocean included caravan routes in Africa, maritime ports of embarkation, nautical routes, ports of disembarkation, and land routes in Asia. Caravan routes, known from records to have arisen or become reified as a result of slaving traffic, crisscrossed much of the hinterland of eastern Africa and southern Asia (Figure 21.4). Although routes sometimes shifted due to circumstances, many were enduring, passing through established towns or collectivization points. Garrisons, watchtowers, rest camps, wells, cairns, and certain tree species often flanked segments of roads or tracks. Many of these routes or their aspects left a material trace (e.g. Wilding 1980; Sidebotham 1991) locatable through aerial photographs, digital satellite imagery, or intensive ground survey supplemented by historical and environmental information. Similar potential projects conducted in Arabian wadis, highland Ethiopia, or sectors of mountainous southern Asia possessing bottlenecks restricting human movement would effectively narrow the landscape area to be explored by archaeologists interested in locating land transit residues.

Slaves who survived overland routes reached their intermediate or final destinations at hinterland markets or coastal depots. Determining the location, layout, and architecture of such built environments (Sims 1978) provides insights into the

Figure 21.4 Slaves being transited from the Ethiopian interior to the coast during the 1840s (from Bernatz, J. (1852) *Scenes in Ethiopia, Volume 2 (The Highlands of Shoa)*, London).

relationship of markets to proximal towns and the areas where slavers restrained Africans or prepared them for sale or transshipment. Slavers, themselves, might be examined through remains associated with residences, depots, and caravanserais. The latter, common in and around towns such as Surat, served as inns for those conducting business or completing journeys. While Chami and colleagues (2004) recently completed the first excavation of a caravanserai in East Africa, other structures and sites associated with slave transit remain ignored by scholars, despite their importance to regional history and their decaying condition.

Investigating routes, nodes, and ports is only one component of a larger endeavor to study regional shifts in political economies associated with slaving. Histories of the sixteenth through nineteenth century indicate that select economies focused on trading slaves were dependent, in large part, on oceanic transport. The search for maritime evidence of trade, including harbors and sunken ships, is yet to begin in earnest despite tantalizing finds, particularly off the coasts of South Africa and western India (Rao 1998). Still, few studies focus exclusively on the Medieval Period and none highlight slaving. For later periods, documents exist capable of assisting archaeologists in locating underwater sites, particularly shipwrecks or localities of maritime accidents, numbering in the hundreds, if not more, in South African waters alone (Werz 1993: 238). Underwater archaeologists should focus on harbors of known slave trade ports, the vicinities of common nautical routes, the shallow-water environments of the Red Sea, Gulf of Aden and Persian Gulf, and the coastal waters of Madagascar and India. Study of vessel logs, port records, and sea charts should be conducted in concert with visual, remote sensing, and intrusive efforts (Guerout 2001). Ancient submerged ports, identified by underwater structures or groups of stone anchors, should be relatively easy to locate. Certainly, greater attention must be focused on finding not only European ships associated with slaving (e.g. East Indiamen), but also traces of Arabian, Indian, and African vessels, some of which lacked metal parts, and, thus, cannot be identified using traditional magnetic technologies (Flecker 2000). Maritime evidence might be linked to slaving through documents or through associations with specific artifact types, such as shackles or items commonly traded for or alongside slaves. The emergence of specialized marine archaeology institutes and training programs, such as the one at the National Institute of Oceanography in Goa, India, are cause for optimism.

Ports in Asia or on pertinent islands where many African slaves disembarked warrant equal attention. Remains exist, especially at sites used over many centuries as, for example, in the vicinity of Aden (Whitcomb 1988; Prados 1994). The limited archaeological work that has been conducted at such ports has not focused on material signatures associated with dispersed Africans. Potential seems particularly high at coastal venues that may have retained slaves prior to their further transport as, for example, at Mukalla in Yemen or Dahlak Kebir opposite the ancient port of Adulis in the Red Sea, where at least one archaeologist claims "numerous rock-cut water cisterns [were] dug to provide water to a transient slave population" (Insoll 1996: 446). Waypoints in Africa and Asia, whether tracks, markets, towns, ports, or shipwrecks merit focused archaeological attention.

Existence, community formation, labor and struggle (component 3)

Once slaves reached their final destinations they began to rebuild their lives in new social and physical environments. Sometimes slaves who had been thrust together were few in number and had dramatically different origins. In other cases African slaves on foreign shores shared localized homelands and developed communities of thousands or more. Regardless of the system involved or the form of exploitation, all slaves—men, women, and children—were reduced to a condition of slavery; *slavery* being the most severe form of exploitation of an individual's labor and reproductive capacities (Lovejoy 1983: 1–22, see also Miers 2003). Owners often employed coercion, sometimes violent, to secure slaves' obedience. In localities where slaves reached significant numbers, the terror of exploitation sometimes resulted in retribution or revolt. However, especially in Islamic lands, slaves endured comparatively less violence and often gained freedom upon integration into their host societies (e.g. Miers and Kopytoff 1977).

Sizable Africa-derived slave communities inhabited numerous sites in Africa and Asia. One such locality is Ankobar, the principal city of the nineteenth-century Kingdom of Shoa in Ethiopia. It possessed palatial ruins and churches in addition to a few hundred proximally concentrated wattle-and-daub slave houses (Pankhurst 1982: 278–283, 290–293). Sites in India and Pakistan ranging from central Indian strongholds to small coastal colonies dating to as early as the thirteenth century were homes to *habshis* and *sidis* (Harris 1971; Gupta 1991). For later periods, Barendse (1998: 48, 98) notes that Goa, Diu, and Vengurla in India were surrounded by settlements of refugee Portuguese slaves primarily from Mozambique. Numerous mines and ports also exploited African slaves. Yet, historic period potential largely remains unexplored. Urban sectors of historic cities, such as Colombo, Sri Lanka, offer additional opportunities, as well as the settlements of other Africa-derived communities resulting from the cultural articulations of dwelling in displacement in Yemen, Mauritius, and Madagascar. At yet other localities there were slave encampments, cemeteries, prisons, and places of worship as well as "freedom villages" (havens for ransomed slaves), such as those at Bagamoyo, Tanzania.

Localities attributable to African slave and freed communities offer archaeologists additional research opportunities. Where did slaves live in relation to their exploiters and can archaeologists differentiate slaves' habitations from those of the wider community? Employing archaeology, among other methods, Donley-Reid (1984) and Markell (1993) provide partial answers to these questions for historic cases in the Lamu Archipelago and South Africa, respectively. How many slaves inhabited certain localities and for what periods of time based on detectable settlements and accumulations of discard? Also, did slaves maintain or remake aspects of their home material cultures through time and to what degree? Can ethnogenesis in diverse slave communities be read in new and generalized material cultures? Archaeology performed at known sites of *habshis* or *sidis*, for example, when placed in context, might identify the emergence of a material signature unique to their Afro-Asian identity and worldview. Did freed Africans revive aspects of their homeland material cultures suppressed by enslavement? Might the "small things forgotten" illuminate slaves' lives (Hall 1993: 187–188)? What do skeletons indicate about identities, demographics, stresses, and origins? In analyzing bones, bone chemistry, and teeth, Cox *et al.* (2001) and Sealy *et al.* (1993) demonstrate archaeologists' capacities to differentiate African slaves from wider populations. And what of labor? In the lower Pangani Basin of East Africa, slaves constructed shallow irrigation canals and processed coconuts and sugar from the late nineteenth century forward. Clove plantations of Zanzibar and historic estate infrastructure in Oman also provide oral and preliminary material evidence of slaves (e.g. Mershen 2001; Croucher 2004). These and other cases offer opportunities to practise historical or industrial archaeologies of slave labor and production by fully integrating material, oral, folkloric, and documentary sources.

Regional African maroon, or escape slave, settlements supply further potential. The best-studied cases of *maroonage* in the western Indian Ocean, including southern Somalia, coastal Kenya, and Mauritius and Reunion, are known only from documentary and oral research (e.g. Allen 1999; Alpers 2003b). In these areas large numbers of African slaves engaged in agricultural labor. Maroons often established remote settlements or built defenses and usually raided proximal towns to exact revenge and obtain supplies. Chowdhury (2003) recently launched an innovative archeological study of maroons on Mauritius, identifying occupation sites as well as artifacts and ecofacts associated with their habitations. Southern Somalia and northeastern Tanzania bear similar sites and remains (Brandt, personal observation; Walz, personal observation). The Mauritian study and other potential projects should further explore artifact assemblages, residential architecture, and defenses while striving to integrate alternative historical resources (Weik and Walz n.d.). Ethnoarchaeology is an additional method that should be employed to locate enduring material culture among descendants of maroons. When investigated properly, material evidence may assist archaeologists in remaking interpretations of escapee communities while adding new information about settlement, architecture, "illicit" activities, diets, and craft production.

Slaves also used open revolt to contest oppressors. One of the greatest slave rebellions in world history, the Great Zanj Revolt of southern Iraq, involved tens of thousands of eastern Africans who rebelled against the powerful Abbasid Empire (Popovic 1999). According to the ninth- to tenth-century Arab historian Al-Tabari, rebel slaves who had been forced to clear and drain salt marshes, destroyed sectors of Abbasid towns, established permanent settlements, developed a military, and minted their own coinage, a few pieces of which have been recovered (e.g. Walker 1933). Records indicate general vicinities of slave work camps, military camps, and cities built during the rebellion in addition to roads, bridges, and canals. Led by Ali bin Muhammad, rebels concealed al-Mukhtara, their capital, in marshes. The walled city contained palaces, prisons, mosques, and other structures built from baked clay bricks (Popovic 1999). Although shifting riverbeds and human waterworks in the area may have destroyed much evidence of the Zanj, it is left to archaeologists to locate and retrieve material vestiges.

The study of slave life, community formation, labor systems, and resistance requires heightened attention to the material record and adjustments to traditional archaeological practice in the wider region. Archaeologists engaged in such work should record all site types in regional surveys, as even small scatters might supply critical evidence of sites used infrequently or for short periods (e.g., maroon hideaways). Furthermore, scholars should invest substantial time in learning about local contexts, including histories of slavery, so they are empowered to recognize material differences between slave and other populations.

Discussion and conclusion

Written, oral, ethnographic, and other sources document the forced dispersal of countless Africans into lands bordering the western Indian Ocean. While this diaspora is known to have occurred, our knowledge of aspects of the slave trade and the lives of dispersed Africans in the East remains grossly incomplete. Archaeology provides one means of extending and refining our knowledge. For archaeologists there are, indeed, many obstacles to overcome, including defining concepts, determining past identities (slave, African, or otherwise) and interpreting finds. In Asia these tasks must be performed without essentializing Africa. The fact that slaves possessed very little and often were absorbed into foreign societies makes the task no easier. The poor preservation of material culture in the tropics presents further impediments. One scholar goes as far as to claim that in sub-Saharan Africa there is a "near-impossibility ... of recognizing chattel-slavery from material remains [alone]" (Alexander 2001: 44, 56–57). Although challenging for a range of reasons, there is *no* basis upon which to dismiss potential before investigations have begun in earnest.

We prefer an approach that considers multiple types of evidence simultaneously, fortifying interpretations that identify aspects of the slave trade and dispersed Africans in the archaeological record. We must remain critical and reflexive, but logical, when investigating the diaspora, considering evidence in its totality rather than type-by-type. Recent studies based on archaeological fieldwork (mentioned above) demonstrate that aspects of the slave trade and slaves' lives can be investigated successfully in Indian Ocean contexts. Other aspects may remain elusive.

As yet, many regions and localities, including those bearing all of the outlined components of enslavement and diasporism, for example Ankobar, remain unexplored. Once scholars recognize certain material patterns associated with African slaves or the slave trade in these and other historic contexts, "... [it will] allow us to search for these patterns in undocumented historic sites, or, by extension, to search for evidence of slavery in preliterate sites" (as Lange and Handler 1985: 28 argue for the New World). Clearly, a movement into "prehistory" does not signal the end of historical or cultural connections, but, rather, an opportunity to extend knowledge beyond known temporal frameworks. African and Afro-Asian settlements might even be located archaeologically in areas where diasporic consciousness was once strong, but has since subsided. In short, where residues are recoverable and where scholars pose questions answerable in archaeological terms, material evidence can shed light on diasporas.

Archaeologists should no longer ignore the Indian Ocean slave trade and African diaspora communities as subjects, nor peripheralize sites, features, or artifacts potentially associated with slaves.[11] This endeavor is made all the more urgent by the increasing pace of heritage destruction in Africa and Asia. Africans, among others, contributed to the making of the modern world from early times and, thus, should be a focus of intensive study in the Indian Ocean world as much as any other group. The individual archaeologist must determine the approach appropriate for exploring slaves and slave systems in a given place and time. However, regardless of context, investigators should search widely for sources, incorporate local scholars and populations into research, and be sensitive to the meanings of histories to local communities as well as the complex of "identity politics" associated with modern nation-states.

One bi-product of research on the African diaspora in the Indian Ocean is the comparative information that it would supply scholars working on other African diasporas. For example, how does evidence of enslavement in East Africa compare to that in West Africa? Are there differences in the nature of residues of slave communities in Islamic and Christian religious contexts? Do trends in material culture retentions indicate different degrees and forms of slave resistance in Asia and the New World? Are there aspects of an emerging material cultural common to African descendants in the East as seems to be the case in the Americas? Posnansky (1999), among others (e.g. Agorsah 1996; Singleton 2001), argues that studies of African communities, including slaves, would benefit from ethnological and archaeological perspectives working across continents and contexts. We support his contentions and suggest in-depth archaeological case studies, including investigative extensions into "prehistory."

We have attempted to raise issues, highlight resources, and generate interest concerning the exploration of African diaspora heritage in the western Indian Ocean and beyond. Empirical archaeological studies of this diaspora, we believe, are capable of influencing diaspora theory. Undoubtedly, more questions than answers have been raised by our modest preamble. Africanist and Asianist archaeologists and their colleagues now bear the responsibility of taking further action to recover, interpret, and compare traces of the regional slave trade and diasporan linkages between Africa and Asia, a task best achieved through scientific practice and a humanistic outlook.

Acknowledgments

We thank Jay Haviser and Kevin MacDonald for encouraging us to publish our chapter. We are grateful to Ned Alpers, Felix Chami, Amitava Chowdhury, Chapurukha Kusimba, and Ian Lilley for supplying copies of papers in advance of their publication. Insightful comments by Ned Alpers, Kevin MacDonald and James Brennan improved the chapter's final form. Any errors or omissions are our own.

Notes

1 We limit our discussion to areas bordering the "western Indian Ocean," including the Red Sea and Persian Gulf.

2 Harris (1971) provides the best-known early treatment of Africans in Asia. Investigations of the slave trade or slavery during specific periods or in certain subregions also exist

(e.g. Pescaletto 1977; Sheriff 1987; Lewis 1990). Interest in this diaspora has expanded since the late 1990s as evidenced by publications (e.g. Jayasuriya and Pankhurst 2003 and contributions in *Slavery and Abolition*) and international conferences. The UNESCO Slave Route Project has raised further archaeological interest in the topic.

3 As Alpers (2000: 85) asserts, "... African voices have been *actively* silenced in this diaspora both by the cultural contexts of their host societies and by the way in which the scholarly production of knowledge has reflected such cultural domination." See Posnansky (1984: 197) for a similar critique of archaeologists' early inattention to the African diaspora in the Atlantic.

4 This situation is changing. The African Diaspora in Asia (TADIA) interest group provides a linkage mechanism for experts in addition to promoting the causes of contemporary Afro-Asian communities.

5 A robust debate about continuity *or* transformation in African cultures and their material correlates, such as that carried out in the New World, has yet to take place in the Indian Ocean arena.

6 Such slave systems included the following:

> the Mascarene Islands (including the Seychelles) are best conceptualized as displaced Caribbean sugar islands; Madagascar ... shares much in common with Asian closed systems of slavery ... Zanzibar and coastal East Africa ... [fit] into broader patterns of Islamic slavery in Arabia and the Persian Gulf ... [O]ne represents a Christian European variety of plantation slavery, another an independently evolved Afro-Asian hierarchical state system model, the last a variation on Islamic slave systems ... we must include colonial slavery at the Cape ... [and] the African open system of slavery ... that characterized the Zambezi *prazos* ... of the Portuguese. In Arabia and South Asia ... Africans were enslaved in somewhat different systems under Islam ... Finally, Africans also turn up as bonded servants in the European administrative emporia of Mozambique and India.
>
> (Alpers 2003b: 51)

Further overviews and details of these slave systems can be found in Harris 1971; Isaacman 1972; Cooper 1977; Watson 1980; Worden 1985; Bissondoyal and Servansing 1989; Lewis 1990; Klein 1993; and Campbell 2004.

7 Lilley (2004) suggests that locating diasporas archaeologically involves identifying both abrupt appearances of new material phenomena in previously inhabited areas as well as evidence for the maintenance of dispersed but coherent communities distinct from both hostland and homeland populations. Lilley further asserts that archaeologists must engage modern nondiaspora dispersals as well as diasporas in order to better grasp material correlates that might identify and differentiate each archaeologically.

8 We provide only an abbreviated review of the regional slave trade. For our purposes, northeastern Africa includes Egypt, eastern Sudan, and the Horn, i.e., present-day Ethiopia, Somalia, Eritrea, and Djibouti. East Africa refers to present-day Kenya, Tanzania, and Uganda, while eastern Africa denotes contemporary Mozambique, East Africa, and the Horn. The Swahili coast embraces the eastern African coast as well as its offshore islands.

9 Scholars posit estimates of the number of African slave who entered areas of the western Indian Ocean (e.g. Martin and Ryan 1977; Lovejoy 1983; Austen 1988). These estimates range widely and focus on the later trade. Primary sources are elusive for earlier periods and overall documentation is poor.

10 A necessary later step, and one that lies fully outside the scope of this chapter, is to make comparisons between pertinent sites and regions.

11 Insoll (1999) does not make significant mention of the archaeological traces of slaving, slaves, and slavery in the Islamic world. As regards artifacts, scholars have located items, such as

those interpreted as shackles, in excavations without effectively integrating these finds into interpretations of sites (e.g. Anfray 1963: plates lxi, lxxxi–lxxxii).

References

Agorsah, E. (1996) "The archaeology of the African Diaspora," *African Archaeological Review*, 13, 4: 221–224.

Alexander, J. (2001) "Islam, archaeology, and slavery in Africa," *World Archaeology*, 33, 1: 44–60.

Allen, R. (1999) *Slaves, Freedmen, and Indentured Laborers in Colonial Mauritius*, Cambridge: Cambridge University Press.

Alpers, E. (1975) *Ivory and Slaves in East Central Africa*, London: Heinemann.

Alpers, E. (1997) "The African Diaspora in the Northwestern Indian Ocean: reconsideration of an old problem, new directions for research," *Comparative Studies of South Asia, Africa & the Middle East*, 17, 2, 62–81.

Alpers, E. (2000) "Recollecting Africa: diasporic memory in the Indian Ocean world," *African Studies Review*, 43, 1: 83–99.

Alpers, E. (2003a) "The African Diaspora in the Indian Ocean: a comparative perspective," in S. Jayasuriya and R. Pankhurst (eds) *The African Diaspora in the Indian Ocean*, 19–50, Trenton: Africa World Press.

Alpers, E. (2003b) " 'Flight to freedom: escape from slavery among bonded Africans in the Indian Ocean world', c. 1750–1962," *Slavery and Abolition*, 24, 2: 51 68.

Anfray, F. (1963) "La Premiere Campagne de Fouilles a Matara (Nov. 1959–Janv. 1960)," *Annales d'Ethiopie*, 5: 87–166.

Austen, R. (1988) "The 19th century Islamic slave trade from East African (Swahili and Red Sea Coasts): a tentative census," *Slavery and Abolition*, 9, 3: 21–44.

Barendse, R. (1998) *The Arabian Seas, 1640–1700*, Leiden: Research School CNWS, Leiden University.

Basu, H. (2003) "Slave, Soldier, Trader, Faqir: Fragments of African Histories in Western India (Gujarat)," in S. Jayasuriya and R. Pankhurst (eds) *The African Diaspora in the Indian Ocean*, 223–249, Trenton: Africa World Press.

Beachey, R. (1996) *A History of East Africa, 1592–1902*, London: I. B. Tauris.

Bissondoyal, U., and Servansing, S. (eds) (1989) *Slavery in the South West Indian Ocean*, Moka, Mauritius: Mahatma Gandhi Institute.

Butler, K. (2001) "Defining Diaspora, Refining a Discourse," *Diaspora*, 10, 2: 189–219.

Campbell, G. (ed.) (2004) *The Structure of Slavery in Indian Ocean Africa and Asia*, London: Frank Cass.

Carter, M., and Gerbeau, H. (1988) "Covert slaves and coveted coolies in the early 19th century Mascareignes," *Slavery and Abolition*, 9, 3: 194–208.

Cassanelli, L. (1982) *The Shaping of Somali Society: Reconstructing the History of a Pastoral People, 1600–1900*, Philadelphia, PA: University of Pennsylvania Press.

Casson, L. (1989) *The Periplus Maris Erythraei: Text with Introduction, Translation, and Commentary*, Princeton, NJ: Princeton University Press.

Chami, F., Maro, E., Kessy, J., and Odunga, S. (2004) *Historical Archaeology of Bagamoyo: Excavations at the Caravan-serai*, Dar es Salaam: Dar es Salaam University Press.

Chaudhuri, K. (1985) *Trade and Civilisation in the Indian Ocean: An Economic History from the Rise of Islam to 1750*, Cambridge: Cambridge University Press.

Chowdhury, A. (2003) "Theoretical reflections on maroon archaeology in Mauritius," *Revi Kiltir Kreol*, 3: 55–59.

Clarence-Smith, W. (1988) "The economics of the Indian Ocean and Red Sea slave trades in the 19th Century: an overview," *Slavery and Abolition*, 9, 3: 1–20.

Clifford, J. (1997) *Routes: Travel and Translation in the Late Twentieth Century*, Cambridge: Harvard University Press.

Cohen, R. (1997) *Global Diasporas: An Introduction*, Seattle, WA: University of Washington Press.

Cooper, F. (1977) *Plantation Slavery on the East Coast of Africa*, New Haven, CT: Yale University Press.

Cooper, F. (1997) *From Slaves to Squatters: Plantation Labor and Agriculture in Zanzibar and Coastal Kenya, 1890–1925*, Portsmouth, NH: Heinemann.

Cox, G., Sealy, J., Schrire, C., and A. Morris (2001) "Stable carbon and nitrogen isotopic analyses of the underclass at the Colonial Cape of Good Hope in the eighteenth and nineteenth centuries," *World Archaeology*, 33, 1: 73–97.

Croucher, S. (2004) "Zanzibar Clove Plantation Survey 2003: Some Preliminary Finds," *Nyame Akuma*, 62:65-69.

DeCorse, C. (ed) (2001) *West Africa during the Atlantic Slave Trade: Archaeological Perspectives*, London: Leicester University Press.

Donley-Reid, L. (1984) *The Social Uses of Swahili Objects and Spaces*, unpublished PhD thesis, University of Cambridge, Cambridge.

Duyvendak, J. (1949) *China's Discovery of Africa*, London: A. Probsthain.

Ewald, J. (2000) "Crossers of the sea: slaves, freedmen, and other migrants in the Northwestern Indian Ocean, c. 1750–1914," *American Historical Review*, 105, 1: 69–91.

Flecker, M. (2000) "A 9th-century Arab or Indian Shipwreck in Indonesian Waters," *International Journal of Nautical Archaeology*, 29, 2: 199–217.

Freeman-Grenville, G. (1975) *The East African Coast: Select Documents from the First to the Earlier Nineteenth Century*, London: Rex Collings.

Gerbeau, H. (1979) "The Slave Trade in the Indian Ocean: Problems Facing the Historian and Research to be Undertaken," in UNESCO (ed.) *The African Slave Trade from the Fifteenth to the Nineteenth Century*, 184–207, Paris: UNESCO.

Gilroy, P. (1993) *The Black Atlantic: Modernity and Double Consciousness*, Cambridge, MA: Harvard University Press.

Guerout, M. (2001) "Submarine Archaeology and the History of the Slave Trade," in D. Diene (ed.) *From Chains to Bonds: The Slave Trade Revisited*, 36–42, Paris: UNESCO.

Gupta, A. (ed.) (1991) *Minorities on India's West Coast: History and Society*, Delhi: Kalinga Publications.

Hall, M. (1993) "The archaeology of colonial settlement in Southern Africa," *Annual Review of Anthropology*, 22: 177–200.

Hall, M. (2000) *Archaeology and the Modern World: Colonial Transcripts in South Africa and the Chesapeake*, London: Routledge.

Harris, J. (1971) *The African Presence in Asia*, Evanston, IL: Northwestern University Press.

Harris, J. (1989) "African Diaspora Connection," in U. Bissondoyal and S. Servansing (eds) *Slavery in the South West Indian Ocean*, 1–5, Moka, Mauritius: Mahatma Gandhi Institute.

Hintjens, H. (2003) "From French Slaves to French Citizens: The African Diaspora in Reunion Island," in S. Jayasuriya and R. Pankhurst (eds) *The African Diaspora in the Indian Ocean*, 99–120, Trenton: Africa World Press.

Hornell, J. (1934) "Indonesian Influences on East African Culture," *Journal of the Royal Anthropological Institute of Great Britain and Ireland*, 64: 305–337.

Hunwick, J. (1978) "Black Africans in the Islamic World: An Understudied Dimension of the Black Diaspora," *Tarikh*, 5: 20–40.

Hunwick, J. (2002) "The Same but Different: Africans in Slavery in the Mediterranean Muslim World," in J. Hunwick and E. Powell (eds) *The African Diaspora in the Mediterranean Lands of Islam*, ix–xxiv, Princeton, NJ: Markus Wiener.

Insoll, T. (1996) "The archaeology of Islam in Sub-Saharan Africa: a review," *Journal of World Prehistory*, 10, 4: 439–504.

Insoll, T. (1999) *Archaeology of Islam*, Oxford: Blackwell.

Isaacman, A. (1972) *Mozambique: The Africanization of a European Institution, The Zambesi Prazos, 1750–1902*, Madison, WI: University of Wisconsin Press.

Jaubert, P. (1975) *La Geographie d'Edrisi*, Amsterdam: Philo Press.

Jayasuriya, S., and Pankhurst, R. (eds) (2003) *The African Diaspora in the Indian Ocean*, Trenton: Africa World Press.

Klein, M. (1989) "Studying the history of those who would rather forget: oral history and the experience of slavery" *History in Africa*, 16: 209–217.

Klein, M. (ed.) (1993) *Breaking the Chains: Slavery, Bondage, and Emancipation in Modern Africa and Asia*, Madison, WI: University of Wisconsin Press.

Kobishchanov, Y. (1979) *Axum*, University Park, PA: Pennsylvania State University Press.

Kusimba, C. (2004) "Archaeology of Slavery in East Africa," *African Archaeological Review*, 21, 2: 59–88.

Lane, P. (2004) "Re-constructing Tswana Townscapes: Toward a Critical Historical Archaeology," in A. Reid and P. Lane (eds) *African Historical Archaeologies*, 269–300, New York: Plenum.

Lange, F., and Handler, J. (1985) "The Ethnohistorical Approach to Slavery," in T. Singleton (ed.) *The Archaeology of Slavery and Plantation Life*, 15–32, New York: Academic Press.

Larson, P. (2001) "The Origins of Malagasy Arriving at Mauritius and Reunion, 1770–1820: Expanding the History of Mascarene Slavery," in V. Teelock and E. Alpers (eds) *History, Memory and Identity*, 195–236, Reduit, Mauritius: Nelson Mandela Centre for African Culture.

Lewis, B. (1990) *Race and Slavery in the Middle East: An Historical Enquiry*, New York: Oxford University Press.

Lilley, I. (2004) "Diaspora and Identity in Archaeology: Moving Beyond the Black Atlantic," in L. Meskell and R. Preucel (eds) *Companion to Social Archaeology*, 287–312, Oxford: Blackwell.

Lovejoy, P. (1983) *Transformations in Slavery: A History of Slavery in Africa*, Cambridge: Cambridge University Press.

McCrindle, J. (1897) *The Christian Topography of Cosmas, an Egyptian Monk*, London: Hakluyt Society.

Markell, A. (1993) "Building on the Past: The Architecture and Archaeology of Vergelegen," *South African Archaeological Society Goodwin Series*, 7: 71–83.

Martin, E., and Ryan, T. (1977) "A Quantitative Assessment of the Arab Slave Trade of East Africa," *Kenya Historical Review*, 5: 71–91.

Mathew, G. (1966) "The East African Coast until the Coming of the Portuguese," in R. Oliver and G. Mathew (eds) *History of East Africa*, Vol. 1, 94–127, Oxford: Clarendon Press.

Mershen, B. (2001) "Observations on the Archaeology and Ethnohistory of Rural Estates of the 17th through Early 20th Centuries in Oman," *Proceedings of the Seminar for Arabian Studies*, 31:145–160.

Miers, S. (2003) "Slavery: A Question of Definition," *Slavery and Abolition*, 24, 2: 1–16.

Miers, S., and Kopytoff, I. (eds) (1977) *Slavery in Africa: Historical and Anthropological Perspectives*, Madison, WI: University of Wisconsin Press.

Newitt, M. (2003) "Madagascar and the African Diaspora," In S. Jayasuriya and R. Pankhurst (eds) *The African Diaspora in the Indian Ocean*, 81–98, Trenton: Africa World Press.

Orser, C. (1998) "The Archaeology of the African Diaspora," *Annual Review of Anthropology*, 27: 63–82.

Pankhurst, R. (1968) *Economic History of Ethiopia, 1800–1935*, Addis Ababa: Haile Sellassie I University Press.

Pankhurst, R. (1982) *History of Ethiopian Towns: From the Middle Ages to the Early Nineteenth Century*, Wiesbaden: Steiner.

Pankhurst, R. (2003) "The Ethiopian Diaspora to India: The Role of Habshis and Sidis from Medieval Times to the End of the Eighteenth Century," in S. Jayasuriya and R. Pankhurst (eds) *The African Diaspora in the Indian Ocean*, 189–221, Trenton: Africa World Press.

Patterson, T., and Kelley, R. (2000) "Unfinished migrations: reflections on the African Diaspora and the making of the modern world," *African Studies Review*, 43, 1: 11–45.

Pescaletto, A. (1977) "The African Presence in Portuguese India," *Journal of Asian History*, 11, 1: 26–48.

Popovic, A. (1999) *The Revolt of African Slaves in Iraq in the 3rd/9th Century*, Princeton, NJ: Markus Weiner.

Posnansky, M. (1984) "Toward an Archaeology of the Black Diaspora," *Journal of Black Studies*, 15: 195–205.

Posnansky, M. (1999) "West Africanist Reflections on African-American Archaeology," in T. Singleton (ed.) *"I, too, am America": Archaeological Studies of African-American Life*, 21–38, Charlottesville, VA: University of Virginia Press.

Prados, E. (1994) "An Archaeological Investigation of Sira Bay, Aden, Republic of Yemen," *International Journal of Nautical Archaeology*, 23, 4: 297–307.

Rao, S. (ed.) (1998) *"Marine Archaeology of Indian Ocean Countries,"* Goa: National Institute of Oceanography.

Ricks, T. (1988) "Slaves and slave traders in the Persian Gulf, 18th and 19th centuries: an assessment," *Slavery and Abolition*, 9, 3: 60–70.

Ross, R. (1988) "The last years of the slave trade to the Cape Colony," *Slavery and Abolition* 9,3: 209–219.

Safran, W. (1991) "Diasporas in modern societies: myths of homeland and return," *Diaspora*, 1: 83–99.

Safran, W. (1999) "Comparing diasporas: a review essay," *Diaspora*, 8, 3: 255–291.

Sealy, J., Morris, A., Armstrong, R., Markell, A., and Shrire, C. (1993) "An historic skeleton from the Slave Lodge at Vergelegen," *South African Archaeological Society Goodwin Series*, 7: 84–91.

Serjeant, R. (1963) *The Portuguese off the South Arabian Coast: Hadrami Chronicles*, Oxford: Clarendon Press.

Sheriff, A. (1987) *Slaves, Spices, and Ivory in Zanzibar*, London: James Currey.

Sidebotham, S. (1991) "Ports of the Rea Sea and the Arabia–India Trade," in V. Begley and R. De Puma (eds) *Rome and India: The Ancient Sea Trade*, 12–38, Madison, WI: University of Wisconsin Press.

Sims, E. (1978) "Trade and Travel: Markets and Caravanserais," in G. Mitchell (ed.) *Architecture of the Islamic World*, 80–111, New York: William Morrow and Company.

Singleton, T. (2001) "An Americanist Perspective on African Archaeology: Toward an Archaeology of the Black Atlantic," in C. DeCorse (ed.) *West Africa during the Atlantic Slave Trade: Archaeological Perspectives*, 179–184, London: Leicester University Press.

Snowden, F., Jr (1970) *Blacks in Antiquity: Ethiopians in the Greco-Roman Experience*, Cambridge, MA: Harvard University Press.

Vernet, T. (2003) "Le Commerce des Esclaves sur la Côte Swahili, 1500–1750," *Azania*, 38: 69–97.

Walker, J. (1933) "A Rare Coin of the Zanj," *The Journal of the Royal Asiatic Society*, 651–655 and Plate V.

Walz, J. (2005) "Mombo and the Mkomazi Corridor: Preliminary Archaeological Findings from Lowland Northeastern Tanzania," in B. Mapunda and P. Msemwa (eds) *Salvaging Tanzania's Cultural Heritage*, 198–213, Dar es Salaam: Dar es Salaam University Press.

Watson, J. (ed.) (1980) *Asian and African Systems of Slavery*, Oxford: Oxford University Press.

Weik, T. and Walz, J. (n.d.) "Marooned in a Forgotten Past: Comparative Archaeological Perspectives on African Maroons in the New World and Africa," Presentation at the 44th Annual Meeting of the African Studies Association, Houston, Texas, November 15–18, 2001.

Werz, B. (1993) "South African shipwrecks and salvage: the need for improved management," *International Journal of Nautical Archaeology*, 22, 3: 237–244.

Whitcomb, D. (1988) "Islamic Archaeology in Aden and the Hadhramaut," in D. Potts (ed.) *Araby the Blest: Studies in Arabian Archaeology*, 177–263, Copenhagen: Museum Tusculanum Press.

Wilding, R. (1980) "The Desert Trade of Eastern Ethiopia," in R. Leakey and B. Ogot (eds) *Proceedings of the 8th Panafrican Congress for Prehistory and Related Studies*, 379–380, Nairobi: Louis Leakey Memorial Institute for African Prehistory.

Worden, N. (1985) *Slavery in Dutch South Africa*, Cambridge: Cambridge University Press.

Index